Introductory Readings on the English Language

RICHARD BRADDOCK

Writing Supervisor
The Rhetoric Program
The University of Iowa

Prentice-Hall, Inc.

ENGLEWOOD CLIFFS, N.J.

1962

Preface

Liberal education has been conceived to promote the student's understanding of himself and the world of which he is both part and product, and to provoke his curiosity in a number of areas of human interest. One of the most significant of such areas is language, for man's communication through language is the basis of his humanity, the function which most clearly distinguishes him from his animal cousins. If a person wishes to understand himself and his world, he must understand something of language as surely as he must understand something of plants and animals, of psychology and sociology, of the earth and its atmosphere, of economics and art. Just as an introductory biology textbook makes a student aware of a subject he has had about him all his life, so does this collection of *Introductory Readings on the English Language* reveal new insights into a very familiar subject. The student who seriously studies these readings will be surprised how much he is learning about a phenomenon which has permeated his entire life.

In the Middle Ages, the language trivium—grammar, logic, and rhetoric—constituted three of the "seven liberal arts." Today, after much systematic study, the subject of language is broader yet, including even more areas than the divisions of this book suggest. Through painstaking analysis and scientific experiment, man is deepening his knowledge of language in significant ways. One of the most exciting of these is the effort to understand the extent to which man's thought is the product of his language, a subject little more than touched upon in these readings. This book is designed to *introduce* the college student to the English language as a highly significant area of his liberal education; many readings are included to afford new information which will provide a foundation for more specialized reading. Some readings are included because they open controversies on which even language scholars disagree, but all the readings have been selected to awaken the student's curiosity about language, to stimulate him to sharpen his ear and eye to the ways in which language is being used and to the ways in which he himself can use language to communicate with clarity, felicity, and responsibility.

The editor of these readings is greatly indebted to the authors and publishers who have permitted their work to be collected here. Compiling other men's ideas is justified by the need for a broadly conceived selection of readings that are both comprehensible and stimulating to the student seeking a liberal education concerning his own tongue. No less indebted is the editor to his wife, Carol, who somehow kept their home running as smoothly as ever while contributing immeasurably to the completion of this compilation. The editor is also indebted to his colleague, John C. McLaughlin, who suggested review questions on the four versions of Matthew 8 but who should not be held accountable for error or infelicity in the present phrasing of those questions.

RICHARD BRADDOCK

Contents

Contents   *vii*

PART I

Historical
Background

*B*asic to an understanding of our own language
is some sense of its place among the languages of the world. Margaret Schlauch provides this perspective in the first selection by
showing how children say "Yes, Mother, I
have three" in many European tongues, by
introducing us to the major Indo-European
languages of the world, and then by review-
ing some of the speculation on the spread of
language from a single point or multiple
points of origin. (Written during World
War II, the Schlauch article touches upon the
contention of the Nazis that German was an
"Aryan"—or "Indo-Germanic"—language,
which somehow was supposed to prove that
the Germans were "purer" than most non-
Germans.)

John S. Kenyon's article extends the historical perspective of the Schlauch article by
showing how English has developed from its
primitive Germanic parenthood to modern

English. Exemplifying the major periods in the development of English are the subsequent versions of the same chapter from the Bible—Matthew 8:1-13—translated into Old English, Middle English, Early Modern, and Late Modern. Finally, a selection from Stuart Robertson's and Frederic Cassidy's book brings the historical perspective to bear on the way words change their meanings, refuting the mistaken notion that every word has a "true" meaning which can be found by studying its etymology.

Several of the selections in this book, including the Schlauch article, illustrate sounds by presenting phonetic symbols, in brackets. The reader may refer to the second selection by John Kenyon, "The Representation of Speech Sounds," for an explanation of these symbols. (The table on pages 78-80 is especially useful for this purpose.) Conversely, the Robertson and Cassidy article provides a basis for understanding Part IV, "Usage," and Part VI, "Semantics." It will therefore be understood that the division of this book of readings into parts does not mean that the parts should be considered in isolation from one another.

MARGARET SCHLAUCH

From The Gift of Tongues, *by Margaret Schlauch. Copyright, 1942, by Margaret Schlauch. By permission of The Viking Press, Inc.*

Family Relationships Among Languages

FAMILIES OF LANGUAGES

In happier times, it was possible to cross the length and breadth of Europe by train in so few days that the journey could still be conveniently measured by hours. Paris to Berlin, fifteen hours; Berlin to Moscow, forty hours; Berlin to Milan, twenty hours. In certain parts of that complex and explosive continent, it was necessary to change one's official language three or four times in the course of a pilgrimage which in the United States would appear to be, in length, a mere uneventful hop. You could cross the English Channel and find yourself greeted within a couple of hours by the slow even courtesy of a Dutch immigration officer; a few more hours and a Belgian would appear at the door of your compartment and, in French idiom sounding somehow un-French, make the same routine demands with a courtesy of a different tang. Then eastwards, you could encounter the clipped precision of German officialdom, followed by softer accents emanating from the speakers of a series of Western Slavonic national languages. And to the south there lay, also easily accessible, the varied music of Mediterranean Romance languages, maintaining a certain insidious charm even as spoken by the stampers of passports and openers of trunks. The landscape might not change perceptibly at the political borders, but there would be a stir in your compartment, a coming and going of people, new phrases to be caught on the wing as travelers passed by in the corridor; and as you sat in your corner eagerly experiencing the linguistic kaleidoscope of the continent, you would strain to catch the first sounds of the new idiom as fresh companions settled themselves about you. The Dutch commercial travelers condoling or congratulating with one another in measured tones on the current market would give place to a group of French *permissionaires* exchanging rapid chaff on the exploits of their leave, in an esoteric professional jargon of considerable gayety; their still-warm places might be occupied by a domestic group on the German border, *Vati,* and *Mutti* complete with *Brüderlein* and *Schwesterlein* who were sure to be the silent, well-behaved recipients of a series of solicitous imperatives. Cries from the station platforms might echo in your mind in rich polyglot confusion at the end of such a long journey eastwards: *"Cigarren! Cigaretten!"—"Paris-Soir! Figaro!"—"Abfahrt!"—"Het is al tien uur."—"A la aduana . . ." "Agua mineral, chocolade . . ." "Priidjite, pozháluista!"*

Certainly these differences in tongue would be bewildering in the extreme to any traveler, until instruction and experience could bring order out of the chaos of aural impressions. But an enthusiast who set out to acquire some smattering of the languages in a series of countries to be so traversed would soon begin to observe some curious parallelisms in the words learnt to designate the same object. For two or even more languages he would find repeated similarities, remote but still perceptible, not only in individual words but in the manner in which these words were put together in sentences. Naïve observers explain these similarities by talking of a vague "mixture" or "corruption." When they come across a sentence in Dutch like *"Ik heb het voor mijnen zoon gekocht"* they are pleased and surprised to observe how much it resembles English "I have bought it for my son" or German *"Ich habe es für meinen Sohn gekauft."* And so they inform you gleefully, with all the assurance of a non-linguist: "Dutch is a funny language; it's a mixture of English and corrupt German."

A Hollander would of course protest vehemently that Dutch is no more corrupt, funny, or mixed than any other national speech in Europe, and he would be quite right. There is another way of explaining its gratifying resemblance to things we already know.

Let us take a single sentence and follow its land-changes, its mutations, over a fairly wide territory—as territories are reckoned in Europe.

Suppose you begin a trip in Sweden, and you find yourself seated with a mother who is anxiously supervising the box lunch of several small children. She turns solicitously to one of them and says, "Did you get any cookies (or apples, or candies)?" And the child replies: "Yes, Mother, I have three." In Swedish that would be, *"Ja, moder, jag har tre."* In Norway, to the west, or Denmark, to the south, it would be almost the same: *"Jà, mor, jeg har tre."*

The slight differences in vowel sound and in sentence melody do not disguise the fact that we are listening to the same words. A moment's reflection will suggest the right explanation. We are not confronted by a borrowing or "mixture" in any case. The three Scandinavian languages mentioned are equally ancient. At one time they were identical, for all practical purposes. A traveler in olden times (let us say the ninth century) could traverse the whole length of Norway or Sweden and pass to the southern extremity of Denmark without any change in his speech. Everywhere he would hear children say: *"Já, móđir, ek hefi þrjá."* (The last word was pronounced [θrjɑ:].) The changes and differences developed during centuries, rather rapidly in Denmark, more slowly in Sweden. As a result, we now have diversity where once there was unity. Three national languages, equally venerable, have replaced Old Scandinavian. They are extremely close relatives, but none could claim parental precedence over the others. If any branch of Scandinavian could exact respect on the grounds of conservatism (that is, fidelity to the parent, the Old Scandinavian) it would be modern Icelandic, spoken in the distant island which Norwegians settled in the ninth century. Here children still say: *"Já, móđir, ek hefi þrjá."* The values of the vowels have changed slightly; that is all.

When the train crosses from Denmark into Germany, a greater change becomes apparent. Here the maternal inquiry elicits the answer, *"Ja, Mutter, ich habe drei."* In Holland or the Flemish-speaking parts of Belgium, tow-headed lads murmur, *"Ja, moeder* (or *moer*) *ik heb er drie."* The cleavage is greater, but the separate words still look distinctly familiar. We can even group the versions of our little sentence to show where two or more languages show particular likeness:

ICELANDIC:	*Já, móđir, ek hefi þrjá.*	
SWEDISH:	*Ja, moder, jag har tre.*	
DANISH:	*Ja, mor, jeg har tre.*	
NORWEGIAN:	*Ja, mor, jeg har tre.*	

GERMAN:	*Ja, Mutter, ich habe drei.*
DUTCH:	*Ja, moeder, ik heb drie.*
FLEMISH:	*Ja, moeder, ik heb drie.*
ENGLISH:	Yes, mother, I have three.

German stands somewhat apart because its consonants show certain peculiarities: it alone has a [t] between vowels (that is, intervocalic) in the word for mother. Still, it is clear that we are still dealing with variations on the same theme.

Just as the Scandinavian examples revealed close kinship among themselves, so all of those in the extended list show some degree of relationship with one another. Sentences betraying the close linguistic ties within this same group could be multiplied indefinitely. Such being the case, we are justified in speaking of a "family" of languages, borrowing a metaphor from the realm of human relations.

PARENT GERMANIC

Detailed comparisons of this sort indicate that all the members of this Germanic group go back to a single parent language, now lost, spoken as a unity somewhere between the first century B.C. and the first A.D. We call this lost parent language Primitive Germanic. Its modern descendants are grouped into what is known as the Germanic family of European languages. English is one of them. The precise geographical location of Primitive Germanic is not known. We can surmise the nature of its sounds (*phonology*) and inflections (*morphology*) with what is probably fair accuracy, however, because of some early literature and inscriptions dating back to a time when the separate descendants had as yet separated very little from one another. . . .

By comparative study it has been established which sounds in the quoted words are most faithful to the original language. We know that English has preserved the initial consonant of the word "three" [θ] as spoken in Primitive Germanic; but that Icelandic, Flemish, and Dutch have kept the consonant at the end of the first person pronoun singular (*ik*), which has been lost in English and transformed in the others. Back of the multiplicity of extant forms we can feel our way to the existence of the single speech called parent Germanic.

ROMANCE LANGUAGES

But now let us continue the journey south. In Belgium our anxious Flemish mother may be replaced by a fellow-country-woman who speaks French. Her child will say something strikingly different from anything heard so far. *"Oui, mère* (or *maman*), *j'en ai trois."* As the train goes southwards towards that fertile cradle of cultures, the Mediterranean basin, it may be routed towards the Pyrenees, or across the Alps into Italy. If it should cross the Iberian peninsula you would hear in Spain: *"Sí, madre (yo) tengo tres"*; and in Portugal: *"Sim, mãe, tenho tres."* But if it should take you across the barrier which Hannibal—even Hannibal—found all but impassable, down the steep slopes to the smiling Lombard plains, you would hear: *"Si, madre, ce n'ho tre."* And even across the Adriatic, on the far side of the Balkan peninsula, hardy descendants of the Roman army and Roman colonists will be saying in Rumanian: *"Da, mama mea, eu am trei."*

The similarities are apparent:

FRENCH:	*Oui, mère, j'en ai trois.*
SPANISH:	*Sí, madre, (yo) tengo tres.*
PORTUGUESE:	*Sim, mãe, tenho tres.*
ITALIAN:	*Si, madre, ce n'ho tre.*
RUMANIAN:	*Da, mama mea, eu am trei.*

The situation is comparable to the one which diverted and possibly mystified you in Germanic territory. You have been traversing lands where the people communicate with one another in tongues clearly descended from a single parent. This time the parent language was a form of Latin: not the solemn speech, stilted and formal, which was reserved for polite literature and speeches in the forum, but the popular or "vulgar" Latin spoken by common people throughout the length and breadth of the Roman territory. Plain soldiers, tavern keepers, itinerant merchants, freedmen, small traders, naturalized citizens of all the polyglot Roman provinces, must have used this form of discourse as an international *lingua franca.* In this idiom they bought and sold, exchanged jokes, flirted, lamented, and consoled with one another. We know from late written documents and inscriptions (especially those on the humbler tombstones of poor folk) just how ungrammatical, rapid, informal, and even slangy this Latin was, compared with the intricate and highly mannered periods of a Cicero. People had become impatient with the many case endings required in classical Latin, and were reducing them to two or three. Even these were treated with playful carelessness. The verb was handled in a different way—a more vivid one—to show changes in tense; and the word order was simplified. Moreover, slang words triumphed completely over traditional ones in some provinces. Ordinary people in Gaul (perhaps emulating the jargon of the army) stopped referring to the human head as *caput,* and substituted *testa* or "pot," from which comes modern French *tête.* It is as if all persons speaking English should have fallen into the way of saying "my bean" for the same object, so that it became the accepted word, while "head" was lost entirely.

The popular Roman speech differed from one province to another because popular locutions do tend always to be regional, and because the Romans came in contact with widely differing types of native speech. Thus the pronunciation and even the grammar were affected by the underlying populations. In one place the Latin word *habēre* continued to be used for "to have"; in the Spanish peninsula, however, it so happened that *tenēre,* meaning "to hold," came to be used in its place in the more general sense of "to have." That is why our imaginary Spanish child says *tengo* instead of any form of the classical *habēre.* The number "three," on the other hand, varies only slightly in the series of Romance sentences quoted. The numbers have remained fairly stable in the various daughter languages perpetuated from vulgar Latin. One of the factors tending to preserve a similarity in them throughout the ages has been their similar experience in developing a strong stress accent during the transition to the Middle Ages. This new accentuation caused similar losses in unaccented syllables in a given word in all Mediterranean areas. There were differences, of course, in the forms that emerged; but certainly not enough to make the results unrecognizably alien to one another.

The neo-Latin languages (if the expression may be permitted) give us another example, therefore, of a family which bears its signs of con-

sanguinity very legibly on the external aspect of each of its members. In
Roman times, Latin itself could claim cousins (in the ancient *Italic*
group) which have since been lost.

THE SLAVIC FAMILY

And here is one further example of language relationship which may
metaphorically be called close consanguinity. In eastern Europe a sharp-
eared traveler on an international train will also have an opportunity to
detect fundamental similarity behind the changing visages of national
speech. A far-flung territory is occupied by peoples speaking *Slavic*
languages and dialects. It would be possible to pursue the transformation of our key sentence addressed to an imaginary Slavic mother to the
east as follows:

CZECHISH: *Ano, matko, man tři.*
POLISH: *Tak, matko, mam trzy.*
RUSSIAN: *Da, matʲ, u menʲá tri.*

When our international train crosses into the Soviet Union, it will
pass through various sections of Russia showing distinct dialect colorings.
Ukrainian, for instance, shows enough differentiation to be dignified as
a national language, with an official spelling of its own. Even an un-
tutored eye, however, can see how close it is to the official language of
Great Russia, the classical medium of literature known to the world
as "Russian." In the Balkan states, South Slavic languages show these
perceptible nuances of our chosen theme. For instance, the Bulgarian
version of it would be: *"Da, maika, imom tri."*

Once again, we are justified in assuming that centuries ago there
was a single language from which these cousins descended. About the
seventh century it was probably still fairly unified. In the ninth century
a southern dialect of this early Slavic (Old Bulgarian) was written
down in a translation of the Bible made by Saints Cyril and Methodius.
The text helps us to get quite a clear picture of parent Slavic, just as
runic inscriptions bring us close to Primitive Germanic, and unofficial
documents of the Roman Empire tell us much about Vulgar Latin.

INDO-EUROPEAN, PARENT OF PARENTS

Slavic, Romance, and Germanic represent three families of languages spoken in Europe today. But surely it must be clear that similarities link these families to one another besides linking the smaller subdivisions within each given family. In *all* the national languages surveyed so far, it will be noticed, the word for "mother" began with the labial nasal [m]; in a considerable number a dental [t], [d], or [d] appeared in the middle of the word after the first vowel. Likewise in *all* of the languages listed, "three" began with a dental [t], [d], or [θ], followed by an [r]. Why is this?

Clearly, at a still earlier period than the days of early (prehistoric) Germanic and Slavonic, and of Vulgar Latin, there must have been a more ancient and inclusive unity which embraced all three.

The same procedure, if pursued farther, would have revealed to us other major families belonging to the same larger embracing unity in Europe and parts of Asia. These are:

Celtic, including Irish, Highland Scottish, Welsh, and Breton. (In modern Irish, "mother" is *mathair* and "three" is *tri.*)

Baltic, including Lettish, Lithuanian, and an extinct dialect once spoken in the territory of modern Prussia (Old Prussian). The word for "mother" is *motina,* not closely related to the cognates already cited. *Tris* for "three" is, on the other hand, an obvious cognate.

Hellenic, including modern Greek dialects, some of which go back to very ancient times. (An ancient Greek dialect, Attic, spoken in the city of Athens, produced a body of literature of enduring splendor. Its word for "mother" was *matér* and for "three," *treîs.* This is the classical language studied in school.)

Albanian, the national language of Albania, with no close relatives outside its own borders. Here "three" is *tre*; but the word for "mother" is not related to the forms in the above languages. A new form, *nona,* has replaced the Indo-European term preserved elsewhere.

Armenian, spoken in Armenia (between Europe and Asia Minor), is, like Albanian, a language with many diverse elements borrowed from outside, but it has an independent history traceable back to the fifth or sixth century A.D. Its word for "mother," *mair,* is easily recognizable as a cognate of the others given; not so, however, is *erek* for "three."

Even in Asia there are languages with venerable histories and rich literary heritage which can be recognized as members of the same linguistic clan:

Indian, including Hindustani, Bengali, Marathi, and Hindi. These dialects are descended from Old Indian, preserved to us in a classical literary form (Sanskrit) which dates back to the fifteenth century B.C. or even several hundred years earlier. Sanskrit, despite its great antiquity, still shows close generic resemblance to its modern European cousins. Its word for "mother" was *mātṛ* and for "three," *tri.*

Iranian, very closely related to Sanskrit, was spoken in the Persian highlands while Indian was spreading over the interior of India. It produced an early literature in the form of Zoroastrian hymns. Since those ancient times Persian has been subjected to large foreign infiltration, notably Arabic, but its structure still reveals its kinship with the other groups listed.

Hittite, a language spoken by people frequently mentioned in the Bible, is now extinct. Cuneiform inscriptions give us enough material to reveal its fundamental character. Some sort of relationship it surely must have had with the members of the broad family of families now being surveyed, but the precise nature of that relationship is still under discussion.

Tocharian, now extinct, is represented by some fragmentary texts (probably antedating the tenth century), which were discovered in eastern Turkestan in a Buddhist monastery. The material is too scanty to permit of definitive analysis, but it shows relationship to the above subsidiary groups.

Our railroad trip beginning with Germanic territory has taken us far afield, even to the shores of the Indus River in Asia. Even so, and despite the most baffling diversities, skilled comparison of key words has been able to establish that the miniature families surveyed do undoubtedly belong to the same large, inclusive family already postulated to account for likenesses observed among Germanic, Slavonic, and Romance (from Old Italic).

Back of the smaller families lay a single family; attached to this single family it is almost certain there must have been a single language. We call the whole family by the name "Indo-European," a term generally preferred today to "Indo-Germanic" or "Aryan," both of which could easily be misunderstood. That is to say, every language mentioned so far is an Indo-European language, no matter what smaller group it may belong to.

HOMELAND OF INDO-EUROPEAN

But if they are all related thus, we must assume that a single definite language, parent Indo-European, gave rise to all of them. This is probably true. Some time before 2000 B.C., in some part of the world, a group which was essentially a single community spoke this single parent language. Later, dialect forms of this tribal language were carried into many different countries, from Iceland to India—by emigration, by conquest, by peaceful transfer. We do not know how this occurred in every case, but the expansion had already begun in earliest historical times.

Where the parent language was spoken, and by whom, is something of a mystery. By studying words that are common to a number of the family groups listed above we can, to be sure, get some idea of the culture these people had before their language was spread over a wide area and differentiated by the divisions, migrations, or conquests of a half-dozen millennia ago. We can surmise that they probably lived in a temperate climate because a number of the descended languages have similar words for spring, summer, autumn, and winter. There are common words indicating a developed (though still simple) agriculture: terms having to do with the plow, spade, sickle, and mill; with carting, sowing, and mowing. For instance, the word for plow is *arðr* in Icelandic, *áratron* in Greek, *arātrum* in Latin, *arathar* in Irish, *árklas* in Lithuanian, *araur* in Armenian. The names of certain plants and animals are supposed to offer some guidance. Parent Indo-European had terms for dogs, cows, sheep, bulls, goats, pigs, and horses; also for wild animals such as the bear, the wolf, and the fox. Hermann Hirt, author of an elaborate discussion of the subject, considers the common words for "eel" in several languages as very important. If the original speakers of Indo-European knew this fish, they could not have lived originally near the Black Sea, where it is not found. Another important word is the old term for the beech tree in the various languages. The words *Buche* in German, *fagus* in Latin, *Bachenis* Forest in a Celtic place-name, and

Phegós (φηγός) in Greek (where it had been transferred, however, to the oak tree), indicate that the beech was a tree known at the time of the parent language. The forms just quoted could all have come from a single root. Now the eastern boundary for the presence of this European tree is a line drawn roughly from Königsberg to the Crimea. Therefore Hirt argues that the parent language must have developed to the west of such a line.

North central Germany, Lithuania, the Danube Valley, and Southern Russia (near the Black Sea) have been suggested in turn as the original homeland of the parent language. India, once regarded as the cradle of our general Indo-European speech, has been relinquished in favor of European territories answering to the geographical clues of the joint vocabularies. Of these it may be said that probability favors those districts in which there are many physical traces of early mankind, such as burial mounds, skeletons, fragments of pottery, signs of human habitation. The Danube Valley is particularly rich in these, and also Germany and Southern Russia. Lithuania can boast an extraordinarily archaic language, similar in many ways to ancient Sanskrit, but its territory is poor in archaeological remains, those mute witnesses to the daily living of people like ourselves who "flourished" (if that is the proper word) in prehistoric times. Lithuania may have been settled early in the age that saw the spread of Indo-European, but it is less likely than other districts to have seen its first development.

No matter where Indo-European developed out of still earlier linguistic stages now hopelessly lost, it is important to remember that we know absolutely nothing about the physical appearance of its first speakers. They have long since been leveled with the dust; we cannot say whether their skin was light or dark, their vanished hair shadowy or bright. Among the broad-skulled and long-skulled and medium-skulled remains of prehistoric man, we cannot tell which—if any—moved their bony jaws in olden times to the sounds and rhythms of the Indo-European parent language. Although most of the contemporary peoples of Europe may be descendants, in part, of members of our postulated Indo-European community, still it is not safe to assume that this community was itself racially homogeneous.

In any event we cannot be sure about what happened in those early ages. It is instructive to think of the mutations of history in the era since writing began. Whole peoples have suffered extinction as nations in past centuries, yet they may perpetuate and hand on the language of the conquerors when the latter in their turn are destroyed or absorbed. A West Indian Negro today can often be found speaking with the faultless accents and intonation of choice classical English; if you closed your eyes you would think he had been nurtured on the playing fields of Eton or by the Cam. He speaks standard English *as his native tongue;* he is aware of nothing alien about it as it leaves his lips; there is no psychological strain involved in employing this particular instrument merely because his ancestors in Africa used a very different one long ago. No doubt flawless Latin was spoken in the streets of Rome by naturalized provincials of many races, showing wide variety in the hues of their epidermises. In somewhat the same way all of us, for that matter, may be using variations of a borrowed instrument. So completely separate are the questions of language and race.

Most scholars would, to be sure, look to one or another of the contemporary peoples of Europe or India or even Persia to find lineal descendants of those who first spoke Indo-European. Yet two well-known authorities, Sigmund Feist (a German) and Vendryès (a Frenchman), have argued that even the Germans of today—who usually claim that honor—do not have the blood of the parent tribe in their veins even though they speak an Indo-European language (which they now choose to call "Aryan"). Feist and Vendryès point out that German (like Dutch, English, and Scandinavian) shows a very great change from the parent speech which lies back of the other Indo-European offshoots. The Germanic family has changed many of the supposed original sounds. Where Latin had *piscis,* Germanic substituted a form like *fisk* (English "fish"); where Latin and Greek had *patēr,* Germanic showed something like English "father." Thus this one particular group looks quite different from its Romance, Slavonic, Hellenic and other cousins because of an unusually complete shift of consonants. According to Feist and Vendryès, the reason is that the Primitive Germanic tribesmen were an alien race trying to learn to pronounce an Indo-European or "Aryan" language. They had trouble with sounds like [p] and [t], and so distorted them to [f] and [θ]. If this theory is sound, the Germans of today would be a non-"Aryan" race (granting that the phrase means anything), speaking an "Aryan" language imposed upon them by conquerors in prehistoric times! The whole question is very speculative. It may be pointed out that if Germanic tribesmen had trouble with [p] and [t] in primitive times, at least their descendants soon made good the loss by developing new [p] and [t] sounds out of Indo-European [b] and [d].

At the moment, however, what interests us most is the evidence of underlying unity, not of divergence, in the Indo-European family. As we shall see, the divergences turn out to be fairly regular when they are closely examined. Because they are more or less predictable by an advanced student, they do not disturb seriously his impressions of the underlying unity which justifies him in regarding the whole majestic array of tongues as a close-knit family. The more acutely one observes the principles of correspondence and divergence, the easier it becomes to learn a new member within the widely scattered group.

Cursory as this review has been, it has probably indicated the approach and even something of the methods used in the study of comparative linguistics.

Comparisons of a similar sort have established family relationships for the rest of the world. For the languages less familiar to us speakers of English a briefer survey will suffice.

.   .   .

SINGLE OR MULTIPLE ORIGIN OF SPEECH?

Already the question has often been asked: "Do we know enough to decide whether all languages, the world over, had a single origin? Is *every* language related to every other?"

It is a fascinating question. The mere possibility of unified origin for all human speech appeals strongly to the imagination. Here indeed would be a most gratifying satisfaction for our natural desire to simplify our understanding of the universe about us by reducing the number of categories under which we conceive of it. There is also something aesthetically grandiose about the thought that the vast symphony of all languages and dialects was elaborated, so to speak, from a single theme.

In the early days of linguistic science, the presuppositions were naturally in favor of monogenesis of speech, because the story of the Garden of Eden, whether understood literally or not, exerted a strong influence on investigators. Then under the spell of Darwinism there was a reaction to a belief in polygenesis, likewise often expressed in dogmatic terms.

Analogies were drawn and misapplied in linguistic science, for which Darwin himself should not be blamed. The chief exponent of linguistic polygenesis was Friedrich Müller, who assumed that the "speech" of animals must have developed gradually into human speech, so gradually indeed that man must have been a diversified type long before the evolution was completed, "and herewith," he argued, "we may be said to have an *a priori* postulate, from the point of view of the history of evolution, of the derivation of human speech (as an ideational and conceptional language based on sounds) from several mutually independent sources."

Today most authors are extremely cautious when they touch upon the unrecoverable epoch when speech originated. They usually avoid committing themselves on the question as to whether this happened once or several times in various parts of the world. In any case, they say, the answer is unimportant, even irrelevant, for the solution of problems significant for us today.

Nevertheless a few individual writers are willing to commit themselves. Alfredo Trombetti, for instance, has presented a lengthy, ambitious argument for monogenesis, fortified with many concrete illustrations. On the basis of extremely wide and detailed study, Trombetti builds up a scheme including wider and wider groups and families of languages, making use of surviving similarities in numerals, pronominal forms, and the like. Such structural words are apt to be conservative of their form, and they are not readily borrowed from one language by another in most cases. He records similarities between numerals in Sudanese-Bantu and Munda-Khmer of the Austro-Asiatic group; between pronouns in Hamitic-Semitic, Dravidian, Munda, and Polynesian; between numerals in Indo-Chinese and Uralic (he says "Ural-Altaic"); between verbs in Dakota (American Indian) and Georgian (in the Caucasian territory). He observes that the greatest similarities are to be found between groups most widely separated on the periphery of a huge circle having its center in India. Therefore he deduces that India was the home and starting point for all races as well as all languages. It is true that Trombetti produces some astonishing parallelisms. But one becomes suspicious of them when one reflects upon the great mobility of language: its proneness to change and transformation. After observing the behavior of vowels and consonants over the very short span of recorded history, one begins to suspect that two words that look alike now are probably unrelated for that very reason—unless they belong to two subgroups in demonstrably close generic relation, and also mean approximately the same thing. English "book" and German *Buch* are indeed cognates, but it is quite accidental that Quiché *buj* or *vuj* (also pronounced [buχ], but with a loose *b*) means the same thing. We know too little about the early history of the languages outside of Indo-European and Hamito-Semitic to commit ourselves too far on the matter of ultimate relationships. For one thing, change operates very slowly in some groups and with almost dizzying rapidity in others. We must allow for this in estimating the value of Trombetti's parallels. The question about a single origin for the diverse tongues of mankind must be tabled until we know more of their earlier forms; and that may be—forever.

JOHN S. KENYON

From American Pronunciation, *tenth edi-tion, by John S. Kenyon. Copyright, 1924, 1935, 1945, 1946, and 1950, by John S. Kenyon. By permission of George Wahr Publishing Co.*

Historical Suggestions

In order to understand many aspects of our modern English it is essential to be able to form some idea of the way in which various features of our language have come to be what they are. It is therefore necessary for the student of phonetics to have some background of the history of the English language. The following facts should be mastered by the student.

1. English is a descendant of the Germanic branch of the Indo-European family of languages. Latin and Greek are sister branches to the Germanic. Since English is descended from the Germanic branch, and French and Spanish from the sister Latin branch, English may be said

to be a cousin of French and Spanish. Since modern German and English are both descendants from the Germanic branch, they are sister languages, more recently related than Latin and Germanic.

The speakers of the English descendant of the Germanic branch migrated from northwestern Europe to England in the fifth century A.D. There the language went on developing. The earliest written records of English we have are from the seventh century. The language from that time till about 1150 is called Anglo-Saxon or **Old English (OE)**. King Alfred, who wrote several important works, may conveniently be taken as the chief representative of the Old English period. From the reign of Henry II (about 1150) to that of Henry VIII (about 1500) the language is called **Middle English (ME)**. Chaucer (1340-1400), in the reign of Richard II, may be taken as the chief representative of Middle English. From about 1500 to the present is **Modern English (MnE),** that from 1500 to 1700 being **Early Modern (EM),** and from 1700 to 1950+, **Late Modern (LM).**

The student should avoid the mistake of applying the term "Old English" to any stage of early English later than 1150. The term is often wrongly applied to Chaucer's English, or even to Shakespeare's. Chaucer's language is Middle English, and Shakespeare's Early Modern. Some try to avoid ambiguity by calling English before 1150 "Anglo-Saxon," a term misleading in other respects. The name was never applied to their language by the Anglo-Saxons themselves, and it unfortunately helps to foster the too prevalent notion that King Alfred's English was a foreign tongue that did not become English till it was united with French. King Alfred and his contemporaries called their language "English," and neither its name nor its essential character was changed by the later assimilation of French and Latin words to its vocabulary. The student should learn these periods carefully, as frequent reference is made to them.

2. Until the Scandinavian Conquests and extensive fusion with the English people (8th-11th cc.), and the Norman Conquest (1066), the words in English were mostly native, i.e., words that had descended from parents to children through the West Germanic branch from the original word-stock of Indo-European. But from their Norwegian and Danish neighbors in England the English borrowed several hundred words, as *fellow, loose, raise,* etc. Likewise a great number of place-

names in England are of Scandinavian origin, from which many family names are derived.

When the Norman French settlers came to England in 1066, they of course brought with them their own language—a northern dialect of French. This was spoken in England until about 1350 in a form gradually changed from its continental original and now called Anglo-French. Because the government and the church in England were then under the control of the Normans, French was the language of the higher classes and of literature, while English continued to be spoken by the native lower classes. About 1350 English again became the language of the ruling class, and French became a possession of only the educated. In the meantime the Central, or Parisian, French had exerted such influence on Anglo-French that Parisian French was now the preferred form in England, and the great body of French loan-words taken into English from about 1250 to 1400 are chiefly of the Central French form. However, a few Anglo-French speech sounds came into English from the French spoken in England and developed into Modern English along with other English sounds.[1]

After about 1250—nearly two hundred years after the conquest—Parisian French words flowed into England in great numbers for nearly two hundred years,[2] and were learned and used as English words alongside the native words. In the main they were pronounced—except for the inflectional endings—as French was at that time pronounced, which was very different from modern French. The accent was at first that of the French, usually near the final syllable, but this soon shifted in many words to a place near the beginning, where most native words were accented, though often in the longer words a secondary accent remained where the main French accent had been. In the following centuries many Latin words, too, were introduced through literature and scholarship, and became assimilated into the English word-stock.

3. Important as are these two great additions—the French and the Latin—to the English vocabulary, they did not otherwise much affect

[1] See §§30 and 35 of "A Brief History of the English Language," pp. lxxxiv-v of *Webster's New International Dictionary, Second Edition.*
[2] The influx, in somewhat lesser numbers, has continued to the present day. See Jespersen, *Growth and Structure of the English Language,* Leipzig, 1905, §95, and A. C. Baugh, in *Modern Language Notes,* February, 1935, pp. 90-93, and his *History of the English Language,* N.Y. 1935, §123, esp. p. 207.

the language. They did not essentially modify the pronunciation of native words, or the grammar and syntax of English. The essential structure of English is today what it was in King Alfred's day, before the Norman Conquest.

Important changes, however, were already going on before the influx of the new borrowed words. They are chiefly of five kinds: (1) Changes in the **meanings** of words—not of great importance in the study of phonetics. (2) Changes in **syntax,** or construction—also of minor importance to phonetics. (3) Changes in **inflectional endings** for number, case, tense, etc. These are of considerable importance to phonetics, for change and loss of inflectional endings have brought about many changes in pronunciation. (4) Changes in **stress.** These have also caused considerable changes in pronunciation—especially in the shifting of the accent in borrowed words. (5) Changes in **consonant and vowel sounds.** These are of central importance to phonetics. Many of the foregoing changes are still going on. They will be referred to as occasion requires.

4. Changes in pronunciation arise from two principal sources—phonetic change and change by analogy. **Phonetic change** is the gradual, progressive, unconscious change in the sounds of words that results in part, at any rate, from our inability to imitate and reproduce perfectly what we hear. Thus the word *stone,* which in King Alfred's time was pronounced "stahn" with *a* as in *father,* changed so gradually that few, if any, realized that any change was going on till it reached its present pronunciation. And so with other phonetic changes. **Analogical change** is quite different in its operation. It can best be exemplified. When a child says *goed* for *went,* he does so not because he has heard *goed,* but because he has frequently heard *showed, snowed, tried, rained, burned,* and many others—all indicating past time by means of a **d** sound at the end. Hence by imitating, not the whole word, but the method of adding endings, he adds the same ending to *go* before he has fully learned the form *went.* Though *goed* is often *heard* in children's speech, the form has never got into general use. But in the past, children and adults have created many such new forms, many of which have become general and have crowded out older forms. For instance, the proper past tense of the verb *step* was formerly *stōp.* But someone at some time first said *stept* instead of *stōp,* in imitation of many verbs that formed their past tense by adding a **t** sound, such as *lost, stopt, walkt,* etc. Many other speakers did the

same thing, till finally everybody gradually abandoned the old form *stōp* and adopted the new form *stept*.[3]

In the same manner a large number of verbs have been changed by analogy from the "strong" to the "weak" conjugation. OE had the same two classes of verbs as MnE—the "irregular" or "strong" verbs like *drive, drove, driven; sing, sang, sung; fall, fell, fallen;* and the "regular" or "weak" verbs like *fill, filled, filled; deem, deemed, deemed; keep, kept, kept*. But from the earliest historical period of the English language the strong verbs have been constantly changing to the form of the weak. The following verbs were originally strong, but by analogy have become weak: *bake, bow, carve, chew, creep, delve, flee, help, laugh, melt, milk, mourn, seethe, shave, shove, spurn, step, swell, wash, yell, yelp, yield;* and about sixty others.

Another example of change by analogy is the plural -*s* of nouns. Formerly only one group of nouns formed their plural by the addition of -*s*. Some made the plural by adding -*en*, as three nouns still do— *oxen, children, brethren;* others by adding -*e*, of which no trace remains; others had the plural identical with the singular, as a few still do—*deer, sheep, swine*. But finally, by analogy of the group that added -*s*, all regular nouns have now come to form their plural in -*s*.

5. Though a **standard literary English** arose in Chaucer's day, it was in the 16th c. that the speech of London, Oxford, and Cambridge gained a place as the **spoken standard** to which the educated in various parts of England tended to conform. But their adherence to this type of speech was never complete, and even today speakers in south England vary considerably in their pronunciation of present-day "Standard English."

Some of the features of standard English in the 17th c., when America was settled, were the following: (1) r was sounded wherever it was spelt. (2) The vowel of *half, last, path, dance* was like that today in *hat, man*. (3) The vowel in *stop, rob* sounded like the short of the one in *father*. (4) The vowels of *hate, spade,* and of *note, rode* were simple vowels, not diphthongs as in present British. (5) The vowel in *due, true* was **ɪu**, not a *yoo* and *oo* sound as in present British. (6) The

---

[3] Strictly, these are not directly changes in pronunciation, but substitution of different grammatical forms. Changes in speech sounds by analogy are rarer; as the British pronunciation of *lather* as lɑðə by analogy of *father, rather;* or the *ĕ* of *friend* from *friendship,* or the *ĭ* of *wind* from *windmill*. See also *Webster,* "Pronunciation," §1.

vowel in *borne* was ō, distinct from the *aw* sound in *born*. (7) The vowel
of *talk, draw* was nearer the *ah* sound than today. (8) The h in *what,
when* was sounded. (9) Words like *dictionary, cemetery, dormitory* had
a secondary accent on the third syllable.

By 1800 the speech of London had so changed from the standard form
that was still used away from the metropolis that it became the basis
of a new standard form, while the older one continued to be spoken in
the more remote districts, especially the North and America, to which it
had been taken in the 17th c. By 1900 the new British type had the
following features among others: (1) r was sounded only before a vowel.
(2) The vowel in *half,* etc., had become that in *father*. (3) The vowel
in *stop, rob* had moved toward that in *talk*. (4) The vowels of *hate,
spade,* and of *note, rode* had become diphthongs. (5) The diphthongs in
due, true had become *yoo* and *oo* sounds. (6) The vowel of *borne* had
become like that in *born*. (7) The vowel in *talk* had gone nearer to ō.
(8) The h sound had gone from *what, when*. (9) *Dictionary,* etc., had
lost the secondary accent.

As shown long ago by W. D. Whitney and E. S. Sheldon,[4] and
recently by Dr. Orbeck,[5] American English came, not chiefly from
British local dialects, but from standard British of the 17th c. The
striking resemblance of General American to Northern British in certain features has been cited to show that GA came from northern England. But these features belonged to 17th c. Southern British. The same
is true of resemblances to GA found in other British local dialects: they
have disappeared from standard British but remained in GA.

Exactly how the three chief types of American English—Eastern,
Southern, and General American—are derived from British is not yet
determined. But there is much evidence that the chief colonial centers,
Boston, New York, Richmond, and Charleston, continuing in closer
cultural contact with London than did the rest of the rapidly increasing
colonial population, shared more of the advancing changes of Southern
British. Hence Eastern and Southern American today are more like
present Southern British than is GA, which preserves more features
of the 17th c. standard British.

[4] See *Dialect Notes,* Vol. I, p. 292.
[5] Anders Orbeck, *Early New England Pronunciation,* Ann Arbor, 1927.

Four Versions of Matthew 8:1-13

From Introduction to the English Language, *Albert H. Marckwardt. Copyright, 1942, by Oxford University Press.* By permission of Oxford University Press.

OLD ENGLISH GOSPELS

1. Sōþlīċe þā sē Hǣlend of þǣm munte nyþer āstāh, þā fyliġdon him miċele menigu.

2. Þā ġenēalǣhte ān hrēofla to him, and hine tō him ġeēaðmēdde, and þus cwæð: 'Dryhten, ġif þū wilt, þū miht mē geclǣnsian.'

3. Ðā āstrehte sē Hǣlend his hand, and hrepode hine, and þus cwæð: 'Iċ wille; bēo ġeclǣnsod.' And his hrēofla wæs hrædlīċe ġeclǣnsod.

4. Ðā cwæð sē Hǣlend to him: 'Warna þē þæt þū hit nǣnegum men ne secge; ac gang, ætīewe þē þǣm sacerde, and bring heom þā lāc þe Moyses bebēad on heora ġecȳðnesse.'

5. Sōþlīċe þā sē Hǣlend in ēode on Capharnaum, þā ġenēalǣhte him ān hundredes ealdor, hine biddende,

6. And þus cweðende: 'Dryhten, mīn cnapa liġð on mīnum hūse, lama and mid yfle ġeðrēaġd.'

7. Ðā cwæð sē Hǣlend tō him: 'Iċ cume and hine ġehǣle.'

8. Ðā andswarode sē hundredes ealdor and ðus cwæð: 'Dryhten, ne eom iċ wierðe þæt þū in gange under mine þeċene; ac cweð þīn ān word, and mīn cnapa biþ ġehǣled.'

9. 'Sōðlīċe, iċ eom man under anwealde gesett, and iċ hæbbe þeġnas under mē, and iċ cweðe tō þissum, "Gang," and hē gǣð; and iċ cweðe to ōðrum, "Cum," and hē cymð; tō mīnum ðēowe, "Wyrċ þis," and hē wyrċð.'

10. Witodlīċe, þā sē Hǣlend þis ġehīerde, þā wundrode hē, and cwæð tō þǣm ðe him fyliġdon: 'Sōþ iċ secge ēow, ne ġemētte iċ swā ġelēafan on Israhel.

11. Tō sōþum iċ secge ēow þæt maniġe cumað fram ēastdǣle and westdǣle, and wuniað mid Abrahame, and Isahace, and Iacobe on heofona rīce.

12. Witodlīċe þises rīċes bearn bēoð āworpene on þā ȳtemestan þēostro; ðǣr bēoð wōp and tōða grīstbītung.'

13. And sē Hǣlend cwæð tō þǣm hundredes ealdre: 'Gā, and ġeweorþe þē swā swā þū ġelīefdest.' And sē cnapa wæs ġehǣled on þǣre tīde.

WYCLIFFE'S MIDDLE ENGLISH VERSION

1. Forsothe when Jhesus hadde comen doun fro the hil, many cumpanyes folewiden hym.

2. And loo! a leprouse man cummynge worshipide hym, sayinge, Lord, ȝif thou wolt, thou maist make me clene.

3. And Jhesus, holdynge forthe the hond touchide hym, sayinge, I wole, be thou maad clene. And anoon the lepre of hym was clensid.

4. And Jhesus saith to hym, See, say thou to no man; but go, shewe thee to prestis, and offre that ȝifte that Moyses comaundide, into witnessing to hym.

5. Sothely when he hadde entride in to Capharnaum, centurio neiȝide to hym, preyinge hym.

6. And saide, Lord, my child lyeth in the hous sike on the palsie, and is yuel tourmentid.

7. And Jhesus saith to hym, I shall cume, and shall hele hym.

8. And centurio answerynge saith to hym, Lord, I am not worthi,

that thou entre vnder my roof; but oonly say bi word, and my child shal be helid.

9. For whi and I am a man ordeynd vnder power, hauynge vnder me kniȝtis; and I say to this, Go, and he goth; and to an other, Come thou, and he cometh; and to my seruaunt, Do thou this thing, and he doth.

10. Sothely Jhesus, heerynge these thingis, wondride, and saide to men suynge hym, Trewly I saye to ȝou, I fonde nat so grete feith in Y[s]rael.

11. Sothely Y say to ȝou, that manye shulen come from the est and west, and shulen rest with Abraham and Ysaac and Jacob in the kyngdam of heauenes;

12. Forsothe the sonys of the rewme shulen be cast out in to vttermest derknessis; there shall be weepynge, and beetynge togidre of teeth.

13. And Jhesus said to centurio, Go, and as thou hast bileeued, be it don to thee. And the child was helid fro that houre.

KING JAMES VERSION

When he was come down from the mountain, great multitudes followed him.

2 And, behold, there came a leper and worshipped him, saying, Lord, if thou wilt, thou canst make me clean.

3 And Jesus put forth *his* hand, and touched him, saying, I will; be thou clean. And immediately his leprosy was cleansed.

4 And Jesus saith unto him, See thou tell no man; but go thy way, shew thyself to the priest, and offer the gift that Moses commanded, for a testimony unto them.

5 And when Jesus was entered into Capernaum, there came unto him a centurion, beseeching him,

6 And saying, Lord, my servant lieth at home sick of the palsy, grievously tormented.

7 And Jesus saith unto him, I will come and heal him.

8 The centurion answered and said, Lord, I am not worthy that thou shouldest come under my roof: but speak the word only, and my servant shall be healed.

9 For I am a man under authority, having soldiers under me: and I say to this *man,* Go, and he goeth; and to another, Come, and he cometh; and to my servant, Do this, and he doeth *it.*

10 When Jesus heard *it,* he marvelled, and said to them that followed, Verily I say unto you, I have not found so great faith, no, not in Israel.

11 And I say unto you, That many shall come from the east and west, and shall sit down with Abraham, and Isaac, and Jacob, in the kingdom of heaven.

12 But the children of the kingdom shall be cast out into outer darkness: there shall be weeping and gnashing of teeth.

13 And Jesus said unto the centurion, Go thy way; and as thou hast believed, *so* be it done unto thee. And his servant was healed in the selfsame hour.

REVISED STANDARD VERSION

When he came down from the mountain, great crowds followed him; ² and behold, a leper came to him and knelt before him, saying, "Lord, if you will, you can make me clean." ³ And he stretched out his hand and touched him, saying, "I will; be clean." And immediately his leprosy was cleansed. ⁴ And Jesus said to him, "See that you say nothing to any one; but go, show yourself to the priest, and offer the gift that Moses commanded, for a proof to the people." [a]

5 As he entered Capernaum, a centurion came forward to him, be-

[a] Greek *to them*

seeching him [6] and saying, "Lord, my servant is lying paralyzed at home, in terrible distress." [7] And he said to him, "I will come and heal him." [8] But the centurion answered him, "Lord, I am not worthy to have you come under my roof; but only say the word, and my servant will be healed. [9] For I am a man under authority, with soldiers under me; and I say to one, 'Go,' and he goes, and to another, 'Come,' and he comes, and to my slave, 'Do this,' and he does it." [10] When Jesus heard him, he marveled, and said to those who followed him, "Truly, I say to you, not even[b] in Israel have I found such faith. [11] I tell you, many will come from east and west and sit at table with Abraham, Isaac, and Jacob in the kingdom of heaven, [12] while the sons of the kingdom will be thrown into the outer darkness; there men will weep and gnash their teeth." [13] And to the centurion Jesus said, "Go; be it done for you as you have believed." And the servant was healed at that very moment.

STUART ROBERTSON AND
FREDERIC G. CASSIDY

From The Development of Modern English, *second edition, by Stuart Robertson, revised by Frederic G. Cassidy. Copyright, 1934, 1938, and 1954, by Prentice-Hall, Inc. By permission of Prentice-Hall, Inc.*

Changing Meanings and Values of Words

. . . Even though it is generally recognized that meanings change, many people still cling, curiously enough, to the quite contradictory notion that words all have "true" meanings, that changes somehow take us away from the "true" meaning, and that the way to find out what

[b] Other ancient authorities read *with no one.*

a word "really means" is to find out what it once meant. This is particularly true in respect to borrowed words in English, the belief evidently
being that the meaning of the word in contemporary English and the
meaning of the Latin or Greek word from which the English word is
derived must be one and the same. A little reflection should show that
an appeal to etymology in order to establish the present meaning of the
word is as untrustworthy as an appeal to spelling in order to establish
its present pronunciation. And for a reason that is almost exactly parallel:
change of *meaning* is likely to have altered the etymological sense, which
is thereby rendered archaic or obsolete, just as change of *sound* is likely
to be unrecorded in the "antiquarian" spelling that so frequently characterizes Modern English. The study of etymology has great value and
interest—a point to which we shall later return—but its usefulness in
settling the question of what a word means is subject to considerable
qualification.

Let us see what results when one ignores the idea that a word may
change its meaning, and appeals to its etymology in order to determine
its present meaning. A handbook of only twenty-odd years ago on "correct English"[1] sets forth the following dictum: *"Dilapidated . . .*
Said of a building or other structure. But the word is from the Latin
lapis, a stone, and cannot properly be used of any but a stone structure."
One might just as reasonably argue that because *candidate* is related to
the Latin *candidus* (white), it cannot properly be used of an aspirant for
political office unless he is clothed in a suit of white material. More
clearly even, one might protest that *holiday* properly describes Christmas
or Easter, but should never be used of Independence Day or Labor
Day; or that *bonfire* should not be applied except where the combustible
material is bone. These arguments are not much more grotesque than
some that have been seriously maintained in defense of an etymological
crotchet, while ignoring the fact of change of meaning. Indeed, one who
argues on this basis is a victim of the "etymological fallacy."

The fact is that what a word once meant is not necessarily what it

[1] *Write It Right,* by Ambrose Bierce, New York (Neale), 1928. The work is
well worth investigating as a striking demonstration of what pedantry, combined with ignorance of linguistic processes, will do for one. To much of it, a
witty definition of Bierce's own is curiously applicable: *"positive*—mistaken at
the top of one's voice."

now means; the etymological meaning has often died out, and a quite new development is the living descendant. This is particularly true of words in common or popular use. Words, after all, are for the most part purely conventional symbols. They mean only what those who are using them agree to make them mean. Exactly the same principles apply to "learned" words, but because their traditional users have generally known the language from which they were borrowed, or of whose elements they were composed, they have tended to preserve the etymological meaning—indeed, it is conventional to use such words with an eye to their source; thus they are less prone to alterations of meaning than are popular words. It is in this way, incidentally, that a cultural tradition holds in check, to some extent, the constant tendency of language to change.[2]

Change of meaning, however, though usually unpredictable, is not utterly arbitrary; as we shall see in a moment, it often proceeds along familiar paths. Furthermore, though it takes place in all languages, it does not proceed at the same rate even in related ones. If we look at cognate words in English and German, for example, which might have been expected to have the same meaning, we often find them widely different, and the difference is most commonly the result of some radical change of sense in the English word. Opposite instances can be found, admittedly, in which the English word has stood still and the German one changed; yet it is usually the latter which is conservative. Examples of this characteristic English shift in meaning are the following: *Schlagen* and *slay* are originally the same word, but the German word retains the general meaning of "smite" or "strike" while the English word has become narrowed to mean "strike with fatal consequences" or "kill."[3] *Knabe* is the cognate in German of Old English *cnapa* or *cnafa,* and has the same meaning, "boy"; but Modern English *knave* has a radically different one; the German *Tier* means any kind of animal, as did the cognate Old English *deor,* but in Modern English *deer* means one particular kind of animal.

[2] Some of this holding in check is unconscious, some conscious; we shall have to postpone to a later chapter the question of the values and judgments upon which conscious attempts to control language are based.

[3] The Latin word *caedere,* though unrelated to English *slay,* has undergone exactly the same specialization of meaning.

GENERALIZATION AND SPECIALIZATION

One very common type of change is that in which the "area" of the meaning is changed. When a word that has referred broadly or inclusively begins instead to refer narrowly or exclusively, this is an example of "specialization" of meaning; the contrary is called "generalization." Interestingly enough, the same word may undergo both processes at different stages of the development of its meaning. *Go,* for example, is a verb of motion that seems as general as possible in meaning, and presumably this is also the basic meaning; early in its history in English, however, it must have specialized, for Old English *gān* sometimes means "walk," and in Middle English *ryde or gon* (ride or walk) is a familiar formula. Although the present meaning is the generalized one, the specialization "walk" was still possible in the late seventeenth century, as we see in these phrases from Bunyan: "I am resolved to run when I can, to go when I cannot run, and to creep when I cannot go." [4]

Borrowed words are quite as likely as native ones to undergo such transformations in meaning. *Virtue*[5] is connected with Latin *vir* (man). Thus, *virtue* first meant "manliness" in general; but its meaning later specialized to stand for the manly quality most in demand in the military state, namely "fortitude" or "warlike prowess"—the meaning familiar in Caesar's *Commentaries.* But a still later Latin meaning is more comprehensive, and it was this very general meaning that was attached to *virtue* when it was borrowed in English through French. One possible specialization was "power," as in "Virtue had gone out of him," or even "magical power," as in "the virtue of the spell" or Milton's "virtuous ring and glass." More commonly, however, the word in English retained a general sense of "noble quality"—though more and more with reference to moral rather than to mental or physical characteristics. But another specialization limits its application to women; for example, "All the sons were brave, and all the daughters virtuous," where *virtuous* is equivalent to "chaste." "A woman's virtue" will today be interpreted

---

[4] Quoted by Bradley, *The Making of English,* p. 182.
[5] This history is given in greater detail in Greenough and Kittredge, *Words and Their Ways in English Speech,* pp. 241-242.

in only the last sense. A curious evolution, indeed, when one recalls that the etymological meaning is "manliness."

The foregoing are particularly striking examples, but hundreds of others could be cited. We find generalization in such everyday words as *picture,* once restricted, as the etymology would suggest (compare: the *Picts,* "painted ones"), to a *painted* representation of something seen, but now applicable to photography, crayon drawing, and so forth; *butcher,* who once slew one animal only, the goat (French *bouc*); the verb *sail,* which has been transferred to *steam* navigation, just as *drive* has been transferred to self-propelled vehicles; *injury,* which once was limited to "injustice"; *zest,* which meant "bit of lemon-peel"; *chest,* which usually meant "coffin"—"He is now deed and nayled in his cheste";[6] *pen,* which meant "feather," but which is now much more likely to mean a writing implement tipped with metal than a quill; *quarantine,* from which the original meaning of a "forty" days' isolation has quite disappeared; and *companion,* which has likewise lost the etymological sense of "one who (shares) bread with" another.

But generalization of meaning does not always stay within bounds; under some conditions the meaning becomes so broad that, in extreme cases, there is hardly any meaning left. We have a whole set of words, used conversationally when we either do not know, or cannot remember, or perhaps will not take the trouble to search for a more precise term: the *what-you-may-call-it* kind of word—*thingumabob, doohickie, jigger,* and so on.[7] Not so long ago *gadget* was imported into the U.S. from England, and has found a very hearty welcome into this company.

Another type, in which generalization goes even farther, has aroused strong opposition from guardians of literary style, who realize that emptiness and "jargon" result from the indiscriminate use of "words that mean little or nothing, but may stand for almost anything":[8] such words are *thing, business, concern, condition, matter, article, circumstance.* As we all recognize at once, these are words that have a fairly exact sense, but which also have acquired the ability to fit into a wide variety of everyday contexts, in which their meaning becomes extremely

[6] Chaucer's clerk, speaking of Petrarch (*Clerk's Prologue,* line 30).

[7] Louise Pound has collected more than 100 such terms now current in popular speech: "American Indefinite Names," *American Speech,* Vol. VI, No. 4 (April 1931), pp. 257-259.

[8] Greenough and Kittredge, *op. cit.,* p. 235.

vague—in fact, almost wholly dependent on the context. The word *deal* is the current American favorite in this group, its gamut of meaning running all the way from perfectly favorable ("Your job sounds like a pretty fine deal") to thoroughly unfavorable ("I won't take part in any of his deals"). This word serves the purpose, and is going through the same general sort of development, that *proposition* did a generation ago.

Even more frequent than generalization, and even more readily illustrated in numberless familiar instances, is the opposite process of specialization. *Steorfan* is an Old English word, cognate with the German *sterben*, which meant "die"; but the standard Modern English meaning ("starve") is a specialized one, namely "die from hunger." Another specialization, "die from cold," is found in certain Modern English dialects: "[he] . . . bid her come . . . sit close by the fire: he was sure she was starved" is from the Yorkshire dialect of *Wuthering Heights* (Chapter XXX). The older meaning of *meat* was "food" in general, as one might suspect from the archaic phrase *meat and drink* and from the compound *sweetmeat*. For the meaning "meat," the older term was *flesh* or *flesh meat*. It is interesting to observe, incidentally, that the German cognate for *flesh, Fleisch,* suggests first of all the specialized sense of "meat"; this is the present meaning, too, of French *viande,* while the English *viands* retains the general sense of "food." *Coast* is a borrowing, through French, from a Latin word for "side" or "rib" (compare Modern English *intercostal*), and once meant "border" or "frontier"—the "coast of Bohemia" was not always an absurdity. But *coast* in present use not only has the usual specialization "seashore"; as employed in the eastern United States, it means specifically "Pacific coast." *Shore,* on the other hand, means, in parts of the east at any rate, "Atlantic shore." [9] In some of the same localities, however, "eastern shore" means what elsewhere would have to be expanded into "eastern shore of the Chesapeake in Maryland," just as in part of New England "the cape" means definitely "Cape Cod." *Token* formerly had the broad meaning "sign," but was long ago specialized to mean a physical thing that is a sign (of something)—as in *love token,* or the metal tokens used on streetcars or buses.

[9] In Philadelphia it is often used in a still more specific sense, "southern New Jersey shore"; it sometimes bears a yet more localized signification: "Atlantic City," which occurs repeatedly in the headlines of Philadelphia newspapers.

An *undertaker* once could undertake to do anything; nowadays he only undertakes to manage funerals. So, to people in general, *doctor* stands only for *doctor of medicine*. *Liquor,* which once was synonymous with *liquid,* is now definitely specialized. *Reek,* like the German *rauchen,* once had the broad meaning "smoke," as it still has in the Scotch dialect; but the standard Modern English use limits it quite definitely to unpleasant exhalations. *Disease* meant "discomfort"—"lack of ease" in general. *Girl* meant "young person (of either sex)." The limitation of *corpse* to *"dead* body" made it necessary to re-borrow the word in its Modern French form *corps* for another possible meaning of "body," and to make occasional use of the original Latin, *corpus,* for still another sense, "complete collection of writings." *Corn,* in general American use, will be immediately understood as "Indian corn" or "maize." But the word itself once meant simply "grain," and so, in other parts of the English-speaking world, it is differently specialized [10]—in Scotland, to mean "oats," and in England "wheat." Keats's allusion to "Ruth amid the alien corn" probably calls up, to many American readers, a very different picture from what the poet had in mind.

What are the factors that account for specialization of meaning? One is, of course, that localities and groups of people have their own specialized associations for words that otherwise may convey a broader meaning. It has been well remarked that "every man is his own specializer." [11] *Pipe,* for example, calls up different ideas in the mind of the smoker, the plumber, and the organist. *Ring* may be thought of in connection with jewelry, opera, politics, or pugilism—even though, in the last connection, the "squared circle" has long since superseded the original truly circular shape. Quite apart from particular or local specializations, however, there are a great many words whose meaning has become specialized for nearly everybody. A second factor that helps to account for both generalization and specialization is the fading of the etymological significance of the word. Thus, to illustrate the one point, *arrive* [< Lat. *ad* (to) + *ripa* (shore)] originally applied to the end of a voyage only, and was used without the preposition, since this was included in the word. Milton's "ere he arrive the happy isle" illustrates

[10] In other Germanic languages, the cognate word has still different specializations in various places: "barley" in Sweden, "rye" in north Germany, and "spelt" in south Germany. (Jespersen, *Mankind, Nation, and Individual,* p. 212.)
[11] Quoted by Greenough and Kittredge, *op. cit.,* p. 251.

a use that is in strict accord with the etymology of the word. When, however, consciousness of the Latin parts that made up the word was weakened, it was no longer used transitively, but in the phrase "arrive at," and with the more generalized application to the end of any journey.

Yet another factor is the competition among synonymous words. The borrowing of the Latin *animal* and the French *beast* meant that, with the native *deer,* English would have possessed three exactly synonymous terms for one idea; it is obviously in the interests of economy that *deer* should have specialized to mean one particular species of animal rather than "animal" in general, and that *beast* should have acquired connotations that limit its sphere. *Bird* and *fowl, dog* and *hound, boy* and *knave, chair* and *stool* are further instances of words that were once synonyms but that have been differentiated in meaning here by the specialization of the second term of each pair.

A further remark about generalization and specialization is suggested by some of the words just alluded to. The degree of specialization which a language exhibits seems to depend on cultural need. In a culture in which the coconut is essential—as in Polynesia—an extremely complex vocabulary is said to have grown up, with different terms for many stages of ripeness of the fruit. So also, the Eskimos have different terms for falling snow, snow on the ground, snow packed hard like ice, slushy snow, wind-driven flying snow, and other kinds.[12] Many similar examples could be cited, for the languages of peoples of undeveloped culture appear to be particularly rich in specialized terms. At one time in the course of the English language it must have seemed desirable to speakers to make verbal distinctions in connection with groups of animals—mostly those of interest to farmers and hunters. An elaborate set of what are called "company terms" was accordingly developed, some (but by no means all) of which survive today. The better known ones include a *herd* or a *drove* of cattle, but of a *flock* of sheep (or birds), a *school* of fish, a *pack* of wolves (or hounds), a *covey* of partridges, and a *swarm* of bees. But there are others far more esoteric,[13] such as *nye*

---

[12] See B. L. Whorf, "Science and Linguistics," *The Technology Review,* Vol. XLII, No. 6 (April 1940), reprinted in *Four Articles on Metalinguistics,* Washington, D.C. (Foreign Service Institute), 1950, p. 6. For further examples see also Jespersen, *Language,* pp. 429-431.

[13] These, and many others, are mentioned in an editorial comment in the *New York Times* for November 20, 1930. All but *doylt* are recorded in the *Oxford Dictionary.*

of pheasants, *cete* of badgers, *sord* of mallards, *wisp* of snipe, *doylt* of tame swine, *gaggle* of geese, *harras* of horses, and *kennel* of raches. There is a similar profusion of names for the same animal (*cow, heifer, bull, calf, steer,* and *ox*), the young of various animals (*puppy, kitten, kid, calf, colt, lamb,* and so forth), and the male and female of the same species (*gander* and *goose, drake* and *duck, horse* and *mare, cock* and *hen, dog* and *bitch*).[14] The need for a generic term is of course particularly felt here, and it is supplied, not quite satisfactorily, by the convention of making either the name of the male (*horse* and *dog*) or of the female (*cow, duck,* and *goose*), or even that of the young of the species (*chicken* and *pig*), perform a larger duty.

ELEVATION AND DEGRADATION

If generalization and specialization may be said to involve a change in the "area" of meaning, elevation and degradation[15] involve the rising or falling of meaning in a scale of values. Thus a word which once denominated something bad (or at least neutral) but comes to refer to something good, has undergone *elevation* of meaning; the reverse of this process, obviously, represents a *degradation* of meaning.

And here a word of warning: we must not confuse the linguistic signal with the thing it stands for, though that error is too often made. It is not the word as such which is bad or good, or which becomes elevated or degraded, but only the meaning which society chooses to put upon it. As we shall see, society often reverses itself in the course of time, and words which were once disapproved may become "respectable," while others that had social favor may lose it. This would not be possible if the value were inherent in the word. With this in mind, then, let us illustrate degradation of meaning.

Many terms that are now descriptive of moral depravity were once quite without this suggestion. *Lust,* for example, meant simply "pleas-

[14] McKnight, *English Words and Their Background,* p. 239, calls attention in greater detail to the lack of generalizing terms in the animal kingdom, and suggests further that the variety of names for sea craft (*sloop, schooner, brig, ship, boat, dinghy, bark,* and so on) is a similar survival of primitive habits of thought.

[15] Elevation is also called *aggradation* or *amelioration,* and degradation is also called *degeneration* or *pejoration.*

ure," as in German; *wanton* was "untaught"; *lewd* was merely "ignorant," "lerned and lewed" being a phrase commonly standing for
"clergy and laity"; *immoral* was "not customary"; *vice,* "flaw"; *hussy,*
"housewife"; *wench,* "young girl"; and *harlot,* "fellow" (of either sex).
In a similar way, words that impute rascality have often been thoroughly
innocent labels: *villain,* for example, was "farm laborer"; *counterfeiter,*
"imitator" or "copyist"; *pirate* (at least in its earlier Greek sense), "one
who adventures or tries"; *buccaneer,* "one who smokes meat"; *ringleader,*
simply "leader" (in a good or a neutral sense); *varlet, knave,* and *imp*
meant merely "boy"; and *sly, crafty,* and *cunning* all implied the compliment "skilful." A perennial form of humor—the city man's ridicule of
the countryman—is witnessed in the degradation of such nouns as
peasant, boor (compare German *Bauer* and Dutch *Boer*), and *churl,*
and in the frequent implication of such adjectives as *bucolic, rural,*
rustic, and *provincial.*

When a word may be applied in two possible ways, one favorable or
complimentary and the other the reverse, it is extremely likely that it
will specialize in the less desirable sense. Thus, *suggestive* is likely to
mean only "evilly suggestive," though it *may* still mean "informative" or
"illuminating," and though the noun *suggestion* has escaped any such
specialization—just as the verb *to harbor* is limited to unworthy or illegal
concealment (as in "harboring a criminal" or "harboring thoughts of
revenge"), while the noun *harbor* retains the old broad and literal
meaning of "haven." *Asylum,* through association with the idea of
"refuge for the insane," has followed a course like that of the verb *harbor.*
A *libel,* in Middle English and early Modern English, was simply a
"brief bit of writing" (from Lat. *libellum,* little book); now it is
definitely limited to something malicious or defamatory. *Doom* once
meant "judgment"; now it means only "condemnation." *Reek,* as we have
seen, can now stand only for unpleasant distillations; *stink* and *stench*
have specialized in the same way from a formerly neutral meaning, and
smell and even *odor* seem likely to follow their lead. A *smirk* was once
merely a smile, without the suggestion of affectation. One could formerly
resent benefits as well as injuries, and *retaliate* for favors as well as
slights; compare with the present meanings of these words the ordinary
implications of the phrase "get even with" or "get square with."

On the other hand, instances of words that have traveled an opposite
path, from the humble to the exalted, or from the base to the refined,

are not far to seek. The institution of chivalry brought about the elevation of *knight* (youth) and *squire* (shield-bearer) ; and *chivalry* itself
was invested by the Romantic Revival with a glamor that the word
(as we see from its source, Fr. *cheval,* horse) did not originally possess.
"Romantic" ideas in the late eighteenth and early nineteenth centuries
were similarly responsible for the gain in dignity of such words as *bard,*
once a term of contempt like *vagabond; minstrel,* once applicable to
juggler and buffoon as well as musician; and *enthusiasm,* in the earlier
eighteenth century akin to *fanaticism.* Like *knight,* other terms for rank
or position have had the good fortune to take on added prestige when
the offices for which they stood changed their character, and when their
own etymological meanings were forgotten. Such is the history of *marshal*
(originally, "horse-servant"), *chamberlain* (room-attendant), *minister*
(servant), *constable* (stable-attendant), *governor* (pilot), and *steward*
(sty-guardian). It is true that in a number of these words the extent
of the elevation fluctuates: *marshal* is a less dignified title when it is
applied to the lone policeman of an American village than when it is applied to the highest ranking officers of the English or the French army;
there is a similar variation between the American and the British connotations for *constable,* just as *steward* may suggest a club attendant as
well as the Lord High Steward of England, or even the royal dynasty of
the *Stewarts* (or *Stuarts*) ;[16] likewise, *governor* may mean the warden
of an English prison or the chief administrative officer of one of our
American states. On the whole, however, the fact that any present
implication of these words represents a gain in dignity over the etymological one is patent enough. So too it is with a number of political and
religious labels: *Tory, Whig, Puritan, Quaker,* and *Methodist* are well-
known examples of names that were originally applied in contempt but
that have taken on dignified associations (though, to some, *Puritan*
and perhaps *Tory* still convey a derisive significance). Archbishop
Trench long ago pointed out that the influence of Christianity elevated
angel from merely "messenger," *martyr* from "witness," and *paradise*
from "park," through the Biblical application to the abode of our first
parents (as in *Paradise Lost* and *"earthly* paradise") to the "blisful
waiting-place of faithful departed spirits." [17] Miscellaneous further illus-

[16] Greenough and Kittredge, *op. cit.,* p. 296.
[17] Archbishop Richard Chevenix Trench, *On the Study of Words,* New York
(Armstrong), 20th ed. (no date), p. 114.

trations of elevation are *pretty* from an early meaning "sly," through "clever," to something approaching "beautiful"; *nice* from an etymological meaning "ignorant," through its earliest English sense "foolish," and later ones like "particular," to its present broad and vague colloquial meaning of "pleasant" or "acceptable"; and *fond* from "foolish" to "affectionate."

The usual view of degradation and elevation has been that the downward path is far the more common. Despite McKnight's protest to the effect that elevation has been less noticed simply because it is less dramatic,[18] there seems to be every reason to agree with the general verdict. Examples of elevation, after all, are far less easy to find than examples of degradation, which indeed meet us at every turn. Besides, most of the words that have been cited as undergoing elevation fall into a few obvious categories, while the types of degradation are extremely various. The truth of the matter would appear to be that degradation has been more noticed not because it is more spectacular but simply because it is omnipresent, as elevation is not. Why should this be so, and why should the use of words be made difficult by a lurking leer, a hint of unpleasant connotation that makes a word that appears to be absolutely right in denotation impossible for a given occasion? It is hard to escape the conclusion that there is a disagreeable commentary on human nature here. How difficult it is for superlatives to retain their superlative force— because the general tendency is to apply them on light occasion and hence to weaken their meaning! So *fair* comes to mean "passable," and indeed is often equivalent to "not good"; and *quite* has passed, in its usual American application at least, from "entirely" or "completely" to moderately." The tendency to procrastinate finds illustration in a whole series of words or phrases—*by and by, presently, anon, immediately, directly,* and *soon* itself—that have "slowed up," changing their meaning from "now" or "at once" to "soon" or "after a time." It is scarcely a far-fetched interpretation to see in the narrowing of *demure* to apply to *mock* modesty, of *genteel* to *spurious* gentility, of *sophistication* to *worldly* wisdom, of *egregious* to notoriety rather than fame, of *sanctimonious* to *pretended* holiness, and of *grandiose* to *tinsel* (itself an example of degradation) grandeur—to see in all these, and dozens of others that

[18] *English Words and Their Background,* p. 292; cf. also Janet Aiken, *English Present and Past,* p. 112, and G. A. Van Dongen, *Amelioratives in English.*

might be mentioned, the workings of human motives like suspicion, contempt, and general pessimism.

QUESTIONS FOR REVIEW OF PART ONE

1. What is the ancestral lineage of the English language?
2. Which consonant and vowel sounds remain the same in all or many of the Indo-European languages from which Miss Schlauch offers translations of "Yes, Mother, I have three"?
3. What is Miss Schlauch's opinion of the Biblical story of the origin of language?
4. What are the names and dates of the three major periods in the development of English, and who was a notable writer from each?
5. When English grammar is primarily Germanic, how did our language acquire so many words derived from Latin?
6. What is the distinction between phonetic and analogical change?
7. In what similar way have the following Old English words in Matthew 8 changed their spelling by the time they appear in Middle English and again in Early Modern? (The pertinent verse is indicated after each word.)

    yfle (6)   heofona (11)   ġelīefdest (13)

8. Notice the following verbs in the Old English Gospels. (The pertinent verse is indicated after each word.) Compare the Middle English forms.

    fyliġdon (1)   ġedrēaġd (6)
    hrepode (3)   andswarode (8)
    ġeclǣnsod (3)   ġehǣled (8)
    ēode (5)

    What grammatical function does the *d* in each verb perform? Does it perform the same function in Modern English? Can you identify the grammatical function of the prefix *ge-*? Does it still serve in Modern English?
9. What are some examples of difference in word order between the sentences of the Old English Gospels and the sentences of the Middle English version?
10. What are some examples of a fallacious use of etymology in finding the "true" meaning of a word?
11. How would you define and exemplify *generalization* and *specialization, elevation* and *degradation*?
12. How do Robertson and Cassidy account for the fact that the meanings and values of words change?

SUGGESTIONS FOR INDIVIDUAL PROJECTS
AND CLASS DISCUSSION

1. The Schlauch article states that English is a member of the Germanic family of European languages. Make the following test of the truth of that statement in regard to vocabulary, recognizing as you do it that you are not testing grammatical relationships. Make a list of twenty common English words. After you have done that, list alongside them their German equivalents and their French equivalents. Decide which per cent of the English words are closer to the German words, which per cent to the French words. You may need to use English-German and English-French dictionaries or to consult such a source as the Britannica World Language Edition of the Funk and Wagnalls *New Practical Standard Dictionary of the English Language*, Volume II of which includes (in Part II) a list of common English words and their translations into six other languages.

2. Conduct a test somewhat similar to the above by listing forty common English words. Then, by consulting the etymological information given in a good dictionary for each of the words, determine which per cent of the words are derived from a Romance language, which per cent from a Germanic language, and which per cent from miscellaneous other languages. Again, remember that this project tests the vocabulary, not the grammatical relationships.

3. After studying in a dictionary the etymology of each of the following Late Modern words, identify the corresponding words in the Old English and Middle English versions of Matthew 8 and explain the nature of the change which has taken place. (The pertinent verse is indicated after each word.) Look particularly for changes in meaning and value, and changes from Old English words to words derived from French (after the Norman Conquest).

    nether (1)   *bid* and *command* (4)
    many (1)   *bid* and *pray* (5)
    companies (1)   *knave* (6)
    Lord (2)   *faith* (10)
    stretch (3)

4. On page 34, Robertson and Cassidy state that "the languages of peoples of undeveloped culture appear to be particularly rich in specialized terms"; and in Footnote 14 they refer to the richness of specialized terms as a "survival of primitive habits of thought." Consider the specialized terms which are used in American for different types of automobiles. Who is more primitive about automobiles—the American or the Eskimo? Who is more primitive about snow—the American or the Eskimo? What if any substitu-

tion would you make in Footnote 14 for "survival of primitive habits of thought"? Looking back at the context of Robertson and Cassidy's full discussion of the proliferation of specialized terms, would you say that the authors deny themselves?

SUGGESTED WRITING ASSIGNMENT

Some people say that the English language has "descended from Latin." In 300-500 words, explain why such a statement is misleading. In your introduction, mention why some people think that Latin, not German, is the parent of English. Then divide the body of your paper according to the types of evidence you are using to show why their notion is misleading. Make your main idea clear in your conclusion.

Consider the historical evidence which Kenyon presents. Compare and contrast the sounds, inflections, and word order of the English sentence, "Yes, Mother, I have three," to such aspects of equivalent sentences in Latin and Dutch. If you know Latin and German (or Dutch) you may wish to make the same comparison with several other English sentences.

PART II

Lexicography

ost people have some reference books in their homes. Although few of us have basic references in biology, chemistry, or meteorology (involved though we all are in life, the elements, and the climate), almost every family has a telephone book, a cookbook, a Bible, and a dictionary. When we are puzzled by an unfamiliar word in our reading, need to check the spelling or pronunciation of a word we are going to use, or wish to discover when Diocletian was emperor of Rome—when we have traffic with words, the road frequently leads to a dictionary. Yet it is surprising how many of us approach a dictionary as if it were a Divine Book. That is, we open it as if we expect to find in it The Truth. If, as is common, we do not understand any but the most rudimentary techniques of dictionary use, we may find something more akin to Mystery than knowledge. Yet somehow we feel as though our souls are the better for it, as if we had been in church—even though we did not understand the sermon.

But a dictionary is not Holy Writ. In the last selection of Part I, Robertson and Cassidy demonstrated that the meanings and values of words tend to change, often very markedly. They also showed that words are the products and expressions of the gamut of human emotions. Their article makes it easier to see why a dictionary can be neither as accurate as a telephone book nor as prescriptive as a cookbook. Dictionaries are the result of human enterprise—a most challenging attempt to record the way man uses words to communicate his knowledge and feelings. It is a tribute to dictionary-makers that their efforts are as accurate as they are.

Because dictionary-making is a human process, our use of a dictionary needs to be based on an understanding of that process. Spencer Armstrong, in the first selection of this part, describes some of the procedures used by better dictionary-makers. Following that, David B. Guralnik, General Editor of the *New World Dictionary,* relates some of the difficulties lexicographers have in recording the feelings which words express. The concluding selection, by Albert H. Marckwardt, deals with the problems involved in recording the sounds of words in dictionary print. A reminder is in order that there is much valuable information about lexicography and language in the introduction of a good college-level or unabridged dictionary. The following selections supplement rather than repeat such information.

SPENCER ARMSTRONG

How Words Get into the
Dictionary

THE DAILY HUNT IN THE WORD-SHOP

Within easy walking distance of Gramercy Park and charming Madison Square Park, at the top of a building flanked by two of Manhattan's busiest thoroughfares, is our word-shop. It isn't very pretentious, our shop; everyone knows of many others whose artistic appointments and decorative graces are far more alluring. We have no velvet curtains as a backdrop for our wares. They are merely words. No suave clerk will usher you across deep carpets to overstuffed divans. Your heels will click against bare concrete floors, and the rustle of paper is the nearest approach to the swish of silks and satins, or rayon taffetas.

Instead of the walls of our shop being tinted in the latest fashion, they are lined with tiers of books, stacks and stacks of books in many languages and from many countries, their thousands of pages crowded with those "adventures of the mind" which make the blood and sinew of the Dictionary. So far from being a barren abode, our shop is, in truth, a rendezvous of the romances of time; within it, day by day and year after year, accumulate almost all the hopes and fears, the hates, the conquests and accomplishments of mankind. For these things, whether they are thought or done, or dimly felt, can be known only if they are *communicated;* and for communication we need—Words.

But words, like nations, have their history, and properly to appraise the rank, dignity, and worth of a claimant to dictionary favor demands high scholarship, great versatility, no little humor, and powers of judgment seasoned by long experience.

Let us eavesdrop on a typical session once held in our shop by one of the high courts of the English language.

The court convenes.

"Here's a new word," announces a clerk.

"No, that's not a new word," interjects one of the justices. "It was well-known about Boston in Miles Standish's time."

"Been seen much since?" asks the chief justice.

A perusal of the records reveals slight usage.

"Once or twice," the clerk responds.

"Much too lazy. To the files with it! Next!"

"*Whoopee* is the next candidate for entry into the dictionary," the clerk continues. "We have a record of its appearance in England about 1530, but it wasn't very popular. Used by John Palsgrave, the busy chaplain of Henry VIII. Shakespeare revived it a couple of times. Found in Kipling later. It was first used to urge action by dogs, then horses. Like *sick 'im* or *gid-ap*. Now it is used as a cheer to excite or express superhilarity. It's been quite popular since—"

Needless to say, *whoopee* is received into the living language by acclamation and the judges go on to the next "case": which (to come to our days) may be anything from a bit of the vernacular like *hep, jive,* or *hubba hubba,* to the new meanings of *ceiling* and *umbrella* and the claims of *fission* as a permanent contribution to the language from the physicists of the atomic age.

Actually, of course, it is not a court at all. It is just a large, busy office, replete with desks and files, archives, telephones and typewriters, staffed by lexicographers, editors, stenographers, and clerks. Very prosaic to the casual eye; quite humdrum, even: but engaged in a business of high import to everyone who uses words, and wants to use them *right*. This is the business of making dictionaries and of keeping them up to date.

GOOD LITTLE WORDS
THAT NEVER ARRIVE

A staff of readers and correspondents is continually searching the press of the English-speaking world, the newspapers, magazines, technical periodicals and books, for virgin words. When an apparent newcomer is discovered, the first task is to ascertain if it is actually new. We first seek its pedigree in Cockeram's *Interpreter of Hard English Words,* published in 1623; in Blount's *Glossographia,* of 1656; or perhaps in Samuel Johnson's famous dictionary of the year of 1755.

If not found in any of the English lexicons of the past, we deem it may be of foreign extraction. For this purpose we have dictionaries in Sanskrit, Maori, Hausa, Hebrew, Arabic, Irish, Hindustani, Afrikaans, besides those of modern languages from French to Japanese. We have, too, complete dictionaries embracing lace making, draperies, politics, textiles, plastics, biochemistry, photography, ethics, botany and a myriad other specific subjects. Then also there are encyclopedias from almost every nation, English-speaking and foreign. So it is a foxy word, parading as a new one in an attempt to elude its past, that can escape the net of this investigation.

But if the new arrival is bona fide, we take it into our care for a few years, place it on file. We watch its use by the people and tally this against its record during the probationary period. Also, in this interim, numerous letters will arrive at our office asking for the meaning of the intruder into the language. At the end of the interval the record of the neophyte is computed, and if the score shows a popular demand, it is awarded a place in the dictionary.

Incorporation in the dictionary, though, is no signal for a word to become indolent. It must work. We have a "word pool" of sizeable proportions in our archives much of whose contents have shown little or no activity in the language for a long time. We keep a tally also on these words that have been abandoned by the public, giving them a sort of indefinite reprieve, waiting for the verdict—resuscitation or oblivion.

Not all new words have to wait so long to get into the dictionary, however. Sometimes the acclaim of a new candidate is so universal and widespread that its inclusion is assured at once. Think of *jeep,* and the now almost forgotten *gremlin.*

Then again some good words never become popular. We have a pet in our shop, orphaned by the world of letters, that has been hungering for admission into the dictionary since the Victorian era. It is a charming little word with the euphonious syllables *meloceus.* The first and last time we met *meloceus* in literature was in Oscar Wilde's *The Picture of Dorian Gray.*

It seems to be a name for a precious gem capable of detecting criminals. If so, in this one word is a theme for a series of *whodunits* (yes, that word has "arrived") that might intrigue the fancy of a Philo Vance or a Hercule Poirot. But nowhere can we find it repeated—never used again.

We have searched the lapidary's lexicons of all ages, we have combed the encyclopedias of many countries, we have sought the assistance of gem lovers from Johannesburg to Maiden Lane; but to no avail. Always we receive the negative answer—unknown. The lips that might offer enlightenment are now still, and we can only suppose that *meloceus* was the coinage of an imaginative mind. Yet, because no writer has felt inclined to give this lovely waif a new lease on life, we have regretfully consigned it to the limbo of lost words.

CONTRIBUTIONS TO THE LANGUAGE

How many words are coined annually? There are no exact figures: who, indeed, can take an accurate census of new arrivals in so vast and fluctuating a world as that of language? In normal times the accepted language may grow at a yearly rate of about 3000 new words—and new meanings for old words, but of these only a small proportion will have the vitality to ensure their eventual appearance in the dictionary. In days of stress, in times of war, or in such years of discovery and invention as preceded and followed the atomic bomb, 5000 or more words will clamor for public attention so that their inclusion in the dictionary is urged by scholar, specialist, and layman alike.

Probably there are at least three times as many words as this, articulated or printed every year, mainly slang, but if they are not stillborn, they soon die for lack of fostering pen to aid them through the vicissitudes of infancy.

Who coins these new words? Today most of those which are legitimate additions to the language emanate from the research laboratories where men are struggling with new ideas, new processes, and new products. Once born, the right word must be found for the new creations—and so we have *biomechanics, cyclotron, narcosynthesis, radar, eniac, teleran,* and hundreds of others, most of them from the rich domains of medicine, chemistry, physics, or related sciences. Nor are these words exclusively technical.

Radio, to take one example only, has fattened the dictionary with more than 5000 new words and compounds—and television is now pushing it hard for the lead. The physicists, not satisfied with the 92 chemical elements of the old periodic table, have added four new ones: *neptunium, plutonium, americium, and curium*—and the hunt still goes on.

Discovering something previously unknown to man, the scientists inadvertently enrich the language. If the find proves extraordinary, the name of the inventor or discoverer is frequently used to commemorate the deed in our speech. Well-known examples of this cognizance are *ohm, watt, curie, bel,* and *ampere.* In other fields are *macadamize, sanforize, sherardize, galvanize, bessemerize,* celebrating in lay speech the doings of Messrs. Galvani, Bessemer, Macadam, Sanford Cluett, and Sherard Cowper-Coles.

There have been many exponents of this art of creating expressive terminology. They have come from almost every station of life, but naturally those who command the public spotlight have their mental offspring registered sooner.

Theodore Roosevelt, reflecting the explorer in his character, minted new words with an agility that kept lexicographers ever on the qui vive. One of his oddest contributions to the language was *chinafy,* coined to express the complete helplessness to which pacifism would reduce America. He could have used the synonymous adjective root, *sinitic,* already in the language; but he created a term that would catch on—and also be forgotten!—more quickly. When the Government was building the Panama Canal he commanded much space in the press crusading to *sanitate* the Zone. This was heralded as a new word, but upon investigation we found that it had been introduced into speech as early as 1811, though used infrequently since.

Woodrow Wilson undoubtedly was about the greatest phraseologist, outside of an advertising agency, that the United States has heard in many generations. *Watchful waiting* and *too proud to fight* are memorable of this expressiveness in arranging new word groupings; but he failed to enrich our mother language with new words.

Franklin Delano Roosevelt, seeking to dramatize our bomber attacks on Tokyo in 1942, but without revealing any military secrets, remarked cannily that the bombers took off from a hidden base in *Shangri-la*. Immediately, the mythical land in Hilton's *Lost Horizon* became a household word and is now even applied to restaurants, garages, *motels* (itself an apt compound of *motor car* and *hotel*), and beauty parlors.

Then there are the curious twins *triphibious,* and *triphibian.* The first was contributed by Leslie Hore-Belisha in a speech made in the House of Commons in 1941, to be revived two years later in another speech by Herbert Morrison. The second was used in a compliment paid to Lord Mountbatten by Winston Churchill in a radio broadcast at Quebec in 1943. Neither of these words is linguistically respectable but both were so immediately understood by association with *amphibious* and *amphibian* that they entered the language at once, where they bid fair to remain for who knows how long?

Even more permanent is the word *quisling,* once the name of the head of the Norwegian Nazi Party, Vidkun Quisling, now impossible to dissociate from its meaning as a person who deliberately betrays his country to a hostile and subsequently occupying power.

And what of the tantalizing contractions that have invaded the language during and since World War II, most of them via the lively sciences of electronics and nucleonics? *Radar* and *loran* many of us easily recognize, but do you know what is behind the letters of *eniac, edvac, shoran, sodar, sonar*, and—this one is just coming into use—*dovap?* Then, of course there were the *Seabees*—alias C.B.'s, members of the Construction Battalions of remote Pacific islands during many hard-fought campaigns against the Japanese.

A DETECTIVE AND A CARTOONIST

There was a young detective in the New York City Police Department some years ago who was acclaimed the handsomest man on the force. This gift of the gods he accepted as a license to strut and swagger a trifle more than his companions. Combined with a flowering of the physical, he was also clever in his appointed tasks. After achieving several successive scoops, his chest measurement seemed to increase perceptibly. In order to relieve the strain on his vest buttons, Chief of Detectives Devery stated to reporters anxious for details of this thief catcher extraordinary that he was a splended officer, but too *chesty*.

Chesty! Again the subheads of the newspapers featured a new word. Forsooth, it became overworked, so widespread was its appeal; but this constant repetition whipped it into the working vernacular of the average person and to-day it is a byword on the tongues of the multitude. Upon retrospection, it is rather difficult to imagine that it hasn't been with us always, but linguistically it is a parvenu.

Another fertile source of new expressions—idioms rather than words— is the studio of the cartoonist, the columnist and the gag man of the motion pictures and the theater; also the campus of the carefree collegian. These are mainly springheads of "slanguage," mothered mostly by a desire to be smart or witty. The issues emanating from this speech incubator, though popular for a brief period, fade into oblivion in the same skyrocketing spirit that marked their ascent.

Snoogling, quilling, snousy, oomph, shmoo, and their like, though humorous and catchy, have no innate lasting qualities and are only mottoes of the moment. Each year brings a veritable horde of such linguistic corruptions that are scarcely worth housingroom in our word-shop; but we offer them shelter for the one gem in a thousand that will rise above its class and become a member in good standing in the society of speech.

. . . But don't think the dictionary wears a high hat. Far from it. In assembling new material we are only hearkening to the edicts of the time-ripened formulas of accepting the best, the most useful. Slang isn't.

Though we do ferret slang from its habitat for investigation, there is a more fertile field, somewhat allied—dialect. A dialect is still considered by many people as degraded and a vulgar variety of speech. But it isn't. Beyond the rim of the city's stir and strife, along the shady lanes and in the nurtured acres of the countryside, there has gradually grown, from time long past, a distinct vernacular. It is rustic, we say, and the pedagogically inclined are apt to sniff at this poor relation of the literary language. Evolved by those who live closest to Nature, it is not only more varied but, within limits, much richer than its more precise counterpart.

The cant of a group, trade, or profession, like the jargon of the gipsy, is alive with terms that are Greek to another. The lawyer, the mechanic, the housewife, the journalist and the laborer, each has a vernacular that mystifies a hearer from another environment.

The dictionary must become the clearing-house of these diversified provincialisms and argots. So we explore the domains of the arts, crafts and trades to report new and unusual words for the purpose of aiding English-speaking people to understand each other.

Again, the language is in a constant state of flux; there is a ceaseless mutation of the meaning of words. *Girl* once meant a child of either sex. *Agony* once meant a wrestling match, or exhibition of combat. *Run* years ago was a simple little word denoting the forceful dashing movement of a being. Now it has expanded until the dictionary lists ninety-four different meanings for it. Thus a writer or speaker may give a new interpretation to a common word which, gaining currency, takes unto itself another significance. These departures from the normal must be captured, for they modify the language: consider the remarkable and, some think, excessive versatility of the word *streamline*.

BUSY WORKERS AT THE WORD-MINT

To the trained eye and ear, words are flowering everywhere, to say nothing of new meanings for old words. In fact, a new profession—the word coiner—has capitalized on the modern demand for personal and business distinction.

Foremost among his clients is the business man who seeks a distinguishing mark for a commodity he is about to market. Perhaps this potential manufacturer solicits the cooperation of an advertising man for this task, for such professionals make a specialty of just the right words, searching hours sometimes in quest of the proper term to express precisely their thoughts; and not without pleasing monetary compensations, it might be added. But however the prospective producer obtains the new term, he guards it with secrecy until it can be registered in the files of the United States Patent Office.

Here then is another fountainhead of many original words that are used glibly by the man on the street, as though they had been extant forever. We have more than 50,000 trade terms in our many special glossaries; but no great proportion are in the dictionary, because most of them have a very limited use, or are discards that have failed to gain the approval of the public. When a coined word is ratified by popular use, however, it may become an exceedingly valuable commercial property, to be misused at one's peril. . . .

WHO'S WHO IN THE DICTIONARY

Not only places of public interest but also names of people, together with an epitome of their deeds, are in the dictionary. Nor is it merely a necropolis of ancient immortals. When a living person pokes his head above the horizon of the average by exploit, or by a position in life which gives promise of continuance in the public mind, he or she becomes the object of attention by the lexicographer.

Every President of the United States is, of course, accorded a notation in the dictionary in the next edition after his inauguration, if he hasn't already been recorded there. Statesmen of prominence, leading scientists, doctors, authors, singers, inventors, everyone whose fame may carry his name into posterity, is carefully watched for the possibility of being listed in the dictionary.

Now that the new word is captured the next stop is to register it in the master-dictionary. This complex volume is an index of practically all human thought. It is really more of a combined loose-leaf file and card index than a dictionary, for it is but a temporary abode for most words, a reservoir of speech housing a host of transients of doubtful vintage that may soon fade from view, unknown and unlamented by the public at large.

These archives could more properly be called a lexicographer's notebook, as they harbor, in seasons, thousands of words which few people will ever see, hear or use. However slight their value may be to the general public they are by far the most important documents in the keeping of the dictionary-maker; for they contain the gathered harvest of his labors, and are very carefully safeguarded against fire or destruction. Were we stripped of this repository of the latest crop of virgin words, all our activities previous to the hour of that catastrophe would be rendered vain and all subsequent steps supremely difficult, if not impossible.

A third step in aiding a word to enter the catalog of speech is the dressing of it in a proper attire—correct spelling. It is somewhat unfortunate that the twenty-six letters of our alphabet are productive of one hundred and seventeen different sounds. The very first letter of the alphabet even has seven different choices of sound values—as in *art, ape, fat, fare, fast, what* and *all,* not to mention the *e* in *obey* masquerading as an *a*. . . .

WORDS THAT PASS IN A NIGHT

When the stranger knocking at the dictionary-door for admission has been properly spelled and pronounced, the next task is to discover what it means. As most of the new words slide almost noiselessly into usage, there is seldom any clue to their meaning other than the few flanking words of context from which they are taken.

A first, second, or third appearance of the new word in print or conversation may disclose no precise sense, because other users slightly shade its significance each time it is used. Repetition, however, soon dispels this divergence of meaning among writers or speakers by some seemingly mysterious transference of thought to a probable single interpretation. If two or more meanings persist, one is almost mathematically certain to gain the greater currency and eventually win first place in the dictionary from its rival.

Slang is always untractable. It is too transient: in the mouths of the many today, superannuated by another wisecrack to-morrow. These fancies we usually list with a lead pencil, in a conviction—born of experience—that they will fail to pass final tests for inclusion in our word-book.

Yet some slang terms may enter the dictionary—in time. *Goon, mike,* and *cheesecake,* for instance, are now recorded, and the verb *to pan,* in the sense of rigorously criticizing somebody or something, is another recent dictionary entrant.

Indeed, some of the slang of today is sure to be used by fastidious writers of a following generation. The process is perennial. *Idiot,* signifying an imbecile, was once slang for a private citizen. *Buncombe,* meaning bombastic speech or any showy utterance for effect, is another. This latter comes from a remark made by a member of Congress from Buncombe County, North Carolina, who confided to a compeer that he was talking "only for Buncombe" when on the floor of the House. He was, apparently, for from this word *bunk* is derived.

Also, definitions must be precise, for space in the dictionary is limited. A word must be so synonymized that it can be replaced in a sentence by its own definition. When the craft was young—we lift this from a seventeenth-century lexicon—a lobster was described as "a little red fish that walks backward." Such interpretation is more like a guessing contest, for a lobster is neither a fish nor, unboiled, is it red, and it doesn't walk backward.

EINSTEIN IN 100 WORDS

What would you do if you were suddenly called upon to describe Einstein's *relativity theory* comprehensively? Or Planck's *quantum theory* or the *exclusion principle* of Pauli? And how would you define such things as *atomic energy, chain reaction,* a *black body* or a *cloud chamber?* Behind each of these deceptively simple terms is a long history of patient observation, strenuous experiment, and the most abstruse mathematical labors—all of them directed toward a fuller understanding of, and control over, the forces of nature.

Not so long ago it was said that only a dozen of the world's most advanced intellects could understand the intricate reasoning behind Albert Einstein's two theories of relativity. But, however difficult and mysterious these theories were, the dictionary-makers had to extract the essence of them. The scholars, scientists, and philosophers of twenty centuries were consulted. The most modern methods of science were enlisted in the quest for popular enlightenment. From the mass of evidence collected it appeared that, despite many forerunners (including an American meteorologist in the service of Uncle Sam) Einstein had given to the word *relativity* its clearest and most rigorous scientific meaning. If you wish to know the gist of this meaning but have neither the time nor the inclination to study the subject, look it up in the dictionary. You will find it tersely explained in less than 100 words.

More briefly, but with equal accuracy, are defined the other scientific terms mentioned above, as well as hundreds more scattered through the alphabet. And if, in your reading or in discussions with others, your curiosity is aroused by such words as *existentialism, logical positivism, totalitarian, genocide, Mach number, geopolitics, airlift,* and so on—try the dictionary! The chances are that it will be ready for your questions:

provided of course, that the word you are looking for has achieved enough currency and shown enough vitality to win its place within the crowded and necessarily selective pages.

Definitions, however brief, must be exact also because Congress and many other legislative bodies enact laws with the help of a dictionary. A mistake may strip the Internal Revenue Department of thousands of dollars in income. Again, as an aid to the classification of a hitherto unclassed product the dictionary is used by the United States Board of Customs Appraisers to determine the nearest general grouping of the new commodity, so that the appropriate toll may be levied against it. If the dictionary should be in error the Government would be the loser.

After a word has been acquired, registered, spelled, defined and otherwise made presentable, comes the final step: examination by the committee on admissions, a group representing a wide range of academic abilities and human interests. As such a group is difficult to maintain in the intervals between full revisions of a dictionary, its varied functions are discharged by our managing editor in association with a permanent staff trained in the manifold technical skills that go into the making of a great reference work.

To gain a place in the dictionary, a word must connote or denote something that is not already in the compendium. As the language grows, this test becomes more and more exacting, finally resolving itself into the necessity of a new word practically performing the work of two other words now in our speech.

Another certificate demanded of new words is the reputation of the person who vouches for them. Under whose authentication do they demand a place in our speech? One utterance of a new word by the President of the United States will speed it into the dictionary, where a thousand repetitions by a nonentity will fail. Next, orators and writers of seasoned popularity are the best endorsers for words that entertain hopes of longevity.

Furthermore, a word must, so to speak, be linguistically decent to enter even the largest general dictionary. Vulgarities, barbarisms, and gutter-speech are excluded, their interests being sufficiently attended to by specialists in such abstruse matters. Similarly with large numbers of technical terms in the medical, anatomical, surgical and psychiatric domains: such words, however legitimate and necessary to those with the requisite *know-how,* form no part of the layman's active vocabulary and may well be relegated to any of the excellent specialized glossaries available in good libraries.

ABSOLUTE ACCURACY ALWAYS

But the lexicographer doesn't make the language in any sense; he merely records the best of it, that which is used or usable. Neither can speakers nor authors force new vehicles of speech into the language; not even the President.

The language is made by that mythical person—the man in the street. It is to him that the committee on admissions turns when preparing its final decision. Popularity is the ultimate test for the entrance into the dictionary of a reputable word.

A candidate lacking any semblance of style or pedigree can attain first rank among the immortal members of the language if it be acclaimed by the voice of the mass. The word may be but a passing fancy; but this position, if attained, is unalterable for the present, no matter how much the gownsman or speech purist may protest. The majority rules in lexicography, and the popular judgment is final. In essence, a dictionary is designed to enable those who so desire to understand all classic and current literature of the English language. Its purpose is to provide a maximum of sound information for the greatest number in a minimum of time.

During this process of word analysis for our speech there is one slogan seared into the minds of the staff—Absolute Accuracy. This is inviolable, because the dictionary is the master-proof chart; all other users of words take its edicts without question. The world's foremost specialists on every subject are consulted on each moot point. Human errors are reduced to a minimum.

But catching and authenticating words, once the dictionary is made, is almost child's play compared with creating such a compendium from blank paper. It is merely watching the parade go by, awarding palms to the new recruits; an endless task, but pleasant.

Indeed, it is a far cry from poor old Samuel Johnson, fuming away in his room on Fleet Street, working almost single-handed at his labors of making a dictionary, then only 50,000 words, to a staff of 380 experts and more than 500 specialized scholars and readers dissecting 100,000 volumes in the building of a modern lexicon. Such was our shop not so many years ago. Really, it wasn't a shop; it was a fact foundry. . . .

DAVID B. GURALNIK

From College Composition and Communication, *IX (May, 1958), 90-93. Copyright, 1958, by the National Council of Teachers of English. By permission of the National Council and the author.*

Connotation in Dictionary Definition

In selecting and writing his definitions, the lexicographer is of course fully aware that he is not actually recording the "meaning" of a particular word, but that he is merely trying to suggest, within the available space, as many of the aspects of the thing defined as will recall it to the reader or will allow him to form an idea of it in his mind. That is to say, a dictionary definition such as "a tool or apparatus for boring holes in wood, metal, stone, etc." does not actually describe any single, particular device. It might suggest a hand drill or a power drill or a dentist's device for evoking exquisite pain, but it does in any case denote, or explicitly mark out, that class of objects to which English speakers have assigned the generic word *drill*. Of course, the more restricted the class, or the fewer the possible number of referents, the more precise the denotation. A proper name is the most restrictive of all. The term *William Shakespeare* will probably suggest the author of a number of enduring plays and poems. Or, if your interests incline in a somewhat different direction, it might recall a skillful member of the Yale backfield in the late thirties. But it will probably have no other "meaning" for most people.

The lexicographer is primarily concerned with pinpointing the possible denotations of a word, and there are those who believe that this is all he can or does do with the "meanings" of words. Such a notion is an erroneous one. The editor is also aware that what the word suggests, that is its connotation, can be fully as important as what it denotes, for he knows that words are not only grammatical tools and symbols, but that they embody as well an ensemble of notions, concepts, and psychological reactions. A politician and a statesman may both be concerned with carrying out the affairs of government, but unless the reader or user of these terms understands that the word *politician* is frequently used in a derogatory sense, with implications of seeking personal or partisan gain, scheming, opportunism, etc., and that *statesman* suggests able, farseeing, principled conduct of public affairs, he cannot have the full meanings of these words. The lexicographer knows clearly in such a case that his responsibility does not end with recording the denotation of these words. It occurs to me, in passing, that age must be the catalyst that invariably transforms the politician into a statesman. We seem to be burdened with an unconscionable number of elder statesmen, but I have yet to hear of an elder politician.

All words, with the possible exception of the particles, convey connotative notions of one sort or another. Very often these connotations are of a highly personal order. To the child who first becomes aware of polka dots as the embellishment of his mother's silk dress, the term *polka dot* may thereafter evoke the sensation of soft silkiness. Some words may have group, in addition to individual, suggestiveness; that is, their connotations may be sharply divided into opposing camps depending on whether the idea denoted is favorably or unfavorably received by the listener. Emotion-charged terms such as *integration, socialism,* and, on another level, *rock and roll* offer extreme examples of violently disparate connotation. It is clear that such individual or group reactions cannot be taken into account by dictionaries. The editor of a dictionary, and especially of a college desk dictionary, is constantly buffeted between the Scylla of excessive terseness and the Charybdis of an unwieldy, too expensive volume.

Other terms, however, may over a period of time acquire specific connotations that are sufficiently widespread to warrant recognition and recording by the lexicographer. The word *propaganda,* which until quite recently meant essentially "any systematic, widespread, deliberate indoctrination or plan for such indoctrination" today requires an annotation like the one in the *New World*: "now often used in a derogatory sense, connoting deception or distortion."

The line of demarcation between the denotative and connotative aspects of a word is not always clearly drawn. Frequently the elements blend and are merged into a single descriptive statement that serves as the dictionary definition. The lexicographer need not feel undue concern where this occurs naturally and easily. The problems of judgment and selection enter where the division is sharp and easily recognized. Here the editor must decide whether the exigencies of space will allow the extra connotative note that could round out the meaning of the term.

In addition to the explicit note, there are other devices used by dictionaries to suggest the connotative aspects of words. In a very large sense, the usage labels attached to many terms and senses constitute one such device. It is one thing to know that *haughty* can mean "lofty or noble," but unless one also knows that this sense is regarded as archaic, he may, if he uses it innocently in normal conversation, find himself misunderstood. In the same way it is only proper that a college dictionary record the word *hight,* meaning "named or called," but unless this too is labeled *Archaic,* the freshman who appropriates this term into his active vocabulary may find himself the victim of condescending smiles. The same situation would apply to words and meanings labeled "obsolete" or "colloquial" or "slang" or "British." Similarly, after some meanings, the dictionary may have a note stating that the word is used ironically (as *pretty,* meaning "fine or good" in *a pretty mess*) or familiarly or vulgarly or hyperbolically or as a counterword of wide application (e.g., *nice,* used as a generalized term of approval). Thus we can see that usage labels serve not only to nail down the period or level to which a term properly belongs, but also to suggest the flavor or odor which the term may emit in its context. This, too, is connotative.

To digress for a moment, one of the suggested topics for discussion today concerns the method used to determine the usage levels for words and meanings. The answer should be obvious, but it may nevertheless bear statement. Such determinations are largely informed opinions, based on the accumulated evidence of the chronology, frequency, and distribution of citations, aided by the ear of the editor himself and by the suggestions of linguistic consultants. Language is not a static thing and words wander casually and easily from one level of usage to another over a period of time. The business of keeping up with these changes is just one of the continuous problems of lexicography.

But to return to my main topic. Sometimes the lexicographer must include some of the connotative affects of a word if only to illuminate its normal extensions in meaning. For example, the staff of our dictionary recently decided that although the word *jungle* denotes most simply "land covered with dense growth of trees, tall vegetation, vines, etc., typically in tropical regions," we shall be required to add the connotative information that jungles are generally inhabited by predatory beasts, so that the extended meaning of this word that has resulted in such Hollywoodisms as *asphalt jungle* and *blackboard jungle* might be properly understood.

Another word recently recorded by the *New World* is *exurbanite,* the coinage of A. C. Spectorsky. At its most elemental level, this word refers to "a person of the upper middle class who lives in the semirural areas beyond the suburbs but who works in the metropolis, especially in the communications fields, as in advertising, publishing, the theater, etc." That is essentially all the word "means." But unless we remark also that "exurbanites are regarded as conforming to social and cultural patterns as standardized as those of suburban life," Mr. Spectorsky's whole point in writing the book—and coining the word—is lost. And for *suburban,* too, we must have a note stating that this word variously connotes a combination of urban and rural features, middle-class conservatism, etc., since the word today is as frequently used for its connotative elements as for its explicit denotation.

A class of words that can and should receive explanatory notes in dictionaries concerning their suggestive tones are the terms of racial and ethnic opprobrium. The lexicographer, we feel, has the moral responsibility to inform the dictionary user that if he persists in using these terms he does so today, in the view of most cultivated people, only by jeopardizing his respectability and good taste.

Still another area in which the dictionary can convey connotation is in the little paragraph labeled "Synonymy" that follows many words of general vocabulary. These paragraphs serving to discriminate among various closely related words are as often concerned with the suggestive differences between these various terms as they are with the denotative differences. Take, for instance, the group *desire, wish, want,* and *crave.* All of these words, collectively, denote a strong longing or yearning, and within the definitions proper for these words it seems pertinent to employ the same or similar wording, often even using one or more of these terms as an approximate synonym for another. But within the synonymy it is possible to offer the extended nuances that make each of these more precisely appropriate in a particular context. The paragraph reads: "*desire,* generally interchangeable with the other words here in the sense of 'to long for,' stresses intensity or ardor (to *desire* success) ; *wish* is not as strong a term as *desire* and has special application when an unrealizable longing is meant (he *wished* summer were here) ; *want,* specifically suggesting a longing for something lacking or needed, generally is a more informal equivalent of *wish* (she *wants,* or *wishes,* to go with us) ; *crave* suggests desire to gratify a physical appetite or an urgent need (to crave *affection*)."

Frequently where specific explanation must be forgone because of lack of space, connotation can be implied through the judicious use of illustrative examples. The discerning freshman soon learns that the phrases or sentences demonstrating the word in action serve not only to elaborate the definition, but often through context suggest the special nuances that the word has acquired in usage. For example, the word *ramble,* in one sense, might be defined: "to grow or spread in all directions." This clearly gives the proper denotation of one use of *ramble.* But if we add the illustrative "as, vines *rambled* over the fence," the graphic image conjured up by the example supplies suggestive tones that may help the dictionary user focus the true "meaning" of the word. Often the etymology will supply an interesting sidelight that can bring a flash of understanding to the student. To know that *supercilious* refers ultimately to raised eyebrows or that *sarcasm* derives from a Greek verb meaning "to tear flesh like dogs" is to have an additional insight into the subtle shades suggested by these words.

I have been speaking of the ways in which dictionaries can and frequently do supply the connotations that are essential to a proper grasp of meaning. But I do not mean to imply satisfaction with the extent to which these techniques have been carried out in existing dictionaries. It is the conviction of our staff that the use of these devices should be extended still further. The chief problem, of course, is one of space. But I believe that a way will be found, perhaps by a reapportionment of the space allotted to the various lexicographical elements and by securing the approval of the user of the dictionaries to such a reapportionment.

For in our opinion it is precisely the inclusion of connotation in dictionary definitions that can lend precision to the student's speech and art to his writing.

ALBERT H. MARCKWARDT

From College Composition and Communication, *IV* (*May, 1953*), *35-38. By permission of the National Council of Teachers of English and the author.*

The Dictionary as a Guide to Pronunciation

For certain features of language, particularly matters of inflectional form and syntax, there are many different kinds of information about current use, both generally available and readily interpreted. For pronunciation there is but one—the dictionary. For just a little less than two hundred years, dictionaries have assumed the responsibility of presenting information about, and guidance in, matters of pronunciation. Samuel Johnson treated this topic somewhat casually, but in the quarter-century which followed the first appearance of his magnificent work, three pronouncing dictionaries of the English language were compiled. Since that time English lexicographers have regularly endeavored to furnish their public with positive aid in the matter of pronunciation.

This involves a number of difficulties which may easily lead to errors of interpretation and judgment, if they are not clearly recognized by those who consult dictionaries on questions of pronunciation. First of all there is the sheer magnitude of the task. Unabridged dictionaries today record approximately half a million words. English is a first or native language for no less than 225,000,000 speakers. According to their titles, many dictionaries claim to reflect the language practices of all or a large portion of this tremendous number.

Fortunately, not all speakers regularly use or pronounce the whole English word stock. If they did, the lexicographer would be faced with the stupendous task of representing or reflecting 112,500,000,000,000 individual word-pronunciations. By comparison even the national debt pales into insignificance. Seriously, however, this means that in collecting information about pronunciation, no dictionary can do more than sample the usage of a relatively small number of speakers for a relatively small proportion of the total English vocabulary. Anything beyond this would be so costly as to be totally impracticable.

The second major difficulty is that which faces the pronunciation editor when he tries to put into two-dimensional black and white, in a form simple enough to be interpreted by the average reader, a series of vocal noises which have at least three or four dimensions or attributes. In addition to its distinctive phonemic quality, the ordinary English speech sound also possesses the features of duration, stress, and pitch, not to mention the way in which it may be joined to neighboring sounds. Ideally, some clue ought to be furnished for all of these; practically this can be done only for a very limited audience, those who have been trained to interpret narrow phonetic transcription. The general-use dictionary must content itself with a very broad approximation to these complexities.

These, then, are two of the very practical and immediate problems which beset the editor of any pronouncing dictionary. He will, of course, approach his task conscientiously and do his best, but it would be a mistake not to realize that he is necessarily operating under limitations.

All lexicographers do not go about their business in precisely the same manner. Consequently, to interpret intelligently the information on pronunciation which is presented in a dictionary, the reader must be aware of the attitude toward several salient editorial problems which each particular dictionary reflects. First of all, what is the editor's conception of the function of a pronouncing dictionary? There is a world of difference between the concept implicit in such a title as *The Five Thousand Words Most Frequently Mispronounced* and the scientific attitude set forth in the second edition of Webster's *New International Dictionary* to the effect that "The function of a pronouncing dictionary is to record as far as possible the pronunciations prevailing in the best present usage, rather than to attempt to dictate what that usage should be." Fortunately, most current dictionaries have followed Webster in attempting to attain something like scientific objectivity, although possibly no one of them succeeds one hundred per cent of the time.

This concept of dictionary function raises a further question. What is one to do about pronunciations which he knows to be in current use by cultivated speakers but which do not appear in the dictionary? Here again the answer is suggested by the Webster preface in the sentence immediately following the one quoted above. "In so far as a dictionary may be known and acknowledged as a faithful recorder and interpreter of such usage, so far and no farther may it be appealed to as an authority." In terms of a specific situation, this means that if the pronunciation of *data* with the vowel of *fat* is widely current among educated people and the dictionary does not record the pronunciation, that dictionary simply ceases to be an authority on that particular point. On the other hand, it must be remembered that the collective experience reflected by any dictionary is unquestionably greater than that of the individual observer; hence the dictionary may properly be assumed to be correct until it is indisputably proved wrong. But this can happen.

It is also important to be aware of the speech situation which is reflected in dictionary pronunciations. Some dictionaries record the informal utterances of cultivated speakers, the language of well-bred ease; others select the language characteristic of decidedly more formal situations. For example, in ordinary conversation the final syllable of *evil* will consist of little more than a syllabic consonant, but on the lecture platform many speakers take great pains to pronounce the unstressed *i* with the vowel of *bit;* in fact, they may have to do this in order to be clearly understood. The most frequent misinterpretation of the dictionary in this connection is to attempt to apply in ordinary conversation the dicta which are intended for the pulpit and the lecture platform.

This also raises the interesting question of what dictionaries of the future will do about formal platform speech. The recent development of voice-amplifying mechanisms has rendered largely unnecessary many of the artificial emphases and distortions which were forced upon speakers of an earlier era in order to make their unamplified voices clear to large audiences. Presumably this change should be reflected by dictionaries now in the process of being edited.

A corollary matter is the question of whether pronunciations are to be recorded in isolation or as they occur in running context. Most of our speech is, of course, in running context; hence, a transcription of a word in isolation is in a sense an artificial abstraction. On the other hand, the influences of neighboring sounds and varying prosodic patterns upon a word are potentially so numerous as to place a severe burden upon the lexicographer if he tries to cover them all.

There is also the question of the regional form of speech which is to be represented. With English the first problem is a national one, the English of England or of America. Frequently the title of a dictionary will give a clue to its policy and coverage, as for example *A Pronouncing Dictionary of American English,* but more often the reader must consult the preface for information on this point. And once the national variety of the language has been determined, we are then faced with the question of which regional form is to be given priority. In general, American lexicographers have not in theory assumed that any one dialect was superior to another, but in actual practice, during most of the nineteenth century many concessions were made to New England pronunciations. It is probably fair to say that, even today, Southern pronunciations are not covered as fully and as conscientiously as other regional forms.

The difficulty of reducing sounds to a series of black and white marks has already been mentioned, and here the reader must learn precisely what the system of symbolization in his dictionary is intended to represent. A symbol may represent one and only one configuration of the organs of speech, as do for example the characters of the phonetic alphabet. Or, on the other hand, a dictionary symbol may signify a whole range of pronunciations, as does, for example, the Webster á, which is used in connection with the entire class of words of the *ask—path—calf* type, whose pronunciation ranges from the stressed vowel of *hat* to that of *art.* In the latter instance, these variant values are clearly set forth in the preface—that great no-man's land of the lexicographer—but they cannot be clearly comprehended by the hasty reader who consults only the running key at the bottom of the page. Similar multiple values are also frequently assigned by lexicographers to symbols representing the stressed vowels of words like *hot, bird,* and *new.* The multiple-value symbol has the advantage of economy; it runs the risk of misinterpretation.

Of course dictionaries frequently do indicate more than a single standard pronunciation for many words. Very often such words fall into well-defined groups posing certain common problems, as for example the variant stress on disyllabics like *robust* and *finance*. Again these may be taken up as a group in the introductory matter, and in the body of the dictionary the reader will simply be referred to the section of the preface where they are discussed, either by a paragraph number or other reference symbol, but this is precisely the kind of mechanism which the casual reader often misses.

There is a final question which is posed by variant pronunciations in the dictionary. Which of the several recommended forms is the consultant to employ? For many years there has been a superstition of decided preference adhering to the first pronunciation, but again a glance at the preface of a good dictionary will easily dispel this notion. The *Webster's Collegiate* tells us that "Each form entered, however, has the support of good usage, and in some cases this usage is nearly or quite equally divided." The *American College Dictionary* is even a little more forthright in its statement that "Any pronunciation in this dictionary is a good pronunciation and may be safely used. If the second or third pronunciation is your natural pronunciation, it is the one to use." Indeed a moment's reflection will make it plain that the number of informants from which pronunciations are collected is so small, and the number of speakers they represent so vast, that a second body of information collected from an equal number of cultivated speakers might quite completely reverse the evidence upon which the editor's final judgment has been based.

Admittedly the dictionary is not a perfect tool, but it is a useful one, and if employed intelligently can dispel much uncertainty, much anxiety, and many wrong notions about pronunciation. In terms of the skill and science which go into their make-up, dictionaries are in all probability ahead of their market at the present time. They will improve only in response to the intelligent demands of their users.

QUESTIONS FOR REVIEW OF PART TWO

1. How are new words coined?
2. Armstrong writes that new words must be "bona fide" or "legitimate additions to the language" before they are included in a dictionary. What do you think he means by "bona fide" and "legitimate"?

3. What are some of the stages in the process of writing a dictionary entry which the Armstrong selection does not fully describe?

4. What is the difference between denotation and connotation?

5. Why is it difficult to provide complete and accurate treatment of connotation in a dictionary?

6. Some individuals and groups have a special stake in seeing that certain words (or certain denotations and connotations) are included in or excluded from dictionaries. From what Armstrong writes about coinage and from what Guralnik writes about connotation, who do you suppose some of these people are?

7. Why is it difficult to provide complete and accurate treatment of pronunciation in a dictionary?

SUGGESTIONS FOR INDIVIDUAL PROJECTS AND CLASS DISCUSSION

1. Drawing from your familiarity with some one specialized area of knowledge, make a list of twenty words that are not generally known, at least not in their specialized meanings. For example, you could list words used by musicians, hot-rodders, criminals, lawyers, farmers, storekeepers, sailboat enthusiasts, space scientists, interior decorators, labor union members, radio hams, or politicians. Then look up each of the words in a good, college-level dictionary to see if the specialized meaning of the word is given. Be prepared to report your findings to the class and to speculate on why some words are included in your dictionary but others are not included. (If you genuinely believe that you are not familiar enough with any specialized area of knowledge to draw your list from words you already know, you may construct a list by consulting one of the specialized dictionaries in the library or by referring to one of the many articles on argot, jargon or cant in back issues of *American Speech*. Handle such references and periodicals carefully, though; it is a serious handicap when people find such basic references misplaced or mutilated.)

2. During the ensuing week, prepare a dictionary entry for a slang word or an example of campus jargon that is not in your dictionary. Carry some 3 x 5 cards with you, and whenever you hear the word write on one of the cards (in quotation marks) the precise sentence in which you hear it. As soon as possible afterward, note, below the sentence, the meaning which the speaker seemed to intend by the word. You may wish to check the meaning with the speaker. Also note the age, sex, and education of the speaker; and characterize the circumstances or social situation in which he used the word (lecture hall, informal class discussion, dormitory bull-session, locker room, formal dance, and the like). After you have assembled ten or

more such citation cards (as lexicographers call them), write on a separate card a succinct definition (or, if necessary, several definitions) of the word, following the format of a vocabulary entry in your dictionary. You may include pronunciation and etymological information in your entry, but that is optional. Write your name in a corner of the entry card, place that card on top of the citation cards, and submit the packet, enclosed in a rubber band.

SUGGESTED WRITING ASSIGNMENT

After completing one of the projects described above, write a 400-500 word theme reporting what you discovered. Plan your paper carefully so that it does not turn into a dull report of the mere steps you went through. Before you begin your rough draft, list (preferably in complete sentences) the general conclusions you can draw from your project. See if you can relate all or most of these conclusions to one over-all statement which you can make the main idea of your paper. Then organize the body of your paper according to the general conclusions, not to the steps of the process. Make each of these conclusions the topic sentence of a paragraph, using specific examples of words or sentences which you discovered in your project as means of explaining the topic sentence. Be sure that you use quotation marks around all quoted sentences and expressions and around words referred to as words rather than for their meaning. If you use any printed references, cite them informally in the body of your paper or formally in footnotes.

PART III

Grammar

 e can rely on a discussion of grammar to end in argument. Why is a subject so familiar to us one on which we tend to disagree? There are several explanations. One is that people frequently are arguing about different things when they use the term. To some, "grammar" means all that is involved in writing (perhaps even in speaking)—the organization and style, even the content of writing, as well as spelling and punctuation. To others (including the editor of this book), "grammar" refers to the forms of individual words and their arrangement in sentences—morphology and syntax. When people using these different conceptions argue about how much grammar should be taught in the public schools, we can see that they are, for the most part, arguing about different things.

Another reason why people disagree about grammar is that, despite using it more or less unconsciously every waking hour, most of them do not know much about it. Some people argue about grammar without having any more understanding of what is involved than they have when they decide which flavor of ice cream to choose. Others are more or less familiar with mistaken notions perpetrated upon an unsuspecting public 150 years ago by scholars who tried to construct an English grammar based upon the grammar of formal Latin. (As we have already seen in the Schlauch article of Part I, those scholars would have done better to select Dutch.) Still others have become more or less informed by studying the ways in which the morphology and syntax of English actually work. Not to be confused with these people are language scholars primarily concerned with "usage." They concentrate on the way individual words and constructions are used by writers and speakers of different locales and social levels, under different circumstances, and at different periods of time. These important concerns are not primarily grammatical, but metalinguistic; they are dealt with in Part IV.

The two chief groups of grammarians today are the "traditionalists" and the "structuralists." Drawing on the sounder notions adapted from the old Latin grammar, the better informed traditionalists have discarded silly ideas not workable in English grammar and have developed some conceptions that go beyond the old precepts of 150 years ago. Two selections which represent the informed traditional point of view are included at the end of Part III: Philip B. Ballard's chapter on "The Sentence" and Janet Rankin Aiken's chapter on "What Is Good Grammar?"

The structuralists, who have done most of their research since World War II, have attempted to overcome the deficiencies of applying Latin grammar to English. They have done this, in so far as they have been able, by discarding the old grammatical concepts and terminology and by studying English grammar with new eyes. For example, they tend not to classify isolated words by the parts of speech, recognizing that a word like "bomb," though listed in dictionaries as a noun or verb, can function as an adjective, as in "the bomb shelter." It is to the credit of L. M. Myers, from whose structurally-oriented *Guide to American English* two selections are included here, that he does not go so far as to refuse to label any word as a part of speech.

Structuralists study grammar with "new ears" as well as new eyes. Recognizing that speech has preceded and shaped writing, they have opened up a new dimension of grammar by listening to its intonations, stresses, and pauses. That is why Part III begins with John S. Kenyon's "The Representation of Speech Sounds," even though it concerns phonology, not morphology or syntax; some knowledge of phonetics is helpful in reading several selections in this book and it is essential to a broad understanding of the English language. George P. Faust's "Terms in Phonemics" then extends and applies phonetic insights to the structure of English words and sentences. The article by Ralph H. Lane and the subsequent comment by Robert A. Caldwell are included to sharpen critical sensitivity to one phenomenon of grammatical change occurring around us at the present time.

JOHN S. KENYON

From American Pronunciation, *tenth edi-*
tion, by John S. Kenyon. Copyright, 1924,
1935, 1945, 1946, and 1950, by John S.
Kenyon. By permission of George Wahr
Publishing Co.

The Representation of Speech
Sounds

Language is primarily speech; primarily, both in origin and in respect
to importance. The first parent speech of our language originated,
gradually developed, split up, in the course of group migrations, into
many sister languages, underwent numberless changes in word-stock,
word meanings, grammar and syntax, and pronunciation, centuries before
any one succeeded in making language visible to the eye in writing.
Written English in our present alphabet is hardly fifteen hundred years
old. In present importance, also, spoken English is far in advance of
written. Even people engaged chiefly in intellectual affairs speak a
hundred words where they write one; with the average man the ratio
of spoken to written is far greater. But the measure of the relative importance of speech and of written or printed language is not quantitative;
a personal interview is far better than a letter to accomplish a practical
end. Speech is a living activity inseparable from personality; written or
printed language is only an imperfect picture of it.

In the study of language we are constantly tempted to forget that
speech is primary, and writing and reading secondary, because speech
is wholly unconscious in its beginning with the individual, and virtually
so throughout life. But our conscious efforts with language—our first
laborious reading, spelling, and writing, the later study of grammar and

74

composition, and of literature, and our study of the printed page in other subjects—all these deal with the written or printed representation of speech to the eye; and so in our conscious intellectual life the written language assumes a prominence all out of proportion to its actual daily importance. Particularly in phonetics is it necessary to remind ourselves at every turn that the real language is speech—spoken groups of words— and not the written or printed signs representing it to the eye.

Though the English people who migrated to the British Isles in the fifth century possessed an alphabet, called runes, when they came, the great body of their literature was not written down, but was composed and spoken orally, and transmitted by memory. In the sixth century the missionaries from Rome who had settled in Ireland began to Christianize England in Northumbria, and thus introduced the **Roman alphabet** into England for the writing of the native language.

A few changes in the use of the letters have been made since the Roman alphabet began to be used to represent English sounds. The OE scribes used for the first sound in *we* the runic character p called *wĕn*. In the thirteenth century this was abandoned and *uu* or *vv* ("double *u*"), and then *w*, was used in its place. A rune þ, called *thorn,* was used for the two *th* sounds now heard in *thin* and *this*. The use of this character for the *th* sound persisted in occasional use till the seventeenth century, though after printing began, the letter *y* was often used when type fonts lacked þ. This is sometimes seen now in imitation of old style, though most people are now unaware that it stands for the *th* sound, and wrongly pronounce it as *y* in *you*.

Until the seventeenth century *u* and *v* were not used as now—*u* for the vowel and *v* for the consonant—but were regarded as merely different forms of the same letter, each of which represented either a vowel or a consonant sound. The usual rule was to use *v* at the beginning of a word for consonant or vowel, and *u* in the middle or at the end as consonant or vowel. Thus in the Authorized Version of the Bible in 1611 we find, "When thou tillest the ground, it shall not henceforth yeeld vnto thee her strength: A fugitiue and a vagabond shalt thou be in the earth" (Gen. 4:12); and this is the usage throughout the Bible and books of the sixteenth century and before. Milton in 1645 followed the present method of using *u* for the vowel and *v* for the consonant, regardless of position in the word. But not till the nineteenth century did dictionaries separate words with initial *u* from those with initial *v*.

Likewise *i* and *j* were formerly merely different forms of the same letter, which had the value either of the vowels in *it* and *ice* or of the first consonant in *jug*. At first ı alone was used, without the dot. When initial, this was often prolonged above the line to keep it distinct from the following letter. This form finally appeared, after printing began, as I. The dot was added to ı, also to avoid confusion with adjacent letters, as today. In medieval European writing, at the end of words i was often prolonged below the line, giving the form j. This was used by English scribes in numerals, as *j, ij, iij, vj, xij,* etc., and at the end of Latin words such as *filij*. (In English words final *i* was replaced by *y*.) These different forms were used as vowel or consonant. Thus we find in the Bible of 1611, "I am iealous for Ierusalem, and for Zion, with a great iealousie" (Zech. 1:14). Again Milton was among the first to adopt the present practice of using *i* for vowel and *j* for consonant, but dictionaries did not separate words with initial *i* and *j* till the nineteenth century, and *u* and *v, i* and *j* were not separated in the British Museum catalog till about 1930.

When English began to be written in Roman letters, the spelling was as nearly phonetic as possible; i.e., each scribe represented his own English sounds by the letter that stood for the Latin sound nearest to his own. But even at first there were some discrepancies. For example, the letter *f* was used both for the sound in *fat* and for that in *over* (then spelt *ofer*) ; *s* stood for the sound in *fast* and in *rise;* þ stood for the sound of *th* in *thin* and in *writhe,* and ð stood for the same also; *g* stood for the sound in *get* and in *yet*. As time went on, there was a constantly increasing discrepancy between sound and spelling. An alphabet remains comparatively fixed, and habits of spelling tend to remain, rather than to change—especially since the use of printing—for they are based on visible and conscious imitation. Speech, on the other hand, is based on unconscious and somewhat imperfect imitation, and so changes by imperceptible and continuous variation. Thus the word *man* is still spelt as it was in King Alfred's time, but has changed in pronunciation from "mŏn" to its present pronunciation. *Hope* in Chaucer's day was pronounced "haw-puh"; but though it has changed to its present sound, it is still spelt *hope* as it was in Chaucer's day. So after English sounds began to be represented in Roman letters, the sounds tended to depart farther and farther from what the letters had at first suggested. It is obvious that if this divergence between sound and spelling continued, the sounds would after a while become entirely different from what the letters had at first suggested. Then either the spelling must fail to serve its purpose, and new letters must be used, or the letters must gradually come to suggest different sounds from those at first associated with them. In fact, the latter is what happened, but not with all the letters at the same time. From the fifteenth to the seventeenth centuries the sounds of English had so changed that it is now true with most vowel sounds and some consonant sounds that the letters do not ordinarily stand for the sounds which had been associated with the Roman letters in English down to the fifteenth century, and in other European languages down to the present time. The change in vowel sounds that occurred from the time of Chaucer to the present is called **The Great Vowel Shift,** and consisted, for the long vowels, in the raising of the tongue for each vowel except the two already highest i: and u:), which became diphthongs.

The attempt in English to keep up with the changing sounds by using the same letters with changed values was not entirely successful. Hence we find in present English that the single letter *a*, for example, represents the different vowel sounds in such words as *name, bare, father, all, village, lunar, sofa;* the letter *e* spells the different sounds in *be, here, there, bed, alert, England, moment, added,* and very often no sound at all, as in *life, make;* and so with other vowel letters. The consonants are more consistent with their spelling: *b, h, j, k, l, m, q, v, z* nearly always denote one sound each, though most of them can be silent. But *c* denotes the sounds in *city, sacrifice,* v. (*z*), *cat, vicious; d* those in *day, walked; f* those in *life, of; g* those in *get, age,* or none, as in *caught; n* those in *fin, finger,* or none, as in *solemn; s* those in *say, rise, sure, measure,* or none, as in *island.* On the other hand, the same sound is often represented by more than one letter; thus the vowel sound in *mate* is represented by *a;* the same sound in *they* by *ey,* in *vein* by *ei,* in *hail* by *ai,* in *break* by *ea,* in *gauge* by *au.* The sound represented by *e* in *be* is represented by *ee* in *see, ea* in *heap, ie* in *believe, ey* in *key, ei* in *seize, i* in *machine, eo* in *people.* The obscure sound at the end of *sofa* may be represented by any vowel letter and by many combinations, as by *a* in *sofa, e* in *fallen, i* in *possible, o* in *gallop, u* in *suppose, ai* in *villain, ou* in *famous, eou* in *outrageous,* etc.

It is obvious from these illustrations that we could not form a definite idea how present-day English is pronounced if we were dependent solely on the current spelling and had not already learned to speak before learning to spell. Much more is it true then, that we cannot *study* pronunciation successfully with only the ordinary spelling to guide us and to represent it with. In order to consider pronunciation scientifically, and to record and communicate the results of our study, we must make use of some system of symbols that shall unmistakably represent the sounds of speech.

In the main, such a phonetic alphabet must meet two requirements: (1) each symbol shall represent only one speech sound; (2) each speech sound shall have a symbol to represent it. Several such phonetic alphabets are in use by phoneticians and lexicographers. The one now most widely used is that of the **International Phonetic Association** (IPA) and is used in this book. The official publication of the IPA is *Le Maître Phonétique* (Quarterly), and contains articles and specimens in various modern languages, printed in this alphabet.

i ɪ e ɛ æ a ɑ ɒ ɔ o ʊ u

ʒ̩ ɝ ɜ ə ʌ aɪ aʊ ɔɪ ɪu ju

p b t d k g f v θ ð s z

ʃ ʒ h tʃ dʒ m n ŋ l

w j r

PHONETIC SYMBOLS

VOWELS

No.	SYMBOL	KEY WORD	PRONUNCIATION
1.	i	*beet*	bit
2.	ɪ	*bit, easy*	bɪt, izɪ
3.	e	*bait*	bet
4.	ɛ	*bet*	bɛt
5.	æ	*bat*	bæt
6.	a	Sc. *cat*	kat. Between æ and ɑ.
7.	ɑ	*father*	fɑðɚ
		fodder	fɑdɚ. General American "short *o*".
8.	ɒ	*fodder*	fɒdə. British "short *o*" (between ɑ and ɔ).
9.	ɔ	*law, horse*	lɔ hɔrs
10.	o	*coat*	kot
11.	ʊ	*pull*	pʊl
12.	u	*pool*	pul
13.	ɝ	ˈ*further*	ˈfɝðɚ. Accented. General American.
		*per*ˈ*verse*	pɚˈvɝs
14.	ɚ	ˈ*further*	ˈfɝðɚ. Unaccented. General American.
		*per*ˈ*verse*	pɚˈvɝs
15.	ɜ	ˈ*further*	ˈfɜðə. Accented. East, South, and England.
		*per*ˈ*verse*	pəˈvɜs
16.	ə	ˈ*custom*	ˈkʌstəm. Unaccented.
		*a*ˈ*bove*	əˈbʌv
17.	ʌ	ˈ*custom*	ˈkʌstəm. Accented.
		*a*ˈ*bove*	əˈbʌv

DIPHTHONGS

No.	SYMBOL	KEY WORD	PRONUNCIATION
18.	aɪ	*ice*	aɪs
19.	aʊ	*house*	haʊs
20.	ɔɪ	*boy*	bɔɪ
21.	ɪu	*abuse*	əbɪuz
22.	ju	*use*	juz

CONSONANTS

Symbols not numbered have their usual names

No.	SYM-BOL	KEY WORD	PRONUN-CIATION	No.	SYM-BOL	KEY WORD	PRONUN-CIATION
		Stops		26.	ʒ	*vision*	vɪʒən
					h	*hail*	hel
	p	*peep*	pip				
	b	*bib*	bɪb			Affricates	
	t	*toot*	tut	27.	tʃ	*church*	tʃɜtʃ
	d	*did*	dɪd	28.	dʒ	*judge*	dʒʌdʒ
	k	*cook*	kʊk				
	g	*gag*	gæg			Sonorants	
					m	*maim*	mem
		Fricatives			n	*noon*	nun
	f	*fife*	faɪf	29.	ŋ	*sing*	sɪŋ
	v	*valve*	vælv		l	*lull*	lʌl
23.	θ	*ether*	iθɚ			Glides	
24.	ð	*either*	iðɚ				
	s	*cease*	sis		w	*wail*	wel
	z	*zones*	zonz		hw	*whale*	hwel
25.	ʃ	*mission*	mɪʃən		j	*young*	jʌŋ
					r	*road*	rod

Note: A phonograph record of the author's speech sounds may be got from National Council of Teachers of English, 508 So. 6th St., Champaign, Ill.

Accent is indicated by the mark (') for **primary accent** and (ˌ) for **secondary,** each placed **before** the accented syllable, as in 'shoeˌmaker 'ʃuˌme kɚ, 'drawing ˌroom 'drɔ ɪŋ ˌrum. Wholly unaccented syllables are not marked, as in 'nation 'ne ʃən, be'fore bɪ'for. When it is desired to indicate a subordinate accent weaker than secondary, this may be indicated by a dot, thus . : ˌmis.under'standing ˌmɪs.ʌn dɚ'stæn dɪŋ, in which four degrees of accent are perceptible by comparison of adjacent syllables —**primary, secondary, light, and no accent.** It is usually sufficient to recognize three degrees only—primary, secondary, and no accent. Syllables with a considerable degree of accent are often left unmarked when adjacent to the syllable that has primary accent, as in 'accent 'æk sɛnt, 'contract 'kɑn trækt. The primary accent mark is generally omitted from words accented only on the first syllable.

The **sign** : after a vowel symbol indicates that the vowel is relatively **long in duration.** The sign ˙ may be used to indicate **intermediate length.** When length signs are systematically used, short vowels are unmarked. In American transcription it is seldom important to indicate length.

The plus sign (+) placed after a symbol (usually a vowel symbol), indicates a pronunciation of it with more advanced tongue position; thus ɑ+ means "advanced ɑ." Similarly the minus sign (−) means "with retracted tongue," as æ−, "retracted æ." The sign ˔ means "with raised tongue," as "ʊ˔," "raised ʊ," and the sign ˕ means "with lowered tongue," as ɛ˕, "lowered ɛ." The signs may be combined; as ɪ˕−, "lowered and retracted ɪ."

In this book spellings are printed in *italics* and sounds in **boldface**. In works where **boldface** is not so used, and in written work, it is customary to place phonetic symbols in square brackets [ ] to distinguish them from ordinary spelling.

In this book the same symbol ɪ is used for both the accented and the unaccented vowel, though they often differ slightly. For the final vowel in words like *easy* many speakers pronounce **i**, fewer in the South and Eastern New England. The author pronounces ɪ in such words.

The vowel in words like *air, care, there* sounds between ɛ in *very* **vɛrɪ** and æ in *bat* **bæt**, *carry* **kærɪ**. Two varieties are in standard use, one nearer to ɛ and the other nearer to æ. It may be written as in **kɛr, ðer** or **kær, ðær**, according as it most resembles ɛ or æ.

The sound a (No. 6) as heard in *cat, man,* etc. in the pronunciation of standard English in Scotland and northern England, is a sound acoustically between æ in *sand* and ɑ in *father*. It occurs in General American only in the diphthongs aɪ and aʊ, and as an occasional unconscious variant of æ. It is used by some speakers in New England and New York City in words like *ask*. In transcription it must not be substituted for ɑ.

The vowel ɒ, which sounds between ɑ and ɔ as it is regularly pronounced in England and locally in America in words with "short *o*" like *not, top, watch, what,* is not often heard in General American, being usually replaced by ɑ.

The symbols ɝ and ɚ each represent simple *r*- colored **vowels**, expressed in current spelling by a vowel letter and *r*, as in *further* **fɝðɚ**. The vowel ɝ occurs only in **syllables of perceptible accent,** as in 'person '**pɝsn**, '*per,vert* (n.) '**pɝ,vɝt,** and is always **syllabic** (is the main vowel of the syllable).[1] The unaccented ɚ is likewise always syllabic, but shorter; as in *better* '**bɛtɚ**, *maker* '**mekɚ**.

The syllabic *r* sound is sometimes transcribed with the phonetic sym-

[1] Many transcribers use the form ɝ with hook at the top as in ɚ. ɝ and ɚ are to be regarded as equivalent, ɝ being easier to write.

bol ɹ̩ (*stirring* stɹ̩ɪŋ, *better* bɜtɹ̩) or with r (bɛtr). But there is the same
reason to use a different symbol for a syllabic r sound (bɛtɚ) than for a
nonsyllabic r sound (*rate* ret, *far* fɑr, *farm* fɑrm) as there is to use a different symbol for a syllabic u sound (*duel* du-əl) than for the corresponding nonsyllabic u sound (*dwell* dwɛl), or a different symbol for a syllabic
i sound (*Bostonian* bɔs'toniən) than for the corresponding nonsyllabic i
sound (*onion* ʌnjən). For the relation of consonant r to the r-colored
vowel ɝ or ɚ is the same as that of consonant w to vowel u or ʊ, and of
consonant j to vowel i or ɪ; the consonants w, j, r being glide consonants,
often called semivowels.

In some former editions of this book the symbol ɚ was used both for a
syllabic vowel (*better* bɛtɚ, *perceive* pɚ'siv) and for a nonsyllabic vowel
forming the latter part of a diphthong (fɑɚ, fɑɚm); but experience
with elementary classes has convinced the author that, in spite of slight
theoretical inconsistency, the practice adopted in *PDAE* (see §26 of
that book) is more practical, in which ɚ stands solely for the r-colored
vowel that forms a syllable either alone (bɛt-ɚ) or with a consonant
(pɚ'siv), and in which r stands both for the consonant (ret, traɪ) and for
the nonsyllabic vowel forming a diphthong with the preceding vowel
(fɑr, fɑrm). When r comes between vowels (*very*), there is even better
reason to use the symbol r, for the sound may be either a consonant
(vɛ-rɪ) or a nonsyllabic vowel (vɛr-ɪ). Both pronunciations occur and
are not easy to distinguish in current speech.

The distinction between consonant r and nonsyllabic vowel r is easily
made by remembering that consonant r always occurs just before a
vowel in the same syllable (ret, tri, bɪ'riv, fæk-tə-rɪ, fæk-trɪ), while vowel
r always immediately follows a syllabic vowel in the same syllable, making
an r diphthong (dɪr, fɑr, fɑrm, fɑr-ðɪŋ); but ɚ always represents a simple monophthongal syllabic r-colored vowel.

Observe that the symbol ə (No. 16), when it is the only vowel of the
syllable, is to be written only in wholly unaccented syllables, as in
above ə'bʌv, *custom* 'kʌs-təm, *sofa* 'so-fə; or in unstressed monosyllables,
as *two of the men* 'tu əv ðə 'mɛn. In the speech of those who "drop their
r's" ə may also be part of an accented syllable, but only the unaccented
part, as in *merely* 'mɪə-lɪ. Hence ə occurs only in unstressed positions.
Likewise the symbol ɚ is to be written only in unstressed positions, either
an unaccented syllable of a word ('bɛt-ɚ, pɚ'siv) or an unstressed mono-
syllable (*two or three* 'tu ɚ 'θri).

On the other hand, the symbols ʒ and ʌ are not to be written in wholly unaccented syllables or unstressed monosyllables. Note the following examples of the correct use of these symbols: *survey* (vb.) sɚˈve, *survey* (n.) ˈsʒˌve; *pervert* (vb.) pɚˈvʒt, *pervert* (n.) ˈpʒˌvʒt; *London* ˈlʌndən; *unless* ənˈlɛs, *unlace* ʌnˈles; *undone and done up* ʌnˈdʌn ən ˈdʌnˈʌp; *misunderstand* ˌmɪsʌndɚˈstænd; *upon* əˈpɑn, *up and down* ˈʌp ən ˈdaʊn; *he heard her* hiˈhʒd ɚ; *her mother, not her* hɚ ˈmʌðɚ, nɑt ˈhʒ.

It should be noted that ə is not only an unaccented substitute for accented ʌ, but for all other accented vowels as well; as in ˈkɑntrækt—kənˈtrækt; kwaɪˈitəs—kwaɪət; moˈmɛntəm—ˈmomənt; ˈmænlɪ—ˈpostmən; ɪmˈpoz—ˌɪmpəˈzɪʃən, etc. Likewise ɚ is the unaccented substitute not only for ʒ, but for the various combinations of accented vowels with a following r. Compare ˈpɑrtɪ—pɚˈtɪkjələ; ˌsɪməˈlærətɪ—ˈsɪmələ; rɪˈkɔrd—ˈrɛkɚd; ˈbordɚ—ˈkʌbɚd.

In transcribing words like *abuse, cure, few,* etc., the student must observe whether he pronounces ɪu or ju, both of which are current. ɪu is never used initially.

For convenience, the letter g is printed for the symbol ɡ, but in written transcription ɡ should always be used.

The symbols m̩, n̩, l̩, called "syllabic *m, n, l,*" indicate m, n, and l sounds that form syllables without any vowel whatever, either alone, as in *stop 'em* stɑp m̩, *listen* lɪs-n̩, *battle* bæt-l̩, or with one or more other consonants, as in o-pm̩, a frequent pronunciation of *open, listened* lɪs-n̩d, *handled* hæn-dl̩d. The sound ŋ can also be syllabic, as frequently heard in *I can go* aɪ kŋ go, where the syllabic marker is omitted for typographical reasons.

Caution: Do not use at all the symbols c, q, x, y. Use only the symbols as given in the tables, which are sufficient to transcribe all the sounds of English. Moreover, these four letters are IPA symbols for certain sounds of other languages (e.g., x is the sound of *ch* in Scottish *loch* lɒx and German *ach* ɑx, and y is the sound of French *u* in *lune* lyn and German *ü* in *fühlen* fyːlən).

Remember that the symbol g stands *only* for the sound in *gag* ɡæɡ, and j only for the first sound in *young* jʌŋ. Do not use either g or j for the sound in *gem* dʒɛm or *judge* dʒʌdʒ.

The following passage, transcribed in a colloquial style in the author's pronunciation, contains all the regular sounds of General American.

Bear in mind that it is not presented as a model of pronunciation, but simply as an example of natural speech in a certain style.

rɪp væn 'wɪŋk!

ðə gret 'ɛrɚ ɪn rɪps ˌkɑmpə'zɪʃən wəz ən ɪn'sɪupərəbl̩ ə'vɜʒən tu ɔl kaɪndz əv 'prɑfɪtəbl̩ 'lebɚ. ɪt 'kudn̩t bi frəm ðə wɑnt əv ˌæsə'dɪuətɪ ɚ ˌpɜsə'vɪrəns, fɚ i wəd sɪt ɑn ə wɛt rɑk, wɪð ə rɑd əz lɔŋ ən 'hɛvɪ əz ə 'tɑrtɚz læns, ən fɪʃ ɔl de wɪð'aut ə 'mɜmɚ, 'ivən ðo i 'ʃudn̩t bi ɪn'kɜɪdʒd baɪ ə 'sɪŋgl̩ 'nɪbl̩. hid 'kærɪ ə 'faulɪŋˌpis ɑn ɪz 'ʃoldɚ fɚ aurz tə'gɛðɚ, 'trʌdʒɪŋ θru wudz n̩ swɔmps, ənd ʌp hɪl ən daun del, tə ʃut ə fɪu skwɜlz ɚ waɪld 'pɪdʒɪnz. hi wəd 'nɛvɚ rɪ'fɪuz tu ə'sɪst ə 'nebɚ, 'ivən ɪn ðə 'rʌfɪst tɔɪl, ənd wəz ə 'forˌmost mæn ət ɔl 'kʌntrɪ 'frɑlɪks fɚ 'hʌskɪŋ 'ɪndɪən kɔrn ɚ 'bɪldɪŋ ston 'fɛnsɪz; ðə 'wɪmɪn əv ðə 'vɪlɪdʒ, tu, jus tu ɪm'plɔɪ ɪm tə rʌn ðɛr 'ɛrəndz, ən tə du sʌtʃ 'lɪtl̩ ɑd dʒɑbz əz ðɛr lɛs ə'blaɪdʒɪŋ 'hʌzbəndz 'wudn̩t du fɔr ðəm. ɪn ə wɜd, rɪp wəz 'rɛdɪ tu ə'tɛnd tu 'ɛnɪˌbɑdɪz 'bɪznɪs bət ɪz on; bət əz tə 'duɪŋ 'fæmlɪ 'dɪutɪ, ən 'kipɪŋ ɪz fɑrm ɪn 'ɔrdɚ, hi faund ɪt ɪm'pɑsəbl̩.

ɪn fækt, hi dɪ'klærd ɪt wəz əv no jus tə wɜk ɑn ɪz fɑrm; ɪt wəz ðə most 'pɛstl̩ənt 'lɪtl̩ pis əv graund ɪn ðə hol 'kʌntrɪ; 'ɛvrɪˌθɪŋ ə'baut ɪt wɛnt rɔŋ, ənd 'wud go rɔŋ, ɪn spaɪt əv ɪm. hɪz 'fɛnsɪz wɚ kən'tɪnjuəlɪ 'fɔlɪŋ tə 'pisɪz; hɪz kauz wəd 'iðɚ go ə'stre, ɚ gɛt ə'mʌŋ ðə 'kæbɪdʒɪz: hi 'kudn̩t 'kipm̩ ət hom; widz wɚ ʃur tə gro 'kwɪkɚ ɪn 'hɪz fildz ðən 'ɛnɪ ˌhwær ɛls; ðə ren 'ɔlwɪz med ə pɔɪnt əv 'sɛtɪŋ ɪn dʒʌst əz i hæd səm 'aut-əv-ˌdor wɜk tə du; so ðət ðo ɪz ˌpætrə'monɪəl ə'stet əd 'dwɪndl̩d ə'we 'ʌndɚ ɪz 'mænɪdʒmənt, 'ekɚ baɪ 'ekɚ, ən'tɪl ðɚ wəz 'lɪtl̩ mor lɛft ðən ə mɪr pætʃ əv 'ɪndɪən kɔrn ən pə'tetuz, jɛt ɪt wəz ðə 'wɜst-kən'dɪʃənd fɑrm ɪn ðə 'nebɚˌhud.

Isolating sounds from words. A difficulty for the beginner is to learn to isolate the separate speech sounds from the combinations in which they occur in speech. The current spelling is deceptive because a single sound may be spelt with more than one letter, as f in *phonetics* fo'nɛtɪks, p in *happy* hæpɪ, θ or ŋ in *thing* θɪŋ, ʒ or ɪ in *journeyed* dʒɜnɪd; or two sounds spelt with one letter, as ks in *tax* tæks; or a sound with no letter, as p in *warm( )th* wɔrmpθ, k in *leng( )th* lɛŋkθ, and t in *eigh( )th* etθ. Some single sounds are always spelt with two letters, as θ or ð with *th,* and others usually so, as ʃ with *sh,* tʃ with *ch* (or *tch*). Hence it is necessary to consider the *sounds* and guard against deceptive spelling. It is best to sound the word without looking at the spelling and listen while repeating it. After the sound is perceived and pronounced separately, select the symbol which expresses it. Remember that the tables contain *all* the separate sounds; avoid confusing one sound with two, as ŋ with ɪŋ.

GEORGE P. FAUST

From College Composition and Communication, *V* (*February, 1954*), *30-34. By
permission of the National Council of
Teachers of English and the author.*

Terms in Phonemics

By means of phonemic analysis, structural linguists try to discover the
sound-system of a language as it is consciously or subconsciously meaningful to the speakers. A new set of terms (and symbols) is forced upon
them partly because they have formed new categories and developed new
techniques and partly because the familiar terms have an aura of association that would act to block understanding if they were used in new
senses. The difficulty is that the new terms themselves have blocked
understanding between structuralists and teachers. The problem of this
article is to remove some of the barriers and show some of the uses
teachers can make of the present knowledge of English structure, with
no attempt to go beyond phonemics.[1]

But the barriers will not fall automatically with the explanation of a
few technical tems. As I have tried to say earlier,[2] we must first persuade
ourselves to accept two basic tenets: (1) that speech is the primary form

[1] In general, this article will follow the analysis in George L. Trager and
Henry Lee Smith, Jr., *An Outline of English Structure* (Studies in Linguistics.
Occasional Papers No. 3), 1951. This is a thoroughly technical piece of work
not recommended for beginners. The best available starting point is Robert A.
Hall's *Leave Your Language Alone!* (Linguistica: Ithaca, N.Y.), 1950. [This
book is also available in the inexpensive Anchor reprint series as *Linguistics
and Your Language.*] If you don't like the social attitudes expressed, ignore
them and concentrate on the very able exposition of linguistics.

[2] "Basic Tenets of Structural Linguistics," *CCC,* December, 1953, pages 122-126.

of language and underlies all writing, and (2) that the concern of structuralists is with the mechanisms of language as a medium, not with the
"message" (meaning) carried by the medium.

These two tenets accepted, let us start by fastening attention on the
p-sounds in the possible expression 'rapid pup.' We will follow the general
practice of putting phonetic symbols in brackets, e.g., [p], and phonemic
symbols between slashes, e.g., /p/. In a phonemic transcription of my
speech without stress and intonation marked, we can set our expression
down as /ræpid pəp/. This is not phonetic, for among other things any
competent phonetician could hear differences among the *p*-sounds as he
listened to me. If he took the first as a phonetic norm, he might transcribe
them in order as [p], [p'], and [p'], with ['] standing for aspiration (a
puff of air that can be felt on the back of the hand held close to the
mouth) and ['] indicating no release by reopening the lips. All three
varieties are called allophones.

To put it as untechnically as I can, ALLOPHONES are phonetically
similar sounds that never get in each other's way. As native speakers of
English, we have learned to use the proper allophones automatically and
to ignore them completely in our own speech and in the speech of others.
This means that *if you know that a word has two pronunciations, they
differ phonemically, not allophonically.* It is only when a foreigner fails
to use the right allophones that we become vaguely conscious that something is wrong: The foreigner, we say, speaks English with an accent.
In all this we are reacting quite normally, and no phonetically untrained
reader should be disturbed if he fails to hear allophonic differences.

Allophones have COMPLEMENTARY DISTRIBUTION, the technical term
that corresponds to "never get in each other's way." This is a tricky term
to handle. Allophones tend to be restricted. That is, [p'] simply cannot
appear at the beginning of a word because we have to reopen our lips to
get on with the word. On the other hand, [p'] does on occasion replace
[p'] at the end of a word. But we speakers react to /pəp/ as the "same"
word, no matter which allophone is used, and any sense of difference here
is likely to be referred to the speaker's attitude, not his dialect. Therefore, the allophones never collide, even when they alternate with one
another, and they complement one another in such a way that in sum
they take care of all the situations in which their phoneme occurs.

Complementary distribution is one side of the coin, CONTRASTIVE
DISTRIBUTION the other. Sounds contrast most obviously when the dif-

ference produces different words. Thus /p/ and /f/ contrast because 'pup' is not 'puff' (/pəf/). *And one contrast anywhere in the language is enough to establish separate phonemes everywhere in the language.* It is known quite definitely that [p] between vowels is voiced in normal American speech and is thus very close to [b] in the same situation—at least as close to [b] phonetically as to initial [p']. But since [p] and [b] are assigned by speakers to different phonemes (cf. the contrast between /pet/ and /bet/), the phonetic similarity is inconsequential. You can test this for yourself. Just invite a friend to pat your 'rabid pup' and see whether his reactions are like those of the friends you have invited to pat your 'rapid pup.'

Here it is necessary to insist that the difference in meaning is the *result* of the difference in sound. Strangers who hear my weakly aspirated initial /p/ (an individual peculiarity) quite easily "misunderstand" me and think, for instance, that my middle initial is B instead of P. The sense of "misunderstand" here is that they have misclassified a sound, with resultant change of meaning.

An error of this sort points up one extremely important difference between phonetics and phonemics. In phonetics a sound can be between a /p/ and a /b/ in the sense that it can have certain characteristics of each, such as the voicelessness of an initial /p/ and the relatively weak aspiration of an initial /b/. The phonetician tries to describe the sound actually produced. But in phonemics there are no gradations. *A sound is assigned to one phoneme or another, and there is no in-between stage.* The linguistic evidence goes to show that we hear in terms of phonemes and listen to only as much of a sound as we need to in order to assign it to an established phoneme. This is a fundamental reason why phonemic transcriptions don't need to distinguish among allophones.

We should now be ready for some definitions. A sound produced is a PHONE. It is a unique historical event, in theory as individual as a fingerprint. Obviously, only a microscopic sample of the phones produced ever get recorded, and yet the patterning of language is such that linguists can classify as confidently as though they had a statistically large sample. In great measure, this is because they have occasion to concentrate on only a few variations. The subclasses into which phones are fitted are ALLOPHONES, each of which, though in complementary distribution, is distinct from all others by at least one phonetic feature. At this level we are still in a region where sounds may be symbolized in phonetic transcription. Next, the allophones are gathered into one class, a PHONEME, which is distinguished by the phonetic similarity of its members and by its contrastive distribution with other phonemes.

To tie all three together, any phone may be called a phone (i.e., an individual sound) or an allophone (i.e., a member of an allophone) or a phoneme (i.e., a member of a phoneme). Imagine that I now hear you say 'pup.' The first sound was a phone, already past history. As long as it remains unclassified, I can call it nothing but a phone. Probably I will next classify it as a member of the phoneme /p/, and now I can call it either a phone or a phoneme. When finally I group it with other members of /p/ that have aspiration, I can also call it an allophone of /p/, and I can describe that allophone phonetically as [p']. In the same kind of way, all other vowel-like or consonant-like phones can be identified as belonging to one or another of the thirty-three phonemes that make up this part of the English sound-system.

For teachers, the usefulness of having a working acquaintance with these phonemes is that it sheds valuable light on many spelling problems. All of us already know, in a relatively unsystematic way, that our students tend to reflect their pronunciations in their writing, but the remedies we have offered have sometimes been unrealistic, to a considerable extent because we have confused letters and sounds. One pronunciation of *often,* now well established, is supposed to be due to the letter *t* in the spelling—some people, apparently, never thought of *soften.* Once we realize that *used to* is regularly pronounced /yuwstuw/, not /yuwzd tuw/, we may be more sympathetic to the spelling *use to,* which is really very sensible, if not orthodox. Of course we should try to impress the conventional spelling but not, I suggest, at the cost of a pronunciation which may be unforced for some speakers but which I never happen to have heard attempted except by teachers. Again, probably many of us tear our hair over students who seem unable to pluralize words like *scientist.* But a great many standard speakers have /-s/ at the end of such words instead of /-st/, and to them the plural presumably sounds just like the singular.[3] It would strike an informed teacher as unreasonable to attempt to modify a standard pronunciation; it would be better to show the students that for spelling such words they cannot trust their

[3] A structurally more accurate way of putting this is that the final consonant cluster /-sts/ is non-existent in the speech of many Americans.

ears. This is the type of situation which a knowledge of phonemics enables a teacher to handle sensibly.

To return to the sound-system, the set of phonemes referred to so far are called SEGMENTAL PHONEMES to distinguish them from another more recently discovered set, the SUPRASEGMENTAL PHONEMES. These consist of stresses, pitches, and junctures—the last being modes of transition from one speech-segment to another. Of course the fact of their existence is not news; the recent knowledge is of their contrastive distribution into phonemes, which has been worked out in considerable detail during the last ten years by Kenneth Pike and others.

STRESS is familiar as what we call accent in dictionaries, where only three relative degrees are necessary, counting the unmarked as weak. (However, you should not expect dictionaries to be accurate on stress. For example, they leave the second syllable of *cargo* unmarked, though it definitely has more stress than the second syllable of *sofa*—as much, in my speech, as the marked second syllable of *blackbird*.) Connected speech has a fourth degree of stress which overrides the others and which we use to establish word-groups. Customary symbols of stress are

$$/ \acute{} , \hat{} , \grave{} , \breve{} /,$$

called primary, secondary, tertiary, and weak.

Whêre's thĕ cárgò

illustrates the four phonemic stresses.

The very idea that relative levels of PITCH are contrastive is a novelty. Here there is nothing like a familiar dictionary to fall back on, and since the proof is somewhat complicated, about all that can be done here is to make the flat assertion that English has four phonemic pitches. The joke 'What are we having for dinner? Mother?' depends on the misuse of pitch levels. In the commonplace 'What are we having for dinner, Mother?' the vocative can be either at the lowest pitch or the next above, but it can never be at either of the two highest pitches. With next-to-top pitch, as in the joke, 'mother' becomes a separate question.[4]

Pitches are usually symbolized by numbers: $/^1,^2,^3,^4/$. Unfortunately,

[4] I am indebted to H. L. Smith, Jr., for this passage, joke included.

there are two systems in use, one that numbers from the top and one that begins at the bottom. Other devices, like dotted lines above and below the text, are also in use.

The phonemes of JUNCTURE, or TRANSITION, are classes of the ways we use to pass from one bit or stretch of linguistic material to the next. If this merely seems a clumsy way of saying something like "get from one phrase or sentence to the next," the reason is that the use of juncture helps to define terms like *phrase* and *sentence.* Therefore we cannot, without circular reasoning, use the terms in describing juncture. As a minor digression, let me point out that our standard practice has been to use circularity, though often at one or two removes. We may use *sentence* to help define *verb,* and then turn around and use *verb* to help define *sentence.* The structuralists try very hard not to fall into this sort of trap.

The four phonemes of juncture are symbolized by /+, |, ||, #/, called plus juncture, single bar juncture, double bar juncture, and double cross juncture respectively. PLUS JUNCTURE, which classically distinguishes 'night rate' from 'nitrate,' can be left behind with the observation that it always occurs at least between secondary stresses, and between a secondary and primary, unless one of the other three junctures is there. (This, of course, like all that follows, is a rule of the language, not of the structuralists; it is a phenomenon observed, not created.) The remaining junctures can be thought of as major, for they serve to establish what is probably the basic rule of English grammar: There is always one, and only one, primary stress between any pair of /|, ||, #/. This rule is completely accurate if the silence before speech is counted as a major juncture and if the speaker is not interrupted. For example, both these versions are accepted by listeners as normal English:

> My ôlder brôther is a plúmber.
> My ôlder bróther | is a plúmber.

SINGLE BAR JUNCTURE can be read as transition across a fairly minor break with pitch sustained to the point of juncture. It is never an uninterrupted speaker's final juncture. DOUBLE BAR JUNCTURE is familiar to us as the rising "question intonation," a thoroughly misleading term. The questions that end in double bar are those without question words, like 'Are you going?' and 'He's here?' In all but perhaps a very few dialects, questions like 'Where are you going?' do not end in double bar.

Polite vocatives always end with double bar: 'I'm going, Mother.' Especially in rather slow speech, the rise of double bar is common within the conventional sentence:

> The sôldiers in Koréa || wânted to gêt hóme.

DOUBLE CROSS JUNCTURE is marked by voice fade-out, and usually a lowering of pitch. It appears where periods have been used in the examples, and at the end of 'Where are you going?' It also appears, at least in some reading styles, before what we have been trained to call a non-restrictive subordinate clause at the end of a sentence.

The implications of the suprasegmental phonemes for teachers are important. Almost all marks of punctuation are juncture signals, as we demonstrate again and again by reading aloud mispunctuated student sentences to show that they sound queer. Some of us, perhaps, sometimes even deliberately misread the student's punctuation because it violates an editorial rule, not a linguistic principle. But almost nobody, within my knowledge, is equipped to give students a sensible explanation of punctuation in terms of major junctures and the arbitrary rules of editors.[5]

Reading styles differ within rather narrow limits, but for the sake of illustration we can arbitrarily pick one in which /#/ is symbolized by a period and /|||/ by a comma. No other junctures are marked by punctuation. If the student gives the reading 'He wasn't there /|||/ therefore I didn't see him,' the comma before *therefore* is right linguistically, however wrong it may be editorially. If he reads 'I didn't go to the dance /#/ because I was too tired,' the proper punctuation linguistically is into two sentences. In the past year and a half, I have marked comma faults and fragments RA for "Read aloud." When the student's reading has been right linguistically, I have been able to show him how to identify the situations in which he cannot trust to his ear for punctuation. Without claiming perfect results, I can say that I have been astonished at how readily students of all levels have taken to my explanations and how often they have asked me why punctuation was never explained to them that way in high school.

Over and above such editorial errors in punctuation, the suprasegmental

[5] By far the best available explanation is that by A. H. Marckwardt in the Thorndike-Barnhart *Comprehensive Desk Dictionary* (Doubleday, 1951), pp. 21-24.

phonemes are important in helping students understand why we group words as we do and how it happens that writing produced by the unwary is often ambiguous. Students can see (and hear) that junctures enclose word groups, and when they understand that the number of junctures increases as the pace of reading slows, they can more and more guard their readers against misunderstanding. 'After eating the baby fell asleep' (which I owe to a former colleague) tends to disappear. This is not simply a matter of punctuation, for often the student either alters the word order ('The baby fell asleep after eating') or makes a substitution ('After its meal the baby fell asleep'). The reason it disappears is that the student has discovered that

After êating the báby . . .

is a possible alternative to

After éating . . .

The sound system of English, then, has a rather direct bearing on what teachers do in the classroom. In particular, familiarity with the segmental phonemes should make for an understanding of spelling difficulties due to dialect and should kill once and for all the notion that unconventional phonemic spelling is a sign that the speller "doesn't speak good English" or "doesn't enunciate his words clearly": When the snow is deep, many of the best people wear

/ártĭks/, not /árk + tĭks/.

And second, acquaintance with the suprasegmental phonemes can help us realize why naive students punctuate as they do and manage to produce some of their howlers. It is not a question of studying speech for its own sake; it is a question of being able to put our fingers quite precisely on what is amiss and of being in a position to help each student accommodate himself to our traditional writing system and its editorial expectations.

L. M. MYERS

From Guide to American English, *second
edition, by L. M. Myers. Copyright, 1959,
by Prentice-Hall, Inc. By permission of
Prentice-Hall, Inc.*

The Patterns of Grammar

The very popular statement that "grammar is a lot of nonsense" contains a great deal of truth, though not quite in the way that is usually
intended. Let's look at some nonsense and see what we can learn from it:

The floog sirily mirlated naxes with a sool pern.

Since most of the words are strange we don't know exactly what this
statement means, but we do know the following things:

1. Whatever happened, the *floog* did it.	Clue—position
2. There was probably only one *floog*.	" no -*s* ending
3. It was done to the *naxes*.	" position
4. There was more than one *nax*.	" -*es* ending
5. The action of *mirlating* is over.	" -*ed* ending
6. *Sirily* tells something about how it was done.	" -*ly* ending
7. *With a pern* tells more about how it was done.	" word *with*
8. There was only one *pern*.	" word *a*
9. *Sool* tells what kind of a pern it was.	" position

We know these things because our language contains a system of
patterns which convey what is called "structural meaning" almost with-

out regard to the dictionary meanings of the particular words used. As
the clues above indicate, the main elements in the patterns of written
English are:

> *Word order,* or relative *position*
> *Word form* (usually, but not always, a matter of endings)
> *Function words* like *a, the,* and *with,* which are more important for what
> they tell us about how other words are used than for exact meanings
> of their own

In spoken English at least three other elements called *pitch, stress,*
and *juncture* must be recognized. These are to some extent implied in
writing, but cannot be indicated as explicitly as the first three. We will
therefore postpone discussing them until we have seen how the more
obvious elements work.

It used to be believed that a language was made up simply of words,
which had only to be arranged according to the logical rules of "universal
grammar" in order to make good sentences. It is now recognized that
there is no such thing as universal grammar. Each language has its own
patterns as well as its own words, and these patterns are matters of
habit rather than logic. We have been exposed to our own particular
patterns of word form, word order, and function words for so long that
we now react to them automatically even when they are filled with
nonsense words. If there were just one dialect of English we could use
them automatically, too, and not have to think about them. But most of
us have grown up in such a confusing mixture of dialects that simple
imitation is not enough. In order to speak and write with accuracy and
confidence we have to make some sort of study of the competing patterns;
and we'd better make the study systematic so that we'll know when we
have covered the ground.

GRAMMATICAL POSITION

In analyzing our nonsense sentence we gave only one clue for each
bit of information, as if the three elements of position, word form, and
function words could be completely separated. Actually they cannot. For

instance, grammatical position is not merely numerical position in a sentence but relative position; and we recognize it by considering word form and function words as well as word order. Take another look at the first four words of our sentence:

The floog sirily mirlated

We know that the *floog* did the *mirlating*—that it is what we call the subject—not by the fact that it is the second word in the sentence, but by taking all the following facts together:

1. When we see a pattern like "The _____ _____ _____ed" we assume that the word ending in *-ed* is the verb, and that one of the two words between *the* and _____*ed* is the subject.

2. Since the word just before the verb ends in *-ly* it almost certainly tells something about the verb and therefore cannot be the subject.

3. Therefore the other possible word—*floog*—is the subject. (Notice that if the sentence had begun "The floog *siliry*" instead of "The floog *sirily*" we would take *siliry* to be the subject and *floog* to be an adjective modifying it.)

It is obvious that the study of grammatical position could become a pretty complicated subject, but we don't have to go into it very deeply. To begin with we are interested only in the way it can help us to classify four important kinds of words.

THE KINDS OF WORDS

We have to classify words in order to discuss them in groups. Even in the last section we had to use the terms *verb* and *adjective,* though we have not yet had time to define these; and if we couldn't say things like "the possessive form of a noun is always written with an apostrophe" it would take quite a while to cover the language. Unfortunately, nobody has ever found a perfect way to classify words in English. The two most obvious ways are by form and by meaning. If we base our classes on either one of these we run into trouble with the other; if we try to use both at once we get a complicated mess; and if we decide to have two separate classifications we find that they overlap so much that it is very difficult to keep them separate.

As a compromise, not perfect but reasonably workable, we will use in this book a system based on three main principles:

1. We will use such familiar *single* terms as *noun* and *adjective* to designate the ways words and word-groups function in sentence patterns.

2. We will use such *double* terms as *inflected noun* or *regular noun* (which means "noun inflected in a certain way") to discuss forms and form changes.

3. We will not bother to classify a word at all unless we have a definite reason for doing so. And if a word happens to be both a noun (by use) and an inflected noun (by form) we will use whichever designation seems to be handiest at the time.

CLASSIFICATION BY POSITION

We began this chapter by analyzing a sentence composed of three familiar words, *a, the,* and *with,* and six nonsense words, *floog, sirily, mirlated, naxes, sool,* and *pern.* We could of course make up any number of similar sentences; and if we made up, say, ten pages of them, we should discover the curious fact that all the nonsense words could be reasonably put into just four classes:

1. Words that pattern like *floog, naxes,* and *pern,* which can be called *nouns.*
2. Words that pattern like *mirlated,* which can be called *verbs.*
3. Words that pattern like *sool,* which can be called *adjectives.*
4. Words that pattern like *sirily,* which can be called *adverbs.*

The nucleus of an English sentence is a combination like *man is* or *girls sang* or *floog mirlated,* in which one word seems to name something and the other seems to say something about it—even if both words are nonsense or completely unknown. In such combinations we call the naming word the subject—and the kind of word that is or could easily be the subject we call a *noun.* The saying word we call the *verb.* Words that seem to describe nouns we call adjectives—*big* man, *young* girls, *sool* pern. And words that seem to describe verbs we call *adverbs*— *probably* was, *merrily* sang, *sirily* mirlated.

Far more than ninety-nine per cent of all the words in English fall into these four classes, and more are being added to them every year. They are therefore called open or unlimited classes. There is nothing surprising about seeing an unfamiliar word in a position that seems to indicate any one of these classes; and even if we are quite sure that the word has no real meaning we somehow feel that we know how it acts.

All the other kinds of words (which we will not classify just now) total only a few hundred all together, and no new ones are being added. We have to know these words individually to react to the patterns of our sentences; and if we replace them by nonsense words the patterns disappear. Let's try it:

> Pra floog sirily mirlated naxes tran oc sool pern.

Possibly the successive endings *-ly, -ed,* and *-es* still suggest some meaning, but there is no longer a firm pattern for the sentence as a whole. Nonsense substitutes for *a, the,* and *with* won't work.

At first glance classification by position may seem a very round-about way of getting at such familiar definitions as "a noun is a word used to name a person, place, thing, or idea," but it has its advantages. These familiar definitions work beautifully in selected sentences, but simply do not apply to the language as a whole unless we stretch them until they are practically meaningless. The reason is that we do not always use the same grammatical patterns to express the same ideas, and it is silly to pretend that we do. Look at the following sentences:

> Sometimes he works and sometimes he loafs.
> His industry and laziness alternate.
> He is alternately industrious and lazy.
> He acts industriously and lazily by spells.

Each of these conveys the same basic information; but the contrast between his working and his loafing is shown in the first sentence by verbs, in the second by nouns, in the third by adjectives, and in the fourth by adverbs. There just is no fixed relation between the meaning conveyed and the grammatical pattern used to convey it; and since we are discussing grammar, not philosophy, we'd better depend on the perceptible patterns.

THE FORMS OF WORDS

The second element in our grammatical patterns is word form. Some words, like *always, into, must, tactics,* and *which,* have only one form; but most words have from two to five different forms called *inflections.* Inflected words fall into four groups, three of which may be divided into *regular* and *irregular* subgroups.

Inflected nouns
  Regular: boy, boy's, boys, boys'
  Irregular: man, man's, men, men's
Inflected pronouns
  All *irregular:* I, me, my, mine, myself
Inflected verbs
  Regular: save, saves, saved, saving
  Irregular: take, takes, took, taken, taking
Inflected adjectives
  Regular: big, bigger, biggest
  Irregular: good, better, best

These are the only kinds of inflection in English. Such endings as *-al, -dom, -hood, -ic, -ish, -ize, -ly, -ment,* and *-ness* are considered to make different words rather than different forms of the same word. (It is much simpler to accept the fact that this is so than to try to decide whether it should be.) They are called derivational suffixes, and will not be discussed here.

There are many thousands of regular nouns and regular verbs, and both groups are still growing. Whenever we adopt a new noun like *sputnik* everybody seems to assume at once that the only reasonable plural is *sputniks,* not *sputnak* or *sputniki.* In other words, we automatically treat it as a regular noun. And if we adopt a new verb, or make a new verb out of an old noun, we treat *it* as regular. As soon as we read that sputniks *orbit* we know that we can also say that they *orbited* or have *orbited,* not that they *orbat* or have *orbiten.* It is therefore only the regular nouns and verbs that are "open." There are about six hundred regular adjectives, and this class might be called "open at one end." Nobody knows why, but whenever we adopt a new two-syllable adjective ending in *-y,* such as *newsy* or *corny,* we give it the regular *-er* and *-est* endings. All other new adjectives are unchanging, and show degrees by *more* and *most.*

Nobody has much trouble with the spoken forms of these three regular groups, and the spelling of the written forms follows rather simple rules which will be given later. The four irregular groups are more difficult, since each word has to be learned individually. Fortunately these groups are much smaller than the regular ones, and are shrinking rather than growing.

Along with the four inflected groups we must consider one group of words that never change form but do have a characteristic form of their own—the *-ly* adverbs like *badly* and *wonderfully*. This is another open class; we feel free to add *-ly* to almost any adjective and thus make a new adverb, if we can find a use for it.

FUNCTION WORDS

Function words are words which are used to form grammatical patterns, and which cannot be changed without changing the patterns. Look at the following sentence:

The old man *had* cheerfully started *the* job *with a* sharp knife.

The words in ordinary type could be varied indefinitely without changing the pattern. We could find dozens of substitutes for *started* or *job,* and hundreds for each of the others. But if we change *the* to *an* or *had* to *has* or *with* to *on* we get a different pattern at once. *The* implies that you know which old man the sentence is about; *an* implies that you don't. *Had* puts the statement in a different time relation from *have.* And the things that you can reasonably do *on* a knife are quite different from those that you can do *with* it.

The difference between function words and others (sometimes called *content words*) are not absolutely sharp or reliable, and you can argue with the statements in the preceding paragraph if you care to. But if we consider the distinction as a matter of convenience rather than of desperate doctrine, we will find it useful. Function words are used principally to make up grammatical patterns; content words are used to fill those patterns and give them specific meanings. You have to know the meanings of the content words in a particular sentence to understand that sentence; but you have to know the ways most function words are used to understand English at all.

It is reasonably easy to divide content words into four classes—nouns, verbs, adjectives, and adverbs. A satisfactory classification of function words is a good deal more difficult. For the moment we will merely indicate three principal types:

1. Auxiliary verbs, like those italicized in the following verb-phrases: *will* go, *could* eat, *has* been, *is* going, *must have* seen.
2. Connectives, including all prepositions (*to, from, with,* etc.), conjunctions (*and, because,* etc.), and many words often called adverbs and pronouns (*there, when, which,* etc.).
3. Certain special modifiers of the kinds sometimes called determiners (*a, the, those,* etc.) and qualifiers (*very, quite,* etc.).

THE PARTS OF SPEECH?

It may seem curious that we have discussed two different kinds of classification of words, one by function and one by form, without even mentioning the "parts of speech." But the fact is that the whole concept of parts of speech depends on a stable relation between form and function which has almost disappeared in our language. The concept can, of course, still be applied to modern English, but it no longer seems to be really useful; and those people who insist most strongly that there *are* parts of speech disagree about whether it is the function classes or the form classes that deserve this name. And those who take form as the basis disagree about whether it is simply the form of the words or the form of the patterns in which the words are used that must be considered.

Since there is no discoverable way of settling this argument (or of stopping it, either) we will simply disregard it. Anybody can call anything he wants to the parts of speech. Meanwhile we will try to make it clear whenever we are talking about form rather than function or function rather than form. When the two overlap (as they often do) we can use either set of terms safely as long as we don't over-generalize. Thus in the sentence "The best cost no more" we can say that *best* is an irregular adjective in form but a noun by function in this sentence; and we can call *cost* an irregular verb or simply the verb without much danger of misleading anybody.

CONVERSION BY SUFFIX

Earlier in the chapter we mentioned that endings other than inflections are called suffixes—for instance, *-dom, -ize, -ly,* and *-ment.* Suffixes are sometimes used to give words different meanings without changing their functional classification. Thus we have *gray* and *grayish,* both normally adjectives, and *man* and *manhood,* both normally nouns. More often suffixes convert words from one classification to another, as in the following examples:

> *Verbs to nouns:* appease–appeasement, serve–service
> *Adjectives to nouns:* free–freedom, happy–happiness
> *Nouns to verbs:* atom–atomize, gas–gasify
> *Adjectives to verbs:* dark–darken, tranquil–tranquilize
> *Nouns to adjectives:* child–childish, man–manly
> *Adjectives to adverbs:* glad–gladly, frantic–frantically

This kind of conversion is common in many languages, including Greek, Latin, and French, from which a great many English words come. It explains many of the related words in the language.

FUNCTIONAL SHIFT

Conversion of a word to a new function *without* the use of a suffix occurs much more often in English than in most other languages. This is known as *functional shift,* and it has gone so far as to make a single classification of words into parts of speech almost meaningless, as we have already suggested. The general tendency is to use any word in any way that is convenient and makes sense, without regard to its original classification. Thus we may use *work* as a noun (a *work* of art), a verb (they *work* hard), or an adjective (his *work* clothes). We cannot use it as a connective, not because of any grammatical rule, but simply because there is no way to do it. And nobody but a historian of the language has any reason to care about what its original part of speech may have been.

If a word shifts its function to that of a noun or a verb, it takes on the regular inflections of its new class. Thus the irregular noun *man* gives us the regular verb *to man*, with the forms *man, mans, manned, manning*. Likewise the irregular verb *to drink* gives us the regular noun *drink, drinks*. In other shifts of function no new inflections are needed.

REASON FOR FUNCTIONAL SHIFT

Quite obviously the underlying reason for functional shift is economy —either the use of a shorter word for a longer one or the use of a word instead of a phrase. Use of the plain form of a verb as a noun eliminates either the *-ing* inflectional ending (*talk* for *talking*) or a suffix (a *serve* for a *service* in tennis) ; and use of a noun as an adjective eliminates a suffix (*wool* clothes for *woolen* clothes, *atom* bomb for *atomic* bomb). On the other hand, use of an adjective as a noun often saves a word or more (*the poor* for *the poor people, the beautiful* for *that which is beautiful*). Verbs converted from nouns are particularly economical, though not always graceful. Thus *to requisition* stands for *to put in a requisition for, to contact* for *to get in touch with*.

When the two kinds of economy conflict, the one that makes the greater overall saving generally wins out—at least in circles where efficiency is more prized than grace. Thus *to certificate* is longer than *to certify*, but shorter than *to furnish with a certificate*. It is therefore often used when the certification consists of supplying a document rather than guaranteeing a statement.

LIMITS TO FUNCTIONAL SHIFT

The fact remains that many functional shifts that might well have taken place have not done so. Sometimes this is because a familiar word that makes a shift unnecessary is already available. Thus the verb *to man* makes it unnecessary to convert *boy, girl, or woman* into verbs. Juveniles or females can *man* a boat. Fifty years ago, when automobiles were still competing with carriages, we used *to auto* down to the beach, since *to drive* was not sufficiently specific, and any other available expression would have been longer. Now that carriages have practically disappeared the one-syllable verb *drive* clearly means to go by automobile. *To auto* is no longer economical, and there would not be enough saving in *to car* to make it worth while.

At other times we have simply failed to make a shift for no discoverable reason. Thus we say *to reward* and *a reward, to punish* but *a punishment.* A noun *punish* may develop in the future, but it has not yet done so. Moreover, some shifts that certainly have developed are often condemned. That is, although the general principle of functional shift is universally accepted, a few individual shifts have become shibboleths. We often hear that *like* must never be used as a conjunction, that *than* and *as* must never be used as prepositions, and that *loan* and *contact* must never be used as verbs.

To object to these uses on the basis of any grammatical theory is simply silly. Thousands of other words have extended their functions in exactly comparable ways, and there is not the slightest reason why this handful should not do the same. If we must condemn such expressions we should do so by making the honest statement that there is a certain amount of prejudice against them—just as there is now a prejudice against calling a man "a certain party" or a woman "an elegant female" —though there is no doubt whatever that *party* and *female* are, in other expressions, acceptable as nouns.

INTONATION PATTERNS

So far we have dealt only with those elements of our grammatical patterns which are visible as well as audible. In spoken English at least three other elements would be perceptible (though not necessarily recognizable by people without some training). These can sometimes be suggested in writing, but cannot be indicated as explicitly as the first three. Compare the two following sentences:

> Jack put salt in his coffee.
> Jack put salt in his *coffee?*

Since these are identical in all three of the elements so far discussed, many people would call them "the same sentence punctuated in two different ways." But, intelligently read, they sound different and they mean different things—which should be enough to make them different sentences. The fact that the differences do not appear as clearly in writing as they do in speech proves only that our system of writing is imperfect—it indicates some differences less clearly than others. If you read both sentences aloud carefully and naturally you will see that they vary in three ways:

1. The first syllable of *coffee* is pronounced more strongly in the second sentence than in the first. This is a difference in *stress*.

2. The same syllable is also pronounced on a higher musical tone in the second sentence. This is a difference in *pitch*.

3. At the end of the first sentence the voice comes down in pitch as it fades into silence. At the end of the second it does not. This is a difference in *juncture*. In order to make the comparison as simple as possible we have shown the difference in stress, pitch, and juncture only at the ends of the two sentences, but they occur throughout. Every syllable that is pronounced at all must be pronounced with some degree of stress and at some pitch; and whenever two successive words are not completely run together the transition between them can be called juncture. Thus *white house* has a kind of juncture not found in *Whitehouse;* the sort of pause often shown by a comma is a second kind; and the rising and falling tones as your voice fades off after different kinds of sentences are two others.

It is possible to indicate all these things consistently by a special system of writing—the stress by accent marks, the pitch by numbers, and the juncture by special symbols. Thus the second sentence might be written as follows:

$$^2\text{Jâck} + \text{pùt} + \text{sâlt} + \text{in} + \text{his} + {}^1\text{cóffee}^3 \uparrow$$

(It might also be indicated in several other ways.) This more complete system of writing is very useful for experts who wish to make a detailed analysis of our sound patterns, but it is a little cumbersome for ordinary use. Most of us would rather get along with just a few hints, such as the italicizing of *coffee* and the question mark at the end. Moreover, experts are still disagreeing about such questions as how many degrees of stress and pitch are significant, and how regular and dependable are our uses of these elements. We are not therefore going into these matters in much detail. But we should realize that the experts are right in principle

—these elements are quite as real as the first three, and at least some of the time they are quite as important.

Stress, pitch, and juncture together make up *intonation*. Every spoken sentence must have its pattern of intonation; and every good written sentence at least suggests one. If you don't believe intonation is as real or as important as the other sounds, perhaps you can remember a time when you were seriously misquoted by somebody who claimed to be repeating exactly what you had said, and who did repeat the same words in the same order—but who changed the intonation pattern so as to give an entirely different meaning.

L. M. MYERS

From Guide to American English, *second edition, by L. M. Myers. Copyright, 1959, by Prentice-Hall, Inc. By permission of Prentice-Hall, Inc.*

Modifiers

A modifier may be defined roughly as a word, phrase, or clause that supplies any kind of additional information (even negative information) about the element with which it is associated. A verb is not considered as modifying its subject. Thus in the sentence, "*Young* Lorenz worked *hard,* but made *no* progress," only the italicized words are called modifiers. If the modifier is a phrase or clause, it may itself contain secondary modifiers:

He saw *a tall* man *in black clothes.*

Here the words *a* and *tall* and the phrase *in black clothes* modify *man;* and within the phrase, *black* modifies *clothes.* In discussing the structure of sentences we shall not usually have to bother about the internal structure of phrases.

We can avoid a good deal of trouble if we realize from the beginning that it is in human minds, not on printed pages, that modification takes place. No word automatically does anything at all to another word; but the relative positions of words stimulate us to make certain associations. When we see a combination like *tall man* we can be quite sure that the writer meant *tall* to refer to *man,* and that any normal reader will take it as he meant it. It is a convenient short-cut to express all this by saying *"tall* modifies *man."* In dealing with this particular pattern—adjective plus noun—the statement is safe because our habits are so uniform that there is very little chance of either a misunderstanding or an argument.

But suppose we encounter a sentence like "He sent the man from Texas." The writer might mean "He sent the Texas man (somewhere or other)"; while a reader might take it to mean "He sent the (unidentified) man out of Texas." Are we justified in taking sides and saying what the phrase *from Texas* "really" modifies?

We could of course "make a rule" that in such sentences the final phrase must always be considered as referring to the word immediately before it, or a different rule that it must always be considered as referring back to the verb. But neither one of these rules would be an accurate description of good usage. The simple fact is that our habits of association are not as regular in this type of construction as in the *tall man* pattern, largely because there is less need for them to be. Let us look at some other examples, and illustrate the natural associations by simple diagrams:

    1. He met a man from New York.

    He   met   a man
    ————————————————
                  |from New York

Here the phrase clearly refers to the complement.

    2. He knocked the glass from the table.

    He   knocked   the glass
    ————————————————
        |from the table

Here the phrase clearly refers to the verb.

3. He sent a present from Paris.

He	sent	a present
	from Paris	

or

He	sent	a present
		from Paris

This might mean that he sent a present-from-London from Paris, or a present-from-Paris from New York; but the most probable guess is that both the present and the sending were from Paris. If this is true, one diagram would be as good as the other.

4. He shot the man from the bank.

He	shot	the man
	from the bank	

or

He	shot	the man
		from the bank

Here the two diagrams represent entirely different situations. Was the shooting done from the bank, or was the man shot an employee of the bank?

In the first two of the four sentences above the particular words used help the grammatical pattern to indicate clearly the intended association. The third sentence, about the present, is technically ambiguous, but there is not much chance of a serious misunderstanding. The fourth sentence, however, when printed alone, could mean either of two quite different things. It would probably be clear if spoken, because the speaker could show by his intonation pattern whether the man or the shooting was from the bank, and a listener would probably follow him. And it might be clear in writing if the context made one interpretation or the other automatic. But as a single written sentence it is completely ambiguous.

Thus we have four sentences containing the same grammatical pattern (as far as a reader can tell without knowing the exact meanings of the words) but indicating quite different relations of ideas. If we try to make a general rule to cover all four we may arrive at something like this:

The reader's natural tendency is to make the easiest association possible. Since the final phrase comes right next to the complement, the obvious first guess is that it refers to the complement. But if this association seems unreasonable, he will carry the phrase one position further back and try it with the verb. A writer should bear this tendency in mind, and arrange his sentence so that no misleading or ridiculous association is easily possible.

Of course we usually make our associations rapidly and subconsciously. It is only when we are puzzled by sentences, or when we deliberately analyze or diagram one, that we consciously consider such problems. We may do this quite informally by saying something like, "Oh yes, I see—*from the bank* goes with *shot,* not with *man.*" Or we may do it (usually at a teacher's request) formally and according to rule.

When we do attempt to analyze formally by rules, we have good reason to ask how sound the rules are. Let us look at another sentence that can be diagrammed in two ways:

John waved a greeting to the man.

John   waved   a greeting
         |to the man

or

John   waved   a greeting
                  |to the man

Here there is not the slightest doubt as to what the whole sentence means; yet we can make diagrams to indicate two quite different theories as to what the phrase modifies. And if we look for comparisons, we can find evidence on both sides:

John's greeting to the man was cordial.

John's   greeting   was   cordial
         |to the man

John threw the ball to the man.

John   threw   the ball
         |to the man

We may, of course, argue about which comparison is closer, and perhaps feel we have proved that one or the other of the diagrams is right.

But this is merely playing a game with definitions. Association of *to the man* with *any* element in the sentence is neither as close nor as uniform as associations of the *tall man* type; and we can't make it so by drawing a picture.

Sometimes the question that arises is not which element a word modifies, but whether it modifies any one element or a combination of several:

Yesterday my brother went to town.

Here we could explain *yesterday* as modifying either the verb *went* or the whole clause *my brother went to town*. It makes a simpler diagram to relate the modifier to a single word; but the more natural thing to say is that it seems to modify the whole clause. Incidentally, this interpretation helps to explain why some modifiers can be put almost anywhere in a sentence, while others have a fixed position.

If there is any moral in all this, it is that a diagram may be a useful way of indicating a connection of ideas, but offers no convincing proof, since people who disagree about what the relations are will naturally draw different diagrams.

POSITION OF MODIFIERS WITH NOUNS

The obvious place to put a modifier is close to the word it modifies; and the two closest positions are immediately before and immediately after. Normally we put a single-word modifier of a noun before, and a phrase or clause modifier after. Thus we should say "A tall man," "The man in the street," and "The man who was here yesterday."

The habit of putting a phrase afterward is so strong that if for any reason we put it first we usually convert it into a single word by the use of hyphens. Thus we write *four-in-hand ties* and *off-the-cuff speeches*. The habit of putting a single word first is not quite so strong. Nobody would say *a man tall,* but we might say either *the only available man* or *the only man available*. The modifier comes first at least nine times out of ten. When it comes after the noun, it is usually because it introduces, or easily could introduce, a phrase. Thus we should say:

A broken bough	A bough broken by the wind
An appropriate sum	A sum appropriate for the purpose

The reason that such words as *appropriate, available,* and *possible* may be used after the noun even when they do not introduce a phrase is that they tend to suggest a phrase in a way that words like *tall* and *beautiful* do not. We should say "He is a possible winner" and not "He is a winner possible." But we might say either "The only possible explanation" or "The only explanation possible," because we are used to such expressions as "The only explanation possible under the circumstances."

MODIFIERS IN SERIES

When two modifiers come before a noun, there are four possible relations:

1. Both may modify the noun independently. If so, the modifiers are usually "leveled" by *and, but, or,* or a comma.

    Old, tired men   *Long* and *boring* books   *Air* or *sea* travel

2. The first may modify the second, while the second modifies the noun.

    Dark green water   *Very old* men

3. The second may modify the noun, while the first modifies the combination.

    A *long comic* book   The *old hired* man   A *new dollar* bill

4. The two may be taken as a unit modifying the noun.

    A *high school* boy   The *land conservation* program
    A *New Deal* politician

It is often a hair-splitting process to decide exactly which of these relations is intended (for instance, in *dark oak table*), and therefore unnecessary to indicate which one you have selected. When there is a chance of misunderstanding, the two more closely related words may be joined by a hyphen.

A *comic-book* salesman   *High-school* expenses
A *comic* book-salesman   *High* school-expenses

Many writers regularly use hyphens to indicate combinations of *modifiers* even when there is no danger of ambiguity.

A *high-school* team   but   The *high school* is new
A *New-Deal* politician   The *New Deal* brought changes.

Such combinations are not usually included in dictionaries as hyphenated words, but they are clearly established in standard usage. If a combination comes into very frequent use it is often written as a single word. Thus we may read *high school* texts, *high-school* texts, or *highschool* texts.

The series of modifiers preceding a noun may be considerably longer than two, whether they all modify the noun or some of them modify others.

A long, interesting, well-documented, and highly important book
The present Scottsdale High School athletic program committee

These longer series involve no further theoretical problems, but anybody with a sensitive ear will probably decide that the second one is at least a word too long.

ADVERBIAL MODIFIERS

Modifiers of verbs can be placed more freely than modifiers of nouns. This is partly because there is usually only one verb in a clause, while there are likely to be several nouns; and partly because it often makes little difference whether we associate an adverbial modifiers specifically with the verb or more generally with the clause as a whole. For instance we might find any of the following orders:

Slowly Emmett walked down the street.
Emmett *slowly* walked down the street.
Emmett walked *slowly* down the street.
Emmett walked down the street *slowly*.

Some readers might prefer one of these sentences to the others, or feel that they all showed some differences in emphasis. But there is no question that the same general information is conveyed by all four, and that a great many readers would consider them completely interchangeable.

Some modifiers are less flexible than others. If we substituted *fast* for *slowly,* we could not use the order "Fast Emmett walked," because a reader would probably think *fast* described Emmett, rather than the way he walked down the street. We should also be unlikely to say "Emmett fast walked," though we might have some trouble in explaining why. Other modifiers might have different numbers of possibilities, and it would make a definite difference where some of them were put.

The fact that there is no satisfactory general rule for such constructions need not trouble us. "Modification" is merely a matter of habitual association; and a position that seems natural to the writer will usually be satisfactory to the reader. There are, however, a few words about which an arbitrary theory has been developed. It is often said that the following pairs of sentences have different "real meanings," approximately as indicated:

> I *only* want ten cents. (I don't expect to get it)
> I want *only* ten cents. (That is all I want)
> I'll *just* see him for a minute. (Not talk to him)
> I'll see him for *just* a minute. (It won't take longer)
> He doesn't *even* have a dollar. (So he can't spend it)
> He doesn't have *even* a dollar. (He has less than a dollar)

The theory is that words like *only, just,* and *even* necessarily modify the words that immediately follow them. But the theory simply isn't true. It describes a habit that we might have developed, not one that we actually have developed. When we hear such sentences, the sensible thing to do is to try to figure out what the speaker actually means. If we want to express such ideas, and have any fear of being misunderstood, we can always say something like "All I want is ten cents" or "My desire for ten cents is merely a wish."

SUCCESSIVE MODIFYING PHRASES

A phrase is usually placed immediately after the word it modifies. This ordinarily causes no trouble; but when two phrases are used, one of them must come first. There is then a possibility that the second may be taken as modifying the last word in the first phrase, instead of the word with which the writer associated it. This may result in an actual misunderstanding or in a ludicrous suggestion.

> There is a man *from Kansas*   *in the car.*

Both phrases clearly refer to *man.*

> There is a man *in the car*   *from Kansas.*

Either the man or the car may be from Kansas.

> The car was identified *as the one stolen*   *by Jim Dodd.*

If Dodd merely identified the car, he might bring a libel suit on the basis of this sentence.

No general rule can be given on which type of phrase should be put first. A writer must remember that the reader will probably associate the second phrase with the nearest word to which it can reasonably apply, which is often the last word in the first phrase. If such an association would lead to misunderstanding, the writer may reverse the phrases. If the result is still unclear, he should completely rewrite the sentence.

GENERAL PRINCIPLES OF MODIFICATION

A comprehensive treatment of the problems of modification would require far more space than we can afford in this book; but careful attention to a few general principles will solve most of them.

1. Modification depends on association of ideas.
2. It's not enough for a writer to prove that his association is possible. Unless he makes it automatic for his readers, his sentence is ambiguous.
3. A written sentence gets no help from intonation. Word order is therefore doubly important.

RALPH H. LANE

From Word Study, *XXX* (*February,
1955*), *1-3. Copyright, 1955, by G. & C.
Merriam Co., publishers of the Merriam-
Webster dictionaries. By permission of
G. & C. Merriam Co. and the author.*

Passing Participles

"Cream cheese, chip beef, and butter pecan ice cream," says the American housewife. The order-taker understands, of course, because the
printed labels on these products usually agree with their spoken names.
Few persons (least of all, the manufacturers) notice that such compound
nouns embrace past participles which have lost final sounds. *Chipped
beef,* in fact, is less often said than read, *buttered pecan* and *creamed
cheese* are so rare in print as to command attention—and *iced cream* in
advertising is unimaginable.

The popular forms, nevertheless, embody the compressed report of a
process once expressed by means of the conventional past participle.
When it remains the final element in a verb phrase, the third principal
part of the verb seldom varies from its recognized form; but when the
word takes a new place immediately before the noun, the ending often
is lost.

An obvious reason for mutescence is the demand for euphony which
certain sound-combinations create. An equally important reason for
this change is the gradual absorption of the verbal by the noun; as a
result, *spice cake* becomes a separate idea from that of mere *cake,* and the
action of spicing, now an accomplished fact, is no longer of primary
importance. In various degrees, this fusion of ideas is noticeable when
degenerated past participles appear before nouns.

In English the tendency toward clipping past participles is well established. We need glance only at *wed, quit,* and *thrust* for reminders that the practice is ancient. Such changes—and the recording of the changes, too—have increased in frequency and rapidity (owing to the growth of literacy), and in this country the natural tendency toward shortening words is accelerated. As a result, dozens of past participles, especially those of weak verbs, are losing final sounds and, in many instances, becoming homonyms of the present tense.

We make continual allowance for some combinations of sounds, ignoring standard spelling. "The form of the word is not fixed, but depends on its service in the sentence," as Kruisinga reminds us (using as examples *jumpt up* and *jumt down*).[1] Adaptability of words accounts for such variations as *salt pork* and *salted peanuts, scallop tomato* and *scallopt oysters, devil crab* and *devil deggs.* Some of these pronunciations are not committed to writing, of course, and the conventional spelling prevails, but it must be noted that *devil crab* and *scallop tomatoes* are appearing on menus as frequently as *deviled eggs* and *scalloped oysters.*

Dual forms exist in hundreds. Persons who speak of *skim milk* still use *had skimmed.* Similarly, *mincemeat, parsley potatoes, potpie,* and *roast chicken* are forms which nobody questions in combination, although few persons would clip the same past participles in verb phrases. A host of like examples may be found in daily speech throughout the United States, especially in language pertaining to food and drink. Everyone has heard *crush pineapple, bottle beer, can peas, butter bread, bake beans, corn beef, hash brown potatoes, mash turnips, pickle peaches, stuff peppers, whip cream, dice carrots,* and *popcorn.*

These combinations illustrate not only the urge toward monosyllabism but also the importance of the finished process in the resulting adjective prefixed to the noun. Process is implicit in *slice tomato, ice water, dry beans, grill bacon,* and *boil dinner,* as well as in compounds like *honey dip donuts* and *open-face pie.* In each instance the compound represents a preference which eliminates a relative clause. *Vacuum pack coffee* is so much less cumbersome than *coffee which has been packed with a vacuum* that a listener willingly ignores the implications. He understands: *fresh coffee* (distinctively different from *coffee*), oblivious to the syntax of *pack.*

The rare example of doubt regarding the shortened participle shows that few persons give it thought and that those few are troubled only

[1] E. Kruisinga, *The Phonetic Structure of English Words* (Berne, 1943), p. 1.

momentarily. A feature writer, in brief exposition of experiments with falling bodies, used *butter-side* five times, *buttered side* once, *buttered bread* twice, and *buttered slices* once.[2] The first of these, although un-quoted, probably passes as folk speech. The author may have surmised that slices actually have no "butter side" until after buttering occurs. *Butter Side Down,* by the late Lothrop Stoddard, furnishes in its title yet a third variation of the slippery idea, without acknowledging the ab-breviated absolute.

One of the most conspicuous examples of the truncated participle is *old fashion.* This compound, indicating a vague process indeed, finds a place on placards advertising salt-rising bread, Dutch apple pie, cock-tails, whipped creams [candy], root beer, hard candy, and one-cent sales —and it is the name of a barbecue stand in North Carolina. Only seldom do we see the fastidiousness of *Ol' Fashion' Beef Stew.* Charitably we assume that a nameless action has provided outmoded individuality, but the process itself no longer interests us.

Words related to the preparation of foods suggest similar usage of terms describing the manufacture of clothing. The innumerable com-pounds which differentiate articles of costume (often fictitious) almost invariably concern specialized treatment, and they seem even more sus-ceptible to the loss of endings. Examples are myriad, but these will suf-fice: *high-heel shoe, patent leather, high-fashion shoes, scotch-grain leather, water-proof sole, close-knit fabric, fur-trim coat, balloon-seat pajamas, print dress, polka-dot tie, clean clothes, luxury trim coats, open crown hat, wing-tip cuff, slim line suit,* and *solid color shirt.* In each case, the modification is a kind of absolute construction; having been altered or made in a particular manner, the article is now inseparable from the attribute which it has acquired.

Building and furnishing also inspire the use of the shortened participle, as in these combinations: *shingle roof, plaster wall, press brick house, gable roof, flat-roof garage, panel ceiling, wainscot room, grill door, brick wall, grass plot, veneer table, lacquer box, enamel tub, ruffle cur-tains, candy-stripe drapes, wide-screen picture, twist broadloom rug,* and *stipple paint.* In these examples, again, the "new" concept takes for granted whatever activity has transformed the substantive, which other-wise would signify only a general idea.

Miscellaneous combinations of the same type include: *copyright photo,*

[2] *Parade.*

cable instructions, money men, phone orders, feature picture, package liquor, horn-rim glasses, black-letter edition, curve ball, white sidewall tires, power mower, wheel chair, two-wheel bike, soft-toe dance, high-tone lady, saw-tooth edge, low price store, and *open-top car.* Once more, it is plain that the added feature converts the original object into another kind of object, endowed with distinguishing qualities.

The abbreviated participles most noticeable today are as yet confined to adjectival uses (although *beat-up* is a strong exception). Storekeepers already are advertising *Melon—Whole or Slice,* which certainly is an indication of the trend. *Has ask* is as common in vulgar speech as *ask price* on the next-higher level. Signs advertising "experience men" and "furnish room" may point likewise to the extinction of the characteristic ending.

Verbals-turning-adjectives lose their *d-* or *t-*sounds readily when they precede *d, t, b, p, f, c,* and *k,* as might be expected. Also, the verb-stems from which they derive are preponderantly of one syllable, a fact which may predispose the speaker to acceptance of a short form in the modifier and, ultimately, in the verb phrase. Paradoxically, these stems are wiry and strong in meaning but weak in inflection; their incisiveness balances the docility with which they may be conjugated.

A few of these modifiers are homonyms of nouns, and in some instances originally were nouns (*radio,* for example, which gave rise to *radioed message* and then to *radio address*). Perhaps the most common word in this anomalous group is *size,* which in multiple compounds rarely carries a final *d,* as in *various size booklets, king-size cigarettes, room size rug, man-size towel, large head-size beret, proper size sheet, over-size vocabulary,* and *big size rocker.* Another homonym which at least temporarily bore the customary ending of the past participle is *uniform,* as now used in newspaper headlines: *Uniform Men,*[3] a usage similar to that in *Reform Church,* as used by a clergyman.[4]

Regardless of the steps by which true participles or analogous forms have reached the position of uninflected adjectives, very few of them present ambiguous meanings. Ambiguity, in fact, undoubtedly will control the shift from verbal to adjective. Whenever *wax floors* implies floors which have received special treatment, most speakers will use the combination. By contrast, *paint wall* seems a remote adaptation, only because

[3] *Chicago Daily Tribune,* 28 September, 1949, p. 1.
[4] *Washington Post,* 31 December, 1949, p. 1B (by Dorothea Andrews, quoting Dr. John Compton Ball, Baptist minister).

the voiced *ed* is more comfortable to the speaker of this phrase. Among the many other verbs which slough endings easily, however, the loss of inflection is proceeding rapidly.

ROBERT A. CALDWELL

From Word Study, *XXXI* (*December, 1955*), *4. Copyright, 1955, by G. & C. Merriam Co., publishers of the Merriam- Webster dictionaries. By permission of G. & C. Merriam Co. and the author.*

Comment on "Passing Participles"

To the Editor of *Word Study:*

Unless I have deceived myself by taking seriously something that was intended to be humorous, Ralph H. Lane's "Passing Participles," WORD STUDY, XXX (February, 1955), is to be deprecated. Three points may be made about it:

1. Mr. Lane shows no awareness of the fact that since at least the early Middle English period the English language has consistently simplified clusters of three consonants, so that such an expression as *chipped beef* is normally sounded and heard as *chip beef.* The semiliterate spelling "chip beef" is, of course, to be explained by reference to this principle.

2. Mr. Lane fails to distinguish between past participles and adjectives formed by means of the bound form *-ed,* which is itself derived from the participle. Such an adjective as *gifted,* for example, derived from the noun *gift,* cannot be made into a past participle by any stretch of the imagination. Many of Mr. Lane's forms, such as *high-fashion shoes,* are to be explained—if they are not rather examples of

conversation—as semiliterate spellings of such adjectives, the semiliterate spelling having then become standard, "correct," by being generally accepted.

3. Mr. Lane fails to recognize the operation of conversion, by which one part of speech is used for another. Though addicted to a pipe, I might on occasion smoke a *king-size cigarette,* though never—if *sized* is a past participle—a *king-sized cigarette,* which could only be one *sized* (glazed or coated) with king. Mr. Lane's *money men* are not the same as *moneyed men.* The latter are wealthy, the former minters, counterfeiters, or speculators of some kind.

The article is an excellent example of why the so-called Bloomfieldian linguist distrusts meaning as a criterion in linguistic analysis. But even in his application of meaning, Mr. Lane has fallen into error; a *waterproof sole* has not been "proofed," it is *proof against* (impervious to) water, and *ice cream,* which has been frozen, is certainly to be distinguished from *iced* (chilled) *cream.*

PHILIP B. BALLARD

From Thought and Language, *by Philip B. Ballard. Published by the University of London Press, 1934. By permission of Mrs. Freda M. Ballard.*

The Sentence

Nobody has any difficulty in picking out sentences from the printed page, for the author (or the printer) has already marked them off. With all the sentences except the first he has placed one period at the head and another at the tail. So a sentence is the discourse between two points; the two points being consecutive full stops. Well, what shall we say to this passage from D'Arcy Thompson's *Day Dreams of a Schoolmaster*?

> Yes, Reader, I am a Hellenist. I am at the end of my third volume,
> and am going to live happy ever afterwards. I have reached Ithaca.
> A little tired and battered. But I have reached Ithaca.

Waiving for the moment the fact that punctuation is largely a matter
of fashion and of personal taste, we have to inquire on what principle
the author (or the printer) cuts up the discourse into lengths called
sentences. What, in fine, is a sentence? Upon this point there is a remarkable unanimity of opinion among the rank and file of grammarians,
and an equally remarkable difference of opinion among philosophers and
psychologists. Dictionaries and grammars tell us boldly and cheerfully
that a sentence is a set of words which express a complete thought. The
only exception I can find is Morris, who says it is a complete thought
put into words. To him a sentence is essentially a thought, and belongs
by right to the first of our three categories; but to the huge majority
it is essentially a group of words, and belongs to the second. But none
of our three categories, thoughts, words, and things, can be studied
in isolation, for they are all three joined together by subtle bonds of
relationship. So that if one is kept in the foreground of consciousness
the other two will be seen lurking in the background. In fact, the set
of words which constitutes a sentence owes all its cohesion and unity
to the thought that stands behind it. The sentence is one because the
thought is one. It seems to follow from this that a separate word cannot
have a whole thought to itself; it has to content itself with a fragment.
There are some, indeed, who go so far as to assert that a word has no
meaning at all, except what it acquires by forming part of the sentence
community.

Those who are prone to glorify the sentence unduly are no less prone
to vilify the word unduly. Bosanquet, in his zeal for exalting the sentence, points out[1] that the ancient Greeks did not separate their words in
writing, and that Aristotle had no simple class name corresponding to
our term *word*. He neglects, however, to add that the Greeks did not
separate their sentences either, and that the only visible units in their
manuscripts were letters. If we are to accept without qualification the
absurd inference that words have no meanings, the only sensible thing to
do is to make a bonfire of all our dictionaries and all our encyclopædias.

Let us carefully examine the assertion that a sentence contains a
complete thought. I open at random a volume of Macaulay's *Essays* and

---

[1] *The Essentials of Logic,* p. 86.

my eye alights on the sentence, *This was denied to him.* Can any one maintain that the thought here is complete? As we are not told what was denied, nor to whom it was denied, we need for the completion of the sense two pieces of information from the outside. So the thought is not complete in the sense of being self-contained. In what sense then is it complete?

With the preceding sentence prefixed the passage runs: *The hand of death was upon him: he knew it; and the only wish which he uttered was that he might die sword in hand. This was denied to him.* We are now given a clue to the meaning of *this* in the second sentence, but we are still left in the dark as to the meaning of *him.* We have, in fact, to go back nearly half a page before we discover that the author is talking all along about Lord Byron. The first of the two sentences contains three statements; the last sentence contains but one. What I want to know is this: on what principle (except that of arbitrary punctuation, which is not a principle at all) can completeness of meaning be withheld from each of the first three statements and granted to the fourth? Why is the thought embodied in *The hand of death was upon him* regarded as incomplete, and the thought embodied in *This was denied to him* as complete? It is beside the mark to say that the first three statements are really sentences. If so, why are they not punctuated as sentences? Neither Macaulay nor his reading public regarded them as sentences; nor would any modern grammarian so regard them. Clauses if you like; predications if you like; but not sentences.

It is, in fact, to its inherent insufficiency that a sentence, as part of continuous discourse, often owes its vitality and fitness. By leaning on other sentences it shares and transmits their warmth. By sending out threads backwards and forwards it helps to knit the whole fabric into one seamless piece. Remove a good sentence from a good paragraph and you leave behind, not a gap with clean-cut edges, but an ugly rent with broken threads at both ends. Even when a sentence seems to stand by itself—when it is a simple remark, or exclamation—its isolation is an isolation of words, not of thought. For its meaning is obscure and incomplete without reference to the circumstances in which it was uttered.

Conscious perhaps of the difficulty he would find in defending the complete thought theory of the sentence, Professor Sonnenschein has taken refuge in vague description, which, nevertheless, he ventures to call a definition; thus: DEFINITION: *A sentence is a group of words which makes sense.*[2] But does not the title of a book make sense? And a head-line in a newspaper? And the rubric of a text? Are the following groups of words sense or nonsense? *The Merchant of Venice, A Tale of Two Cities, Football Results, Big Fire in the City, Assassination of Bulgarian Prime Minister.* And does not a paragraph in a book, or a stanza of a poem, or indeed the book or the poem itself, consist of a group of words, and do not those words make sense? Not always perhaps, but as a general rule? No, no, this definition will never do. As a definition it is not only wrong, but is not even usefully wrong.

I do not, mark you, deny the unity of the sentence; what I do deny is that its unity is a unity of thought. And I further deny that it is the only unit in language. The word has a unity of its own; and so has the paragraph. And so in poetry have the foot, and the line, and the stanza.

If the unity of the sentence is not to be found in the realm of thought, where is it to be found? The answer given by Dr. Alan H. Gardiner is that it is in the realm of will or purpose. In his book *The Theory of Speech and Language* he draws a distinction between speech and lan-guage, regarding language as the science, and speech as its application. Speech, in fact, is language in action. In consonance with this terminology he considers the word to be the unit of language, and the sentence the unit of speech. And here is his definition of a sentence: *A sentence is a word or set of words revealing an intelligible purpose.*[3] To meet the objection that this affords no quantitative criterion, and that it would apply to a sermon as well as to a sentence, he extends his definition as follows: *A sentence is a word or set of words followed by a pause and revealing an intelligible purpose.*[4] The purpose is a communicative pur-pose. The speaker tries to influence the listener in some way; he tries to make him attend to the same thing as he himself is attending to, or to think the same thought, or to accept the same point of view. Or, if the sentence happens to be a command or a question, the aim may be to get the listener to do something or to supply some sort of information.

The reason for the pause and for its incidence has evidently exercised the author's mind, for later on in the book he has another shot at a defi-nition, viz.: *A sentence is an utterance which makes just as long a com-*

[2] *A New Grammar,* Part I, p. 11.
[3] *The Theory of Speech and Language,* p. 98.
[4] *Ibid.*

munication as the speaker has intended to make before giving himself a rest.

One fails to be wholly satisfied with this definition, for the pause (or rest) is by no means as distinctive a mark as one could wish. It is too freakish and lawless; and its length is too variable. There is not only the pause direct, but the pause rhetorical and the pause unintentional— the pause when one can't help it. The pause rhetorical is of two kinds, both purposive: one being a laudable device for lending force to a word or a phrase, the other a piece of sheer pomposity; as, for instance, when a platform orator spreads his speech like this: *Mr. Chairman—ladies and gentlemen—I stand here—on this auspicious occasion—as a representative—of a dense constituency.* The next kind of pause comes when the speaker is trying to think of a word and hesitates till it comes. Then again there is the pause of the speaker who rushes his sentences and runs them into one another—a pause which, though it may come in the right place, is so brief as to escape detection. So not only has the pause other things to do besides marking the end of a sentence, but it does not always do the marking itself well.

And yet one cannot help perceiving that there is a difference in the "feel" of the pause that comes at the end of a sentence—a difference that marks it off from every other sort of pause. To be able to explain that "feel" would be to discover the secret of the sentence. The best we can do is to travel in a circle and come back to the speaker's purpose, and then note the fact that the pause is only one of his means of indicating his intention to close the sentence at that point. He has other means; they all combine to suggest his saying: This is a sentence because it is my will and pleasure that it should be a sentence. It is as much of my full purpose as I care to reveal at the very moment—as much of my meaning as I wish to deliver in one handful. In speaking he conveys all this by his intonation, his gestures, and the pause at the end. In writing he says it with a full stop—or should say it with a full stop.

When Scott wrote,

> The way was long, the wind was cold,
> The minstrel was infirm and old.

he meant the lines to be one sentence. But a modern prose writer might

well mean the same words to be three sentences; in which case he would
punctuate them like this: *The way was long. The wind was cold. The
minstrel was infirm and old.* Not that there is anything specially modern
in this punctuation. It may be paralleled by a few passages from Lamb
and by many passages from Macaulay. And indeed the most punctilious
of purists would never think of challenging sentences with so complete an
equipment of subject and predicate and so free from any mark of sub-
ordination. He would, however, look askance at Kipling's recurrent
Which is another story being given the full status of a sentence. And as
for D'Arcy Thompson's *A little tired and battered,*[5] that would simply
be condemned as a piece of illiteracy. And yet if our theory is sound, these
suspects have all the necessary credentials and are in point of fact sentences good and true.

Although I cannot regard Dr. Gardiner's definition as free from imperfections, I consider it the best we have. By shifting the focus of attention from thought to purpose he has, I believe, given us the right clue to
the unity of the sentence; and has led us to see why so many of our
old disputes have proved so sterile. For if it can be demonstrated that a
sentence may fulfil its proper function as a medium of will or purpose
without consisting of a subject and a predicate, and if it can further be
demonstrated that it need not possess even a finite verb, then it is no
longer possible to identify a sentence with a predication. And demonstrated it can be. Dr. Gardiner has shown quite clearly that in certain
circumstances the word *Rain!* may form a sentence by itself,[6] and that
What a bore! is no less adequate as a sentence than as a response.

And Jespersen, having traced the sentence back to its beginnings among
our remote progenitors, has judged it to consist of a series of sounds
which is neither a word nor a group of words but the snatch of a song—
a wordless song.[7] Songs without words revert to original music, and
"hey-and-a-ho-and-a-hey-nonino" reverts to original speech. Man, in
fact, began speaking in auditory signs (probably musical) which were
used as wholes and were only gradually, and after long ages, differentiated into words. But these wholes were always sentences—always used
as means of influencing the thoughts, feelings, and acts of others. Even
in the grammatical textbooks of to-day the word-sentence receives some

---

[5] See p. 120.
[6] *Op. cit.,* p. 71 ff.
[7] *Language,* p. 432 ff.

recognition; for they commonly teach that *Yes* and *No* are to be regarded as sentences in themselves.

Samuel Butler goes further still. He maintains that we may have a sentence without words at all. In support of this view he tells a story of Mrs. Bentley, wife of the famous Dr. Bentley of Trinity College, Cambridge. When she wanted beer, instead of sending a written or an oral message to the college buttery, she sent her snuff-box. That brought the beer. For it had been agreed between Mrs. Bentley and the butler that the snuff-box should mean *Beer, please*. There were here the conditions necessary and sufficient for authentic language—a sayer, a sayee, and a covenant. "It may sound strange to say," the author goes on to remark,[8] "that one might take a pinch of snuff out of a sentence, but if the servant had helped him or herself to a pinch while carrying it to the buttery this is what would have been done; for if a snuff-box can say 'Send me a quart of beer' so efficiently that the beer is sent, it is impossible to say that it is not a *bona fide* sentence."

There is little doubt that the sentence, as used by our primitive forbears, though heavily charged with will and emotion, was but lightly loaded with thought. It was later in the history of the race, when the pressure of practical needs began to abate, that language, which had proved so potent an instrument of will, began to be used more freely as an instrument of thought. The speaker, instead of always suggesting to the listener: I want you to act like this, got into the way of suggesting: I want you to think like this. And it was, I venture to assert, through his desire to make his listener think in a certain way that he began to mould his speech into that particular pattern of subject and predicate to which we give the name predication. For thinking and predication seem to go hand in hand. And since no sentence can convey a purpose without communicating thought, it follows that every sentence, however primitive or elemental, can be expressed as another sentence which contains at least one subject and one predicate.

A sentence has a meaning, and the words of which it is composed have meanings. How are these meanings related? How do the meanings of the separate words contribute to the meaning of the sentence? For it is the meaning of the sentence that is the goal; the words themselves are but sign-posts pointing to that goal. And down comes any arm of the sign-

[8] *Selected Essays* (Jonathan Cape), p. 235.

post that happens to point in the wrong direction. For each word as it is uttered yields up just as much of its meaning as will tend to make the whole sentence intelligible; the rest is suppressed. And when the last word is uttered the goal is reached and the sentence is understood. That at any rate is what happens when we construct our sentences—when we build them up out of words. But we don't build up all our sentences afresh; we use many of them ready-built. Some of them indeed are not open to analysis except at the risk of being misunderstood. They belong to the clichés which I described in the last chapter. *Don't mention it* is a good example. If the separate words are taken as clues to the meaning of the sentences they will prove false clues. The sentence does not mean *Don't* plus *mention* plus *it;* for it is scarcely more than a deprecatory gesture which implies: *You make too much of my slight services.* It is an expression which the speaker rolls off in one piece and which the listener must bolt whole: if he chews it he will get the wrong sense.

A short time ago I called at a picture-show to see a few water-colour drawings that took my fancy. The assistant, a punctiliously polite young man, followed me round the gallery and responded to all my remarks with the formula *Not at all.* "I like that picture, but the price is beyond my purse." *Not at all.* "I think I'll bring my wife to look at them." *Not at all.* I left him bowing at the door and muttering *Not at all, not at all.* Now *Not at all* taken literally was not at all what he meant. His tone of voice and general demeanour showed me that it was merely a polite and reassuring gesture. Sometimes it seemed to be saying: *We don't in the least mind if you don't buy any of the pictures. These hard times, sir—we quite understand.*

A Frenchman who had spent a few years in England and had made sturdy efforts to acquire the English tongue confessed that there was one word which completely baffled him. He had heard it on everybody's lips, but had utterly failed to find it in any dictionary. The word was *Zattle-doo.*

The sentence has an advantage over the word in being able to convey a general sense of its meaning by the mere intonation or cadence with which it is spoken; in other words, by its tune. If somebody asks you a question and you reply, *I don't know,* you do not say the words at a dead level; you give them a tune. Sometimes, indeed, you give the tune without the words; you just hum them. And you are understood just the same. It's not an improvised tune; it's a conventional one—one that

has accompanied the words times without number. So often, indeed, that
the tune alone conveys the sense just as well as the tune and words together. There is sometimes more than one tune for the same set of words;
there is, for instance, more than one for *I don't know*. But it is never
an arbitrary tune which anyone can change at will. It has always been
fixed and made familiar by social custom and abundant practice. In
using these tunes in this way we are back again at the place where, according to Jespersen, the sentence started its long career down the ages.

The fact that these cadences are conventional, and that the English
conventions are different from the French, and the French different from
the German or the Italian, sets up a linguistic barrier between nation
and nation, second only in strength to that of the vocabularies themselves. So strange are French cadences to the Englishman's ear that he
may be quite familiar with French literature, and quite familiar with
the sounds of individual words, and yet fail deplorably to follow a simple
French conversation. He does not know the tunes. I myself read French
far more easily than I read Welsh; yet I can understand nearly everything that is said in Welsh, however rapidly it is spoken; and precious
little of what is rapidly said in French—unless of course it is spoken by
an Englishman; then I understand it quite well. The reason is simple:
I know the English tunes, and I know the Welsh tunes, but I don't know
the French tunes.

It is clear, therefore, that the sense of a sentence is not always built up
from the senses of the component words. Sometimes several words are
welded together and have to be taken *en bloc*. Sometimes the whole sentence has to be taken *en bloc*. And the *en bloc* meaning of the sentence
may even contradict the cumulative meaning of the individual words. If
I say, *Mr. X is lazy and never does more work than he can help,* everybody understands what I mean and sees nothing strange about the expression. But if I had said, *Mr. X never does more work than he cannot
help,*[9] he would have thought I was talking nonsense. Yet it is the first
sentence that is nonsense, and is accepted as sense only because convention has given the whole sentence a meaning which the meanings of the
separate words do not justify.

Another instance. A small boy is accused of an offence, plausibly denies his guilt, and gets off. Somebody remarks, *I shouldn't wonder if the*

[9] The sense becomes clearer if the sentence is expanded thus: *Mr. X never
does more work than that which he can't help doing.*

young rascal hadn't done it after all. That remark would be taken by the listeners to mean the same as if he had said, *I shouldn't wonder if the young rascal had done it after all.* Here we have two logically contradictory sentences saying precisely the same thing.

If further proof be needed that intimations of meaning, and pretty strong intimations too, come from sources other than the words, let the following experiment be tried. A places six pennies in the palm of his hand, and shows them to B. Then a conversation like this takes place:

A. How many pennies have I in my hand?
B. Six.
A. I say there are five.
B. I say there are six.
A. Will you give me a penny if I am wrong.
B. Certainly.
A. Well, I am wrong. Hand over the penny.

It is amazing how readily people fall into this simple trap. B is so ensnared by the general situation together with the form and cadence of the question, *Will you give me a penny if I am wrong?* that he interprets the question as though it had been either *Will you give me a penny if you are wrong?* or *Will you give me a penny if I am right?* He responds to the expected question, not to the actual question.

To sum up, the meaning of a spoken sentence is something towards which several forces converge, and to which several factors contribute. The most generous contribution comes as a rule from the component words. But the words do not always act singly; they sometimes combine into groups known as clichés, formulas, or stock phrases; and each of these groups delivers a unitary meaning which sometimes owes little or nothing to the individual words of which it is composed. The group functions as a single word. Then again the meaning of many familiar salutations, responses, and set forms of expression is partly conveyed by the cadence—by the modulation and melody of the speaker's voice. And there are times when the cadence can carry the whole of the meaning. Finally, the context—not merely the verbal context but the whole situation, the full *mise en scène* of the little drama—often makes it easy to interpret many a sentence which, if spoken on an empty stage, would have been wholly unintelligible.

JANET RANKIN AIKEN

What Is Good Grammar?

If you have ever glanced through an old collection of sermons—and it is more fun to do so than you might perhaps imagine—you may have noticed one odd fact. The preacher has given more space to the works of the devil than to the works of God. Heaven may be sketched, but the other place is anatomized. Virtue may be praised, but vice is recapitulated. This plan of procedure is evidently intended to promote goodness, as though good were the absence of bad.

The practicing grammarian, that is to say, the grammar teacher, follows a somewhat analogous method. He may give his pupils a sketch or plan, more or less accurate, of the general structure of the English language. He may give examples of sentences (very stupid sentences for the most part) which are grammatically virtuous. But by far the greater portion of the teacher's energy is likely to be devoted to the detection, denunciation, and prohibition of grammatical sin. To him, whether or not he would say it in just those words, good grammar is grammar which is not incorrect.

Certainly it is of the greatest importance that we get and keep a clear idea of what goodness in grammar really is. But I have no intention of being subversively original by emphasizing goodness and minimizing evil. And so I propose to begin in the true preacher-teacher fashion, by giving a brief explanation of the nature of grammatical depravity.

Grammar which is really bad is a negative rather than a positive thing. Basically, it is the failure to achieve the primary purpose of all speech— that is, clear communication.

When we speak or write, we have an idea to convey, and for that idea there may be one or several adequate expressions in words. But when we distort, mutilate, or suppress that expression by leaving some essential out, putting some superfluity in, or twisting our words so that they do not mean what we intend them to mean, we are grammatically sinful.

Ambiguity is the primary sin against the English language. Laying yourself open to misunderstanding or simply to lack of understanding indicates that you have not yet learned how to speak English. And ambiguity occurs in many an innocent-appearing Judas of a sentence, such as *Harry was talking to a man with a smile on his face.* You do not know which of two things that sentence means, and neither does any one else. It is bad English.

Another depraved sentence is *Mary and Joan talked until she cried.* Who is she? No one can tell whether the word refers to Mary or to Joan. It does not convey an idea clearly, and therefore it is bad English grammar.

All of us have some time or other felt the helpless exasperation brought on by some ambiguity in our personal correspondence. All of us have asked desparingly, "But what does Aunt Anne mean? Does she mean that Bill is coming here Wednesday or that she is going to Maine Thursday—or what?"

Occasionally an ambiguity, like a Raffles or a Robin Hood, is so monumental as to compel a sort of admiration. Here is an example from a piece of statistical writing in the field of medicine. It is intended to be used as a column heading: "Three pairs of beds for expectant mothers suffering from tuberculosis and their infants for every 100,000 population."

Frequently ambiguity is funny. The pun is essentially just ambiguity with a comic effect, and the pun, intended or unintended, is found in the most unexpected places. For example, the Bible could not be called precisely hilarious, and yet there is hilarity in 1 Kings 13:27 (I leave the italics as I found them): "And he spake to his sons, saying, Saddle me the ass; and they saddled *him.*"

Ambiguity, incongruity, misunderstanding enter into both comedy and tragedy; both literary forms are conditioned on misunderstanding of

Y habló a sus hijos, y díjoles: Enalbardádme un asno.
Y ellos se le enalbardaron. /[...] Sellatemi l'asino.
Ed essi ~~glieł~~ sellarono.

words, of emotions, of facts, of life itself. But in the great middle ground of everyday living clear thinking is at a premium and ambiguity has no place. In speech, clarity is essential.[1]

But we have only begun with our catalog of speech sins. Beside the cardinal sin of general ambiguity, *a second* is omission, which appears in *Some men like food better than their wives.* Here again there is ambiguity; again the sentence might mean either of two things; but here the trouble lies simply in the lack of a word or two—*do* at the end, or *they like* in the middle would straighten the thing out. An initial *it* is needed in *Being a rainy day, I stayed home.* Of course you know what that sentence means; but it does not say it. What it says is that I was a rainy day.

Redundancy or needless repetition is another very common sin against grammatical perfection. Like ambiguity, it may appear in innocent guise, for example, in *Besides, I also must go too.* To a discriminating mind that sentence with its piled-up affirmatives is fully as bad as its converse, *None of us never went nowhere.* The double or multiple negative is to be condemned because it is redundant, and the multiple affirmative is bad for the same reason, as are *return back, continue on,* and scores of other such expressions to be found in student compositions and elsewhere.

A fourth sin against good grammar is disorder, or right words out of place. *Your letters make me want to finish my lessons very badly,* wrote one student to me. And then there is *the animal's back which seemed to be a horse.* Strictly speaking, *I only had a dime* and *I don't think I'll go* for *I had only a dime* and *I think I shan't go* are of this order of faults. But these are venial, being so widely practiced as to be acceptable to even the grammar teacher. They are "white lies."

Disorder, redundancy, omission, ambiguity in general. These are the four by-ways into which we stray from the highroad of good English, the four means by which the end or purpose of all speech is defeated. These are the immoralities of grammar.

But it is important to recognize the fact that morality, which con-

---

[1] There is a curious distinction between speech which is bad in structure and speech which is bad in intent or content, which should be remarked in passing. Grammar is not concerned with what you mean to say, so long as you make that meaning plain. You may be lying; you may say "Moons are green cheese." Or you may be inciting your hearer to dastardly crime. Your grammar is good if your words express your evil meaning clearly and completely.

cerns the central aim or nature of language (or life), is one thing, and
the conventions, those forms which human beings have agreed shall be
observed in their particular day and generation, are another thing. And
just as the preacher draws no very clear line between immorality and unconventionality in his sermons, so the grammarian lumps together actual
linguistic sin with the failure to observe accepted speech forms, a failing
which we shall now consider.

In grammar as in life, it sometimes seems as if it were more important to observe the conventions than the moralities themselves. Most
grammar teachers would rate *Harry was talking to a man with a smile
on his face* higher than the perfectly clear but unsanctioned *Neither are*
and *I done it.* Convention in speech thus becomes fully as important as
morality. It is as important as modernity in dress, as manners at a wed-
ding, as precedence at a diplomatic function.

The word which describes or explains unconventionality in grammar
is *substitution*—the replacing of one word or construction by another.
It is easy to see that substitution is not of itself bad or inimical to the
progress of a language. Substitution has given us our natural gender,
our easy grammar; it has given us an English superior by far to the
dialects spoken in the England of a thousand years ago, and there is no
reason to suppose that its effect will have been otherwise a thousand years
hence. Two or three centuries ago people began the harmless substitution
of *spoke* for *spake,* and now it is *spoke,* and *spake* is obsolete in actual use.
Even more recently people began speaking of a humorous person as one
who could evoke smiles, instead of one who was capricious and moody;
the substitution of meanings is now complete. And perhaps if enough
speakers on the radio and elsewhere go on saying *mitigate against* when
they mean *militate against,* the former phrase may also become good conventional English.

Once in a long time a substitution involves a lack of clarity and is
therefore immoral. When I read *The colors glew vividly* in a student
composition, I had to stop and think before realizing that *glew* was a
substitution for the past of *glow.* But ordinarily there is no difficulty of
this sort. *Have wrote, ain't,* and *lay down* are as clear as *have written,
am not,* and *lie down.* Their sin is that they are unconventional English.

It is impossible even to enumerate the substitutions which may occur in
the practice of English. Grammars report and denounce only the more
widespread, such as *like* for *as* (*Do it like I do*), *come* for *came* (*I come*

yesterday), *learn* for *teach* (*Learn him his lesson*), and so forth. But often substitution is individual and spontaneous, as when one or another of my students writes of a rendering shriek, a solution hovering into view, the wavering palm-trees, metering out punishment, a chicken coupe, an uprighteous man, an irrepraviable loss, a salmon canary, a carefully tendered garden, a college which was foundered in 1825. I confess that I have a weakness for some of these substitutions, and find the best of this sort poetic as well as humorous. It is the stereotyped, uneducated, uninspired substitutions such as *learn* for *teach* which we can profitably lose.

And now, having defined grammatical immorality and grammatical unconventionality, shall we approach a step nearer to the question asked in the title of this chapter? Shall we inquire what good grammar is? Is it just grammar which is not bad?

It is a change in grammatical theory which has made the question a poignant one. In the very old days the English grammarian had a doctrine based squarely on the rules of a dead and therefore unchanging language, namely Latin, and hence this doctrine could also be rounded and unchanging. The very old grammarian could be an autocrat, benevolent indeed to those who trembled, but terrible toward any who evaded or transgressed his Latinized plan of English.

Little by little people came to realize that Latin with all its charms was not the same as English and could not be considered adequate to express the spirit of a different tongue. So a new theory of linguistic purity began to take shape. A grammarian named Noble Butler, who in 1874 published his *Practical and Critical Grammar of the English Language,* put the prevailing theory fairly neatly in the preface, where he said, "Words and forms which have been established by the usage of the great writers should be regarded as among the elements of the language."

The words have the modern ring. They carry conviction to the modern mind, which is strongly inclined to worry less and less over rules and to allow in English whatever can get itself adopted by reputable writers. At least Butler's principle gives us a definite standard upon which to work, and thus it is calculated to evoke applause from both those who know grammar and those who don't. We can all understand usage even if we have never studied Latin.

So let us set up as a working hypothesis the dictum: good grammar is what the best writers use.

Let us all stand with Butler long enough to ask the next and obvious question, who are these great writers whose usage is to form the standard of correctness? Taking three centuries as the spread of Modern English, perhaps we may begin with Shakespeare and the King James Bible and come down to the present via Milton, Pope, Johnson, Wordsworth, Scott, Dickens, Kipling, and Shaw, to name a few more or less at random. If these are not the great writers of English, who are?

The question is never answered in so many words in the *Practical and Critical Grammar,* but reading this worthy volume through, we are forced to admit, however regretfully, that Butler could not have had these models in mind when he wrote that sentence in his preface. He does not really wish us to mould our English after that of Shakespeare, the Bible, or any of the others I have mentioned. Indeed, at the end of our study of his book, we are forced to the peculiar and somewhat disconcerting conclusion that by "great writers" Noble Butler must mean almost exclusively Noble Butler. Certainly he cannot mean Shakespeare. Shakespeare could force an actor to say "Thou and I am one." He could speak of the "most unkindest cut." In what is probably his most quoted soliloquy the words "must give us pause," have only the doubtfullest of subjects and would certainly suffer correction at the hands of any living grammar teacher. Books have been, and more could be, compiled about the liberties Shakespeare took with the grammar of English. Modern authorities could never give Will a passing grade, much less make him a model for the rest of us.

And the King James Bible too contains dozens of what Noble Butler lists as errors. Every day or two I must correct students who say "That little stream has flown along;" but Job can say "Whose foundation was overflown with a flood." I tell students not to use two subjects with a singular verb, but James can write "Out of the same mouth proceedeth blessing and cursing." Regretfully we must admit that the Bible is no certain candidate for the "great writers" group.

Time and space would fail me if I started the job of checking up on Milton, Pope, Johnson, and the others I mentioned as possibly great. And anyhow it is not necessary, because this job has been done so often. Pick up the second volume of Jespersen's *Modern English Grammar,* to name only one such compilation, and you will find examples from all these worthies enough to make a grammarian's hair curl.

Not one of the classic writers of English measures up to the grammarian's standard in his writing. It is pitifully easy to catch Milton nodding, or to find the Great Panjandrum out. Not a single one of the great authors of English literature chose to make, or perhaps was able to make, his language free from errors in grammar.

So easy and exhilarating is it to snoop out grammatical slips in whatever victim one chooses to select, that boner-hunts have become a popular sport. Recent compilations give classic or stock examples of funny English, and more hitherto unquoted ones, from newspapers, magazines, and novels. They sample slips of all the popular varieties from the *one-of* mistake (*one of the best books that has appeared*) to the split infinitive.

The authors tell the public that they have been on this sort of boner-hunt for many years, but if so, either they have suppressed most of their findings or they have been extraordinarily unobservant; for a year or two of looking would yield boners enough to fill not a book but a library. There is nothing easier than to find vulnerabilities in an author's verbal expressions. I remember well a most distinguished scholar of my acquaintance, to whom a reader sent three closely typed sheets all filled with errors in punctuation, wording, and construction, from his most recent book. When I asked him what he thought of the criticism, he grinned and replied, "I just thought, what a proof reader that man would make!"

But when the last boner-hunt is over and the latest author convicted of deadly sin against his mother tongue, what becomes of the "usage" standard so neatly formulated by Noble Butler in 1874? Can we really entrust our language to these guides who have been shown to be so fallible? Shall we begin to say *overflown* with Job and *to slowly trace* with Byron? Does the usage standard mean that we may begin taking the same liberties with English which Shakespeare took? Or shall we set up yet another standard for good English?

One of these very modern boner-hunters, the linguist Ernest Weekley, may help us. He advocates neither a return to the Latin standard for English nor an adherence to the usage criterion. He says, "If the first duty of the writer is to make himself clear, the second is to avoid unpleasing clumsiness." And as these are the only two duties he mentions, one may perhaps assume that he thinks those are all there are. Clarity and simplicity combine to form this linguist's ideal.

On the whole this standard of Mr. Weekley's hits fairly close to the heart of the matter. At least it permits us still to consider Shakespeare a good writer and the Authorized Version of the Bible good English. It justifies Milton and Pope if not Johnson, whose writing is under a cloud at present anyhow. Kipling, Shaw, Dickens, and Scott all come well within the pale.

I am not just sure that the grammarians themselves do. While their writings are for the most part clear, they must often be labelled clumsy. I would rather write a boner such as *the least worn of the two* than this: "Apart from such pleonasms as are sanctified by long usage, and even these should be used sparingly, a pleonastic statement is as objectionable as one that is left incomplete." Why sanctified? And what is long usage if not merely usage? And what is the construction of the apart-phrase or the these-clause in that sentence? Parentheses might have helped.

However, it is better to know what should be done in English than neither to know nor to practice good writing. And anyhow, the standard of clarity and simplicity is good, because, as I said, it has to do with the spirit rather than the letter. It judges the effect of what one writes rather than merely the words one uses.

One might add to Mr. Weekley's enumeration. There is the elementary necessity of having an idea before beginning to write at all. Too many writers, elementary and advanced, neglect this necessity. There is the essential quality of friendliness, or the ability to get on good terms with the reader. If I were writing a manual on the writer's art I should list this quality as of the very first importance. And then after all the other essentials have been listed, there is always the final essential quality of genius to make words live and last.

Good grammar is not merely grammar which is free from unconventionalities, or even from immoralities. It is the triumph of the communicating process, the use of words which create in the reader's mind the thing as the writer conceived it; it is a creative act, a reproductive animus. Despite all his defects in individual words and phrases this sort of grammar permeates even the triumphant art of Shakespeare himself.

Good grammar may admit a judicious number of the substitutions rejected by grammarians. It is almost certain to favor functional shift, or the transfer of words from their usual use to another. It is likely on the whole to avoid the four cardinal sins against English, detailed at the beginning of this chapter. But it is bold and free. It commands the rules rather than bows to them.

QUESTIONS FOR REVIEW OF PART THREE

1. What are some of the changes which have been made in the use of letters since the Roman alphabet was first used to represent English sounds?

2. What is the phonetic spelling of your name? Of your instructo name? Of the title of this book?

3. The following diagram presents, in condensed form, the long vowel sounds of Middle English. (The pronunciations of the sounds are keyed by the Late Modern words in parentheses.)

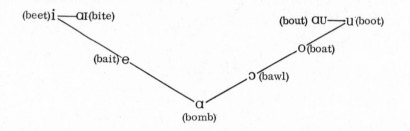

When the Great Vowel Shift took place after the time of Chaucer, long vowel sounds shifted one place higher on the triangle, though the spelling did not change. (In Middle English, the highest long vowels were [i] and [u], and those sounds became the diphthongs [aɪ] and [aʊ]; for example, ME *lif* [liːf] became MnE *life* [laɪf], and ME *hous* [huːs] became MnE *house* [haʊs].)

How, then, were the vowels in these words pronounced in Middle English?

seed	home
made	doom
meat	goat
five	down
need	root

4. What are ten words in "Rip Van Winkle" which you pronounce differently than Kenyon does? After you list the words, correctly spelled, add Kenyon's pronunciation and your own in phonetic spelling.

5. What are the differences between phones, allophones, and phonemes? Think of some examples other than those given in the Faust article.

6. What are the suprasegmental phonemes? What term does Myers use instead of "suprasegmental phonemes"?

7. What are some sentences in which you might be tempted to insert unnecessary commas where single bar or double bar junctures occur!

8. In the following passage from "Jabberwocky," a poem in Lewis Carroll's *Through the Looking-Glass,* as which part of speech would you label each nonsense word?

> 'Twas brillig, and the slithy toves
> Did gyre and gimble in the wabe:
> All mimsy were the borogoves,
> And the mome raths outgrabe.

9. How do you explain the fact that newly coined nouns and verbs automatically are treated as regular in inflection?
10. What is functional shift? What are some examples of it?
11. What "general principles of modification" does Myers offer?
12. What are some original examples of sentences with movable modifiers? With fixed modifiers?
13. How can the use of diagramming as a teaching device be abused?
14. To what extent do you think each of the three Caldwell criticisms of the Lane article is justified?
15. What do you suppose Myers would say about the controversy between Lane and Caldwell? Review "The Patterns of Grammar" and "Modifiers" in preparing your answer.
16. In what respects does the Ballard article anticipate the view of structural grammarians that sentences (or "utterances," as C. C. Fries terms them in *The Structure of English*) are best identified by intonation patterns?
17. What place does the meaning of the words have in Ballard's definition of a sentence?
18. What are some sentences in the Ballard article which would be considered non-sentences by some definitions? How do these sentences differ from the kinds of utterances which even a liberal grammarian would call sentence fragments?
19. What, according to the Aiken article, are the four major grammatical sins?
20. Of the examples of "substitution" in the Aiken article, which would Kenyon describe as examples of analogical change?
21. How do you explain the fact that the Aiken article offers more suggestions on how not to write poorly than it does on how to write well?

SUGGESTIONS FOR INDIVIDUAL PROJECTS
AND CLASS DISCUSSION

1. A speech text, published five years before this book of readings, includes a list of "common mispronunciations" and states "The correct form is indicated within parentheses." Of the following pairs of words selected from the list, which ones are *acceptable*

alternative pronunciations listed in your dictionary, and which (at least according to your dictionary) may properly be labeled "incorrect–correct" as indicated by the author of the speech text?

Misplacing of Accent

ac'climate (acclim'ate)	hospit'able (hos'pitable)
applic'able (ap'plicable)	in'quiry (inquir'y)
compar'able (com'parable)	irrefut'able (irref'utable)
despic'able (des'picable)	lamen'table (lam'entable)
exquis'ite (ex'quisite)	prefer'able (pref'erable)

Addition of Sounds

barbarious (barbarous)	heighth (height)
cyupon (coupon)	of-ten (of[t]en)
grievious (grievous)	warsh (wash)

Sound Substitutions

boquet (bouquet)	dipthong (diphthong)
brochr (brochure)	hōmage (hŏmage)
click (clique)	longgevity (longevity)
crooks (crux)	prespiration (perspiration)
dictionûry (dictionary)	tedjus (tedious)

Make a table of three columns. In the first, list the correct spelling of each word; in the second, give the pronunciation you employ (using phonetic spelling, not diacritical spelling); in the third, label your own pronunciation as "acceptable" or "unacceptable" according to your dictionary. (After reading Marckwardt's article on dictionary pronunciation, you should not expect your answers to agree with those of a student using a different dictionary and you may have some comments on the pronunciations your dictionary records. You may also have some comments on the technique used by the author of the speech text for recording the pronunciations he has in mind.)

2. Write ten or twelve noun phrases in which various adjectives— expressing color, age, intensity, size, and other qualities—modify the noun. See if you can determine whether or not there seems to be a natural tendency to place such adjectives in a given order according to their qualities. (For example, is the order of size-age-color in "little old gray shawl" borne out in other noun phrases?) Where do words which are nouns in form but adjectives in function usually occur in such lists of modifiers? Where do adverbs usually occur?

3. The Lane article reports an increasing tendency to clip the *-ed* from past participles. Test the truth of this by conducting one ro more of the following studies:

    a. A comparison of -*ed* clipping now and thirty years ago in cook-
       books or in food, clothing, or building material advertisements.
    b. Lists of participles clipped and not clipped in advertisements,
       menus, and other types of signs and placards in the business
       district.
    c. A study of whether or not various speakers articulate the final
       consonants of participles audibly.

SUGGESTED WRITING ASSIGNMENT

The Caldwell criticism is negative, almost implying that there
was nothing true in the Lane article. From what you know of the
history, pronunciation, and grammar of the English language, and
from what you yourself have observed about the clipping of participles (preferably by undertaking Project 3 above), write a positive
criticism of the Lane article. That is, clarify or extend Lane's
remarks rather than merely refute them. If you do point out errors
in his article, do it constructively and impersonally.

Usage

*A*lthough it is easy to write that grammar is concerned primarily with morphology and syntax, usage with the appropriateness of words and constructions in various situations, it is impossible to distinguish perfectly between grammar and usage. "What Is Good Grammar?" is concerned with both grammar and usage, as is the first selection in Part IV —"The Varieties of English," by Porter G. Perrin, an article designed to give a relatively brief but comprehensive treatment of usage for writers. The two articles which follow take opposing views toward usage. In his "Bargain Basement English," Wilson Follett, an author and editor, attacks a type of usage which he terms "at best tolerable and at worst revolting." In "Grammar for Today," Bergen Evans, professor of English at Northwestern University and regular participant in the television program entitled "The Last Word," responds to the Follett attack.

PORTER G. PERRIN

The Varieties of English

We began to learn our language by imitating what our parents said, and soon we picked up enough words to make our wants known and then to talk with others. At first our parents were so pleased to have us talk that they accepted some of our infantile contributions to the English vocabulary. Milk might be *nuck,* a hammer an *agboo,* an elephant an *umpy-dump.* We used our own forms of words and our own syntax: One youngster, struggling with irregular verbs, said, "Mother did gave me a lot of pants. She shouldn't have gaven me so much pants this summer." For a while the grown-ups thought this sort of language was cute, but by the time we were four or five, they began to expect us to talk about as they talked, and so far as we could talk that way, we did.

In school we added to our skill in using English by learning to read and write. We studied "grammar," which told us that "It is I" and other expressions were correct and "It is me" and a lot more were not. If a reason was offered, it was generally something like "The verb *to be* is followed by a predicate nominative." We may have tried to follow this grammar in the schoolroom, but outside we talked about the same way we always had. Some of us, though, began to realize that English, which we supposed we just talked naturally, was a pretty complex matter and that opinions about it differed, sometimes violently.

By the time we reach college and find that we are almost ready to take our places in public affairs we begin to have some concern for our language. We want to feel confident in our pronunciation and our choice of words. When we sit down to write something, we want to have control of the language, to be able to use it readily and presentably. And we want to be able to speak and write effectively in the more mature communication situations in which we find ourselves.

Confidence and effectiveness in the use of English come in part from a realistic knowledge of the possibilities of language. We need to know how to choose the forms of expression which are most effective for us, and we need to practice so that the sort of English we want to use comes easily and becomes a habit. The habit of using good English is formed not so much by memorizing rules and trying to apply them as by reading the work of good writers and listening to good speakers, occasionally noticing how they gain their effects. But to observe language profitably we need some conscious knowledge of how it works and some specific guidance; a composition course and a book like this can help.

We all use English with ease and with a good deal of effectiveness in the situations in which we feel at home. But when we meet new people, perhaps from a different social circle or a different part of the country, or when we have to give a talk or write an important letter, a paper for a college course, or something that will be printed, we may become acutely conscious of *how* we are speaking or writing. Fortunately the greater part of our language raises no questions; it can be used at any time, under any circumstances: the ordinary names of things (*dog, dresses, politics*) and of acts (*walking, swimming, voting*) and thousands of other words are in general usage; most of the forms of words are pretty well standardized (*theirs, people's, lived*), as well as the order of words in phrases and sentences. But some questions about usage do come up. Sometimes we have to make choices among words and forms and constructions, and because our choices contribute to the impression our talk or piece of writing makes, they are important.

These questions about English usage arise chiefly because there are different varieties of the language that cannot be used with equal effectiveness in every situation. The questions may be simple, like Is it all right to say "It's *me*," "Go *slow*," "It's *real* interesting," or "It's *laying* on the table"? Does *phony* fit in this sentence? Is *solon* better than *congressman* here? Or the questions may be more complicated,

like Should this be one sentence or two? How can I show the connection
between these ideas? Are these words specific enough? What is the best
order for these ideas?

The answers to some of these questions are clear-cut and definite,
but the answers to others vary with the circumstances. English, like
every other widely used language, is not one single group of words and
constructions, everywhere and always the same, but a variety of such
groups that have much in common but are still far from uniform. There
are two reasons for stressing these varieties in this book: one is to show
the immense resources our language offers, and the other is to help form
habits of easy and automatic choice in your actual usage—habits that
will be appropriate to the varying situations you meet. A mature use of
English means speaking and writing the sort of English that is appropriate to the situation in which you find yourself, for *English is not
just "good"; it is good under certain conditions.*

SOURCES OF VARIATION
IN ENGLISH

The varieties of English that you find around you are all natural
growths, and students of the language are able to describe and in part
account for them. Understanding the principal sources of the differences
will give you perspective on the language and will help guide you in
making some choices.

Variations Due to Time.   It is natural that a language used by
millions of people over centuries of time should change. Occasionally
changes are relatively sudden and far-reaching, as after an invasion by a
nation with a different language, but ordinarily they are slow and barely
noticeable—slightly different pronunciations, new shadings in the meaning of words, and gradual shifts in grammatical constructions. You know
from reading older literature that English has changed a good deal
in the centuries during which it has been written down.[1] A play by
Shakespeare needs a good many notes to tell us what some of the words
meant to the people who first heard the plays over three hundred fifty

[1] For further discussion, see Otto Jespersen, *Growth and Structure of the
English Language* (various editions); George H. McKnight, *English Words
and Their Backgrounds* (New York, 1923); *Oxford English Dictionary, Dictionary of American English.*

ight n. (ME & AS *wiht*; akin to Gmn *wicht*, creature; IE *weġti*- thing) [Archaic] a human being; person, now sometimes used humorously.

years ago. If we go back far enough, English seems like a foreign language, though we may recognize in the older forms the ancestors of some of our current words. Language changes as naturally and as steadily as other customs do—in clothes, food, literary fashions.

Words, forms, or constructions that are no longer in use are called *obsolete*. No one today refers to a *bottle* of hay, or uses *can* in the sense of *know*, or *coy* in the sense of *quiet*. Usages which are now disappearing from the language are called *archaic*. Fashion has just about driven out *betrothed* in favor of *fiancée*. Archaic expressions survive in some situations, such as the *thou* and *saith* of church services. A few archaic or even obsolete words are used in set phrases, such as "much *ado*," "in good *stead*," and many are preserved in uneducated or dialect speech after they have disappeared from other varieties of English. *Learn* in the sense of *teach*, *you was* in the singular, *he don't*, and the double negative were all once in general and reputable use. It is often hard to tell when a word or construction is sufficiently uncommon to be called archaic; a good many words not so labeled in dictionaries are really used very rarely (like *betimes*, *deem*, *doff*).

Because we learn our language chiefly by imitating what we hear and read, obsolete and archaic usage offers few problems, but occasionally in trying to "improve" his language a student will use an archaic expression, and sometimes a strained effort at humor produces words like ↑ *quoth* or *wight*.

We do not need to know the whole history of our language, but realizing that it has a history should help us adjust to reading older literature and will explain many of the peculiarities of the current language (in spelling and verb forms, for instance) that we will need to consider in this book.

Words, constructions, and styles are still changing. Recent years have seen the addition of many words (*baby sitter, bathyscaphe, astronautics, blip*, names for scores of new chemical compounds, and so on),[2] the dropping of some from general use, and a tendency toward more concise idioms and constructions.

People used to shy away from new words until they had "proved themselves a permanent part of the language." It is true that dictionary editors watch for new words in books and magazines and include

[2] *American Speech* treats many new words as they appear, and the annual supplementary volumes to the principal encyclopedias have lists of such words.

them if they continue to be used. But users of the language don't need to be so hesitant. The use of a word should depend on its fitness rather than on its passing a probationary period; dictionary recording comes only as the result of use. Obviously the name of a new invention or of a new social situation is needed immediately and should be freely used. No apology is necessary for words like *televise, iron curtain, deep-freeze, fringe benefits, newscast.*

While new words for new things are natural additions to our vocabulary, it is wise to hesitate before adopting new words for things that have already been named. This is especially true of the abstract words (such as *recreational facilities, urban area, causal factors*) that higher education and occupational specialization seem to be substituting for the common words for some activities and situations.

New words used to make their way into literary usage rather slowly, but most writers today use a new word whenever it is appropriate. (*Pecking order,* for instance, was used in fiction by Aldous Huxley and Ford Madox Ford almost as soon as zoologists had begun to use it.) It is important for a writer to make the fullest possible use of the current language. When you write naturally, from your observation of language, you usually write current English, and you should aim for no other kind.

Variations Due to Place.   No language is spoken exactly the same way in all parts of the country or countries in which it is used. We can easily spot an Englishman because some of his pronunciations and some of his words and constructions are different from ours. We can also very often tell what part of the United States a person comes from by listening to him talk. Differences in words, pronunciations, stress, phrasing, and grammatical habits that are characteristic of fairly definite regions are called *regional dialects;* more accurately, a dialect is speech that does not attract attention to itself in the region where it is used. A pronunciation, a word or meaning of a word, or an idiom that for usually traceable historical reasons is current in one region and not in others is called a *provincialism* or a *localism.*

Dialects are not peculiar to backward regions, for the "Oxford accent" forms a minor dialect and the people of Boston and of New York speak differently from each other. Nor are dialects the result of lack of education or social standing. An educated Westerner will speak somewhat differently from a Southerner or New Englander of a similar degree and quality of education. A dialect may show traits of differing British dialects spoken by early settlers or of foreign language spoken by large numbers of people in the region, as in Dutch sections of Pennsylvania or in the Scandinavian sections of the Middle West. It may show traits of a neighboring language or of the language of an earlier settlement: the dialect of the Southwest contains Spanish elements; of New Orleans, French elements.

There are fewer differences among the dialects of the United States than would be expected in a country of such size, many fewer than exist among the dialects in much smaller Great Britain.[3] The relative freedom of movement of the American people, transportation facilities that have prevented even the Rocky Mountains from marking a linguistic boundary, the educational system, the circulation of books and national magazines, and more recently radio and television—all keep people who are thousands of miles apart speaking substantially the same language.

Three major speech areas of the United States have been traditionally recognized: *Eastern* (New England and a strip of eastern New York), *Southern* (south of Pennsylvania and the Ohio River, extending west of the Mississippi into Texas), and *Western* (extending from New Jersey on the Atlantic, through the Middle West and the whole of our Pacific coast), sometimes called *General American,* or *Northern.* As a result of the work being done on *The Linguistic Atlas of the United States and Canada,* the boundaries are being more exactly drawn, subdivisions indicated, and lines of influence between areas shown. The major speech divisions have been renamed *Northern, Midland,* and *Southern,* but their lines have not been carried far enough westward so that they can take the place of the traditional areas in amateur discussion. Regional varieties exist within each of the three main areas, as in the Ozarks or in New York City, but the differences between the speech of California

---

[3] See Baugh, Ch. 11, especially §250; Bloomfield, Ch. 19; *Dictionary of American English*; Otto Jespersen, *Mankind, Nation and Individual from a Linguistic Point of View* (Oslo, 1925); G. P. Krapp, *The English Language in America* (New York, 1925), pp. 225-73; Mencken. Many articles in the magazine *American Speech* record facts of various American dialects. Linguaphone album L-19 has recordings of twenty-four American dialects. For some results of work on the *Linguistic Atlas,* see Hans Kurath, *Handbook of the Linguistic Geography of New England* (Providence, 1939), *A Word Geography of the Eastern United States* (Ann Arbor, 1949), and E. B. Atwood, *Survey of Verb Forms in the Eastern United States* (Ann Arbor, 1953).

and Illinois are fewer than the differences between either of these and, say, Georgia or Massachusetts. Roughly one twelfth of the population speaks Eastern, one sixth Southern, and three fourths Western or General American.

A professional student of American English observes many differences among these regions that the ordinary person might miss, but we are all aware of some of them. Some New Englanders use a broad *a* (äsk, gräss, päst) where most Americans have short *a;* they usually slight *r* (*bän* for *barn*). A Westerner has a distinct, perhaps even a prolonged, *r,* after vowels as well as before. Like most Americans he has *ä* for the *o* in *hot, lot, cot.* Like many Americans he rounds the *o* in *hog, frog, log.* Beginning in New York State, most speakers of the Western type do not distinguish *hoarse* and *horse, mourning* and *morning,* pronouncing *ōr* (like the word *ore*) in all. A Southerner from the lowlands (as distinguished from the hill country and the hillbillies) does not sound *r* after vowels (for example, *suh* for *sir, douh* or *doh* for *door*). The long *i* both in the lowlands and the hills may suggest *ä* as in the popular spelling *Ah* for *I.* Southerners from the hills usually pronounce *r* after vowels—as all fanciers of hillbilly music know. Each region—Eastern, Southern, and Western—also has its characteristic stress and speech rhythm.

In vocabulary, different words will be found for many common objects. Which of the following is used in your locality, or is some other word used?

         bag–sack–poke   gumshoe–overshoe–rubber
         piazza–porch–stoop–veranda   seesaw–teeter-totter–teeterboard
            doughnut–fried cake–cruller–fat cake–nut cake–cookie

The accompanying map shows several words that are used within the relatively small limits of New England for the common earthworm: *angleworm, angledog, easworm* (for *eastworm*), *fish worm.* In other regions it is known by some of these names and by others as well.

Besides these varying names for common objects, each region has special words for local features of the landscape or for occupations that are more or less local: *coulee, hogback, sierra, mesa; mesquite, piñon; mule skinner, vara* (a surveyor's measure in the Southwest). And there are local idioms like the Southern "I would *like for* you to do it," or

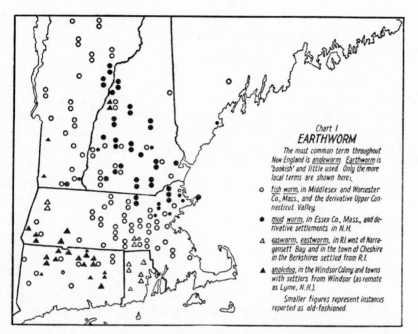

Chart I
EARTHWORM

The most common term throughout New England is *anglewarm*. *Earthworm* is 'bookish' and little used. Only the more local terms are shown here:

○ *fish worm*, in Middlesex and Worcester Co., Mass., and the derivative Upper Connecticut Valley

● *mud worm*, in Essex Co., Mass., and derivative settlements in N.H.

△ *easworm, eastworm*, in R.I. west of Narragansett Bay and in the town of Cheshire in the Berkshires settled from R.I.

▲ *angledog*, in the Windsor Colony and towns with settlers from Windsor (as remote as Lyme, N.H.).

Smaller figures represent instances reported as old-fashioned.

From *Handbook of the Linguistic Geography of New England*, p. 38

like those for telling time—New Englanders generally say quarter *of* four, Southerners quarter *till* four, and Westerners quarter *to* four.

Increased travel, education, and reading are probably reducing the dialectal variety in the United States, just as they are blotting out the dialects of Great Britain. Words peculiar to a local terrain or to local occupations will probably survive, since they fill a real need and usually have no equivalents in other dialects. The frequent use of localisms on radio and television and in stories may help make one region more tolerant of the language of others, and it may very well introduce into general use words formerly characteristic of a particular locality.

People's attitudes toward the use of localisms vary greatly. Some believe that they should be weeded out; others believe that a person should retain as much as possible of the flavor of his native speech. It is a problem each person will have to settle for himself on the basis of appropriateness and effectiveness. An educated person will tend to shed the more conspicuous local pronunciations of his youth, and he may have little occasion to use purely local words. But conscious effort

to change his speech to a different pattern will often result in an unhappy combination of elements from both. Natural, gradual, unconscious
change is best.

Localisms are more appropriate in speech than in writing. Conspicuously formal writers tend to avoid them. Their words come characteristically from the general or specifically formal parts of the vocabulary;
distinctive localisms would be used only for special effects and might be
placed in quotation marks. In General and Informal English (defined
in later sections of this chapter), localisms have more place. They are
necessary to narrative, both in histories and accounts of personal experience and in stories and plays. Consider this description of a meal from a
novel of Florida:

> There were poke-greens with bits of white bacon buried in them;
> sandbuggers made of potato and onion and the cooter he had found
> crawling yesterday; sour orange biscuits and at his mother's elbow the
> sweet potato pone. He was torn between his desire for more biscuits
> and another sandbugger and the knowledge, born of painful experience,
> that if he ate them, he would suddenly have no room for pone. The
> choice was plain.–MARJORIE KINNAN RAWLINGS, *The Yearling*, p. 12

Many young people first become conscious of their native speech
when they go away to school or college. They should study their speech
if it attracts attention, but they need not abandon it just because class-
mates remark about it. They should try to find what in it is suitable and
effective and what seems to defeat easy communication. We would hate
to see everyone's speech smoothed to the colorless, placeless tones of a
network radio announcer.

Differences Between Speaking and Writing.   Basically language
is spoken; its written symbols develop long after speech is established.
We learn to speak before we learn to write, and most of us throughout
our lives will listen and speak more than we read and write. But listening and speaking, reading and writing (not to mention the even greater
use of language in "thinking," about which we know so little) are related, overlapping skills, and a serious lack in one is likely to affect the
others. In a language like English, with a voluminous amount of written
and printed material, the relations between speaking and writing are
complex and so far have not been sufficiently studied to let us discuss them
very exactly.

First we should realize that writing is a greatly simplified representation of speech. We can represent words fairly well by spelling, at least well enough for a reader to recognize them, and we can indicate some major groupings of words by punctuation, especially sentences, clauses, and the longer phrases. But the stress and slight pauses and various "tones of voice" that carry so much of our meaning in speech, qualifying, emphasizing, even sometimes reversing the meaning of the words themselves (as "Oh, I'm very fond of him" can be said so as to mean "I dislike him") cannot be directly represented on paper. This fact shows that writing is not simply a representation of speech, and it never has been. Representing speech fully on paper is a problem for linguists, who need to record it exactly for study, rather than for writers, who need to convey their meaning to readers.

There are several nonlinguistic reasons why writing has developed some characteristics of its own. Readers are often at a distance and may be strangers, with backgrounds different from the writer's. They will probably read silently, no doubt rapidly, and they will expect to find what they read in a form easy to follow. This is one reason for stressing clearness and precision in writing. Another reason is that writing lies on the page and can be examined closely, while speech goes by rapidly. This has led to establishing standards for the written language which, though they have a fairly wide range, are much more uniform than standards for speech. Most of the details of written form have been developed by printers and publishers, who naturally enough wish for consistency in what they publish, and they enforce the details through copy editors and proofreaders, who tidy up copy to meet the standards. This standardization allows for wide circulation of printed matter, one of its greatest assets. Any writer who presents his copy for others to read is expected to approach (though not to meet in every respect) these standards by writing clearly and following the most definitely established conventions of published writing.

Two of the more conspicuous differences between oral and written style are in vocabulary and sentences. The vocabulary of conversation is likely to be somewhat limited. We do not draw on our full stock of words, partly because we do not talk much about some of the subjects we write about, partly because we use phrases or clauses instead of single words (*practices that are not desirable* instead of *undesirable practices* or even *malpractices*), and partly because we can convey our meaning without very exact words. Instead of trying to find exact words in describing something or giving our opinions, we fall back on *good, bad, pleasant,* perhaps even on *nice,* and express the degree of our meaning by tone of voice, gesture, or facial expression. In writing we need more exact words to make up for lack of this support. It might be better if we used more exact words in conversation, but searching for words while we are talking is likely to take the life out of our speech and make it seem formal and aloof. Usually the added exactness of writing does not depend on rare words but just exact ones, as in this simple descriptive statement:

> At the top of the pole crouched a shivering gray kitten, mewing faintly and clinging desperately to the wood with her claws.—WILLA CATHER, *O Pioneers!* p. 5

The grammar of speech is more variable and less exact than that of writing, at least of edited, publishable writing. We use pronouns rather casually, omit prepositions (*a couple birds*), use only a few connectives, sometimes relying heavily on *and* and *so,* and yet we make ourselves clear. Many of the matters marked on student papers are simply such traits of spoken language transferred to paper. Spoken sentences are usually shorter than written, or if they are long it is because one statement is added to another rather than because clauses are built together with subordinating conjunctions. Written sentences need to show the relationship between their parts more carefully, to give the reader more guidance in following them through.

But written English is not a different language from spoken. All these differences are in relatively small matters of style that can be tended to in revising a paper. It is usually best to write nearly as you speak and then test what you have written by reading it as a stranger might, making sure that you are telling him what you mean so exactly that he can understand it without hearing you say it, and that you are in general following the conventions of printed English. The best basis for your writing is your better speech, reshaped a little so that it can stand scrutiny on paper. Some languages have entirely different forms for speech and writing, but in English, and especially in present-day English, the relationship is close. We sometimes say someone "talks like a book," meaning that his talk is uncomfortably elaborate or stiff; it is more often a compliment to say "he writes as he talks." Letters and accounts of personal experience are likely to be quite close to speech; term papers for courses and most academic work need to be in the more formal tradition of writing. It is best to be ready to use as wide a range as possible, drawing on both spoken and written English. The ideal has been put this way: "One would like to think that all of us will come to the stage of refusing to write what we would not, indeed could not, say, though that, of course, is not to limit our writing to what we actually do say." [4]

Differences Due to Use. Many words of similar meaning, though they are in current and general use, cannot be used interchangeably in all situations. Consider the following groups:

> indigent, impecunious, underprivileged, in want, penniless, poverty-stricken, *poor*, hard up, broke, flat
> spent, fatigued, weary, exhausted, *tired*, worn-out, played out, used up, dog tired, all in, pooped
> stripling, youth, lad, *boy*, youngster, kid, punk

Similarly, many idioms and constructions represent the same idea but suggest different varieties of speech:

> dare not, daren't, *do not dare*, don't dare, dassent
> were it not for, if it were not for, *if it was not for*, if it wasn't for, if it wan't for

Poor, tired, and *boy, do not dare* and *if it was not for* certainly belong to the central part of the language and might be used by anyone in any circumstance; the same is true of the words near them in these series. But as we move away from these central expressions, the words become somewhat more limited, until those at the ends would be found only in quite formal or quite informal situations. Probably most of us would not use *indigent, spent, stripling*—they suggest old-fashioned or rather bookish usage. We all might use *broke, all in, kid* in casual company but not when we were talking to someone on whom we wanted to make a good impression. These differences are due not to the meaning of the words but to the circumstances in which they have been generally used and which they suggest. That is, their quality depends on the social situations in which they have been and are predominantly used.

There is no well-established system of naming these varieties of Eng-

---

[4] Bonamy Dobrée, *Modern Prose Style* (Oxford, 1934), p. 229.

lish, though they have been often discussed.[5] In this book four principal varieties are presented, *General* English, *Formal* English, *Informal* English (the three together making up *Standard* English), and *Nonstandard* or *Vulgate* English. These varieties are defined in the table on pages 158–159, and because they are so important in everyone's judgment of his own language, they are elaborated in the next four sections of this chapter.

Although differences are easily observable between these varieties, they must not be thought of as mutually exclusive but as relatively different, shading into each other. A passage may be considered Formal because it has a few conspicuous traits characteristic of that variety, and thus a Formal "feel" or "tone," even though the language of most of the passage is in General usage. Although people's judgment of the boundaries will differ somewhat, the principal characteristics of the varieties are pretty clear, and the illustrations in the following sections should make it possible to distinguish them.

GENERAL ENGLISH—UNLIMITED USE

Most speaking and writing situations call for General English, the great central body of words and constructions of our language. In speech we find it in good conversations, in discussions, in most talks to general audiences; in writing we see it in letters, in newspapers and magazines, in plays and novels, and in books of all sorts for general circulation—in most of what we read.

General written English lies close to good speech, but it is not speech exactly reproduced, partly because the resources of the written language are somewhat different. The words are likely to be from the central vocabulary, of wide currency in both speech and writing (*roomy* rather than *spacious, rainfall* rather than *precipitation*). They are likely to be concrete, close to experience, referring to things, people, actions, and events more than to abstractions, and familiar to a large number of readers. The constructions are likely to reflect those of speech (*look*

[5] See, for instance: Bloomfield, p. 52, 149 ff.; Fries, *AEG,* in which usage is treated according to social varieties; John S. Kenyon, "Cultural Level and Functional Varieties of English," *College English,* 1948, 10:1-6; Marckwardt and Walcott; Pooley, Ch. 3.

into, give up, take over), and the sentences are relatively short, one or two clauses without interrupting phrases or involved movement.

General English is especially appropriate to narratives of personal experience and to presentation of people and action, whether in fiction or factual accounts. In the following paragraph about life on a Pacific island, the sentences are short, averaging twenty words, but not monotonous. With thirteen verbs and seven nouns or modifiers made from verbs (*cooking, cleaning, surging*), and with some phrases that suggest speech (*paddle off, right on the beach, when hungry*), the passage gives an active and immediately understandable picture.

> Life drifts along more or less becalmed in these native villages. There are no pressing duties to be done. The men paddle off to their fishing grounds when they feel like it, and when they return the catch is distributed and often eaten right on the beach without so much as cooking or cleaning the fish. The older men sit cross-legged on the sand, chipping away on logs with a kind of adz, out of which eventually they fashion their canoes. The children move around in little animated groups, surging back and forth like schools of minnows. When hungry, they tear their fish apart with fingers and teeth, or break open a coconut and gnaw the white meat out of the fragments.–DAVID BRADLEY, *No Place to Hide*, p. 161

Ideas, too, though they are by nature abstract and are often presented in Formal English for rather restricted groups of readers, may be expressed in General English. The following definition of the word *sign,* a term important in philosophical discussions of meaning, is presented concretely for general readers by a professor of philosophy. The early specific details lead to the generalization at the end. The constructions are based on verbs (*the way we will dress*), in simple, direct sentences, averaging twenty-two words. (The longest sentence, the third, is a series of clauses.)

> What do all these events have in common that causes us to lump them together as signs? One core similarity: *they all influence the way we tend to react toward something other than themselves.* The alarm tells us the time, the sight of our face in the mirror informs us about our appearance, the newspaper tells us what has happened in the world, the pressure from the oranges or the odor of eggs determines which one we will select, the note to the milkman tells him how we wish him to act. The appearance of the sky or the words of the weather report influ-

ence the way we will dress, the way we will behave outdoors. We do not
put on our raincoats indoors nor raise an umbrella between us and the
newspaper. We eat not the menu but rather what its printed words
stand for. Signs denote something other than themselves, other things
or other aspects of the thing of which they are a part. The marks on
the newspaper stand for happenings in China; the rate of our pulse
beat stands for the condition of our heart. Signs influence our beliefs,
our preferences, our feelings, our actions with respect to what they
signify. They dispose us to react to something other than themselves in
one way rather than another.–CHARLES MORRIS, from *The Open Shelf;*
reprinted with permission of Prentice-Hall, Inc.

The most likely danger of General English is flatness, though this
often comes from flat or obvious subject matter as much as from the
language. In this passage from a short story the language is a compressed
form of what we all might say (except perhaps *the world leaps into proportion*), but it has the quality of feeling that we associate with literature:

   The man who expected to be shot lay with his eyes open, staring at
the upper left-hand corner of his cell. He was fairly well over his last
beating, and they might come for him any time now. There was a yel-
low stain in the cell corner near the ceiling; he had liked it at first, then
disliked it; now he was coming back to liking it again.
   He could see it more clearly with his glasses on, but he only put on
his glasses for special occasions now—the first thing in the morning, and
when they brought the food in, and for interviews with the General.
The lenses of the glasses had been cracked in a beating some months
before, and it strained his eyes to wear them too long. Fortunately, in
his present life he had very few occasions demanding clear vision. But,
nevertheless, the accident to his glasses worried him, as it worries all
near-sighted people. You put your glasses on the first thing in the morning and the world leaps into proportion; if it does not do so, something
is wrong with the world.–STEPHEN VINCENT BENÉT, "The Blood of
the Martyrs," *Thirteen O'Clock*, p. 23

General English is hard to describe by itself, partly because its characteristics are so familiar to us, but it will become clearer by comparison
with the other varieties that follow. Obviously it has a wide range, shading off into Formal English in one direction and Informal in the other.
It is the most useful variety, without the limitations of the others, and
since it has such wide currency and in fact can reach practically all read-

ers, it is the most necessary to master, and is the proper goal of instruction.

FORMAL ENGLISH—LIMITED USE

Formal English is typically found in books and articles of mature interest, intended for circulation among a somewhat restricted group, among teachers, ministers, doctors, lawyers, and others of general or specialized intellectual interests. It is found also in addresses and other formal talks and often colors the conversation of people who do a good deal of reading, but it is more characteristic of writing than of speaking.

Although Formal English will contain a good many traits of General English, it will show enough of the Formal vocabulary and constructions to give it a definite tone. The vocabulary has many words little used in ordinary speech, specialized words from various scientific and scholarly fields and words of more general meaning associated with the literary tradition (like *desultory, ubiquitous, redoubtable*). It uses a good many abstract nouns, which summarize rather than present experience directly (*comfort, distinction, research*). For people familiar with the words, they often carry a good deal of suggestiveness (*bosky, ominous, paradox, transcend*) and often have some appeal of sound or rhythm (*quintessence, immemorial, memorable*).

In Formal English the constructions are usually filled out; short cuts characteristic of General and Informal English are not taken. Contractions are avoided, relative pronouns are not omitted, prepositions and conjunctions are likely to be repeated in parallel constructions, and so on. Sentences tend to be somewhat longer than in General writing, binding more ideas together. They may be elaborately constructed with parallel and balanced clauses, the word order may be different from the usual English pattern, and modifiers may come between the main elements of subject, verb, and object. Allusions to literature and to events of the past are as common as to current affairs.

This does not mean that Formal writing is stiff or dull, though there is danger that it may be; but the nature of the language of Formal writing makes its appeal somewhat limited. It often demands considerable concentration and presupposes in the reader an interest in specialized

Nonstandard English
(Limited use)
Chiefly spoken
Language not much touched by school instruction; often conspicuously local; not appropriate for public affairs or for use by educated people

Typical uses:
Conversations of many people at home, with friends, on the job
Representations of this speech in stories, plays, movies, comic strips, on radio and television

Informal English
(Limited use)
More often spoken than written
Speaking and writing of educated people in informal situations; often includes shoptalk or slang and some localisms

Typical uses:
Casual conversation
Letters between intimates; diaries, personal writing; writing close to popular speech, as in fiction and some newspaper columns

Comments:
1. Informal, General, and Formal English together make up Standard English.
2. The varieties are to be thought of as shading into each other—not as sharply defined and mutually exclusive. A passage might be regarded as Informal, for instance, if it had several conspicuous traits characteristic of that variety even though the greater part of the passage was in General English.
3. Usage is said to be *divided* when choices exist between two usages in General English, both of which are in good standing (for example, the spellings *catalog* or *catalogue,* or a comma or no comma before the *and* of the last item in a series).
4. *Slovenly* (impoverished speech, often including obscenity and pro-

Varieties of English

General English (Unlimited use) *Both spoken and written* Speaking and writing of educated people in their private or public affairs	Formal English (Limited use) *More often written than spoken* Speaking and writing for somewhat restricted groups in formal situations
Typical uses: Conversation; talks to general audiences Most business letters and advertising News and feature stories, newspaper columns Magazine articles and books on subjects of general interest Most fiction and other literature for general circulation	*Typical uses:* Addresses and lectures to special audiences Some editorials and business writing Literature of somewhat limited circulation: essays and criticisms, much poetry, some fiction Academic writing: reference works, dissertations, term papers, some textbooks Scientific and technical reports Books and articles dealing with special subjects for professional groups and experts

fanity) may be regarded as the extreme of Nonstandard and *Stilted* (pretentious and unnecessarily heavy speech or writing—"gobbledygook") may be regarded as the extreme of Standard English.

5. The varieties are characterized by some differences in word forms, in pronunciation, in vocabulary, in grammatical constructions, and by the avoidance of certain locutions (as Standard English avoids double negatives). The chief differences, and the easiest to discuss, are in vocabulary.

6. Labeling a usage as belonging to any one of the varieties is meant to indicate that it is characteristically used as the description of that variety suggests, that its connotation comes from this use, and that it is not characteristic of another variety. Such labeling is not intended to prevent a word's use under other conditions but does suggest that it may be conspicuous in another variety and that its connotation should be intended.

subject matter or in general ideas and some awareness of our cultural tradition. The special audience for which it is written will not only follow the material but, if it is really well expressed, will appreciate the style as well. To some readers, one appeal of Formal English is its very difference from everyday language.

Two examples will show some of the traits of Formal English. In the first, from an impersonal, scientific book on some psychological aspects of painting, the sentences average twenty-four words in length, but though they combine several facts, they move directly. The chief Formal trait is the vocabulary. Some of the words are essential to the subject (*expressive appearance, perceptual classification*), and others are not likely to be used by the average person, although he understands them (*spontaneously, animate, inanimate, dynamics, manifest*). *Linnean classification* is an allusion to a system of botanical classification.

> Some objects and events resemble each other with regard to the underlying patterns of forces; others do not. Therefore on the basis of their expressive appearance, our eye spontaneously creates a kind of Linnean classification of all things existing. This perceptual classification cuts across the order suggested by other kinds of categories. Particularly in our modern Western civilization we are accustomed to distinguishing between animate and inanimate things, human and non-human creatures, the mental and the physical. But in terms of expressive qualities, the character of a given person may resemble that of a particular tree more closely than that of another person. The state of affairs in a human society may be similar to the tension in the skies just before the outbreak of a thunderstorm. Further, our kind of scientific and economic thinking makes us define things by measurements rather than by the dynamics of appearance. Our criteria for what is useful or useless, friendly or hostile, have tended to sever the connections with outer expression, which they possess in the minds of children or primitives. If a house or a chair suits our practical purposes, we may not stop to find out whether its appearance expresses our style of living. In business relations we define a man by his census data, his income, age, position, nationality, or race—that is, by categories that ignore the inner nature of the man as it is manifest in his outer expression.– RUDOLPH ARNHEIM, *Art and Visual Perception*, pp. 368-9

In a somewhat more personal way, the second passage presents an important idea of social development. The words carry a good deal of force and suggestiveness (*high* in a special sense, *guardians of culture, time-honored, outrage*), and some are of rather restricted currency (*occupational disease, disparate, diverse*). Most of the meaning is carried by nouns and adjectives. The sentences are longer, averaging thirty-seven words, but their parts are closely and naturally related.

> All such perversions of high traditions are intensified by traditionalism, the occupational disease of guardians of culture. The guardians tend to forget that tradition has always been the great enemy of the founders of great traditions: that Socrates was a radical who did corrupt the youth of Athens by impiously urging them to question the time-honored ways; or that the teachings of Christ were an outrage to precisely the most cultivated, respectable, God-fearing people of his time; or that the American Revolution was strictly a revolution, illegal, violent, and bloody. In particular, the traditionalists abuse our Western heritage by singling out some one school of thought as the 'essential' or 'true' tradition; whereas diversity and nonconformity are the very soul of this heritage. It is the richest tradition that man has ever known simply because it includes so many disparate elements from diverse sources, and has never been at rest.–HERBERT J. MULLER, *The Uses of the Past*, p. 58

There are some conspicuously formal types within Formal English. Some highly individual styles in literature require detailed study to be understood because of the unusual use of words and the uniquely personal associations of words as well as various departures from the typical patterns of current English. In the quite different styles characteristic of scholarly and scientific writing at its best, a precise and specialized vocabulary is employed in a compact, impersonal statement. And beyond these are abuses of Formal English: the cumbersome, archaic, and highly repetitious language of most legal documents, and the pretentious, abstract, and equally repetitious style of some bad academic writing and of much of the official writing of government and business, popularly and appropriately known as gobbledygook.

But as the two paragraphs just quoted show, Formal English often presents important and illuminating ideas worth thinking about. The ability to read Formal English is a requirement for educated people and one of the abilities to be cultivated in college. Although a good deal of writing is more Formal, or at least more difficult, than it needs to be, we have to face the fact that our intellectual growth demands its mastery. In some college writing, as in term papers for advanced courses, the writing is appropriately Formal, though it should not be excessively so, never to the extent of seeming affected. A development toward somewhat more Formal expression will naturally come with increased experience in reading college-level material.

INFORMAL ENGLISH—LIMITED USE

Informal English is at the other side of General English and grades off into Nonstandard English. When we write for our own convenience or amusement or when we talk or write to members of our family or to friends, we use English with more freedom than when addressing strangers or people with whom we are only slightly acquainted. When Informal English is used publicly, it presupposes a regular relationship of some sort between user and receiver; it may be used in a recurring radio program or newspaper column, or for a distinctly informal situation or subject: amusing little experiences, comment on social foibles, sports, humor.

Informal English has considerable range, sometimes including distinctly Formal traits for contrast or Nonstandard forms for accuracy or novelty. Most conspicuously it uses words and phrases characteristic of familiar conversation, words often marked *Colloquial* in dictionaries or not recorded at all (*comeuppance, in-laws, digger-upper, arty, doohickey*); or words of special currency at the moment (*do-it-yourself, egghead, gung ho, run-around* as a noun); informal coinages for common things or situations (*emcee, boy friend, dog sit* on the analogy of *baby sit*); clipped words (*decal, hi-fi, prefab*). It may include more localisms than General English ordinarily would, shoptalk (words from occupations like *mike, hypo, close-up*), and slang, words continually being formed and given a temporary currency in offhand or flashy speech: *date bait, draft bait, blooper, bobble, boo-boo, fluff*. Since writer and reader usually have a good deal in common, much can be taken for granted—in material, in allusion to common experiences, and in the special current connotation of words.

The carelessness we sometimes permit ourselves in writing letters is not a legitimate characteristic of Informal English, which has its chief use in lively conversation and in some writing where the subject and situation warrant a light touch, as in this columnist's comment on the prevalence of candle heating devices for the table:

Gone are the days when a man got his coffee all saucered and blowed and at the right temperature, only to have the latter drop so rapidly that the beverage was stone cold by the time he got his handle-bar mustache parted and ready. . . . Now a man saucers and blows the stuff and puts it on a little iron cradle over a lighted candle, where the brew starts boiling once more in nothing flat. Then he has to begin all over again. It's going to be hard on commuters until they get the hang of the new gimmick. . . . The ironmonger is jubilant and the fire insurance companies will be as soon as they get hep to this situation and jack up the rates. It makes for a nice, lively business cycle, with the boys at the firehouse scarce able to get through a checker game before the siren sounds again.—INEZ ROBB, "Candle Is Remarkable Invention," *Seattle Post-Intelligencer*, Feb. 6, 1954, p. 11

General, Formal, and Informal English together make up what is known as *Standard English*. Standard English presents, then, a wide range of usage, offering a writer many choices of words and constructions—choices which in any given paper will set its tone and define its possible audience. Some principles to guide these choices will be discussed in the last section of this chapter.

The basis of Standard English is social, the "differences due to use" described on pages 153–154. Its basis has been well described by Professor Fries:

On the whole, however, if we ignore the special differences that separate the speech of New England, the South, and the Middle West, we do have in the United States a set of language habits, broadly conceived, in which the major matters of the political, social, economic, educational, religious life of this country are carried on. To these language habits is attached a certain social prestige, for the use of them suggests that one has constant relations with those who are responsible for the important affairs of our communities. It is this set of language habits, derived originally from an older London English, but differentiated from it somewhat by its independent development in this country, which is the "standard" English of the United States. Enough has been said to enforce the point that it is "standard" not because it is any more correct or more beautiful or more capable than other varieties of English; it is "standard" solely because it is the particular type of English which is used in the conduct of the important affairs of our people. It is also the type of English used by the *socially acceptable* of most of our communities and insofar as that is true it has become a social or class dialect in the United States.—C. C. FRIES, *American English Grammar*, p. 13

The attention given to encouraging the use of Standard English in schools and colleges is intended to help young people prepare themselves to take their part in public affairs, to speak and write for educated people, and so to continue or broaden their range of possible social contacts. Writing in composition courses is practice for later work in college and after college.

NONSTANDARD ENGLISH—LIMITED USE

The everyday speech of many people, relatively untouched by school instruction or by the tradition of printed English, makes up Nonstandard or Vulgate English, the name popularized by H. L. Mencken in *The American Language* and given in *Webster's International Dictionary* as the third sense of *vulgate*.[6] This speech variety is a very real and important part of the English language and is studied by linguists with the same seriousness with which they study other varieties. It is not made up of lapses from any brand of reputable or Standard English but is a different development from the same language stock, representing a selection of sounds, words, forms, and constructions made under different social conditions. It works very well in carrying on the private affairs and occupations of millions of people and is consequently worthy of study and respect. Its avoidance in business, government, or literature is due to social rather than to linguistic causes. It is not ordinarily printed, since, for various historical and social reasons, the printed language is a selection of words, forms, and constructions considered appropriate to public affairs and so to Standard English.

Nonstandard English is most conspicuously different from the other chief varieties of English in the use of pronoun and verb forms and in the freer use of localisms. Many of its words have a longer history in English than the more genteel words that have replaced them in "society." Many of the forms and constructions have a continuous history back to a time when they were reputable: Chaucer could use a double negative occasionally; *ant* (*are not*) and *he don't* were reputable until less than a century ago; what is popularly referred to as "dropping the *g*" in verb forms spelled with *-ing* is a continuation of

[6] See Leonard Bloomfield, "Literate and Illiterate Speech," *American Speech,* 1927, 2:432-9; Fries, *AEG;* Mencken.

an original participle ending. Many other features of Nonstandard English are equally natural developments of the language that by some accident or dialect or other circumstance did not become adopted in Standard English.

Nonstandard English is primarily spoken. Its forms (like *ain't, dassent, scairt, you was*) are not particularly conspicuous when we hear them spoken rapidly and with appropriate, not exaggerated, emphasis. They appear in many radio and television programs, in plays, and in the conversation of stories. You will find them, often intensified, in many comic strips. Occasionally a Nonstandard form is used in humor or for special effect, as in Josh Billings' epigram: "It isn't so much the ignorance of mankind that makes them ridiculous as knowing so many things that ain't so."

The monolog of the barber in Ring Lardner's story "Haircut" is a fairly accurate representation of Nonstandard. A few traits of pronunciation are shown (though the *of* in "she'd of divorced him" has no relation to the preposition *of* but is the spelling of the normal contraction of *have*—"she'd've divorced him"), adverbs without the *-ly* ending, *seen* for *saw, beat her to it,* and so on.

> Jim didn't work very steady after he lost his position with the Carterville people. What he did earn, doin' odd jobs round town, why he spent pretty near all of it on gin, and his family might of starved if the stores hadn't of carried them along. Jim's wife tried her hand at dressmakin', but they ain't nobody goin' to get rich makin' dresses in this town.
>
> As I say, she'd of divorced Jim, only she seen that she couldn't support herself and the kids and she was always hopin' that some day Jim would cut out his habits and give her more than two or three dollars a week.
>
> They was a time when she would go to whoever he was workin' for and ask them to give her his wages, but after she done this once or twice, he beat her to it by borrowin' most of his pay in advance. He told it all round town, how he had outfoxed his Missus. He certainly was a caution.—RING LARDNER, "Haircut," *Roundup*, p. 25

Schools carry on their work in the language of the upper social classes, Standard English. Students who go into the professions, into many branches of business, and into most white-collar jobs continue to use Standard English more or less consistently. Those who go into manual labor and the less well-paid and less socially elevated jobs often return to the use of Nonstandard English. Naturally and necessarily, though, speech is gradually losing many of its Nonstandard traits because of the increased number of white-collar jobs, the greater number of contacts between white-collar and other workers, and the increasing effects of education.

In the lower schools, where pupils are likely to be in daily contact with Nonstandard speech, it forms a serious problem. This is seldom true at the college level, though the speech of many college students is cruder than their social standing would warrant and is consequently a poor background for their writing.

The objection to this variety is not that its grammar is "bad," but that Nonstandard words and constructions are not appropriate to the readers for whom college students and college graduates write or to the subjects they are handling. Complex ideas and dignified subjects cannot be discussed adequately in the vocabulary of Nonstandard English. Nonstandard is necessary in writing the conversation of many characters in stories, or at least it should be approximated, and it should be used occasionally to give a note of realism to portraits of real people who naturally speak it. But most other uses are inappropriate in college writing. When an expression in this book is marked "Nonstandard," it should not be used except for good reason. Many Nonstandard practices are discussed in the next two chapters.

WHAT IS GOOD ENGLISH?

To a student of language, all varieties of English are equally a part of the language, and one variety is to be observed and studied as much as another. But to a *user* of English the varieties are by no means equal. They differ in the impression they make on people and in the sort of ideas they can communicate.

Every educated person naturally wants to speak and write what may be called "Good English," just as he wants to "make a good personal appearance" and to "be intelligent." But the great range and diversity of the English language raises numerous questions about usage. The problem of English usage is much like the problems which face us in almost everything we do that comes under the eyes of others, in our manners, in the jokes we tell, in our food, in our living quarters, in our political ideas. In dress, to take the most convenient parallel, we gradually develop something we call taste or judgment, in part by imitating others, consciously or unconsciously, in part by consulting people who are supposed to know what is good form, in part by following our own preferences in design and color and fabric. Our usual dress lies between the extremes of work, sport, and formal clothes. It is comfortable; it reflects something of the taste of the wearer; it is appropriate to going about personal affairs, to work in stores and offices, to college classes, to informal social affairs. But a person needs to have and to be able to wear several kinds of clothes, and he needs to know for what occasion each is appropriate. In the same way, anyone who is going to take his place in public, business, or social affairs needs to know the resources of the various sorts of English and when they can profitably be drawn on. For answers to questions about English usage, you can often consult books, especially dictionaries and handbooks. You can ask people who write well; you can ask teachers who have made the study of the language part of their professional training. And you can always be watching what effective writers do—how the language is handled in the better books and magazines. This observation is especially important, because, as in dress and in manners, more or less conscious imitation of those you approve of or wish to be associated with will bulk large in forming your own habits. Few will ever write with real ease unless they listen and read a good deal and so unconsciously absorb the ways of their language by direct experience.

Basis of Good English Set by the Purpose of Communication. Of course, anyone may talk to himself or write for his own amusement, relief, or "self-expression"; or he may wish to deceive or puzzle, and then his usage is his own affair. And a writer may experiment as much as he wishes, as James Joyce and Gertrude Stein and others have done, creating for themselves a limited audience willing to study out their meaning in spite of handicaps. But the ordinary and principal function of language is effective communication, making someone understand or feel something, or getting him to do something that we want him to do.

This fundamental purpose in speaking and writing prevents usage, complicated as it is, from falling into chaos, and sets the broad limits of Good English. We use words in the meanings they have acquired from their past use, and we try to make our statements in understandable patterns. From this point of view, Professor Fries defines the basis of Good English:

> . . . language is a means to an end and that end is specifically to grasp, to possess, to communicate experience. Accordingly, that is good language, good English, which, on the one hand, most fully realizes one's own impressions, and, on the other, is most completely adapted to the purposes of any particular communication.–C. C. FRIES, *What Is Good English?* p. 120

In other words, so far as the writer's language furthers his intended effect, it is good; so far as it fails to further that effect, it is bad, no matter how "correct" it may be.[7]

Since Good English is English that serves the definite intention of a person to communicate something to another person or group, the answer to most questions of usage can be found by considering the appropriateness of the word or expression to the immediate purpose. This appropriateness is threefold: to the subject and situation, to the expected listeners or readers, and to the writer or speaker himself. Considering these will yield *principles,* rather than *rules,* to guide actual usage.

Appropriateness to Subject and Situation.   In conversation we automatically adjust our language as well as our topics to the situation in which we find ourselves. Similarly, our talks and papers, whether they are assigned or voluntary, should have a suitable tone. The language of an informational paper for a popular audience will be somewhat different from that of the discussion of an idea or from that of a plea for action or even from a talk for a general audience. The tone of the language depends chiefly on the variety of English used.

Good judgment in choosing the variety of English is one of the signs of a practiced and mature writer. Slang may fit in a letter or in a popular newspaper column; it is usually out of place in discussing a serious or elevated subject. Most fiction is General or Informal. Writing on a technical or professional subject is more likely to be Formal. The language of a church service and of religious and philosophical discussion is Formal.

Students—all writers, for that matter, who try for language appropriate to subject and situation—come at last to the same resolve: *to treat simple subjects simply,* or, in terms of our varieties of English, to treat them in General English. Most subjects are relatively simple,

---

[7] Fries, *AEG,* Ch. 1 (an unusually good statement); Fries, *The Teaching of English* (Ann Arbor, 1949), Ch. 5; Otto Jespersen, *Mankind, Nation and Individual from a Linguistic Point of View* (Oslo, 1925), Ch. 5; Pooley, Part I.

He shouldn't exclude the desire to be humorous (à la S.J. Perelman, say) as a factor here.

or at least the writer is going to give only a simplified version of them. Much of their interest is lost when the language is Formal. Amateur writers are often not content to be themselves but assume a dialect that is really foreign to them, too Formal to be appropriate to their subjects. A boy with a few shrewd remarks to make on modern suicides began this way:

> Through the ages, people have been accustomed to making a premature departure from this "vale of tears" by manifold means. Some favored hanging or a certain type of strangulation; others have been partial to poison, gunshot, or any of a variety of other methods.
>
> However, during recent years a radical change has occurred in the gentle art of self-elimination. This has been due in a large part to the advent of tall buildings. They are seemingly attracted by a strange fascination for the height in combination with a desire to put a spectacular end to their relation with this world.

He may seriously have believed that this kind of writing was better than saying in some simple way that hanging, poisoning, and shooting have given way to jumping off tall buildings, and then going directly into his subject. He might even object to being told that his sentences were bad English, worse perhaps than if they had contained actual Nonstandard expressions. Such errors could be quite easily corrected, but his inflated and pompous paragraphs must be completely rewritten to be acceptable.

Students should also avoid writing too Informally in papers which discuss serious subjects. But the better students in a composition course often err in the direction of overly Formal writing, probably because of the emphasis on Formal correctness throughout their school careers.

Teachers and students will not always agree in their judgments of particular passages, though they will agree on a surprising number of them. But once students understand the principle of appropriateness they will never again return either to unnecessary pomposity or to unsuitable lightness. They will soon come to appreciate the simple appropriateness of this account of an interview with a dean:

> "I guess you're next, son," he said, motioning me into his office. Walking to a chair he had pointed out beside his desk, I sat down. "Well," he said, leaning way back in his swivel chair with his hands folded across his waist, "what seems to be your trouble?" "The trouble,

sir, is that I have a couple of F's as you already know." He didn't smile so I was sorry I said that. Pulling out my deficiency report from a pile on his desk he read it with frowning eye-brows. Looking up at me he said, "How much studying have you been doing?" "Practically none, sir," I said in a weak cracking voice. Laying down the report he started in on a long speech on studying. He looked me straight in the eye and I tried to glare back at him but couldn't. I shook my head every once in a while and said, "That's right," to show him that I was listening. He went on to explain how I should make out a time schedule and stick to it, how I should write out notes on little cards and carry them around with me so that I could review them at spare moments, outline this and outline that. Go to your professors and ask them for suggestions—they'll tell you how and what to study, get your tutor to help you. After he had finished, he got up, slapped me on the back and said, "So, son, get down to work and you'll pull through all right." "Thank you, sir, and good-day," I said as I rushed out of the office. Back to my room I slowly plodded, hands shoved deep in my pockets, chin on my chest, feeling very guilty indeed. Slumping into my chair I lit my pipe and began to think. "Gotta get down to work," I thought. "Guess I'll start—next week."

The tone of a passage should be consistent unless the writer has special reason for departing from it. The lines between the varieties of English cannot be drawn precisely, but a conspicuous lapse from Formal to Informal or from Informal to Formal should ordinarily be avoided. These examples show obvious and awkward lapses:

> Formal to Informal: If our Concert and Lecture program this year is not superior to that of any other college in the country, *I'll eat every freshman lid on the campus.*
> Informal to Formal: *I was bowled over* by the speed with which the workmen assembled the parts.

Some writing—in *The New Yorker,* for example, and in many newspaper columns—fuses distinctly Informal words with quite Formal ones. The expressions are unified by the vigor and smoothness with which they are brought together and are not lapses from appropriateness. Consistency is not so important as the fundamental appropriateness to the situation. But, in general, one variety of English should be kept throughout a piece of writing.

Both in a composition course and out of one, keep a Formal style for complex or scholarly subjects and an Informal style for light or humorous ones; write in General English on most matters. If you know the variety of English that is appropriate for the piece of writing you are doing, this advice is relatively easy to follow. You can settle for yourself most problems of appropriateness to subject and situation simply by considering what the usual tone is in such articles.

Appropriateness to Listener or Reader. If you are trying to reach a particular type of reader, you will adjust both your subject matter and your expression to him. To reach him, to really get your points across, you have to be more than merely intelligible: you have to meet him pretty much on his own ground. You already do this automatically in your letters, writing in somewhat different ways to different persons. You no doubt adjust your expression to the expectations of different teachers. Certainly in many other situations you pay some attention to the language you believe is expected of you.

Some types of writing are in theory completely adjusted to their readers, notably directions to be followed, newspaper writing, and advertising. Although we realize that they often fail, either from cheapness or from dullness and unintended Formality, in a general way they do meet their readers' expectations.

Themes are sometimes difficult to write because you lose the sense of having a reader. It is better to try to visualize some particular audience, to direct your paper to some magazine, or, more commonly, to write for the class of which you are a member. Directing your paper to the members of your class will help you select material that will interest and inform them or at least will appeal to a certain part of the group, and it will help you judge what words and what kinds of sentences are appropriate. Remember that you are not writing for everyone but for a selected audience. Novels are for readers of differing tastes, and even the audiences of best sellers like *The Robe* and *The Wall* were not identical. For practice work in which you can choose your style, a firm General one is probably best, for many people prefer it and anyone can be reached through it.

CLEARNESS. Since your aim is to convey some fact or opinion or fancy or feeling to a person or a group, appropriateness to a reader means clear expression. This means exact words and, for the most part, words that lie within the knowledge of the person you are addressing. If the subject requires words that may not be familiar to him, their meaning can usually be made clear from the way they are used. If not, you can throw in a tactful explanation or in extreme instances resort to formal definition.

Clarity also requires careful sentence construction. Experienced readers can take more elaborate sentences than those who read little or who read hurriedly. But anyone will be pleased with direct, straight-forward sentences. Matters of clarity should be carefully checked in revision.

CORRECTNESS. A large part of a beginning writer's adaptation to a reader is avoiding errors that might attract unfavorable attention. People tend to judge us by superficial traits, in language as in other matters. Spelling, for example, bulks larger in most people's judgment of writing than it reasonably should. Certainly many people take delight in finding what are (or what they consider to be) errors in language, especially in the writing or speech of those supposed to be educated or of anyone soliciting their favor. Courtesy demands that a writer should do his best in anything he is submitting to another: soiled manuscript, many interlineations, confusion of common forms like *its* and *it's,* mis-spelling of common words (*similiar* for *similar*) are ordinarily the result of carelessness or thoughtlessness. The chief reason for mastering the "minimum essentials" of English forms is to meet the expectations of educated readers. You should not worry about these matters as you write, but you should reserve some time for revision to bring the paper to the best state you are capable of.

LIVELINESS. There is so much unavoidable dullness in the world that any reader will appreciate some liveliness in writing, in the expression as well as in the material. Striving for novelty is dangerous, and its results are often self-defeating. But students frequently hide behind a flat sort of language, squeezing all the life out of their writing until it sounds as though it was written by someone three times their age. Your words need not be out of the ordinary, just those that might be used in an active conversation. Your sentences should not be formless or dragged out; they should suggest an alert interest. Refer to things people do and say, use plenty of lively detail to demonstrate ideas and to keep up inter-est, and pay special attention to the beginnings and endings of your papers.

Some professional writers have set themselves the rule "Don't write anything you couldn't read yourself." Following this principle means that you will choose your best available material, write it as interest-ingly as you can, and make it genuinely readable. If you promise yourself that you won't turn in a paper that you couldn't read yourself with interest and perhaps profit, you will be accepting responsibility for your work, doing composition of actual college grade—and you will be permanently improving your control of expression, laying a sure foundation for continued growth in Good English.

In general, satisfy your reader's expectations insofar as you believe they are worthy of respect. One warning is needed: Don't aim at your reader's worst, compromising yourself and insulting him. Visualize him in his better moments and write for him as he is then.

Appropriateness to Speaker or Writer. In the speaker-listener or writer-reader relationship, the speaker or writer actually dominates. He makes the choices; his judgment or unconscious sense of fitness finally controls. Your language in the long run represents your personality, and you are finally responsible for the language you use. To take this responsibility you first need to make every effort to inform yourself of the possibilities of the English language by observing what is actually spoken and written, by using dictionaries and other reference works, and by consulting people who have studied English as a language. Then you can apply this information in your own work according to your best judgment. There is nothing mysterious about the matter; it is just a natural process of learning and applying what is learned.

The most important step in beginning to improve your language habits is to watch your own speech and writing to see what their good qualities are and what shortcomings they may have. Can you confidently pronounce the words you need in conversation or recitation? Does your language tend to be Formal, or is it predominantly Informal or General? Do you rely too much on slang or on trite words, or do you lapse into Nonstandard expressions? When you talk or write to someone older than yourself or when you write a paper for a college course, do you choose the best part of your natural language, or do you assume an entirely different sort of English?

And, finally, is the language you use consistent with the rest of your conduct? If you are a rather casual person, informal in dress and manner, we should expect your English also to be somewhat Informal; if you are conventional in dress and manner, we should expect your English to be more Formal. It is necessary for you also to realize the direction in which you are moving, for young people, especially in college, are changing, becoming more flexible in their ideas and manners or more positive and conventional, or making some other change. Their language should be moving similarly. In your first papers in a composition course you should write as naturally as you can, so that both you and your instructor can see the present state of your language and so that you can decide together on the direction your growth should take. Such growth will in part be in the direction of increased sincerity, of greater appropriateness to yourself.

As a result of this approach to Good English you should have confidence in writing. The greatest handicap in writing is fear—fear of pencil and paper, fear of making a mistake, fear of offending the reader's (teacher's) taste. The opposite attitude, cockiness, is a nuisance and is equally at odds with good writing, but not so many students suffer from that as from inhibitions about their language. As yet psychologists can't tell us much about the mental activity involved in thinking or writing, but some of them believe that the fundamental condition for effectiveness is a positive feeling of readiness—which amounts really to a sort of faith that when you prepare to write, language appropriate to the occasion will come. A wide knowledge of the possibilities of current English, backed up by sufficient practice in writing for definite readers and sufficient care in revision, should increase your confidence. Only with such confidence can you write your best and give that extra something that places your writing above mere competence, that makes it really Good English.

It is obvious that the three sorts of appropriateness here suggested for arriving at Good English (appropriateness to the subject and situation, to the listener or reader, and to the writer or speaker) will not always be in harmony. When they conflict, the solution will have to come through the writer's judgment. The subject may seem to demand words that are not appropriate to the reader. The writer can usually solve such a problem either by finding simpler words or by explaining the necessary but unfamiliar ones. The reader's expectation and the writer's natural manner of expression may be different. Such a conflict can be solved by the writer—deciding how essential to his purpose his own turns of expression are, whether he can honorably yield to the reader's expectation or whether his usage is so necessary to his sense of the subject that compromise is impossible. In the long run the writer's sense of fitness, his pride in his work, will resolve most such conflicts.

Good English, then, is not primarily a matter of rules but of judgment. You are not struggling under a series of prohibitions; you are trying to discover among the magnificent resources of modern English what best suits your purposes. Your desire to communicate something is fundamental; it sets the limits beyond which you will not ordinarily go. This general limitation is made more specific by considering whether the variety of usage and the particular expressions are appropriate to the subject and the situation, to your expected readers, and, finally and most important, to yourself.

WILSON FOLLETT

From The Atlantic Monthly, *CCV* (*February, 1960*), *73-76. Copyright, 1960, by the Atlantic Monthly Company. By permission of the Atlantic Monthly Company and the author.*

Bargain Basement English

Linguistic scholarship, once an encouragement to the most exacting definitions and standards of workmanship, has for some time been dedicating itself to the abolition of standards; and the new rhetoric evolved under its auspices is an organized assumption that language good enough for anybody is good enough for everybody. We have come into a time when the ideals preached and, sometimes, practiced by exalted authority can only take shape in uses of English that are at best tolerable and at worst revolting. Such official pressure as is now put on the young learner is no longer in the direction of forcing him to ask himself whether his way of saying something could have been made better at a bearable cost— as, in a language so rich and various as ours, it generally could have. Everything now taught him concentrates on the lowly question, Will it do at a pinch?

For the handiest possible conspectus of what the new ideal is, one can do no better than to glance at a recent comprehensive manual of rhetorical practice. *A Dictionary of Contemporary American Usage,* by Bergen Evans and Cornelia Evans, comes from authors of prestige and influence, one of them a university professor of English and conductor of a radio and television program devoted to questions of spoken and written usage, the other a writing consultant in the Department of Health, Education, and Welfare and a prize-winning novelist. The reason for turning to this 570-page, 600,000-word volume is not that its publisher proclaims it to be "up-to-date, complete, authoritative"—an assertion of three attributes inherently unattainable by any such work compiled by mortals—but rather that it is declared with strict accuracy to be "based on modern linguistic scholarship." It is essentially a popularization of findings about modern English arrived at and promulgated by contemporary philologists, semanticists, virtuosos of historical and descriptive (as opposed to prescriptive) grammar and morphophonetics, and learnedly implacable assailants of the discarded idea that to speak or write well means hard work, the taking of sometimes painful thought, the constant rejection of labor- and thought-saving alternatives, and the practice of canons that are mastered only by arduous self-cultivation and discipline.

The Evanses manage to convey, along with many shrewd discriminations and salutary warnings often very engagingly phrased, an over-all impression that acceptable usages are arrived at by a process about as automatic as breathing; that to torment oneself with questions of better and not so good is to be a seeker after gratuitous trouble and, what is worse, a purist; and that the way to attain effective expression is to keep our ears open, bank on our natural and inescapable linguistic inheritance, and cultivate an English that will make us indistinguishable from the ostensibly educated surrounding majority. Let us see where anyone will come out if he accepts and applies the combination of what these authors recommend, what they defend or condone, and what they do themselves. He will come out speaking and writing an American English faithfully represented by the scattering that follows:

"Ask whoever you see." "He had as much or more trouble than I did." "He works faster than me"; "he is taller than me." "More unique." "Different than." "The reason is because. . . ." "I can't imagine it being him." "Let's you and I"; "let's you and me." "Bob as well as Frank were there." "Neither D. nor A. are at home"; "neither he nor I are timid"; "either of them are enough to drive a man to distraction"; "neither of them had their tickets"; "I do not think either of them are at home"; "each carried their own pack"; "each of the men were willing to contribute." "Every member brings their own lunch"; "either the boy or the girl left their book." "I cannot help but think." "Nobody was killed, were they?" "Less than three." "If one loses his temper." "We did not find a one." "The sheriff with all his men were at the door." "Not one of them were listening." "Some grammarians claim that this is not permissible." "He allowed that we were right." "Refer back to." "Back of" (behind). "Between each house"; "between every pause." "He blamed it on me." "I haven't but a minute to spare." "I don't doubt but that you are surprised." "Who did you see?" "Who are you looking for?" "Children whom we know are hungry." "Everyplace"; "anyplace"; "someplace"; "someway"; "noplace"; "I have looked everyplace." "It is not I who is angry." "These kind of men are dangerous." "You don't know Nellie like I do." "It is you who will be blamed for it, not them." "That's her at the door now." "A minimum of sufficiency." "We most always go shopping on Saturday." "Very amused." "Overly cautious." "Datas"; "phenomenas"; "much data"; "very little data"; "the data is now in." "I asked him what was he doing." "The rationale for his attack on the President." "As regards." "Somebody left their umbrella." "I will get one someway." "There will only be him left." "Subsequent to his release from the Air Force he got a job with a commercial air line." "A continuous use [of a word in a specified way] is vulgar." "He went no further than Philadelphia." "Neither of these reasons justify the use of the present tense." "He failed, due to carelessness."

This little anthology could be several times multiplied from the same source; thus much will do to imply a general pattern. Some of the specimens are patently better, or less bad, than others. Say of the whole, if you wish: "Some of it might be worse." There is no point in using a microscope on the gradations or on the merits of the arguments used to defend this locution or that. It is enough if we perceive—as we cannot very well escape doing—that collectively they define a stratum of diction that invites defense and seems to require it, one that it is now fashionable to defend with all the resources of specialized learning. No one could possibly contemplate any such handful and then declare its components above challenge and in no need of condoning; no one could associate them with an unremitting effort to discover and to utilize the best that our common language is capable of. A collection of the same size could hardly vary much from this one if it deliberately set out to specialize in the marginal, the dubious, the suspect. What it seems to represent is the pattern of habits deliberately adopted by the educated when they set out to show that they are no better than anyone else, if as good. It goes to show the lengths to which we can carry conformism and the terror of being noticeable in a society that is (as Bierce said of the republic long before H. L. Mencken was heard of) daft with democracy and sick with sin.

If anyone wanted to execute a piece of writing that would be from beginning to end the densest possible concentration of what the elder rhetoricians classified as solecisms, he could hardly do better than to attune his prose to the dicta laid down in *A Dictionary of Contemporary American Usage*. The book is an astute, artful, and tireless harvesting of whatever in American speech is barely tolerable to those who do not make a virtue of pushing either tolerance or intolerance to pathological extremes. And it is a translation into practical advice of what the most erudite philologists and lexicographers have for some time been telling us about the sources of health and vitality in our language. The great nuclear principle seems to be that we should speak and write not as well as we can learn how, but ignobly enough to escape notice.

Now, a resort to this kind of first aid may result in some tactical advantage to the purveyor of insurance or real estate, the chairman of a fund-raising campaign, the soapbox orator, the candidate for minor office. Even that advantage can be doubted: there seems to be a fairly powerful undertow of envious popular respect for the man who uses language with easy distinction, provided that he does it in quiet assurance with no air of showing off or of spitting on his hearers to see if they can swim, as the rude old Yankee folk saying has it. An instance is the standing that ex-Governor Adlai Stevenson seems to have with all classes of his fellow countrymen, whether they applaud his political opinions or not. But whatever the practical momentary advantages of slovenly diction, what is its long-range bearing on education, on the language itself, on its literature? Will, say, two or three consecutive generations of calculated effort to speak and write without excellence enhance the prospect of our producing an Irving, a Hawthorne, a Melville, a Henry James, a Howells, a Sarah Orne Jewett, a Willa Cather? Or will it tend to blight that prospect? Did the virtue of English prose, from Sir Thomas Browne and the King James translators to Bernard Shaw, come out of the acceptance of language on the permissive or lowest-common-denominator basis—out of a preoccupation with what was tolerable, what could barely be endured in default of better?

Is it not one of the shames of modern scholarship that it has so little to say for what is really good, what is best, and so much to say for what is merely allowable or defensible? Scholarship is trying, of course, to discount the factor of taste as nonscientific; but is it scientific to discount it? Taste is the faculty of criticism, the faculty of intelligent choice; and to it belongs the last word about any given use of language. After all, the argument from usage carries only a permissive force, not a mandatory one. Even if it were possible to prove an overwhelming preponderance for "He failed, due to carelessness" and "You don't know Nellie like I do," the proof could mean only that one may use these expressions without being condemned. There would be nothing to say that anyone has to use them, and all of us would still have the freedom of "His failure was due to carelessness" or "Carelessness caused him to fail" and "You don't know Nellie as I do" or "the way I do," which will never raise any problems or any eyebrows.

Nobody is under compulsion to like a construction just because it exists or to use it if he does not like it. This is a principle that applies equally to present and to past usages. We have the whole range of linguistic resources at our disposal; and there is no virtue in flirting with ways of expression that we think dubious or inferior when there are alternative ways—as there always are—to which no exception can be taken. The formation of any style, even a bad one, is an affair of constant acceptances and rejections; and everyone has to lean on his own taste for acceptance of the better and rejection of the worse.

The discussion of usage was probably never shrouded in more fog than it is now. Those who want to fling wide the gates to all manner of laxity maintain firmly that change is the great inescapable law, that the only criterion is what people are doing with language *now,* and they can find no words severe enough for resistance to change, especially when resistance takes the form of quoting classic sources; but if they can unearth in Chaucer or Wycliffe or Donne or Hazlitt some parallel to whatever change is being resisted, they cite it as if it settled the matter forever. Whether the use cited was typical or exceptional in that author is a question not raised; it is enough that the passage exists. The Evanses give us a list of twenty authors, Shakespeare to Maugham—a list as easily extended back to Chaucer—who use *like* as a conjunction, but there is no attempt to show that any one of them regularly or even frequently used it so. A dictionary that illustrates a secondary meaning with a quotation may, for all we can tell, be using the only known occurrence of the word in that sense.

The radical, the innovator, the grammatical iconoclast and libertine is ready to beat down all opposition as tradition-bound and ridiculously conservative, but he is equally ready to demonstrate that whatever is objected to has been English for four or five hundred years. Both forms of argument are supposed to be unanswerably crushing. If some locution now current defies a past consensus, so much the worse for the past; but at the same time any locution ever written by a good writer is *ipso facto* attack-proof, and if a precedent can be adduced for anything, however shabby, the case is closed.

Actually not everything ever written by a good writer, or even by quite a number of good writers, is good, any more than everything ever written by a bad writer is bad. Every good writer has committed himself at one time or another to practices without which he would have been a better writer. It is our privilege to pick and choose, alike from the superior and the inferior, alike from the past and the present. For the winnowing of the past we have the guidance of perspective in addition to taste; for the present, taste alone has to suffice. For taste there is no substitute, nor is there any excuse for not using as much of it as we have. The unexpressed excuse that underlies most refusals to use it is the delusive feeling that every demolition of a barrier, old or new, is a freeing of the language from needless restraints and a further emancipation of its users.

What is overlooked is that language and its users grow by restraints, too. Especially in a time when looseness of many kinds is a dominant fashion, it may be salutary to cultivate a tightness and exactitude not customarily demanded. Linguistic resources are expanded not only by the seizing of new liberties as fast as they become available but also by the rejection of liberties that may be only license. A writer is not alone what he writes; he is likewise everything that he will not write because he finds it not good enough, and his power may be as much a function *crotchet* (here) An odd, whimsical, or stubborn notion

of his renunciations as of his self-indulgences. The libertarians will pity him as self-deprived and call his austerity a crotchet, but he and we are the gainers by his discriminations, and the language may be the loser by the indiscrimination of the loose constructionist.

In no domain is there a clearer illustration of the power of negative choice than in the domain of diction. Good writing has always been marked, and is marked today, by selection of words for their central and not their peripheral meanings. A word, particularly an abstract word, has a core of meaning from which it gradually spreads over associated meanings, perhaps in several directions, until it overlaps words that have likewise spread out from entirely different, possibly remote centers.

The liberalistic view now regnant ranks all such extensions as improvements of language, all as equally good. But the fine writer or speaker is habitually aiming at bull's-eyes, not at general target areas, and he does not care for the idea of shelling the woods with language. His dictionary gives *apparent* as one synonym of *evident,* and vice versa, but he still finds an important kind of integrity in applying *apparent* to the thing that seems to be so whether it is or not and in saving *evident* for that which both seems to be and is so. *Infer* once meant exactly what *imply* means now—it is generally, perhaps always, so used in the seventeenth-century plays of John Ford—but the two words have developed a clear differentiation whereby *imply* goes with the transmitting end and *infer* with the receiving end of the same process of deduction; smoke *implies* fire, but when you smell smoke you *infer* fire. It is a clear loss, not a gain, when we ignore the differentiation in such sentences as these from the best-selling murder story of the decade: "The defense is trying to infer that the prosecution is trying to conceal something." "And surely you do not mean to infer that it would be an unjust verdict if X were acquitted on the ground of temporary insanity?" *Infer* is being so chronically abused by many who should know better that lexicography no longer quite sees what to do with it, but a decent writer sees, and he is well aware that the widespread confusion makes the English vocabulary not richer, but poorer. True, "language grows," as Greenough and Kittredge said in 1901, "by the felicitous misapplication of words"; but there is no profit to be had out of misapplication per se, without the felicity—a reservation that brings us straight back to the necessity of taste.

The obvious and growing indifference of many publishing houses to hundreds or thousands of such distinctions as those illustrated cannot be called one of the more gladdening signs of the times. No practicing editor of any great competence ever sees a book manuscript for which he could not do appreciable favors if he had a free hand and time, and ninety-nine of any hundred published books could have profited by good offices that they never received. But these phenomena, depressing as they are, seem not quite so shocking as the latter-day hospitality of the very learned to every popular usage that volunteers to make the language more fuzzy, inarticulated, and fumbling.

What steadily preoccupies everyone fit to be called a writer is the possibility of improving everything in his work that is improvable. In no other way can he contribute his much or his little to the effectiveness of language as an instrument of precision combined with power. The linguistic scholarship that impedes and discourages where it might help him is operating beneath its privilege, not to say beneath its obligation. Let those who choose define usage as what a swarm of folk say or write by reason of laziness, shiftlessness, or ignorance; the tenable definition is still what the judicious do as a result of all that they can muster of conscious discrimination. It is time we had a philosophy of usage grounded in the steadfast conviction that the best, whether or not we have it in us to attain it, is not too good to be aspired to.

BERGEN EVANS

From The Atlantic Monthly, *CCV*
(*March, 1960*), *79-82. Copyright, 1960, by
the Atlantic Monthly Company. By permission of the Atlantic Monthly Company
and the author.*

Grammar for Today

In 1747 Samuel Johnson issued a plan for a new dictionary of the
English language. It was supported by the most distinguished printers of
the day and was dedicated to the model of all correctness, Philip Dormer
Stanhope, Fourth Earl of Chesterfield. Such a book, it was felt, was
urgently needed to "fix" the language, to arrest its "corruption" and
"decay," a degenerative process which, then as now, was attributed to the
influence of "the vulgar" and which, then as now, it was a mark of
superiority and elegance to decry. And Mr. Johnson seemed the man to
write it. He had an enormous knowledge of Latin, deep piety, and
dogmatic convictions. He was also honest and intelligent, but the effect
of these lesser qualifications was not to show until later.

Oblig'd by hunger and request of friends, Mr. Johnson was willing
to assume the role of linguistic dictator. He was prepared to "fix" the
pronunciation of the language, "preserve the purity" of its idiom, brand
"impure" words with a "note of infamy," and secure the whole "from
being overrun by . . . low terms."

There were, however, a few reservations. Mr. Johnson felt it necessary
to warn the oversanguine that "Language is the work of man, a being
from whom permanence and stability cannot be derived." English "was
not formed from heaven . . . but was produced by necessity and en-
larged by accident." It had, indeed, been merely "thrown together by
negligence" and was in such a state of confusion that its very syntax
could no longer "be taught by general rules, but [only] by special
precedents."

In 1775 the *Dictionary* appeared. The noble patron had been given a great deal more immortality than he had bargained for by the vigor of the kick Johnson had applied to his backside as he booted him overboard. And the *Plan* had been replaced by the *Preface,* a sadder but very much wiser document.

Eight years of "sluggishly treading the track of the alphabet" had taught Johnson that the hopes of "fixing" the language and preserving its "purity" were but "the dreams of a poet doomed at last to wake a lexicographer." In "the boundless chaos of living speech," so copious and energetic in its disorder, he had found no guides except "experience and analogy." Irregularities were "inherent in the tongue" and could not be "dismissed or reformed" but must be permitted "to remain untouched." "Uniformity must be sacrificed to custom . . . in compliance with a numberless majority" and "general agreement." One of the pet projects of the age had been the establishment of an academy to regulate and improve style. "I hope," Johnson wrote in the *Preface,* that if "it should be established . . . the spirit of English liberty will hinder or destroy [it.]"

At the outset of the work he had flattered himself, he confessed, that he would reform abuses and put a stop to alterations. But he had soon discovered that "sounds are too volatile and subtle for legal restraints" and that "to enchain syllables and to lash the wind are equally undertakings of pride unwilling to measure its desires by its strength." For "the causes of change in language are as much superior to human resistance as the revolutions of the sky or the intumescence of the tide."

There had been an even more profound discovery: that grammarians and lexicographers "do not form, but register the language; do not teach men how they should think, but relate how they have hitherto expressed their thoughts." And with this statement Johnson ushered in the rational study of linguistics. He had entered on his task a medieval pedant. He emerged from it a modern scientist.

Of course his discoveries were not strikingly original. Horace had observed that use was the sole arbiter and norm of speech and Montaigne had said that he who would fight custom with grammar was a fool. Doubtless thousands of other people had at one time or another perceived and said the same thing. But Johnson introduced a new principle. Finding that he could not lay down rules, he gave actual examples to show meaning and form. He offered as authority illustrative quotations, and in so doing established that language is what usage makes it and that custom, in the long run, is the ultimate and only court of appeal in linguistic matters.

This principle, axiomatic today in grammar and lexicography, seems to exasperate a great many laymen who, apparently, find two hundred and five years too short a period in which to grasp a basic idea. They insist that there are absolute standards of correctness in speech and that these standards may be set forth in a few simple rules. To a man, they believe, of course, that they speak and write "correctly" and they are loud in their insistence that others imitate them.

It is useless to argue with such people because they are not, really, interested in language at all. They are interested solely in demonstrating their own superiority. Point out to them—as has been done hundreds of times—that forms which they regard as "corrupt," "incorrect," and "vulgar" have been used by Shakespeare, Milton, and the Bible and are used daily by 180 million Americans and accepted by the best linguists and lexicographers, and they will coolly say, "Well, if they differ from me, they're wrong."

But if usage is not the final determinant of speech, what is? Do the inhabitants of Italy, for example, speak corrupt Latin or good Italian? Is Spanish superior to French? Would the Breton fisherman speak better if he spoke Parisian French? Can one be more fluent in Outer Mongolian than in Inner Mongolian? One has only to ask such questions in relation to languages other than one's own, languages within which our particular snobberies and struggles for prestige have no stake, to see the absurdity of them.

The language that we do speak, if we are to accept the idea of "corruption" and "decay" in language, is a horribly decayed Anglo-Saxon, grotesquely corrupted by Norman French. Furthermore, since Standard English is a development of the London dialect of the fourteenth century, our speech, by true aristocratic standards, is woefully middle-class, commercial, and vulgar. And American speech is lower middle-class, reeking of counter and till. Where else on earth, for instance, would one find crime condemned because it didn't *pay!*

In more innocent days a great deal of time was spent in wondering what was the "original" language of mankind, the one spoken in Eden, the language of which all modern tongues were merely degenerate remnants. Hector Boethius tells us that James I of Scotland was so interested in this problem that he had two children reared with a deaf and dumb nurse on an island in order to see what language they would "naturally" speak. James thought it would be Hebrew, and in time, to his great satisfaction, it was reported that the children were speaking Hebrew!

Despite this experiment, however, few people today regard English as a corruption of Hebrew. But many seem to think it is a corruption of Latin and labor mightily to make it conform to this illusion. It is they and their confused followers who tell us that we can't say "I am mistaken" because translated into Latin this would mean "I am misunderstood," and we can't say "I have enjoyed myself" unless we are egotistical or worse.

It is largely to this group—most of whom couldn't read a line of Latin at sight if their lives depended on it—that we owe our widespread bewilderment concerning *who* and *whom.* In Latin the accusative or dative form would always be used, regardless of the word's position in the sentence, when the pronoun was the object of a verb or a preposition. But in English, for at least four hundred years, this simply hasn't been so. When the pronoun occurs at the beginning of a question, people who speak natural, fluent, literary English use the nominative, regardless. They say "Who did you give it to?" not? "Whom did you give it to?" But the semiliterate, intimidated and bewildered, are mouthing such ghastly utterances as a recent headline in a Chicago newspaper: WHOM'S HE KIDDING?

Another group seems to think that in its pure state English was a Laputan tongue, with logic as its guiding principle. Early members of this sect insisted that *unloose* could only mean "to tie up," and present members have compelled the gasoline industry to label its trucks *Flammable* under the disastrous insistence, apparently, that the old *Inflammable* could only mean "not burnable."

It is to them, in league with the Latinists, that we owe the bogy of the double negative. In all Teutonic languages a doubling of the negative merely emphasizes the negation. But we have been told for a century now that two negatives make a positive, though if they do and it's merely a matter of logic, then three negatives should make a negative again. So that if "It doesn't make no difference" is wrong merely because it includes two negatives, then "It doesn't never make no difference" ought to be right again.

Not so: German Es macht nichts, not *Es ma nicht nichts, Swedish Jag såg ingen därinne, no *Jag såg inte ingen därinne, etc.

Both of these groups, in their theories at least, ignore our idiom. Yet idiom—those expressions which defy all logic but are the very essence of a tongue—plays a large part in English. We go to school and college, but we go to *the* university. We buy two dozen eggs but a couple *of* dozen. *Good and* can mean *very* ("I am good and mad!") and "a hot cup of coffee" means that the coffee, not the cup, is to be hot. It makes a world of difference to a condemned man whether his reprieve is *upheld* or *held up*.

There are thousands of such expressions in English. They are the "irregularities" which Johnson found "inherent in the tongue" and which his wisdom perceived could not and should not be removed. Indeed, it is in the recognition and use of these idioms that skillful use of English lies.

Many words in the form that is now mandatory were originally just mistakes, and many of these mistakes were forced into the language by eager ignoramuses determined to make it conform to some notion of their own. The *s* was put in *island,* for instance, in sheer pedantic ignorance. The second *r* doesn't belong in *trousers,* nor the *g* in *arraign,* nor the *t* in *deviltry,* nor the *n* in *passenger* and *messenger.* Nor, so far as English is concerned, does that first *c* in *arctic* which so many people twist their mouths so strenuously to pronounce.

And grammar is as "corrupted" as spelling or pronunciation. "You are" is as gross a solecism as "me am." It's recent, too; you won't find it in the Authorized Version of the Bible. *Lesser, nearer,* and *more* are grammatically on a par with *gooder. Crowed* is the equivalent of *knowed* or *growed,* and *caught* and *dug* (for *catched* and *digged*) are as "corrupt" as *squoze* for *squeezed* or *snoze* for *sneezed.*

Fortunately for our peace of mind most people are quite content to let English conform to English, and they are supported in their sanity by modern grammarians and linguists.

Scholars agree with Puttenham (1589) that a language is simply speech "fashioned to the common understanding and accepted by consent." They believe that the only "rules" that can be stated for a language are codified observations. They hold, that is, that language is the basis of grammar, not the other way round. They do not believe that any language can become "corrupted" by the linguistic habits of those who speak it. They do not believe that anyone who is a native speaker of a standard language will get into any linguistic trouble unless he is misled by snobbishness or timidity or vanity.

He may, of course, if his native language is English, speak a form of English that marks him as coming from a rural or an unread group. But if he doesn't mind being so marked, there's no reason why he should change. Johnson retained a Staffordshire burr in his speech all his life. And surely no one will deny that Robert Burns's rustic dialect was just as good as a form of speech as, and in his mouth infinitely better as a means of expression than, the "correct" English spoken by ten million of his southern contemporaries.

The trouble is that people are no longer willing to be rustic or provincial. They all want to speak like educated people, though they don't want to go to the trouble of becoming truly educated. They want to believe that a special form of socially acceptable and financially valuable speech can be mastered by following a few simple rules. And there is no lack of little books that offer to supply the rules and promise "correctness" if the rules are adhered to. But, of course, these offers are specious because you don't speak like an educated person unless you are an educated person, and the little books, if taken seriously, will not only leave the lack of education showing but will expose the pitiful yearning and the basic vulgarity as well, in such sentences as "Whom are you talking about?"

As a matter of fact, the educated man uses at least three languages. With his family and his close friends, on the ordinary, unimportant occasions of daily life, he speaks, much of the time, a monosyllabic sort of shorthand. On more important occasions and when dealing with strangers in his official or business relations, he has a more formal speech, more complete, less allusive, politely qualified, wisely reserved. In addition he has some acquaintance with the literary speech of his language. He understands this when he reads it, and often enjoys it, but he hesitates to use it. In times of emotional stress hot fragments of it may come out of him like lava, and in times of feigned emotion, as when giving a commencement address, cold, greasy gobbets of it will ooze forth.

The linguist differs from the amateur grammarian in recognizing all of these variations and gradations in the language. And he differs from the snob in doubting that the speech of any one small group among the language's more than 300 million daily users constitutes a model for all the rest to imitate.

The methods of the modern linguist can be illustrated by the question of the grammatical number of *none*. Is it singular or plural? Should one say "None of them is ready" or "None of them are ready"?

The prescriptive grammarians are emphatic that it should be singular. The Latinists point out that *nemo,* the Latin equivalent, is singular. The logicians triumphantly point out that *none* can't be more than one and hence can't be plural.

The linguist knows that he hears "None of them are ready" every day, from people of all social positions, geographical areas, and degrees of education. He also hears "None is." Furthermore, literature informs him that both forms were used in the past. From Malory (1450) to Milton (1650) he finds that *none* was treated as a singular three times for every once that it was treated as a plural. That is, up to three hundred years ago men usually said *None is.* From Milton to 1917, *none* was used as a plural seven times for every four times it was used as a singular. That is, in the past three hundred years men often said *None is,* but they said *None are* almost twice as often. Since 1917, however, there has been a noticeable increase in the use of the plural, so much so that today *None are* is the preferred form.

The descriptive grammarian, therefore, says that while *None is* may still be used, it is becoming increasingly peculiar. This, of course, will not be as useful to one who wants to be cultured in a hurry as a short, emphatic permission or prohibition. But it has the advantage of describing English as it is spoken and written here and now and not as it ought to be spoken in some Cloud-Cuckoo-Land.

The descriptive grammarian believes that a child should be taught English, but he would like to see the child taught the English actually used by his educated contemporaries, not some pedantic, theoretical English designed chiefly to mark the imagined superiority of the designer.

He believes that a child should be taught the parts of speech, for example. But the child should be told the truth—that these are functions of use, not some quality immutably inherent in this or that word. Anyone, for instance, who tells a child—or anyone else—that *like* is used in English only as a preposition has grossly misinformed him. And anyone who complains that its use as a conjunction is a corruption introduced by Winston cigarettes ought, in all fairness, to explain how Shakespeare, Keats, and the translators of the Authorized Version of the Bible came to be in the employ of the R. J. Reynolds Tobacco Company.

Whether formal grammar can be taught to advantage before the senior year of high school is doubtful; most studies—and many have been made—indicate that it can't. But when it is taught, it should be the grammar of today's English, not the obsolete grammar of yesterday's prescriptive grammarians. By that grammar, for instance, *please* in the sentence "Please reply" is the verb and *reply* its object. But by modern meaning *reply* is the verb, in the imperative, and *please* is merely a qualifying word meaning "no discourtesy intended," a mollifying or de-imperatival adverb, or whatever you will, but not the verb.

This is a long way from saying "Anything goes," which is the charge that, with all the idiot repetition of a needle stuck in a groove, the uninformed ceaselessly chant against modern grammarians. But to assert that usage is the sole determinant in grammar, pronunciation, and meaning is *not* to say that anything goes. Custom is illogical and unreasonable, but it is also tyrannical. The least deviation from its dictates is usually punished with severity. And because this is so, children should be taught what the current and local customs in English are. They should not be taught that we speak a bastard Latin or a vocalized logic. And they should certainly be disabused of the stultifying illusion that after God had given Moses the Commandments He called him back and pressed on him a copy of Woolley's *Handbook of English Grammar.*

The grammarian does not see it as his function to "raise the standards" set by Franklin, Lincoln, Melville, Mark Twain, and hundreds of millions of other Americans. He is content to record what they said and say.

Insofar as he serves as a teacher, it is his business to point out the limits of the permissible, to indicate the confines within which the writer may exercise his choice, to report that which custom and practice have made acceptable. It is certainly not the business of the grammarian to impose his personal taste as the only norm of good English, to set forth his prejudices as the ideal standard which everyone should copy. That would be fatal. No one person's standards are broad enough for that.

QUESTIONS FOR REVIEW OF PART FOUR

1. What is the distinction, if any, between the words in the following pairs?

   obsolete—archaic   coinage—neologism

dialect—localism	solecism—barbarism
colloquialism—slang expression	obscenity—profanity
gobbledygook—impropriety	idiom—localism

2. How does Perrin distinguish General, Formal, Informal, Standard, and Vulgate English?

3. What is Perrin's definition of "good English"? What are some of his suggestions for achieving it?

4. Are Follett and Evans writing about the same thing? That is, are they both considering spoken English or written English or what? Does either acknowledge that the kind of usage he advocates is appropriate in some circumstances but not in all? Does either make clear to which circumstances he refers?

5. Do the Follett and Evans articles follow the advice of their respective authors? That is, is each article written in the kind of usage advocated by its author?

6. With whom do you think Perrin would be most likely to agree— Follett or Evans? Why? To which of the three articles in Part Four do you think the Aiken article is closest in agreement? Why?

SUGGESTIONS FOR INDIVIDUAL PROJECTS
AND CLASS DISCUSSION

1. Note some of the local and regional expressions, different from your own, used by a fellow student from another region of the country. Be prepared to report them to the class, explaining which seem to be local expressions and which regional.

2. Look up in a composition handbook or a dictionary twenty of the expressions to which Follett objects. Indicate with a usage label ("informal," "vulgate," etc.) what attitude that source takes toward each expression.

3. By consulting *A Dictionary of Contemporary Usage*, determine what attitude the Evanses take *in their book* toward the kind of expressions Follett condemns. Do they tolerate or advocate the use of such expressions by others? Do they use them in their own writing? Copy verbatim (in quotation marks) a few sentences which substantiate your findings, and report the results to the class.

4. What standard (or standards) of usage do you think you should follow in the papers you write for this course? Before you formulate an answer, think of the standards advocated in the Aiken and Perrin articles. Consider the reasons behind Follett's view and the reasons behind Evans' view. It would be good to illustrate what you mean by quoting from your own previous papers or from the writing of a classmate with whom you exchange papers.

SUGGESTED WRITING ASSIGNMENT

Write a 400-500 word paper comparing and contrasting the levels of usage employed in two different periodicals, one published for a popular audience, the other for a more limited audience. For example, you might select *Science Digest* as a popular magazine, *Scientific American* as a magazine for more educated readers; or you might select the *New York Daily News* as a popular newspaper, the *New York Times* as a newspaper for a more limited audience. Study sentence length and complexity, vocabulary level, and the other matters with which Perrin deals. Be sure that you organize the body of your paper according to principles of systematic division and that the entire paper culminates in a general idea which controls the content and organization. Cite clearly the sources you use, carefully using brief quotations (in quotation marks) to illustrate what you mean.

PART V

Punctuation
and Spelling

D istinctively manifested in writing rather than speech, punctuation and spelling nevertheless grow out of speech and are often strongly affected by it. This realization has led some structural grammarians to use their strong interest in function and in intonation patterns to re-examine these "mechanical" features. Harold Whitehall does this in "The System of Punctuation," classifying punctuation according to four types of function instead of according to the appearance of the punctuation marks themselves. "Simplifying Your Punctuation Problem," by Fred Flanagan and Stan Merritt, follows the Whitehall article with some facetious suggestions which should prove useful to overenthusiastic writers. The articles by Helen Bowyer and Louis Foley consider the pros and cons of simplifying the English spelling system—that amazing product of fourteen centuries of invasion, invention, and inveterate human change.

HAROLD WHITEHALL

The System of Punctuation

The traditional purpose of punctuation is to symbolize by means of visual signs the patterns heard in speech. Grammarians of the eighteenth century, strongly conscious of pause but little observant of tone and juncture, thought that the comma indicated pause for a time count of one, the semicolon for a time count of two, the colon for a time count of three, and the period for a time count of four. Nowadays, we know that pause is simply pause, that pause is often optional, and that when present it combines with preceding junctures to build up what may be regarded as an audible punctuation of words, word-groups, and sentences when we are speaking. To these combinations of speech phenomena, the common punctuation marks of writing (.), (?), (;), (—), (,) bear a correlation which is at best only approximate. Moreover, modern English punctuation has become an intricate system of conventions, some logical, some indicating separations or connections of context, all of crucial practical importance. Its most important purpose is "to make grammar graphic." As a kind of visual configurational feature of grammar, punctuation cannot be properly understood unless the other grammatical features of the language are also understood.

Punctuation is employed in the following functions:

a. To *link* sentences and parts of words.
b. To *separate* sentences and parts of sentences.

194

    c. To *enclose* parts of sentences.
    d. To *indicate* omissions.

We can thus speak of *linking, separating, enclosing,* and *omission* punctuation in the full realization that each function contrasts directly with all the others. It follows, therefore, that when the same marks of punctuation are used in different functions they are very much like words used in different functions: the grammatical meanings of the marks are *different*. The *separating period* (.) is quite distinct in functional use from the *omission period* (.) ; the *linking dash* (—) is functionally distinct from the *omission dash* (—) ; the single *separating comma* (,) is functionally distinct from *enclosing commas* (, . . . ,). In an ideal punctuation system, such differences would be clarified by the use of different marks of punctuation. Yet let us be realistic. Man has been speaking for well over 700,000 years. Man has been practicing alphabetic writing only for about 3450 years. Man has punctuated, in the modern sense, for less than 250 years. He has still not mastered an ideal punctuation. In the system as it stands, the distribution of the marks is as follows:

a. For *linking,* use:

    ;   the semicolon
    :   the colon
    — the linking dash
    - the linking hyphen

b. For *separating,* use:

    .   the period
    ?   the question mark
    !   the exclamation point
    ,   the separating comma

c. For *enclosing,* use:

    , . . . ,   paired commas
    — . . . —   paired dashes
    (. . .)   paired parentheses
    [. . .]   paired brackets
    ". . ."   paired quotation marks

d. For *indicating omissions,* use:

    '   the apostrophe
    .   the omission period (or dot)
    —   the omission dash
    . . .   triple periods (or dots)
    . . . .   quadruple periods (or dots)

Linking punctuation. The semicolon (;), colon (:), and dash (—) are symbolic conjunctions capable of linking subject-predicate constructions without need of conjunctions proper. They differ chiefly in the way they direct emphasis. Semicolons distribute it more or less equally between preceding and following statements; colons throw it forwards towards following statements; dashes throw it backwards towards preceding statements. Since they function as symbolic conjunctions, none of these marks is associated with any distinctive tone pattern of the language. In most cases, indeed, statements preceding any one of them would be read with the final h—l [high to low] tone-pause pattern characteristic of period punctuation. The hyphen differs from the other linking punctuation marks in that it is used to link parts of the words only. The semicolon, colon, and dash may occur in combination with a final quotation mark, in which case they are always placed *outside* the quotation mark.

The *semicolon* (;) is the symbolic conjunction used to link subject-predicate groups that could otherwise occur as separate sentences, particularly if they are parallel in structure and in emphasis:

> The girl is pretty; you will like her.
> I am out of work; I need financial help.
> I was ill that day; nevertheless, I tried to complete the work.
> He was a close friend of the family; moreover, he had a position open.

It is conventionally used to link word groups containing heavy internal comma punctuation:

> My outfit included a rifle, a shotgun, a water bag, and a bedroll; but I did not forget to include a few good books.
> I liked *The Ordeal of Richard Feverel*, by Meredith; *Oliver Twist*, by Dickens; and Oscar Wilde's fine comedy *The Importance of Being Earnest*.

When the semicolon occurs in conjunction with quotation marks, it is placed *outside* them:

> I was reading Shelley's "Adonais"; I did not wish to be disturbed.

The *colon* (:) is the symbolic conjunction used when emphasis is to be thrown forward upon the word-group or word that follows it:

> It was just as I thought: he had stolen the money.
> My outfit included these necessaries: a rifle, a shotgun, a water bag, and a bedroll.
> I could think of only one word to describe him: cad.

In keeping with its general function of *anticipation,* the colon is conventionally used to introduce the chapter figure of a Bible reference, the page number of a volume reference, the minute figure of a clock reference, and the body of a letter following the salutation:

Numbers III:21 (or 3:21)
American Speech 12: 46-49
10:15 A.M.
Dear Sir:

Like the semicolon, it is always placed *outside* a final quotation mark:

I found one leading literary tradition in "Adonais": pastoral tone.

The *dash* (—) is the symbolic conjunction to be used when the word-group or word following it is considered to be subsidiary to, a reinforcement or example of, or an unexpected addition to what precedes it. It directs the reader's attention backward:

A year's work at Harvard—that was what he hoped for.
A rifle, shotgun, ammunition—these were the essentials of my outfit.
He comes to dinner, eats your food, smokes your best cigars—then borrows your money.
He was very crude—crude and utterly crazy.

The dash is conventionally used before the name of the author of a quotation:

Here lies our sovereign lord, the King.
Whose word no man relies on;
Who never spoke a foolish thing,
And never did a wise one.
                    —Anonymous

The dash should *not* be used as a kind of coverall punctuation mark for all linking and separating functions.

The *hyphen* (-) links parts of words together. It is most characteristically used to indicate that contiguous words form compounds not marked by stress modification.

a *well-beloved* woman
my *commander-in-chief*
his *better-than-thou* attitude

The conventional uses of the hyphen are these:

a. To indicate that the beginning of a word on one printed line is linked to the rest of the word on the next.

b. To link the elements of compound numbers from twenty-one to ninety-nine:

> *thirty-four* horses
> *sixty-seven* dollars

c. To link the elements of fractions:

> He had a *two-thirds* lead in the election.

Today we tend to write either separately or as single units those words which were formerly hyphenated:

> my *commander in chief*
> a *wellbred* woman

Separating punctuation. The period separates sentences only. The exclamation mark (!) and the question mark (?), normally used to separate special types of sentences, are also used occasionally to separate parts of sentences. The comma separates *parts* of sentences only. Thus, there is every reason why the period, as sentences separator, should never be confused with the comma, as sentence-part separator, or with the semicolon, the sentence linker. All the separating punctuation marks are roughly correlated with stress-juncture and tone-pause patterns heard in speech, and it is probable that learning to hear the patterns will direct you towards the appropriate punctuation:

> John was coming(.)
> John was coming(?)
> John was coming(!)
> John was coming(,) and I still had to dress.

When they occur in combination with final quotation marks, all the separating punctuation marks are placed *inside* them. In this respect, they contrast directly with the linking punctuation marks which are placed *outside.*

The *period* (.) has the one function of separating declarative subject-predicate sentences (including mild commands) from following sentences. It symbolizes the fall from high to low pitch (h—l) followed by breathing pause. Its grammatical meaning is "end of declarative utterance":

> The mountains enclose a valley.
> Please return the books as soon as possible.

The period can occur after statements not in subject-predicate form if they conclude with the h—l tone-pause pattern.

> The more, the merrier.
> To resume.

It is always inserted *before* end quotation marks:

> He said to me, "Mother is coming."

The *question mark* (?) separates questions and quoted questions from a following context. It symbolizes two quite distinct final tone-pause patterns of actual speech:

a. A fall from high to low tone (h—l) used when a question contains an interrogative word or word order:

> l———h
> Why did you go to the theater?

b. A rising high tone, usual when a question does not contain an interrogative word or word order:

> l———h
> You went to the theater?

The grammatical meaning of the question mark is "answer needed":

> Are you leaving tonight?
> Is John coming?
> You are in Professor Brown's class?
> "Where is the salt?" he demanded.

It is always inserted *before* end quotation marks:

> He said, "Is this what's wrong?"

The *exclamation point* (!) separates exclamatory sentences or exclamatory words from a following context. It symbolizes various final tone-pause patterns based upon sharply rising or falling tone or a combination of these, or unexpectedly level tone, used in speech when an utterance is surcharged with emotion:

> What a marvelous morning!
> Listen! I hear John coming.

It is always inserted *before* end quotation marks that occur *within* a sentence, but it is placed outside quotation marks at the end of a sentence when the whole sentence is exclamatory:

> "I am finished!" he yelled.
> How horrible was their shout, "We're coming to kill you"!

The *separating comma* (,) originally indicated that a part of a sentence preceding or following it was in some way separated from the remainder. Where it corresponds to anything in speech at all, it generally symbolizes internal grammatical juncture followed by pause in slow-tempo speech. Its use, however, is now highly conventionalized: the comma is often used where speech shows internal juncture unaccompanied by pause but where its omission might lead to misunderstanding. The comma never appears between the main structural elements, the *must* parts, of sentences; i.e., it is never used between the subject and verb, between the verb and a complement, or between two complements, and it is never used before movable modifiers of a sentence if these appear *after* the verb; in short, it is never used to indicate optional internal grammatical junctures. The grammatical meaning of the comma is "dissociation." It is inserted:

a. After each word or word-group in a series terminated by *and, or;* here it may symbolize the high rising tone pattern (h):

> I took bread, butter, tea, and salt with me.
> His cunning, his devious treachery, or his ruthlessness will be enough to make him fight successfully.

b. Between subject-predicate word-groups linked by the coupling conjunctions *and, but, or, not, yet*:

> The book is quite good, and it is relatively inexpensive.
> The food and service were good, yet I was hard to please.

c. After any movable modifier thought of as displaced from a normal end-of-sentence position:

> Instead of the expected twenty, only ten came to the party.

But:

> Only ten came to the party instead of the expected twenty.

d. Before any other modifier or modifying word-group thought of as out of its normal sentence position:

> We thought of Goldsmith, poor but genial.
> Talent, Mr. Micawber has; money, Mr. Micawber has not.

e. After an introductory word, word-group, transitional adverb, or vocative expression:

> *This done*, we left the place immediately.
> She didn't like the idea; *nevertheless*, she said she would visit us.
> *Mother*, I have brought my friend to be our guest.

f. After a subject-predicate word-group introducing a direct quotation:

> He exclaimed, "I had no idea that you were in the room."

g. Between elements in sentences and word-groups which might cause confusion if thought of as combined:

> My words are my own; my actions, my ministers'.
> *a bright, blue hat* contrasted with a *bright blue hat*

h. Between items in dates, addresses, books and author references, etc.:

April 1, 1950
Mary Johnson, Cleveland, Ohio
Oliver Twist, by Charles Dickens

The comma is always inserted *before* end quotation marks:

"I am tired of your incompetence," he roared.

Enclosing punctuation. Paired commas, paired dashes, and parentheses are used to enclose elements outside the main structure of a sentence. They represent a triple scale of enclosure, in which paired commas enclose elements most closely related to the main thought of the sentence and parentheses those elements least closely related. Brackets are merely a specialized type of parentheses. Question marks are used principally to enclose the report of words actually spoken.

Paired commas (, . . . ,) have the following uses:

a. To enclose modifying word-groups of the subject-predicate type which are not regarded as essential to the identification of the word which they modify. Such groups are usually called *non-restrictive*.

NON-RESTRICTIVE: This invention, *which our army rejected*, became Germany's surprise weapon.
RESTRICTIVE: The invention *which our army rejected* became Germany's surprise weapon.

In the first example, the identification is supplied by *this;* the modifying group *which our army rejected* is thus properly enclosed in paired commas. In the second example, the modifying group is needed to identify *invention*.

b. To enclose interpolated words and word-groups, especially when those are transitional adverbs or groups with the function of transitional adverbs:

Your ideas, *however*, are scarcely valid.
Your ideas, *as a matter of fact*, are scarcely valid.
Your ideas, *I conclude*, are scarcely valid.

Paired dashes (— . . . —) enclose elements less closely related to the main thought of a sentence than those enclosed by paired commas but more closely related than those enclosed by parentheses:

My friends—at that time mostly workers—took me to task for my social attitudes.

They replace paired commas when the enclosed word-group has heavy comma punctuation of its own:

The artillery—devastating in its sound, fury, and effect—suddenly opened up on us.

Parentheses enclose material which is obviously outside the main scope of the sentence:

These words (*we might call them determiners*) are important in English but of little importance in many other languages.

Parentheses are used conventionally to enclose the figures numbering parts of a series, and, in legal contexts, to enclose figures expressing monetary value:

The aims of this course are: (1) to analyze the structure of American English; (2) to examine the resources of its vocabulary; (3) to sketch the history of American English.

The signer agrees to pay the sum of one hundred dollars ($100.00).

Brackets ([. . .]) are a special kind of parentheses with the following uses:
a. To insert interpolations in quotations:

As Jarrold said, "It [poetry] is an attempt to express the inexpressible."

b. To insert pronunciations written in the symbols of the International Phonetic Association (IPA):

The usual pronunciation of *bait* is [bet].

They also enclose parenthetical matter already in parentheses.

Quotation marks (". . .") enclose direct quotations from speech:

"You may say that," said my father, "but you don't believe it."

They may be used with caution to enclose references to specific words, slang expressions, hackneyed expressions, familiar and well-worn phrases, and terms you do not like:

> My life is one "if" after another.
> His car had the "teardrop" shape of that period.
> While "on campus," Jones was something of a "rod."
> The "liberal arts" curriculum becomes increasingly illiberal.

They are also used to enclose the titles of poems, plays, essays, paintings, etc. (but not the titles of complete volumes or of major works, which are indicated by italics):

> I read Shelley's "Alastor" with distinct pleasure.
> I particularly admired El Greco's "Toledo."
> He was much impressed by the story "Clay" in Joyce's *Dubliners*.

Omission punctuation. Originally, the *apostrophe* (') indicated the omission of a letter no longer pronounced or deliberately suppressed in pronunciation. This is what it still indicates when used with the possessive singular forms of nouns, contracted forms of verb helpers (auxiliaries), and words with an omitted initial letter:

> the Lord's Prayer (earlier, the Lordes Prayer)
> He's not coming, and he won't come.
> a blot on the 'scutcheon

Its conventional uses are as follows:
  a. It precedes *s* in the plurals of figures, signs, symbols, and letters:

> My 8's are difficult to decipher.
> There were three x's in this quotation.
> I have difficulty in writing r's.

  b. It precedes *s* in plurals of words which have no normal plural form:

> There were too many if's and but's about the matter.

c. In a purely symbolic function corresponding to nothing actual in speech, it indicates possessive plurals of nouns:

> The generals' orders had to be obeyed.
> the college girls' escorts

d. It indicates the possessive singular forms of nouns already ending in *s*:

> Dr. Caius' (or Caius's) words
> Moses' pronouncements

e. It indicates the possessive singular forms of group names:

> Thomas, Manchester, and Scott's *Rhetoric*
> Chase and Sanborn's coffee

f. It indicates the omission of initial centuries in dates:

> the class of '38

The *omission period* or *dot* (.) indicates the omission of several letters, particularly when words are abbreviated:

> Mr. V. S. Johnson
> Ph.D.
> I enjoy the plays of G.B.S.

It is not used after contractions indicated by the apostrophe, after Roman numerals, after numbered ordinals, after nicknames, or after per cent (for *per centum*); it is now often omitted after the abbreviated names of government agencies, labor organizations, and the like:

> He'll go.   a five per cent bonus
> XXIV   CIC
> 5th, 6th, 7th   FTC
> Dick, Mick, and Ned

When a sentence ends with an abbreviated word, one period punctuates both the abbreviation and the sentence:

I was talking to Richard Hudson, Ph.D.

Triple periods or *dots* (. . .) indicate a more or less extensive omission of material at the beginning of, or within, a quoted passage; followed by a period (. . . .) they indicate omission at its end:

> . . . language is . . . the thought itself, its confused cross currents as
> well as its clear-cut issues. . . .

Triple periods are often used to indicate omission deliberately left to the
reader's imagination:

> He took her slowly in his arms . . . from that moment she was his.

In recent advertising practice, this use is greatly extended in order to
create appropriate atmosphere:

> Fly to Britain . . . Europe . . . and beyond.
> Industries are discovering . . . with a rush . . . that the Genie of
> "Opportunity" is at their beck and call.

The *dash* (–) as used in omission punctuation indicates the deliberate
suppression of letters in a person's name in order to avoid positive statement of identification:

> My informant, a certain Professor *M*–, vouches for the truth of this
> report.

In earlier writing it was often used to indicate omissions in oaths, etc.:

> "D—n," he said. "I'll see you hanged yet."

No attempt has been made here to deal with all the minute points of
punctuation. Such matters as the use of capitals and italics are treated
under the appropriate headings in a dictionary: they are matters of
format rather than punctuation although they serve a very real purpose in
the transference of spoken to written distinctions. What has been attempted here is to present punctuation proper as a system of symbols each
one of which contrasts with all others in function. Ideally, the writer

should be able to ignore the grammar book or the dictionary when he is faced with a punctuation problem; what he needs most of all is an understanding of the entire system as it determines the individual application.

FRED FLANAGAN AND STAN MERRITT

From Printers' Ink, *CCXVIII (February 7, 1947), 160. Copyright 1947, by
Printers' Ink Publishing Company. By permission of Printers' Ink.*

Simplifying Your Punctuation Problem

The task of writing today's advertising copy has become, we feel, increasingly difficult because of the feebleness inherent in our present system of punctuation—its total inadequacy to express the nuances of meaning so important to the advertiser in the dawning era of competitive selling.

Consider, for instance, the exclamation point! Too often this one mark of punctuation is called upon to perform tasks which are beyond its capabilities—however hard it may strive. Take this typical headline: "Sudsi-wudsi for dandy dudsies!" How weak! How ineffectual the little exclamation point! Here is a headline that *sings* with excitement, that cries out for punctuation in keeping with its message! So—we suggest adding what we call the *flabbergasterisk* (⋇). Notice the difference ⋇ Here we have a punctuation mark that strikes a happy medium between a normal exclamatory value and one of greater impact.

But even the flabbergasterisk is not always enough. Occasionally we are called upon to express more intense heights of emotion, such as in the headline "Everybody . . . yes everybody, chews CHEWIES—E-Y E C C!" Observe how feeble the exclamation point, how limited in its scope. Even the flabbergasterisk cannot express the full dramatic content of this epic caption. For such cases we have developed a still more powerful punctuation mark—the *stupendapoint* (⌇).

This last headline brings up another problem, which, though it may not in itself be a matter of punctuation in the strictest sense of the term, is nonetheless, we feel, of vital importance to the worker with words. Note the underline beneath the word <u>everybody</u>. Completely unimaginative ⌇ The simple underline may be adequate in some cases. But here, where the entire impact of the headline depends so completely on what mental inflection is induced in the reader, it is obvious that the writer's purpose can be better served by use of the fluctustress (～～～).

A related problem arises when, as occasionally happens, even in the most sparkling copy, a word or group of words are included which have comparatively little importance. For moderate unimportance, we employ the de-emphaline (a line over the word or group of words, as contrasted with the well-known <u>underline</u>). Cases of maximum unimportance, where no attention at all need be paid, call, of course, for the use of the ignoramon (the direct antithesis of the fluctustress). Needless to say, the ignoramon should seldom, if ever, be employed in connection with the name of your clients' products or services⌇

Now we face the problem of the semi-colon and the colon—useful devices in themselves—but falling far short of ideal equipment for the painter in prose. On many occasions one may find himself hesitating— harried by the difficulty of attempting to express slight shadings in the degree of division depicted by this means of punctuation. For such cases what more simple solution than the demi-semi colon (⁏), the super colon (⁝), or the summa colon (.;.).

Confusing, also, to the writer is the dual function of the apostrophe, which may either express possession or denote elision. Simple it is, and of far less complexity to replace the apostrophe with either the possessapoint (△) or the abbrevapoint (▽). Note the ease of interpretation when these simplified symbols are used in the following sentence: John△s house is in Po▽k▽psie.

In an <u>article of this</u> length, designed simply as an introductory treatise, we cannot, of course, go too deeply into the ramifications of this simple, <u>practical</u>, new form of punctuation. We have not space here to discuss such important new departures as the undash (|), the superiod (⊙), the maxiperiod (−⦙−), the pre-enthesis (<), the post-enthesis (>), or

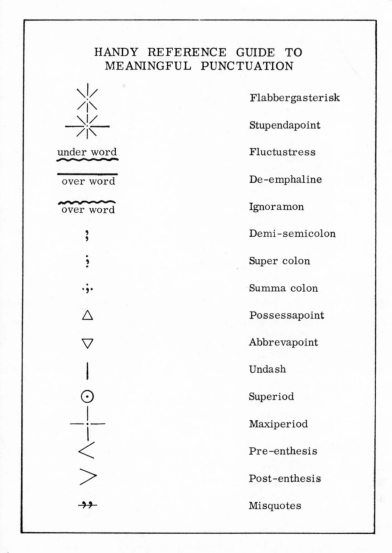

	Flabbergasterisk
	Stupendapoint
under word	Fluctustress
over word	De-emphaline
over word	Ignoramon
;	Demi-semicolon
;	Super colon
.;.	Summa colon
△	Possessapoint
▽	Abbrevapoint
|	Undash
⊙	Superiod
	Maxiperiod
<	Pre-enthesis
>	Post-enthesis
	Misquotes

the particularly useful misquotes (→→). Rather ; let this brief resumé indicate to the creator of copy the trend he must follow to compete today in the marts of trade .;. to put publication copy on the same high plane of intelligibility and forcefulness that has been attained by the radio commercial—⚹— For ; working with these new tools ; we can forge into

our written copy as much distinction .;. as much clarity ; as much <u>mean-</u>
<u>ing</u> to the reader as is possible to the radio announcer through use of the
<u>spoken</u> word–¦–

HELEN   BOWYER

From Phi Delta Kappan, *XXXX (June,*
1959), 378-380. Copyright, 1959, by Phi
Delta Kappa, Inc. By permission of Phi
Delta Kappan and the author.

It's Not Johnny!

Small wonder that Soviet education is so successfully challenging ours.
At least in the basic academic subjects. These subjects demand reading
ability. And this ability comes earlier and incomparably more easily in
the U.S.S.R. than here.

In the first grade of U.S.S.R. schools (we are told by the Council for
Basic Education) after three months of learning to read and write a
vocabulary based on all thirty-three characters of the Russian alphabet,
children move on to short prepared passages and stories from famous
Russian authors.

Naturally they do. Russian uses those thirty-three characters so inconfusably it would be a dull little Moscovite who couldn't so move on
to this introduction to quality reading. Neither then nor later do they
roadblock him with anything like the chaos of long *a* spellings which
stymie our Johnny in *age, gauge, say, they, pain, vein, reign, seine, eight,*
straight, fete, café, matinée, crochet. Or betray his natural expectation
of "like cause, like effect" with anything like the muddle of *oo* transcriptions which bewilder our youngster in *who, do, too, you, two, true, grew,*
shoe, through, lose, bruise, choose. What young Vanya gets is rapid and
mind-satisfying assimilation of sound-sign relationships almost as self-evi-
dent as those which bless the speech of the far-flung Spanish world.

Thousands of teachers here have had the happy experience of teaching Spanish as a foreign language in our high schools, but to get the full educational significance of its spelling you have to teach it as the mother-tongue to Spanish-speaking beginners in a Spanish-speaking land. This I did down in Mexico, both with children and with adult illiterates, and I am still nostalgic for the magic with which my first few months were touched.

So obviously do Spanish letters and digraphs correspond with the basic sound each is authorized to transcribe that it would have taken sheer ingenuity in my small Juanitos and Marias to dodge correct word calling. As for my older beginners, all I had to do was ground them in their benign *alfabeto,* give them a little delighted practice in dipthongs, consonant blendings, and syllables, then sit back and watch the charmed phenomenon of word recognition emerge. And how light-heartedly they could take to writing. Never a worry as to the doubling or not doubling of a consonant, as in our *mellow, melon; dragging, dragon; lemming, lemon.* Never an *ff, ph,* or *gh* usurping the office of a simple and sufficient *f,* as in our *staff, graph, laugh.* And never a silent consonant unlawfully disguising an otherwise easily-pronounceable word, as with our *gnash, knot, limb, solemn, listen.* One said *restar*—naturally; then one wrote *restar*—not *wrestar.* One thought *seudo*—ergo, one spelled it that way, not *pseudo.* One called oneself *Imanuelo* or *Ana*—who in his senses would sign the name *Immanuelo* or *Anna?* [1]

What wonder that the Mexican first grader gets the hang of word calling well within his beginning year and has all the rest of his school life free for word meaning and word relationship in sentence, paragraph, and verse? He has time for grammar, composition, literature, history, geography, and science on a level our youngsters don't begin to tackle, grade for grade. At the end of his eleven-year elementary preparatory courses he has the easy equivalent of a year in a better American college.

Much the same principles apply in Russia, whatever the difference in detail. The Russian alphabet has a few more characters to match up with its basic speech sounds, but as long as sign and sound match inconfusably, a few more or less make no great difference. Which is a fortunate fact

[1] Mexican Spanish does, of course, have the silent *h*—*horo, honor, hueco,* etc. But it is *always* silent; it constitutes no problem. I believe that the only reason the Mexican alphabet retains it is that it still has a sound in some parts of the Spanish world. *She could have asked a less ignorant person, and her "belief" would have evaporated.*

for us. To regularize our English spelling, we could hardly reduce its basic units below thirty-seven, and many phoneticists prefer thirty-nine or forty.

As things are, we bog down our hapless young with . . . have you ever asked yourself how many basic units? In its "Common Spellings" (page xiv) the *American College Dictionary* lists a flabbergasting 251. All the more flabbergasting for the overlappings they sport. For example, an *ea* serves with equal aplomb in *break, breakfast, heart, pear, pearl, appear.* An *sh* sound cavorts through spellings as diverse as *she, ocean, machine, special, sure, conscience, nauseous, tension, issue, mission, nation.* An *oo* spreads itself blandly over *look, loom, brooch, blood.* An *ou* serves quite without bias in *four, tour, sour, courage, could.*

Need we marvel, then, that, free from anything approximating this sound-sign bedlam, the young Sovieteer can read his way to such a foundation in grammar, composition, literature, history, geography, and civics as we cannot, in our senses, expect of his age-mates here. As for science, why wouldn't he leave them even farther behind? Not only does he have open sesame, like my young *Mejicanos,* to the steadily growing vocabulary his science studies demand, but, like them also, he has been consistently slanted to the scientific attitude by the lettering in which that vocabulary comes. Order, predictability, precision, conservation of time and effort, these are the *sine qua non* of any scientific grounding worth spending our tax dollars on. And with every new word Juanito met in his reading, with every fresh sequence of consonants and vowels Maria matched up with basic sounds, plastic young minds were being exercised in these invaluable attributes. Never, not from his first grade clean through his *Preparatoria,* would Juanito have his sense of consistency desensitized by anything like the jungle of long *o* spellings which confront our Johnny in *oh, go, row, doe, though, beau, comb, foam, Rome, host, ghost.* Nor is Maria's sense of cause and effect eroded by anything comparable to the welter of long *i* renditions in our *aisle, isle, island, eye, eyot, aye, ice, lie, lysol, rye, riot, rhyme, guy, guise, by, bison, decline, align, anodyne.*

So with Vanya and his sister in their Soviet classrooms. They have been attuned to the basic requirements of the scientific attitude from their first year by the sound-sign tie-up of what they read in their schoolbooks and write in their school exercises. Attuned incidentally, all but automatically—attuned, that is, in the most effective and enduring manner known to man. Can we doubt that with every year of this intimate process their developing young minds become better and better instruments for the thinking required by the algebra, geometry, trigonometry, biology, physics, chemistry which form so large and exacting a part of their upper grade curriculum? It is a curriculum so much more intensive and faster-paced than ours that in ten years they get a more thorough preparation for professional study than most of our young get in twelve.

Where, there, air, care, bear, prayer—err, were, her, sir, whirr, fur, purr, myrrh, word, curd, courage, work, jerk, shirk, lurk. Along with the irrecoverable time such muddledom steals from our primary children, along with the strains on perception, on memory, on nervous energy, what lasting effect does it build up these first three crucial years?

*Bit, busy, build, been, sieve, women, hymn—*where the simple short *i* must be dug up out of eight different spellings, seven of which are more commonly employed for other sounds.

*Edge, age, gem, jam, tragic, exaggerate, spinach, egregious—*where much the same sorry situation holds for the simple vocable *j*.

Has there ever been any careful study of what such continuous overriding of the higher mental attributes in learning the mere mechanics of reading may do to one's ability to get the subject matter of it? It is serious enough that our youngsters should take three whole years to build up a reading vocabulary of 1,000 to 1,200 words, as against the free range of their grade-mates in Mexico and Russia. And serious enough that through this highly formative period their reading must be restricted to such stuff as can be tailored out of the laboriously rising level within this sorry total. But has something even worse happened to them?

This illogical, contradictory, redundant makeshift for a rational spelling has been put over on our children with all the connotations of the natural, the necessary, the desirable, the approved. And their defenseless little minds have accepted it—or tried to—on the same basis as the truly acceptable symbols found in arithmetic and in what they get of music notation. Have we, then, to the extent of that acceptance, slanted them to illogic, dulled them to inconsistency, blurred them as to cause and effect, habituated them to imprecision, to false analogy, to waste of time and effort, to uncertain and superficial performance of their mental tasks? In short, have we conditioned them *against* that scientific attitude which Russian spelling conditions for. If so, what hope that those lesser innovations which the Sputniks have startled us into considering—

smaller classes, a longer school year, more homework, promotion by achievement instead of by age—can bring them abreast of their Soviet counterparts? Russia has these things in *addition* to a phonetic alphabet.

I submit that a basic and indispensable step to overtaking Russia, be it in science or the humanities, is to make the reading in our classrooms as readable as hers. Some half century ago, Benn Pitman, brother and colleague of the inventor of the Pitman shorthand system, published an alphabet quite equal to the need—and out of nothing but our present letters with dots over five of them instead of two. And today our Simpler Spelling Association proposes one which dispenses even with those dots and still keeps its sound-sign relationships simple and inconfusable. As does the only slightly differing scheme in the demonstration which follows.

Read it with *ae, ee, ie, oe, ue* pronounced as in *phaeton, fee, fie, foe, fuel*—with *aa* and *au* as in *bazaar* and *cause*—with *oo* and *uu* as in *food* and *wood*—with *oi* and *ou* as in *oil* and *out*—with *th* as in *thin* or *beneath*, and *zh* as in *vision*. Give all other digraphs and all single vowels and consonants the sounds most commonly given now. Notice, however, that in the transcription of such words as *chiefly* and *very*, a short *i* replaces the final *y* and that everywhere *t* and *z* replace *d* and *s* whenever they more truly represent the sound.

> "A loef ov bred," the Waulrus sed,
> "Iz hwot wee cheefli need,
> Pepur and vinegur, besiedz,
> Aar veri guud indeed,
> Nou, if yoo'r redi, oisturz, deer,
> Wee wil begin too feed."

> "But not on us," thee oisterz kried
> Turning a litl bloo,
> "Aftur such kiendnes, that wuud bee
> A dizmal *thing* too doo,"
> "The niet iz fien," the Waulrus sed,
> "Doo yoo admier the vue?"

> "Gosh," laft Rae Yung, "kan yoo vizhon that litl seen?"

Here, in these seventy-five words, are all of the (only) forty basic spelling units our youngsters would ever need to learn for the reading, writing, and spelling of their mother tongue. They constitute an alphabet even simpler than the Russian, if seven units longer. With this approximately even break in their reading—in their basic learning tool, that is—couldn't our youngsters come up with the brains, the application, and the interest to equal their Soviet age-mates in whatever studies the promise and the threat of this new age demand of both?

Naturally, we should have to do our part by providing them with the smaller classes, the longer school year, the winnowing and orienting examinations which keep young Russians working so close to their potentiality. Whatever the personal or social difficulties involved, one wonders if the financial would be so staggering—if the billions that now go down the drain of our reading problem and its sorry chain reactions wouldn't go quite some way to meet the cost.

LOUIS FOLEY

From Word Study, *XXXV* (*April, 1960*), *1-5. Copyright* ©, *1960, by G. & C. Merriam Co., publishers of the Merriam-Webster dictionaries. By permission of G. & C. Merriam Co. and the author.*

Upsetting the Alphabet-Cart

One time a good many years ago, rather suddenly it became my responsibility to take over the management of an enterprise of some importance employing a number of people. My predecessor in that position, before finally relinquishing it to me, offered me a piece of prudent counsel which I have never forgotten, and which has since proved applicable to many other situations.

"You will make some changes here," he said, "and no doubt you should. All I want to say is that there were reasons for adopting everything in the present system. Some of those reasons may have ceased to be valid. I think you will improve the arrangements more effectively, however, if you will first take the trouble in each instance to understand why we have been doing things just the way we have."

No such thoughtful hesitation appears to inhibit the iconoclastic energy of the people who from time to time come forward with enthusiastic proposals for sweeping reforms in English spelling. They are not much interested in bothering to look into the reasons why our words happen to be spelled as they are.

Recently a retired teacher, full of admiration for the spelling systems of Russian and Spanish, where "obviously," she finds, "letters and digraphs correspond with the basic sound each is authorized to transcribe," has pleaded for a complete overhauling of our spelling as "a basic and indispensable step to overtaking Russia, be it in science or the humanities." On the surface her arguments may seem plausible to many readers. The whole matter, however, is far from being the simple, open-and-shut affair that she apparently takes it to be.

The more truly one knows different languages, the more clearly one ought to realize that each is a world of its own. Each has evolved along its own peculiar lines into a system that works—for those who really understand it. The fact that each system may look strange indeed to those who see it from outside and consider it from a detached point of view does not prevent it from making sense to those who are naturally accustomed to its ways.

The familiar charge against our English spelling is that it is not phonetic. Certainly it is not "obviously" so as various other languages are. By its very nature it cannot be written phonetically in any such forthright manner as most other languages can. But let us be extra careful not to make too much of a fetish of phoneticism for its own sake; it is not the whole story of reading and particularly not for the modern silent reader of English. At any rate when we view it understandingly, we may discover that in its own subtle ways our spelling manages to be considerably less unphonetic than some people think.

In certain other languages, we requote, "letters and digraphs correspond with the basic sound each is authorized to transcribe." After all, to a certain extent at least, one might make a similar claim for English, only with the corollary that the authorizations are more elastic, more comprehensive—and especially, different. But every language has its own set of sound values for the various letters, virtually never interchangeable with those represented by the same letters for other languages.

The alleged cockeyed spelling of English words is no mere matter of spelling; the real peculiarity is in the unique character of the language. To make our spelling really phonetic would require transcriptions that only trained phoneticians could decipher. Nor are we referring to such evident facts as regional differences of pronunciation which may be equally correct, nor even the way the sounds of words vary with emphasis, shades of meaning, or placement in the word-order of a sentence. These considerations would suffice to make any would-be phonetic spelling of English arbitrary enough, but they only touch the surface.

For the most part, the sort of words whose spelling is most strikingly illogical or unphonetic are not the words which even the least literate people have any difficulty in writing correctly. Individuals who find whimsical satisfaction in misspelling *night* as *nite* do not do so from ignorance or because the correct spelling is in any way difficult. They simply think it is cute to take the word out of its proper category, perfectly familiar to everyone, which includes *light, fight, fright, might, right, sight, bright,* and others. What has really happened, of course, is that such words as these were long ago distorted from their former pronunciation, which in some cases persists to the present day in certain dialects.

Neither is there any problem in learning the accepted written form of a numerous class of words which were arbitrarily altered by pedantic tinkering. However different the purpose, in spirit those earlier attempts at artificial revamping of our language were not unlike the efforts of present-day zealots of simplified spelling. In their enthusiasm for everything classical, sixteenth-century scholars were fond of adding etymological letters to words in order to preserve some flavor of their remote Latin or Greek ancestors—from which they had not directly come into English at all. Words which had remained in the language for centuries in approximately the same form in which they had come from French were thus doctored into fake antiques. So *b* was inserted into *debt* and *doubt* to suggest Latin *debitum* and *dubitare* respectively; *l* in *salmon* (from French *saumon*) to allude to Latin *salmo; l* in *fault* (from French *faute*) in memory of Latin *fallere;* and so on. This was not done with any idea of changing the pronunciation; as late as the eighteenth century, in the meticulous verse of Alexander Pope, *fault* was regularly rimed with words like *thought, ought,* or *sought.* Eventually, however, the modified spelling did sometimes change the spoken word, as happened with the *d* put into *aventure* or *amiral,* for instance. The latter (like some other examples of armchair etymologizing) is amusing because it represents a totally wrong guess. The French word had nothing to do with *admirare,* but came from the Arabic title *amir.* Yet among all the many words in English which were subjected to such whimsical tinkering—which never had any business being spelled as they are—it would be hard to find any about which even an uneducated person has any hesitation as to the correct form.

The basic fact underlying the real difficulty of English spelling is a built-in quality of the language which lays it open to unlimited corruption of pronunciation, and which seems to have been steadily exaggerated as time has gone on. In most languages all syllables are equally distinct and forceful or at least nearly so. If they do employ an *accent de force* ●n certain syllables, that is merely something added; it does not detract from the distinctness of the others. English, however, is spoken with unusual stress on the accented syllables, which bob up with regular frequency, and correspondingly extreme neglect of the unaccented ones. So whatever theoretical vowel we write in an unaccented syllable, most often it subsides into "uh" or even tends to disappear entirely. This is why supposedly literate people confuse *affect* and *effect,* for example, or *accept* and *except;* as actually spoken, the words are virtually indistinguishable, though the context naturally prevents confusion of meaning. An indirect result of this hectic quality of our speech appears in the violent distortion of "OFFense" and "DEfense" which has become standard practice with athletic coaches and sports announcers. Evidently they feel this to be necessary for clarity, though they would not so twist the words if they were speaking of "causing offense" or "self-defense."

The silent letters which the advocates of simplification find so repellent often do perform a real function. In some cases they might be compared to the *pierres d'attente* which stick out like teeth along the façade of a building; they are there so that the building which is ultimately to be built alongside will fit in perfectly when the time comes. So the *n* in *solemn* plays its part in *solemnity* and *solemnize;* that of *damn* becomes active in *damnable,* as does that of *condemn* in *condemnation,* or that of *column* in *columnar.*

When the French word *gouvernement* was anglicized to the extent of losing a syllable with the dropping out of its second *e,* the resulting combination of *rnm* became difficult to pronounce. Consequently in popular speech the *n* simply disappears. Listen to any broadcast from Washington, and you will hear constant reference to the "goverment." In ordinary conversation it usually bogs down to "guhmnt." Yet in *governing* the *n* immediately functions again, even with a careless speaker.

Often enough, however, similar corruption of pronunciation is an obvious cause of misspelling. Common examples are *accidently, incidently, occasionly,* and the like. An instance appears, in fact, in the article from which we quoted, where *diphthong* is spelled *dipthong.* Whether it was the author or the typesetter who was to blame, mispronunciation was the evident cause, as it is when *diphtheria* or *naphtha* is similarly mistreated.

A tempting target for the self-appointed reformers would be words like *pneumatic, pneumonia,* or *psychology.* But have you ever seen these words misspelled? Certainly they do not cause any difficulty for foreigners learning English, for in the cognate words in various languages —French, German, Italian, Portuguese, and others—the *p* is really pronounced, as lazy-lipped English-speaking people find it too much trouble to do.

There may be a real and intelligible reason for the spelling of a word without its being a phonetic reason. Often the explanation—plain enough if one knows the word—is the word-family to which it belongs or the associations of its meaning. Thus *supersede* has no connection with *cede* but is related to *sedentary* and others of the "sitting" group; *consensus* has nothing to do with *census* but is based on the idea of *sense.* Or consider the word *grammar*—one of the most frequently misspelled. From a merely phonetic point of view it might as well be written *grammer, grammir, gremmor, grammur,* or simply *gramr.* It associates, however, with *grammatical* and *grammarian,* where the *a* comes sharply into focus. No doubt the reason why *separate* has for generations been a stumbling-block for so many people is that no word in its family— *separable, separation, separatist*—has the accent on the second syllable to bring out the *a.* It is clear, of course, if one thinks of the French verb *séparer* or Latin *separare.*

Silent letters may indeed function phonetically, and some of the ways in which they do so are part and parcel of the regular system of English spelling. Curiously enough, the failure to grasp these well-established principles is the real cause of a great deal of the misspelling of college students today. Here again we have to do with the peculiar importance of our accented syllables. In an accented syllable, in whole classes of

words, doubling or not doubling the consonant marks the quality (not
the length) of a preceding vowel. This makes the difference between
sniped and *snipped,* or *spiting* and *spitting,* or *stoped* and *stopped.*
Fitted requires two *t*'s, but not *benefited,* because in the latter the syllable *fit* is not accented. If *transferred* were given only one *r,* it would
look as if it rimed with *interfered* or *persevered. Traveler,* if the *l* were
doubled, would suggest a rime with *propeller.* Yet despite the wide application of this clear and simple principle, such misspellings as *occured*
or *equiped* or *omited* are among the commonest in students' papers everywhere. Surely this sort of heedlessness is something for which we *can*
blame Johnny—or perhaps his elementary teachers.

Our apologist for spelling reform finds "flabbergasting," for instance,
the fact that "an *sh* cavorts through spellings as diverse as *she, ocean,*
machine, special, sure, conscience, nauseous, tension, issue, mission, na-
tion." In *machine,* of course, the *ch* has simply kept its French value, as
it has done in many place-names given by French explorers: *Michigan,*
Chicago, Cheboygan, Charlevoix, Champlain, Ponchartrain, and so on.
British people generally pay no attention to the distinction, but it never
bothers Americans. In all the others except *she* the *s* sound which causes
no trouble in French (Latin in the case of *nauseous*) simply became
corrupted by the sloppy mushiness of diction which somehow spread
more and more through English speech during several centuries. But
here is the point: no one has any difficulty in learning to spell these
words! And except *she* the cognates of these words in various other
languages make them the very easiest kind for foreigners—whose only
fault might be a tendency to pronounce them more nearly as they
should have continued to be.

Would our spelling reformers have us undiscriminatingly lump off
together phonetically all such homonyms as *cite, site, sight,* or *done* and
dun, or *son* and *sun,* or *reed* and *read,* or *break* and *brake,* or *fir* and *fur,*
or any number of others? If so, they seem unaware of the operation of
semantics. Spoken words, uttered in a live situation in the presence of
physical objects which supply obvious context, can be perfectly clear
without thought as to their mere spelling. For the silent reader it is
quite another story. To destroy all the word associations created by differentiation of spelling could only produce confusion worse confounded.
As is continually demonstrated by printed jokes involving puns, we are
naturally aware of the sounds of the words we read, but at the same

time their visual effect contributes largely to our immediate recognition
of their meaning.

As a supposedly clinching demonstration of all that "our youngsters
would ever need to learn for the reading, writing, and spelling of their
mother tongue," the author offered these verses:

"A loef ov bred," the Waulrus sed,
"Iz hwot we cheefli need,
Pepur and vinegur, besiedz,
Aar veri guud indeed,
Nou, if yoo'r redi, oisturz, deer,
Wee wil begin too feed."

"But not on us," thee oisterz kried
Turning a litl bloo,
"After such kiendnes, that wuud bee
A dizmal thing too doo."
"The niet is fien," the Waulrus sed,
"Doo yoo admier the vue?"

Are we actually expected to take this seriously? To pretend that it
is phonetic is merely ridiculous. Even on its own arbitrary basis it is
thoroughly inconsistent. If *litl,* for instance, why not *pepr, vinegr, aftr,*
and *dizml?* In these and other items it is apparent that the basic phenomenon of English speech—the role of the accented syllable—is ignored. To
suggest any such self-conscious illiteracy as an improvement over our
established practice is utterly absurd. And again, not a word here presents the slightest problem in its traditional form.

HELEN BOWYER

From Word Study, *XXXVI* (*December,*
1960), *4-6. Copyright* ©, *1960, by G. & C.*
Merriam Co., publishers of the Merriam-
Webster dictionaries. By permission of
G. & C. Merriam Co. and the author.

Upsetting the Alphabet-Cart:
A Rejoinder

Dear Dr. Foley:

Will you take another look at this World English transcript of mine
which you so decried in your "Upsetting the Alphabet-Cart" last April?
As stated in my *Phi Delta Kappan* article of the June before, it spells
itself with just forty basic characters (single letters and digraphs) each
matched with one and only one of our forty basic speech sounds. I again
present them as all our youngsters would ever need to learn for the reading and writing of their mother tongue. Pronounce *ae, ee, ie, oe, ue* as in
maelstrom, heel, hie, hoe, hue—aa and *au* as in *bazaar* and *because—oo*
and *uu* as in *fool* and *full—ou* as in *out—*final *i* as in *pity—zh* as in
*version—*italicized *th* as in *think.* Give all other letters and digraphs the
sounds you most commonly give them now.

"A loef ov bred," the Waulrus sed,
"Iz hwot wee cheefli need,
Pepur and vinegur, besiedz,
Aar veri guud indeed,
Nou, if yoo'r redi, oisturz, deer,
Wee wil begin too feed."
"But not on us," thee oisturz kried,
Turning a litl bloo,
"Aftur such kiendnes, that wuud bee
A dizmal thing too doo."

222

"The niet iz fien," the Waulrus sed,
"Doo yoo admier the vue?"
"Gosh," laft Jae Yung, "kan yoo vizhon that litl seen?"

If your reaction is still, "Are we actually expected to take this seriously?" I unabashedly answer, "We are." We take its *one sign, one sound* principle seriously every time we consult our dictionary for the pronunciation of a word. The only essential difference between its respellings and World English is that, while the former uses diacritics to indicate the values of most of its vowels, the latter uses nothing but plain a, e, i, o, u, alone or combined into vowel digraphs. In their treatment of the consonants and consonant digraphs, the two systems are practically at one. Both dispense with *c, q, x,* but incorporate *zh* and a second *th*. Both drop all silent consonants and reduce doubled ones to singles. In short, save for the different configuration of the corresponding vowels, I might almost as well have taken the vocabulary of my *waulrus-oistur* colloquy from the respelling of my Merriam-Webster as to have built it up from my World English key. So, if you still feel that "to pretend that it is phonetic is merely ridiculous," will you take the matter up with our scholarly publishers? And, if you still think my use of *litl* but not *pepr* makes the demonstration "thoroughly inconsistent," will you consult the world-accredited *New International*? There on page 1444, full in the sight of men and angels, stands *little* respelled as I have it, while on page 1841 *pepper* brazens out its simplification, not as the *pepr* for which you fulminate, but as *pepĕr, -ĕr* being a regular Webster rendering of the syllable for which I as regularly use *ur*.

But what of all this? Let World English be ever so "one sound, one sign," our traditional spelling doesn't need its brash iconoclastic aid. Such, at least, was the burden of your April onslaught on my *Kappan* article. "For the most part," you averred, "the sort of words whose spelling is most strikingly illogical or unphonetic are not the words which even the least literate people have any difficulty in writing correctly." With this sort you include the unsounded *gh* clan—*light, fright, might,* (and one supposes) *height, wright, freight, aught, bought, taught, thought, though, bough, slough.*" No one ever comes a cropper with that *gh* through ignorance! Anyone who writes *nite* for *night* just does it to be "cute." (And doubtless it would be the same if he wrote *slew* or *slue* for *slough*). As for that long category through which our *sh* sound cavorts as erratically as in *ocean, motion, mention, tension, fashion, passion, cau-*

tious, nauseous, anxious, spacial, palatial, sure, issue, conscience, sentience, machine, not a soul under the canopy but takes them in his stride. And when it comes to silent letters, at times they're a positive asset. How would we ever grapple with *solemnity* and *damnation* if it weren't for those silent—but forward-looking—*n*'s in *solemn* and *damn.* The case for *debt, doubt, salmon, almond, indict, scene, sign, ghastly, knowledge, isle, listen, wreathe, myrrh, ptomaine, mnemonic, phthisis, sword* may not be so instantly apparent, but we have only to bone up on what the fifteenth-century printers did to this one or the sixteenth-century classicists did to that one on some or other happenstance of their history, to make their spelling no problem at all.

And it's no use for us self-appointed reformers to drag in *pneumatic, pneumonia,* or *psychology.* Has anyone, you ask, ever seen these words misspelled?

Sorry, but I have. And *rheumatic, phlegmatic, ammonia, psychometry.* And shorter ones in droves like *eye, rye, riot, rhyme, guy, guise, climb, limn, thyme.* Not to mention *busy, dizzy, build, guild, gild, woman, women, care, air, prayer, where, pear, their.* You see, among the "least literate" of our people bulk some twenty million elementary-school children whose present and future are surely as vital to us as is that of any twenty million to phonetic Russia. And the billions of mistakes per annum they total in their reading, writing, spelling, and the effect of this on their education as a whole, is something the Russian school authorities must eye with sardonic astoundedness. "And the acres of print," you can almost hear them jibing, "their pundits put out on THE CHALLENGE OF SOVIET EDUCATION! And their kids with a basic learning tool of 250 jumbled spelling units, and ours a streamlined 36!"

My *Kappan* article rather stressed these odds, but they seemed to make no dent in your conviction of the inviolable all-rightness of our orthographic *status quo.* Inviolable, that is, to all properly constituted persons who are "interested in bothering to look into the reasons why our words happen to be spelled as they are." So, if Johnny graduates from sixth grade, still woozy on *choose, lose, bruise, whose, booze, ruse—goose, truce, sluice, deuce—aisle, mile, style, guile, lisle,* let's be careful to lay the blame where it belongs. On the boy's own heedlessness, that is to say, or on that of his primary- and middle-grade teachers. Chances are they didn't adequately ground him in the Roman, Saxon, Norman derivations of his words, or even drill him in their cognates in modern Portuguese, German, French.

There's not a dictionary in the country which agrees with you. Least of all those prepared for school children of his age and less. Take the Merriam-Webster *Elementary* of 1956. Not only by the care and skill and thoroughness with which it trains its young clientele in the use of its entries and respellings does it place the blame for Johnny where it basically belongs—it comes out with that placement in this unequivocal wise. Taking *way, weigh* and *people, leopard* as examples, it says: "These two groups of words illustrate two things: (1) That the same sound may be spelled in more than one way and (2) that the same spelling may be pronounced in more than one way. . . . If you hear a new word, you can't be sure how it is spelled. . . . If you see a new word, you can't be sure how it is pronounced."

A pretty situation, wouldn't you admit, into which to plunge a six-year-old to whom *all* the words he sees are new? With *on* transmogrifying itself into the *ōn* of *only*, the *un* of *onion*, and the incredible *wun* of *one*. With *speak, break, breakfast* taking on from there, along with *but*, *put—dull, pull—most, toast—new, sew—howl, bowl*. With *s, c, z* playing fast and loose with *his, fizz—rinse, since—rise, size*, and *t* sliding in and out of *such, Dutch, which, witch, oft, often*. And no firmer footing in the next grade, or the next. Is it *double, bubble*—or are the vowels the other way around? And what of *vigor, trigger—acre, Quaker—lemon, demon—novel, shovel, oval?* Need we wonder if his reason revolts, his memory goes on strike, his attention gives up the struggle, and he ends up with that one third of our high-school enrollment who will never read above fifth-grade norm?

Our fifth-grade norm, be it understood. Not that of phonetic Italy, Finland, Siberia, and the far-flung Spanish world.

If I am a little fervent in all this, I have the background for it. Teaching English as a foreign language in the schools of Mexico City gave me an outside view of the time-consuming, memory-burdening, reason-flouting make-up of our spelling. Teaching Spanish as the mother tongue to illiterates there gave me a glimpse of the magic a comparable phoneticism could bring to our reading problem—the Number One headache of our schools.

LOUIS FOLEY

From Word Study, *XXXVI* (*February,*
1961), *5-6. Copyright* ©, *1961, by G. & C.*
Merriam Co., publishers of the Merriam-
Webster dictionaries. By permission of
G. & C. Merriam Co. and the author.

The Alphabet-Cart Jogs On

The real difficulty with English is not its mere "spelling" but its
peculiarities of *pronunciation*. It has built-in characteristics which lay
it open to corruption of pronunciation such as does not threaten other
languages to any comparable extent. Aside from our shifty set of betwixt-
and-between sounds and our commonly vague syllabication, our way of
galloping from one stressed syllable to another renders the "vowels" of
unaccented syllables for the most part merely theoretical. In the word
unemployment, for instance, as actually spoken in a sentence, can anyone
claim there is really more than one vowel? How much of an "a" does
one hear in *dismal* or *admire?* The -*us* of Mrs. Bowyer's "Waulrus"
is not pronounced like the pronoun *us*. Except in very special constructions ("he finally came *to*"), *to* is not pronounced like *too*. In some points
the proposed changes seem actually less "phonetic" than present usage.

With "seen" doing duty for *scene,* the logic of a whole family of
words, as well as common ground shared with various other languages,
would be destroyed, and to what profit? Presumably there would no
longer be any distinguishing of *right, write, wright,* and *rite*—worlds
apart in association though they be. And it has been my observation that
people who confuse homonyms are often really confusing *ideas*. I have
seen this with *accept* and *except,* or *affect* and *effect,* and other such
pairs which as actually spoken are indistinguishable. Apparently, undis-
criminating persons have for such false twins a fuzzy sort of meaning

which covers both. When we read that Mr. Luther Hodges has "a *flare* for comedy as well as commerce" (*Life* magazine, December 12, 1960, p. 32), it is clear that the writer not merely confused this word with *flair* but did not understand the true meaning of the latter term. Procrustean handling of all homonyms—real or supposed—could only produce confusion worse confounded.

It makes a good paper argument to point to the same "simplified" spellings being used in dictionaries for some of the common words in question. Of course a dictionary has to be consistently exact throughout, but does anyone ever look to see how these common words are *pronounced?* The question would hardly arise.

Like our irregular verbs, unusual plurals, and "flat" adverbs, most of our real curiosities of spelling survive in common words which we know from our childhood. They do not figure much in lists of "words frequently misspelled." Very largely the words which make up such lists are ones which have definite reasons for being as they are. It is surprising how many of the commonest misspellings are due to careless unawareness of clear principles of our system which can be steadily applied.

If spelling reformers wish to accomplish a practical improvement more profoundly phonetic than most of their radical schemes, let them work for more consistency in the handling of compound words. A mere hyphen can register great difference in grammatical construction and totally different meaning, as well as the difference in sound which goes with change of accentuation. To see this peculiarity of our language one has only to compare "a rolling *stone*" or "an entering *wedge*" with *parking*-meter or *bowling*-alley, for instance. Yet whereas we often see true compounds written as if they were separate words, at the same time the prepositional phrase "under *way*" is frequently written solid as if it were a unit like "*under*wear," and the English sub-titles of foreign movies regularly confuse the two separate words *all right* with totally different locutions involving an inseparable prefix such as *also, almost, although,* and the like.

Written or printed language is far more than merely "phonetic." As people have come to read more and more, the visual effect of words has acquired vastly greater power of instantly creating connotation. Nor is this a very new thing. A good while ago there were written very entertaining stories which could no more be read aloud than one could read a cartoon. For a couple of off-hand examples we might mention *The Love-*

Letters of Smith, by H. C. Bunner (about 1890), and *A Hamerton Typewriter,* by Eliza Orne White.

One wonders whether the proponents of a complete overhaul of our spelling system can possibly have envisaged the results they would bring about, if their schemes were imposed upon us. Imagine a generation of children accustomed from their earliest schooling to the supposedly easier, more "phonetic" employment of our alphabet. Reading of anything previously printed would be for them a matter of painful deciphering. Serious new mechanical deterrents would be placed in the way of their ever becoming familiar with any literature even a little earlier than their own time. Eventually, were they not to remain relatively illiterate, they would have to learn the traditional spelling after all, at an age when it would naturally be more difficult—like a foreign language—even aside from their hostile conditioning. They could hardly even *find* words in any standard dictionary or in any of the innumerable bilingual lexicons. Incidental disguising of many word-relationships would destroy various aids to vocabulary-building. Understanding the development of our language, so necessary to depth of linguistic consciousness, would become considerably more difficult. And the English language, already peculiar enough in comparison with other tongues, would be rendered more provincial than ever. For a large share of the words that would be most radically altered would be the ones whose "unphonetic" appearance —by arbitrary standards—reveals their relationship with cognates in other languages and makes them much easier for foreigners to learn.

If we admire the success of other peoples in making their children literate, we might do well to imitate the spirit rather than the letter. It is much deeper things than conventions of spelling that make the difference.

QUESTIONS FOR REVIEW OF PART FIVE

1. What does Whitehall believe are the four major functions of punctuation? Do you find his classification more or less helpful than the classification in your composition handbook (or dictionary)?

2. Compare the Whitehall article and a composition handbook on the treatment of other punctuation marks with final quotation marks. In fact, compare Whitehall's last example of the use of the exclamation point to his next-to-last statement in the introductory paragraph on separating punctuation. Do you find any discrepancies?

Can you explain why there are these discrepancies? Which system makes more sense to you?

3. If, in a wild moment, you were to add the new punctuation marks in the Flanagan-Merritt article to Whitehall's system, to which of the four major functions would you assign each of the new punctuation marks?

4. From what you have learned about Samuel Johnson in the Evans article, would you say that Johnson would have encouraged or discouraged the supporters of the proposal in "It's Not Johnny!"?

5. In his first article, Foley writes "To make our spelling really phonetic would require transcriptions that only trained phoneticians could decipher." Referring to Faust's discussion of phones, allophones, and phonemes, would you say that Faust would agree or disagree with Foley's statement?

6. Which do you think wins the argument over the "phonetic" respelling of "little," "pepper," and "vinegar"—the Foley or the Bowyer article?

SUGGESTIONS FOR INDIVIDUAL PROJECTS
AND CLASS DISCUSSION

1. Ballard's article contains some unconventional sentence patterns; consequently, it is not surprising that his punctuation occasionally is unconventional. Find six examples of such punctuation and comment on the effectiveness of each.

2. From the first Foley article, list (correctly spelled) the words with which you occasionally have spelling difficulty. After each word, note Foley's suggestion for remembering the correct spelling.

3. Listed here are some examples of variant spellings. Drawing on what you know about spelling, pronunciation, and etymology (using the etymologies in your dictionary or in the *Oxford English Dictionary* when necessary), explain why each variation exists and why you prefer one variant over another. If you think you have no preference, remember that you will use only one of the spellings when you write the word in a paper.

adviser, advisor	cigaret, cigarette
aesthetic, esthetic	cocoanut, coconut
burden, burthen	collectable, collectible
buses, busses	dandriff, dandruff
calk, caulk	endorse, indorse
catalog, catalogue	fetid, foetid
catchup, catsup, ketchup	fulfil, fulfill
catharsis, katharsis	gaiety, gayety
chammy, chamois, shammy,	gipsy, gypsy
shamois, shamoy	good-by, good-bye

instalment, installment   peddler, pedlar, pedler
judgement, judgment   spacial, spatial
lollipop, lollypop   today, to-day
mediaeval, medieval   whiskey, whisky
moustache, mustache

SUGGESTED WRITING ASSIGNMENT

Review those portions of the Whitehall article which show how
to link and separate subject-predicate groups with a semicolon,
colon, dash, period, or comma. Construct six sets of five sentences,
each set working from the same pair of independent clauses punctuated with each of the five marks. Make sure that most of the
sentences are fairly good sentences, but place a star before the one
in each set which seems to you most effective, a zero before the
one least effective. Here is an illustrative set:

1. All that I am, I owe to my parents; they gave me my
   body, shaped my mind, and warped my disposition.
* 2. All that I am, I owe to my parents: my body, my mind,
   and my warped disposition.
3. My body, my mind, and my warped disposition—all that
   I am, I owe to my parents.
0 4. All that I am, I owe to my parents. They gave me my
   body, shaped my mind, and warped my disposition.
5. All that I am, I owe to my parents, for they gave me my
   body, shaped my mind, and warped my disposition.

(Note: If you disagree with the editor's preference, see if you can
explain the basis for your choice, while he hides behind the page.
Note that in several of the sentences a dash could well be substituted for the comma before "and warped my disposition." Why?)

PART VI

General Semantics

*G*eneral semantics is the study of the meanings of words. It is relatively little concerned with etymology and with the roots and affixes of words and is, therefore, not the same as vocabulary study. Instead, it is concerned with the ways in which meanings of words shape the responses of people to their environments and to each other. A very popular study in the 1940's, the excessive claims for it by some of its devotees brought general semantics into disrepute with many teachers and scholars. Now that the initial fervor and reaction have subsided, it is possible to consider the genuine insights of general semantics without the necessity of taking sides in a controversy. That is what Charlton Laird does in "Thinking about Words," in which he introduces the reader to "the nature of meaning" and "meaning and symbol." Explanations by S. I. Hayakawa of the abstraction

process and of the classification process follow, and Part VI
concludes with a consideration by Anatol Rapoport of various
ways of defining concepts.

CHARLTON LAIRD

Thinking about Words

THE NATURE OF MEANING

We have discussed meaning, and the developments of meaning, but
without asking ourselves what it is, or how a given symbol, a sound or an
arrangement of letters, comes to "mean." How is it that, as you pass your
eyes over this page, you experience ideas similar to those I was thinking
when I hit the typewriter keys?

That you and I should experience these ideas because I write and you
read is amazing enough, but the phenomenon becomes the more staggering when we add that a word has no meaning in any strict sense. Presumably a dollar has value, even though a fiat value which shifts in relation to purchasing power. But no Bureau of Standards for Words of
Doubtful Worth determines their semantic weight and measure; no
United States Linguistic Treasury guarantees the value of a word, not
even of a word as presumably precise as *minute,* which is exactness itself
when compared with a slippery symbol like *Communist* or *Americanism.*
A man calls to his wife, "Are you coming?" and she replies, "In a
minute." He then knows what to expect, not by his knowledge of the
meaning of the word *minute* but by his knowledge of the semantic and
other habits of his wife. She may mean that she is on her way and has
only to grab her purse off the closet shelf, or she may mean that she has

yet to finish with her lipstick, but that she will be along soon enough
so that he need not have implied they were already late. Or she may mean
a dozen other things, depending upon the way she uses words, the way
she happens to be feeling, or the way she expects her husband to interpret
her answer. She probably does not mean to say that she will arrive at
the end of the sixtieth second. She does not mean to use *minute* in this
way even if she says quite precisely, "The egg will be boiled in one
minute," and certainly she does not mean to say that the egg will be
boiled in one fourteen-hundred-fortieth part of a revolution of the earth,
nor to take into account the fact that the sidereal and calendar years,
along with their subdivisions, do not coincide. That is, the word *minute*
is a counter, which a speaker or writer uses for a purpose, and a reader
or hearer interprets in his own way, which is not likely to coincide with
the "meaning" intended by the user.

This was not always the accepted attitude toward meaning. Thinkers
about language formerly assumed, as many laymen do today, that words
have meanings and that these meanings can be determined and recorded
in books. The philosopher Voltaire wrote, "All languages being imperfect, it does not follow that one should change them. One must adhere
absolutely to the manner in which the good authors have spoken them;
and when one has a sufficient number of approved authors, a language
is fixed." Voltaire is here assuming, of course, not only that a language
can be fixed—which all modern students of language would deny—but
that study will reveal the stuff so accurately that we can know what to
fix. To a degree, of course, this last is still the assumption. Lexicographers cannot feel that they are honest men—and as a group they are
uncommonly honest—unless they believe that a word can be defined well
enough to put it into a dictionary. And publishers can sell few dictionaries unless the public believes that words are definable. But we now
suppose that the meaning of a word has a practical, not an actual, reality.

Certain properties of words are more determinable than others, and
of these the most measurable is the *referent,* which represents a concept
so new that the word is likely to appear only in recent dictionaries. It
is the object to which a word refers. If you and I were marooned in a
desert, and you were to cry "Airplane!" I would know what sort of
craft you were referring to, and if I then saw flying toward us a power-
propelled vehicle manned by a pilot and kept aloft by the aerodynamic
forces induced by propulsion, I would recognize the object. That is, *air-*

plane would have a common referent for us. Furthermore, no other referent would be possible; neither of us would suppose that the referent of *airplane* could be the kangaroo rat we were trying to snare for food or the cactus on which we were carefully not sitting.

The uniqueness of the referent need not be obvious. Suppose again that you and I are awaiting rescue when three flying objects approach us from different directions, and you say "Airplane." I am looking in another direction and see a helicopter. Can a helicopter be a referent of *airplane?* If I now look in another direction and see a guided missile, could that be a referent of *airplane?* Or, more generally, if I were to say, "That is not the truth," you and I and Pontius Pilate might not be able to agree as to what constitutes truth. But granted that we could agree that of two statements one was "true" and the other "false," we should then be able to agree as to which was the referent of *truth.*

Speaking generally, then, a word has only one sort of referent, and all users of the language who are familiar with the word agree as to the referent. But speakers agree on little else, for what we call the "meaning" of the word is in us, not in the word, and can be called up only by the word or by the referent of the word. Again, consider you and me waiting on the desert. The word *airplane* fills you with delight; you envisage rescue, cold water, food, a return to your home and friends. I view the airplane with horror, because I detest all airplanes, and I would rather die starved on the sand than smashed into a mountain. Furthermore, I am confident that a jeep squadron is coming. Then, as the plane approaches, your emotions change again, because you recognize the type of plane, and you are sure it is being piloted by your best friend. Meanwhile, my attitude changes, also, because I recall that in a craft of this type I once crashed and thereby acquired my horror of all planes. And so it goes. *Airplane* is not a word in the sense that it is something you and I have in common in its entirety. The referent we have in common, but the impact of the word is yours or mine or any man's, so that, speaking specifically enough, none of us has any word he can share in its entirety with anybody else.

Thus words have no fixed meanings; they have the power of designating referents and of stimulating awareness of meaning in individuals. We use words as though they were dippers, the same dippers for everybody, but the stuff that is dipped up with the dipper depends upon the body of stuff from which it is dipped. And when we use words we are always dipping into ourselves.

In a sense, of course, I am saying here only that we live in an infinitely varied world, where, if we are to make sense of ourselves and our surroundings, we must reduce infinity to order. No two typewriters are alike, although the same mechanically controlled machines make them. No man ever takes two identical steps, and yet we walk by the similarity in our steps, not by their minute differences. The similarities in your notion and mine of what *airplane* means permit us to express ourselves and to approximate the meanings that other people are trying to express. Our experience with words is so vast, and we have done so much— most of it unconscious—to order and generalize this experience, that we can use words as though we all agree as to what they mean and what they are good for. On that ill-founded though useful assumption mankind makes laws and enforces them, builds houses and sells them, proposes marriage, and discusses God. We live by a world of meaning which has no real foundation outside ourselves.

Thus we communicate by the overlapping areas of our meanings, but we do not always rely only on the overlappings. Words can cause fights as well as friendships. Suppose I say, "Professor Snicklepoof? Oh, yes, quite a radical thinker." By this I may mean to compliment the professor by suggesting that the quality of his mind recalls the etymology of the word, Latin *radix,* root. He goes to the roots of things. Or I may mean, presumably *because* Professor Snicklepoof goes to the roots of things, that he is startlingly original and thus evolves ideas other thinkers would miss. If I use the phrase "radical thinker" only in the presence of those who will understand my implications, all may be well. But to some people *radical* can imply no good. To them it suggests a dangerous person, different from the norm in a subversive way, and probably unpatriotic, blasphemous, and immoral.

This uncertainty of meaning can lead to private differences or international disaster. Most such misunderstandings are unintentional, but the ambiguous use of words can be deliberate. Poets get some of their best effects by studied ambiguity. Andrew Marvell wrote,

> The grave's a fine and private place,
> But none, I think, do there embrace.

Here *private* has overtones. Certainly the grave is private; the occupant is alone with the worms. Not a secluded canoe in the shade of the willows, not a parked car on a lonely road, not a dim-lit sofa after the parents have gone to bed can supply such privacy as does the grave, and Marvell suggests that no one puts his grave to such uses as privacy sometimes promotes. But not all studied ambiguity is artistic; some of it is deliberately deceptive. Prior to the second world war, Japan promoted a "Go-Prosperity League," but the Chinese who were the victims of the invasion feared that most of the prosperity was to be Japanese. Similarly, few non-Communists today believe that the current Russian government means peace when they say *peace*. When an advertiser says that his product is "the world's finest," he does not necessarily believe what he says; he may use *world's* and *finest* for their impacts, not because he knows no better.

This use of meaning, the distortion of words to gain the private ends of the distorter, has of late attracted wide attention. The term *General Semantics* often connotes this study of the psychological, sociological, and political implications of meaning, whereas *semantics* is more commonly used to suggest the study of meaning in all its branches. General Semantics is one of the important growths in linguistic understanding in the past quarter century, and if it seems not at the moment to be growing much, it has made the world, particularly the American portion of the world, more aware of the nature of language and of the dangers and potentialities it possesses. General Semantics is one of the reasons that distinctions among the word, the referent, and the meaning are more than academic.

MEANING AND SYMBOL

Words, even if they have no measurable meaning, are the means by which we make meanings workable. How is this done? Some answers are easy: man develops meaning because that is what man is, a meaningful animal; evolution from the brute to the human is the growth of the sense of meaning; what the opposable thumb is to man as a tool-using animal, a sense for meaning is to man as a thinking animal; the use of words is the man, and thus every man has the vocabulary he deserves. This is intriguing if a bit general. And perhaps we must be general to be accurate; if the growth and use of meaning are varied, as life is varied, then meaning may be so complicated and elaborate that no simple statement about it can be meaningful. But we might try.

At the moment, two approaches appear more than normally inviting, if for no other reason than because they are almost diametric in method and philosophy. One is furthered by people who are not students of language in the older sense at all—psychologists, neurologists, mathematicians, and especially mechanically-inclined students called communications engineers. They rely mainly upon two approaches: the study of neurons and the study of frequencies of words by means of counting machines, electric brains, and the like.

First to those who study neurons, popularly called "nerves." The neurons are message carriers; they report that a finger in contact with a flaming match is too hot, and they order the match dropped. But what made the decision to drop the match, as against other possible decisions, for example, to endure the pain or to amputate the finger? Presumably this is done by the "brain," but the brain seems also to be neurons. How does the brain make decisions? A current theory is that neurons are memory paths with binary choices; that is, they can decide for or against, and thus any action is the result of a large number of yes/no answers. Similarly, meaning is the result of a large number of choices, and a child has "learned" a word when his neurons have developed enough memory paths to make a sufficiently large number of yes-decisions as against no-decisions, and he becomes capable of using the word intelligibly and of reacting to the word roughly as his elders would react to it.

But how do the neurons acquire the basis for the yes-decisions? Here the mathematicians and the communications engineers come in. They prefer to call a word a *morpheme,* or a *phrase*—terms with which we shall deal later, but they can be accepted for the current discussion as synonyms of *word*—and they would define its meaning in terms of the probabilities of its occurrence in relationships with other morphemes and phrases having their own probabilities of occurrence. For instance, the child learns to say *the orange juice* and not *orange juice the* or *orange the juice,* because he hears *the* in the first of these contexts and not in the other two. Obviously, this is true. Is it then also true that the child learns to distinguish the different usages of *truth* in "The truth is here obscure," and "I will tell the truth, so help me God" because his neurons have made binary choices? If so, he must recall so many instances of the word *truth* that it can be identified in either

"meaning" by its context, the context determined by tabulated instances
of the neighboring morphemes. Any but an electric brain would boggle
at building and using a vocabulary by such an astronomical number of
binary choices. Of course, the communications engineer could retort
that our brains probably are electric, anyhow, and an even better retort
might be that if we boggle at this definition of meaning, we boggle at
all the others too. As yet we have discovered no reliable unit of meaning, and, without a unit, how can we measure?

This statistical approach to language can, of course, be applied to other
aspects of language than vocabulary—to grammar and usage, for instance
—and we shall need to consider it when we treat those subjects; but
meanwhile we might notice another theory which shuns mechanical
tabulators and approaches philosophy and art. I am referring to the supposed role of symbol in language.

As an example, let us start with two straight lines, like this: / /.
They probably mean little to you. Now let us change the angle of
the lines so that they cross each other, X. Suddenly they have acquired
"meaning." They are now the cross with which a voter indicates his
choice, the X that marks the spot, or a letter of the alphabet. If we now
rotate these lines they become, among other things, a plus sign or the
way an illiterate signs his name (John Jones, His Mark); and if we
elongate one of the lines, they become an indication of the Cross, of Christ,
of the Christian Church, of salvation, and of various things associated with
religion and ecclesiastical architecture. Now broaden them a little: **+**.
If you color them red, they suggest an organization devoted to mercy.
Color them blue or white and they may suggest health insurance or hos-
pitalization. The original two lines could be put in a number of other
significant relationships, T, V, ʌ, >, <, but in some relationships they
would, for most people, mean almost nothing, ⌐ ʌ.

That is, X and + are symbols, but ʌ, practically speaking, is not.
Of course it might become so. Suppose that we became acutely aware
that in modern society everybody depends upon, or let us say *leans*
on, others. We depend upon the milkman for coffee cream and upon
the pilot for a safe landing, and they in turn depend upon dairy
farmers and the makers of radar controls. Now suppose we represent
the person upon whom we lean, whether it is Mother or the milkman,
by an upright line, and the dependence of other people by a leaning

line. We have ʌ, which could become a symbol for the interreliance of human beings in modern society.

That is, a symbol is anything that becomes vested with meaning, significance, the ability to affect men's thoughts, feelings, and actions in ways not to be accounted for by the object itself. All words are symbols, of course. Nothing in the sound or the printing of the words *tire, hire,* or *pyre* makes them incapable of the impact of the shouted word *fire. Fire!* has symbolic powers that *Tire!* and *Hire!* do not; it implies "Save me from the fire!" or "Help me put out the fire before it spreads." But to a degree all words have this power, or they are not words, and in a sense that is what makes them words, that they are symbols for a number of things, especially for meanings.

Man is a lover of symbols. All the higher animals make some use of them, but none so much as man; perhaps he is civilized because he loved symbols and became capable of building them in quantity and variety. Certainly language must have been born when a sound became a symbol, when a cry of fear became a warning of the source of the fear, or a sign of delight meant "I love you."

Furthermore, man is a lover of order. Living in a confused and frightening world he seeks order, hoping that order will promote his understanding and perhaps lessen his fear. A love of order promotes the search for God, the belief in science, the devotion to art, the need for philosophy, the love of mankind, which are all in varying degrees answers to the need for order, intellectual and emotional. Meaning is our means of conscious order, and words—or symbols, if you wish to call them that—are the means of ordering meaning. Man finds order by generalizing, and he embodies his generalizations in words.

Are words, then, only the nuclei for symbol-clusters, and meaning only man's answer to his need for order, an order he finds through symbol? This is at least a pleasant way to think of vocabulary, but it has the limitations notable in some other observations about meaning, that it is neither detailed nor specific. We may yet have to rely on the binary choices of neurons, the choices being counted by an electric calculator, to know anything specific about meaning. On the other hand, the two approaches are not incompatible. Symbol may show us *why* we have words and the electric brain *how* we have words. Both questions are worth answering.

S. I. HAYAKAWA

Abstraction

BESSIE, THE COW

The universe is in a perpetual state of flux. The stars are in constant motion, growing, cooling, exploding. The earth itself is not unchanging; mountains are being worn away, rivers are altering their channels, valleys are deepening. All life is also a process of change, through birth, growth, decay, and death. Even what we used to call "inert matter"—chairs and tables and stones—is not inert, as we now know, for, at the submicroscopic level, it is a whirl of electrons. If a table looks today very much as it did yesterday or as it did a hundred years ago, it is not because it has not changed, but because the changes have been too minute for our coarse perceptions. To modern science there is no "solid matter." If matter looks "solid" to us, it does so only because its motion is too rapid or too minute to be felt. It is "solid" only in the sense that a rapidly rotating color chart is "white" or a rapidly spinning top is "standing still." Our senses are extremely limited, so that we constantly have to use instruments such as microscopes, telescopes, speedometers, stethoscopes, and seismographs to detect and record occurrences which our senses are not able to record directly. The way in which we happen to see and feel things is the result of the peculiarities of our nervous systems. There are "sights" we cannot see, and, as even children know today with their high-frequency dog whistles, "sounds" that we cannot hear.

It is absurd, therefore, to imagine that we ever perceive anything "as it really is."

Inadequate as our senses are, with the help of instruments they tell us a great deal. The discovery of microörganisms with the use of the microscope has given us a measure of control over bacteria; we cannot see, hear, or feel radio waves, but we can create and transform them to useful purpose. Most of our conquest of the external world, in engineering, in chemistry, and in medicine, is due to our use of mechanical contrivances of one kind or another to increase the capacity of our nervous systems. In modern life, our unaided senses are not half enough to get us about in the world. We cannot even obey speed laws or compute our gas and electric bills without mechanical aids to perception.

To return, then, to the relations between words and what they stand for, let us say that there is before us "Bessie," a cow. Bessie is a living organism, constantly changing, constantly ingesting food and air, transforming it, getting rid of it again. Her blood is circulating, her nerves are sending messages. Viewed microscopically, she is a mass of variegated corpuscles, cells, and bacterial organisms; viewed from the point of view of modern physics, she is a perpetual dance of electrons. What she is in her entirety, we can never know; even if we could at any precise moment say what she was, at the next moment she would have changed enough so that our description would no longer be accurate. It is impossible to say completely what Bessie or anything else really *is*. Bessie is no static "object," but a dynamic process.

The Bessie that we experience, however, is something else again. We experience only a small fraction of the total Bessie: the lights and shadows of her exterior, her motions, her general configuration, the noises she makes, and the sensations she presents to our sense of touch. *And because of our previous experience, we observe resemblances in her to certain other animals to which, in the past, we have applied the word "cow."*

THE PROCESS OF ABSTRACTING

The "object" of our experience, then, is not the "thing in itself," but *an interaction between our nervous systems (with all their imperfections) and something outside them.* Bessie is unique—there is nothing

else in the universe exactly like her in all respects. But our nervous
systems, automatically *abstracting* or selecting from the process-Bessie
those features of hers in which she resembles other animals of like size,
functions, and habits, *classify* her as "cow."

When we say, then, that "Bessie is a cow," we are only noting the
process-Bessie's resemblances to other "cows" and *ignoring differences.*
What is more, we are leaping a huge chasm: from the dynamic process-
Bessie, a whirl of electro-chemico-neural eventfulness, to a relatively
static "idea," "concept," or *word,* "cow." The reader is referred to the
diagram entitled "The Abstraction Ladder," which he will find on
page 244.[1]

As the diagram illustrates, the "object" we see is an abstraction of the
lowest level, but it is still an abstraction, since it leaves out characteristics of the process that is the real Bessie. The *word* "Bessie" (cow$_1$)
is the lowest *verbal* level of abstraction, leaving out further characteristics—the differences between Bessie yesterday and Bessie today,
between Bessie today and Bessie tomorrow—and selecting only the
similarities. The word "cow" selects only the similarities between Bessie
(cow$_1$), Daisy (cow$_2$), Rosie (cow$_3$), and so on, and therefore leaves
out still more about Bessie. The word "livestock" selects or abstracts
only the features that Bessie has in common with pigs, chickens, goats,
and sheep. The term "farm asset" abstracts only the features Bessie has
in common with barns, fences, livestock, furniture, generating plants,
and tractors, and is therefore on a very high level of abstraction.

The reason we must concern ourselves with the process of abstracting
is that the study of language is all too often regarded as being a matter
of examining such things as pronunciation, spelling, vocabulary, grammar, and sentence structure. The methods by which composition and
oratory are taught in old-fashioned school systems seems to be largely
responsible for this widespread notion that the way to study words is to
concentrate one's attention exclusively on words.

But as we know from everyday experience, learning language is not
simply a matter of learning words; it is a matter of correctly relating
our words to the things and happenings for which they stand. We learn

[1] The "abstraction ladder" is based on "The Structural Differential," a diagram originated by A. Korzybski to explain the process of abstracting. For a
fuller explanation both of the diagram and the process it illustrates, see his
*Science and Sanity: An Introduction to Non-Aristotelian Systems and General
Semantics* (1933), especially Chapter XXV.

the language of baseball by playing or watching the game *and studying what goes on*. It is not enough for a child to learn to *say* "cookie" or "dog"; he must be able to use these words in their proper relationship to nonverbal cookies and nonverbal dogs before we can grant that he is learning the language. As Wendell Johnson has said, "The study of language begins properly with a study of what language is about."

Once we begin to concern ourselves with what language is about, we are at once thrown into a consideration of how the human nervous system works. When we call Beau (the Boston terrier), Pedro (the Chihuahua), Snuffles (the English bulldog), and Shane (the Irish wolfhound)—creatures that differ greatly in size, shape, appearance, and behavior—by the same name, "dog," our nervous system has obviously gone to work *abstracting* what is common to them all, ignoring for the time being the differences among them.

WHY WE MUST ABSTRACT

This process of abstracting, of leaving characteristics out, is an indispensable convenience. To illustrate by still another example, suppose that we live in an isolated village of four families, each owning a house. A's house is referred to as *maga;* B's house is *biyo;* C's is *kata,* and D's is *pelel*. This is quite satisfactory for ordinary purposes of communication in the village, unless a discussion arises about building a new house—a spare one, let us say. We cannot refer to the projected house by any one of the four words we have for the existing houses, since each of these has too specific a meaning. We must find a *general* term, at a higher level of abstraction, that means "something that has certain characteristics in common with *mago, biyo, kata,* and *pelel,* and yet is not A's, B's, C's, or D's." Since this is much too complicated to say each time, an *abbreviation* must be invented. Let us say we choose the noise, *house*. Out of such needs do our words come—they are a form of shorthand. The invention of a new abstraction is a great step forward, since it *makes discussion possible*—as, in this case, not only the discussion of a fifth house, but of all future houses we may build or see in our travels or dream about.

A producer of educational films once remarked to the writer that it is impossible to make a shot of "work." You can shoot Joe hoeing potatoes, Frank greasing a car, Bill spraying paint on a barn, but

ABSTRACTION LADDER

Start reading from the bottom *UP*

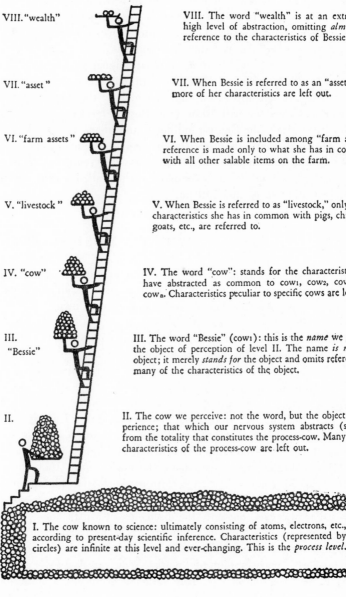

VIII. "wealth"

VIII. The word "wealth" is at an extremely high level of abstraction, omitting *almost* all reference to the characteristics of Bessie.

VII. "asset"

VII. When Bessie is referred to as an "asset," still more of her characteristics are left out.

VI. "farm assets"

VI. When Bessie is included among "farm assets," reference is made only to what she has in common with all other salable items on the farm.

V. "livestock"

V. When Bessie is referred to as "livestock," only those characteristics she has in common with pigs, chickens, goats, etc., are referred to.

IV. "cow"

IV. The word "cow": stands for the characteristics we have abstracted as common to cow_1, cow_2, $cow_3 \ldots cow_n$. Characteristics peculiar to specific cows are left out.

III. "Bessie"

III. The word "Bessie" (cow_1): this is the *name* we give to the object of perception of level II. The name *is not* the object; it merely *stands for* the object and omits reference to many of the characteristics of the object.

II.

II. The cow we perceive: not the word, but the object of experience; that which our nervous system abstracts (selects) from the totality that constitutes the process-cow. Many of the characteristics of the process-cow are left out.

I. The cow known to science: ultimately consisting of atoms, electrons, etc., according to present-day scientific inference. Characteristics (represented by circles) are infinite at this level and ever-changing. This is the *process level*.

never just "work." "Work," too, is a shorthand term, standing, at a higher level of abstraction, for a characteristic that a multitude of activities, from dishwashing to navigation to running an advertising agency to governing a nation, have in common.

The indispensability of this process of abstracting can again be illustrated by what we do when we "calculate." The word "calculate" originates from the Latin word *calculus,* meaning "pebble," and comes to have its present meaning from such ancient practices as that of putting a pebble into a box for each sheep as it left the fold, so that one could tell, by checking the sheep returning at night against the pebbles, whether any had been lost. Primitive as this example of calculation is, it will serve to show why mathematics works. Each pebble is, in this example, an abstraction representing the "oneness" of each sheep—its numerical value. And because we are abstracting from extensional events on clearly understood and uniform principles, the numerical facts about the pebbles are also, barring unforeseen circumstances, numerical facts about the sheep. Our x's and y's and other mathematical symbols are abstractions made from numerical abstractions, and are therefore abstractions of still higher level. And they are useful in predicting occurrences and in getting work done because, since they are abstractions properly and uniformly made from starting points in the extensional world, the relations revealed by the symbols will be, again barring unforeseen circumstances, relations existing in the extensional world.

ON DEFINITIONS

Definitions, contrary to popular opinion, tell us nothing about things. They only describe people's linguistic habits; that is, they tell us what noises people make under what conditions. Definitions should be understood as *statements about language.*

> *House.* This is a word, at the next higher level of abstraction, that can be substituted for the more cumbersome expression, "Something that has characteristics in common with Bill's bungalow, Jordan's cottage, Mrs. Smith's tourist home, Dr. Jones's mansion . . ."
> *Red.* A feature that rubies, roses, ripe tomatoes, robins' breasts, uncooked beef, and lipsticks have in common is abstracted, and this word expresses that abstraction.

Kangaroo. Where the biologist would say "herbivorous mammal, a marsupial of the family Macropodidae," ordinary people say "kangaroo."

Now it will be observed that while the definitions of "house" and "red" given here point *down* the abstraction ladder (see the charts) to *lower* levels of abstraction, the definition of "kangaroo" remains at the same level. That is to say, in the case of "house," we could if necessary go and *look* at Bill's bungalow, Jordan's cottage, Mrs. Smith's tourist home, and Dr. Jones's mansion, and figure out for ourselves what features they seem to have in common; in this way, we might begin to understand under what conditions to use the word "house." But all we know about "kangaroo" from the above is that where some people say one thing, other people say another. That is, when we stay at the *same* level of abstraction in giving a definition, we do not give any information, unless, of course, the listener or reader is already sufficiently familiar with the defining words so that he can work himself down the abstraction ladder. Dictionaries, in order to save space, have to assume in many cases such familiarity with the language on the part of the reader. But where the assumption is unwarranted, definitions at the same level of abstraction are worse than useless. Looking up "indifference" in some cheap pocket dictionaries, we find it defined as "apathy"; we look up "apathy" and find it defined as "indifference."

Even more useless, however, are the definitions that go *up* the abstraction ladder to higher levels of abstraction—the kind most of us tend to make automatically. Try the following experiment on an unsuspecting friend:

> "What is meant by the word *red?*"
> "It's a color."
> "What's a *color?*"
> "Why, it's a quality things have."
> "What's a *quality?*"
> "Say, what are you trying to do, anyway?"

You have pushed him into the clouds. He is lost.

If, on the other hand, we habitually go *down* the abstraction ladder to *lower* levels of abstraction when we are asked the meaning of a word, we are less likely to get lost in verbal mazes; we will tend to "have our feet on the ground" and know what we are talking about. This habit displays itself in an answer such as this:

"What is meant by the word *red?*"

"Well, the next time you see a bunch of cars stopped at an inter-section, look at the traffic light facing them. Also, you might go to the fire department and see how their trucks are painted."

"LET'S DEFINE OUR TERMS"

An extremely widespread instance of an unrealistic (and ultimately superstitious) attitude toward definitions is found in the common aca-demic prescription, "Let's define our terms so that we shall all know what we are talking about." . . . the fact that a golfer, for example, cannot define golfing terms is no indication that he cannot understand and use them. *Conversely, the fact that a man can define a large number of words is no guarantee that he knows what objects or operations they stand for in concrete situations.* People often believe, having defined a word, that some kind of understanding has been established, ignoring the fact that *the words in the definition often conceal even more serious confusions and ambiguities than the word defined.* If we happen to discover this fact and try to remedy matters confused, go on to define the words in the definitions of the defining words, and so on, we quickly find ourselves in a hopeless snarl. The only way to avoid this snarl is *to keep definitions to a minimum and to point to extensional levels wher-ever necessary—and in writing and speaking, this means giving specific examples of what we are talking about.*

Ultimately, no adequate definition of "apple pie" can be given in words—one has to examine and taste an actual apple pie. The same goes for more abstract words. If we have never felt love, if we have never felt strongly about a moral principle nor felt the satisfactions of seeing a moral principle observed, we may verbally define "love" or "justice" until doomsday, but we shall still not know what they mean.

CHASING ONESELF IN VERBAL CIRCLES

In other words, the kind of "thinking" we must be extremely wary of is that which *never* leaves the higher verbal levels of abstraction, the kind that never points *down* the abstraction ladder to lower levels of abstrac-tion and from there to the extensional world:

> "What do you mean by *democracy?*"
> "Democracy means the preservation of human rights."
> "What do you mean by *rights?*"
> "By rights I mean those privileges God grants to all of us—I mean man's inherent privileges."
> "Such as?"
> "Liberty, for example."
> "What do you mean by *liberty?*"
> "Religious and political freedom."
> "And what does that mean?"
> "Religious and political freedom is what we have when we do things the *democratic way.*"

Of course it is possible to talk meaningfully about democracy, as Jefferson and Lincoln have done, as Charles and Mary Beard do in *The Rise of American Civilization,* as Frederick Jackson Turner does in *The Frontier in American History,* as Lincoln Steffens does in his *Autobiography,* as David Lilienthal does in *TVA: Democracy on the March*—to name only the first examples that come to mind—but such a sample as the above is not the way to do it. The trouble with speakers who never leave the higher levels of abstraction is not only that they fail to notice when they are saying something and when they are not; they also produce a similar lack of discrimination in their audiences. Never coming down to earth, they frequently chase themselves around in verbal circles, unaware that they are making meaningless noises.

This is by no means to say, however, that we must never make extensionally meaningless noises. When we use directive language, when we talk about the future, when we utter ritual language or engage in social conversation, we often make utterances that have no extensional verifiability. It must not be overlooked that our highest ratiocinative and imaginative powers are derived from the fact that symbols *are* independent of things symbolized, so that we are free not only to go quickly from low to extremely high levels of abstraction (from "canned peas" to "groceries" to "commodities" to "national wealth") and to manipulate symbols even when the things they stand for cannot be so manipulated ("If all the freight cars in the country were hooked up to each other in one long line . . ."), but we are also free to manufacture symbols at will even if they stand only for abstractions made from other abstractions and not for anything in the extensional world. Mathematicians, for example, often play with symbols that have no extensional content, just to find out what can be done with them; this is called "pure mathematics." And pure mathematics is far from being a useless pastime, because mathematical systems that are elaborated with no extensional applications in mind often prove later to be applicable in useful and unforeseen ways. Mathematicians, however, when they are dealing with extensionally meaningless symbols, usually know what they are doing. We likewise *must* know what we are doing.

Nevertheless, all of us (including mathematicians), when we speak the language of everyday life, often make meaningless noises without knowing that we are doing so. We have already seen what confusions this can lead to. The fundamental purpose of the abstraction ladder, as shown both in this chapter and the next, is to make us aware of the process of abstracting.

THE DISTRUST OF ABSTRACTIONS

We may, using our abstraction ladder, allocate statements as well as words to differing levels of abstraction. "Mrs. Plotz makes good potato pancakes" may be regarded as a statement at a fairly low level of abstraction, although, to be sure, it leaves out many characteristics, such as (1) what one means by "goodness" in potato pancakes, and (2) the infrequent occasions when her pancakes fail to turn out well. "Mrs. Plotz is a good cook," is a statement at a higher level of abstraction, covering Mrs. Plotz's skill not only with potato pancakes, but also with roasts, pickles, noodles, strudels, and so on, nevertheless omitting *specific* mention of what she can accomplish. "Chicago women are good cooks," is a statement at a still higher level of abstraction; it is one that can be made (if at all) on the basis of the observation of the cooking of a statistically significant number of Chicago women. "The culinary art has reached a high state in America," would be a still more highly abstract statement, and if made at all, would have to be based not only on the observation of the Mrs. Plotzes of Chicago, New York, San Francisco, Denver, Albuquerque, and Chattanooga, but also on the observation of the quality of meals served in hotels and restaurants, the quality of training given in departments of home economics in high schools and colleges, the excellence of the writings on culinary art in American books and magazines, and many other relevant facts.

It is to be regretted, although it is understandable, that there exists a tendency in our times to speak contemptuously of "mere abstractions." The ability to climb to higher and higher levels of abstraction is a distinctively human trait, without which none of our philosophical or scientific insights would be possible. In order to have a science of chemistry, one *has* to be able to think of "H_2O," leaving out of consideration for the time being the wetness of water, the hardness of ice, the pearliness of dew, and the other extensional characteristics of H_2O at the objective level. In order to have a study called "ethics," one has to be able to think of what ethical behavior has in common under different conditions and in different civilizations; one has to abstract that which is common to the behavior of the ethical carpenter, the ethical politician, the ethical businessman, the ethical soldier, and that which is common to the laws of conduct of the Buddhist, the Judaist, the Confucian, and the Christian. Thinking that is most abstract can also be that which is most generally useful. The famous injunction of Jesus, "And as ye would that men should do to you, do ye also to them likewise," is, from this point of view, a brilliant generalization of more particular directives—a generalization at so high a level of abstraction that it appears to be applicable to all men in all cultures.

But high level abstractions acquire a bad reputation because they are so often used, consciously or unconsciously, to confuse and befuddle people. A grab among competing powers for oil resources may be spoken of as "protecting the integrity of small nations." (Remember the "Greater East Asia Co-prosperity Sphere"?) An unwillingness to pay social security taxes may be spoken of as "maintaining the system of free enterprise." Depriving the Negro of his vote in violation of the Constitution of the United States may be spoken of as "preserving states' rights." The consequence of this free, and often irresponsible, use of high level abstractions in public controversy and special pleading is that a significant portion of the population has grown cynical about *all* abstractions.

But, as the abstraction ladder has shown, *all we know is abstractions.* What you know about the chair you are sitting in is an abstraction from the totality of that chair. When you eat white bread, you cannot tell by the taste whether or not it has been "enriched by vitamin B" as it says on the wrapper; you simply have to trust that the process (from which the words "vitamin B" are abstracted) is actually there. What you know about your wife—even if she has been your wife for thirty years—

is again an abstraction. Distrusting all abstractions simply does not make sense.

The test of abstractions then is not whether they are "high" or "low level" abstractions, but *whether they are referrable to lower levels.* If one makes a statement about "culinary arts in America," one should be able to refer the statement down the abstraction ladder to particulars of American restaurants, American domestic science, American techniques of food preservation, and so on down to Mrs. Plotz in her kitchen. If one makes a statement about "civil rights in Wisconsin," one should know something about national, state, and local statutes, about the behavior of policemen, magistrates, judges, academic authorities, hotel managers, and the general public in Wisconsin, whose acts and whose decisions affect that minimum of decent treatment in the courts, in politics, and in society that we call "civil rights." *A preacher, a professor, a journalist, or politician whose high level abstractions can systematically and surely be referred to lower level abstractions is not only talking, he is saying something.* As *Time* would say, no windbag, he.

"DEAD-LEVEL ABSTRACTING"

Professor Wendell Johnson of the State University of Iowa, in his *People in Quandaries,* discusses a linguistic phenomenon which he calls "dead-level abstracting." Some people, it appears, remain more or less permanently stuck at certain levels of the abstraction ladder, some on the lower levels, some on the very high levels. There are those, for example, who go in for "persistent low-level abstracting":

> Probably all of us know certain people who seem able to talk on and on without ever drawing any very general conclusions. For example, there is the back-fence chatter that is made up of he said and then I said and then she said and I said and then he said, far into the afternoon, ending with, "Well, that's *just* what I told him!" Letters describing vacation trips frequently illustrate this sort of language, detailing places seen, times of arrival and departure, the foods eaten and the prices paid, whether the beds were hard or soft, etc.

A similar inability to get to higher levels of abstraction characterizes certain types of mental patients who suffer, as Johnson says, "a general blocking of the abstracting process." They go on indefinitely, reciting

insignificant facts, never able to pull them together to frame a generalization to give a meaning to the facts.

Other speakers remain stuck at higher levels of abstraction, with little
or no contact with lower levels. Such language remains permanently
in the clouds. As Johnson says:

> It is characterized especially by vagueness, ambiguity, even utter
> meaninglessness. Simply by saving various circulars, brochures, free
> copies of "new thought" magazines, etc. . . . it is possible to accumu-
> late in a short time quite a sizable file of illustrative material. Much
> more, of course, is to be found on library shelves, on newsstands, and
> in radio programs. Everyday conversation, classroom lectures, political
> speeches, commencement addresses, and various kinds of group forums
> and round-table discussions provide a further abundant source of *words
> cut loose from their moorings.* [Italics supplied.]

(The writer heard recently of a course in esthetics given at a large
middlewestern university in which an entire semester was devoted to
Art and Beauty and the principles underlying them, and during which
the professor, even when asked by students, persistently declined to name
specific paintings, symphonies, sculptures, or objects of beauty to which
his principles might apply. "We are interested," he would say, "in
principles, not in particulars.")

There are psychiatric implications to dead-level abstracting on higher
levels, too, since it is inevitable that, when maps proliferate wildly without any reference to a territory, the result can only be delusion. But
whether at higher or lower levels, dead-level abstracting is, as Johnson
says, always dull:

> The low-level speaker frustrates you because he leaves you with no
> directions as to what to do with the basketful of information he has
> given you. The high-level speaker frustrates you because he simply
> doesn't tell you what he is talking about. . . . Being thus frustrated,
> and being further blocked because the rules of courtesy (or of attend-
> ance at class lectures) require that one remain quietly seated until the
> speaker has finished, there is little for one to do but daydream, doodle,
> or simply fall asleep.

It is obvious, then, that interesting speech and interesting writing, as
well as clear thinking and consequent psychological adjustment, require
the constant interplay of higher and lower level abstractions, and the

constant interplay of the verbal levels with the nonverbal ("object") levels. In science, this interplay goes on constantly, hypotheses being checked against observations, predictions against extensional results. (Scientific *writing*, however, as exemplified in technical journals, offers some appalling examples of *almost* dead-level abstracting—which is the reason so much of it is hard to read. Nevertheless, the interplay between verbal and nonverbal, experimental levels does continue, or else it would not be science.) The work of good novelists and poets also represents this constant interplay between higher and lower levels of abstraction. A "significant" novelist or poet is one whose message has a high level of *general* usefulness in providing insight into life; but he gives his generalizations an impact and a power to convince through his ability to observe and describe actual social situations and states of mind. A memorable literary character, such as Sinclair Lewis's George F. Babbitt, has *descriptive* validity (at a low level of abstraction) as the picture of an individual, as well as a *general* validity as a picture of a "typical" American businessman. The great political leader is also one in whom there is interplay between higher and lower levels of abstraction. The ward heeler knows politics only at lower levels of abstraction: what promises or what acts will cause what people to vote as desired; his loyalties are not to principles (high-level abstractions) but to persons (e.g., political bosses) and immediate advantages (low-level abstractions). The so-called impractical political theorist knows the high-level abstractions ("democracy," "civil rights," "social justice") but is not well enough acquainted with facts at lower levels of abstraction to get himself elected county register of deeds. But the political leaders to whom states and nations remain permanently grateful are those who were able, somehow or other, to achieve simultaneously higher-level aims ("freedom," "national unity," "justice") *and* lower-level aims ("better prices for potato farmers," "higher wages for textile workers," "judicial reform," "soil conservation").

The interesting writer, the informative speaker, the accurate thinker, and the well-adjusted individual, operate on all levels of the abstraction ladder, moving quickly and gracefully and in orderly fashion from higher to lower, from lower to higher—with minds as lithe and deft and beautiful as monkeys in a tree.

S. I. HAYAKAWA

Classification

GIVING THINGS NAMES

The figure below shows eight objects, let us say animals, four large
and four small, a different four with rounded heads and another four
with square heads, and still another four with curly tails and another
four with straight tails. These animals, let us say, are scampering about
your village, but since at first they are of no importance to you, you
ignore them. You do not even give them a name.

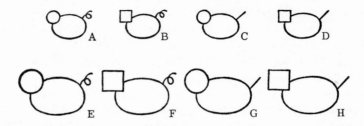

One day, however, you discover that the little ones eat up your grain,
while the big ones do not. A differentiation sets itself up, and abstracting
the common characteristics of A, B, C, and D, you decide to call these
gogo; E, F, G, and H you decide to call *gigi.* You chase away the *gogo,*
but leave the *gigi* alone. Your neighbor, however, has had a different

experience; he finds that those with square heads bite, while those with round heads do not. Abstracting the common characteristics of B, D, F, and H, he calls them *daba,* and A, C, E, and G he calls *dobo*. Still another neighbor discovers, on the other hand, that those with curly tails kill snakes, while those with straight tails do not. He differentiates them, abstracting still another set of common characteristics: A, B, E, and F are *busa,* while C, D, G, and H are *busana*.

Now imagine that the three of you are together when E runs by. You say, "There goes the *gigi*"; your first neighbor says, "There goes the *dobo*"; your other neighbor says, "The goes the *busa*." Here immediately a great controversy arises. What is it really, a *gigi,* a *dobo,* or a *busa?* What is its *right name?* You are quarreling violently when along comes a fourth person from another village who calls it a *muglock,* an edible animal, as opposed to *uglock,* an inedible animal—which doesn't help matters a bit.

Of course, the question, "What is it *really?* What is its *right name?*" is a nonsense question. By a nonsense question is meant one that is not capable of being answered. Things can have "right names" only if there is a necessary connection between symbols and things symbolized, and we have seen that there is not. That is to say, in the light of your interest in protecting your grain, it may be necessary for you to distinguish the animal E as a *gigi;* your neighbor, who doesn't like to be bitten, finds it practical to distinguish it as a *dobo;* your other neighbor, who likes to see snakes killed, distinguishes it as a *busa*. What we call things and where we draw the line between one class of things and another depend upon the interests we have and the purposes of the classification. For example, animals are classified in one way by the meat industry, in a different way by the leather industry, in another different way by the fur industry, and in a still different way by the biologist. None of these classifications is any more final than any of the others; each of them is useful for its purpose.

This holds, of course, regarding everything we perceive. A table "is" a table to us, because we can understand its relationship to our conduct and interests; we eat at it, work on it, lay things on it. But to a person living in a culture where no tables are used, it may be a very big stool, a small platform, or a meaningless structure. If our culture and upbringing were different, that is to say, our world would not even look the same to us.

Many of us, for example, cannot distinguish between pickerel, pike, salmon, smelts, perch, crappies, halibut, and mackerel; we say that they are "just fish, and I don't like fish." To a seafood connoisseur, however, these distinctions are real, since they mean the difference to him between one kind of good meal, a very different kind of good meal, or a poor meal. To a zoologist, even finer distinctions become of great importance, since he has other and more general ends in view. When we hear the statement, then, "This fish is a specimen of the pompano, *Trachinotus carolinus*," we accept this as being "true," even if we don't care, not because that is its "right name," but because that is how it is *classified* in the most complete and most general system of classification which people most deeply interested in fish have evolved.

When we name something, then, we are classifying. *The individual object or event we are naming, of course, has no name and belongs to no class until we put it in one.* To illustrate again, suppose that we were to give the *extensional* meaning of the word "Korean." We would have to point to all "Koreans" living at a particular moment and say, "The word 'Korean' denotes at the present moment these persons: A_1, A_2, A_3 . . . A_n." Now, let us say, a child, whom we shall designate as Z, is born among these "Koreans." *The extensional meaning of the word "Korean," determined prior to the existence of Z, does not include Z.* Z is a new individual belonging to no classification, since all classifications were made without taking Z into account. Why, then, is Z also a "Korean"? *Because we say so.* And, saying so—fixing the classification— we have determined to a considerable extent future attitudes toward Z. For example, Z will always have certain rights in Korea; he will always be regarded in other nations as an "alien" and will be subject to laws applicable to "aliens."

In matters of "race" and "nationality," the way in which classifications work is especially apparent. For example, the present writer is by "race" a "Japanese," by "nationality" a "Canadian," but, his friends say, "essentially" an "American," since he thinks, talks, behaves, and dresses much like other Americans. Because he is "Japanese," he is excluded by law from becoming a citizen of the United States; because he is "Canadian," he has certain rights in all parts of the British Commonwealth; because he is "American," he gets along with his friends and teaches in an American institution of higher learning without any noticeable special difficulties. Are these classifications "real"? Of course they are, and *the effect that each of them has upon what he may and may not do constitutes their "reality."*

There was, again, the story some years ago of the immigrant baby whose parents were "Czechs" and eligible to enter the United States by quota. The child, however, because it was born on what happened to be a "British" ship, was a "British subject." The quota for Britishers was full for that year, with the result that the newborn infant was regarded by immigration authorities as "not admissible to the United States." How they straightened out this matter, the writer does not know. The reader can multiply instances of this kind at will. When, to take another example, is a person a "Negro"? By the definition accepted in the United States, any person with even a small amount of "Negro blood"—that is, whose parents or ancestors were classified as "Negroes"—is a "Negro." *It would be exactly as justifiable to say that any person with even a small amount of "white blood" is "white."* Why do they say one rather than the other? Because the former system of classification *suits the convenience of those making the classification.*

There are few complexities about classifications at the level of dogs and cats, knives and forks, cigarettes and candy, but when it comes to classifications at high levels of abstraction, for example, those describing conduct, social institutions, philosophical and moral problems, serious difficulties occur. When one person kills another, is it an act of murder, an act of temporary insanity, an act of homicide, an accident, or an act of heroism? As soon as the process of classification is completed, our attitudes and our conduct are to a considerable degree determined. We hang the murderer, we lock up the insane man, we free the victim of circumstances, we pin a medal on the hero.

THE BLOCKED MIND

Unfortunately, people are not always aware of the way in which they arrive at their classifications. Unaware of the characteristics of the extensional Mr. Miller not covered by classifying him as "a Jew" and attributing to Mr. Miller all the characteristics *suggested* by the affective connotations of the term with which he has been classified, they pass final judgment on Mr. Miller by saying, "Well, a Jew's a Jew. There's no getting around that!"

We need not concern ourselves here with the injustices done to "Jews," "Roman Catholics," "Republicans," "red-heads," "chorus girls," "sailors," "brass-hats," "Southerners," "Yankees," "school teachers," "government regulations," "socialistic proposals," and so on, by such hasty judgments or, as it is better to call them, fixed reactions. "Hasty judgments" suggests that such errors can be avoided by thinking more slowly; this, of course, is not the case, for some people think very slowly with no better results. What we are concerned with is the way in which we block the development of our own minds by such automatic reactions.

To continue with our example of the people who say, "A Jew's a Jew. There's no getting around that!"—they are, as we have seen, confusing the denoted, extensional Jew with the fictitious "Jew" inside their heads. Such persons, the reader will have observed, can usually be made to admit, on being reminded of certain "Jews" whom they admire—perhaps Albert Einstein, perhaps Hank Greenberg, perhaps Jascha Heifetz, perhaps Benny Goodman—that "there are exceptions, of course." They have been compelled by experience, that is to say, to take cognizance of at least a few of the multitude of "Jews" who do not fit their preconceptions. At this point, however, they continue triumphantly, "But exceptions only prove the rule!" [1]—which is another way of saying, "Facts don't count." In extremely serious cases of people who "think" in this way, it can sometimes be observed that the best friends they have may be Isaac Cohens, Isidor Ginsbergs, and Abe Sinaikos; nevertheless, in explaining this, they will say, "I don't think of them as Jews at all. They're just friends." In other words, the fictitious "Jew" inside their heads remains unchanged *in spite of their experience.*

People like this *cannot learn from experience.* They continue to vote "Republican" or "Democratic," no matter what the Republicans or Democrats do. They continue to object to "socialists," no matter what the socialists propose. They continue to regard "mothers" as sacred, no matter which mother. A woman who had been given up both by physicians and psychiatrists as hopelessly insane was being considered by a committee whose task it was to decide whether or not she should be committed to an asylum. One member of the committee doggedly refused to vote for commitment. "Gentlemen," he said in tones of deepest

[1] This extraordinarily fatuous saying originally meant, "The exception *tests* the rule"—*Exceptio probat regulam.* This older meaning of the word "prove" survives in such an expression as "automobile proving ground."

reverence, "you must remember that this woman is, after all, a mother." Similarly such people continue to hate "Protestants," no matter which Protestant. Unaware of characteristics left out in the process of classification, they overlook, when the term "Republican" is applied to both the party of Abraham Lincoln and the party of Warren Harding, the rather important differences between them: "If the Republican party was good enough for Abe Lincoln, it's good enough for me!"

COW₁ IS NOT COW₂

How do we prevent ourselves from getting into such intellectual blind alleys, or, finding we are in one, how do we get out again? One way is to remember that practically all statements in ordinary conversation, debate, and public controversy taking the form, "Republicans are Republicans," "Business is business," "Boys will be boys," "Women drivers are women drivers," and so on, are *not true*. Let us put one of these back into a context in life.

> "I don't think we should go through with this deal, Bill. Is it altogether fair to the railroad company?"
> "Aw, forget it! *Business is business*, after all."

Such an assertion, although it looks like a "simple statement of fact," is not simple and is not a statement of fact. The first "business" *denotes* transaction under discussion; the second "business" invokes the *connotations* of the word. The sentence is a *directive,* saying, "Let us treat this transaction with complete disregard for considerations other than profit, as the word 'business' suggests." Similarly, when a father tries to excuse the mischief done by his sons, he says, "Boys will be boys"; in other words, "Let us regard the actions of my sons with that indulgent amusement customarily extended toward those whom we call 'boys,'" though the angry neighbor will say, of course, "Boys, my eye! They're little hoodlums; that's what they are!" These too are not informative statements but *directives, directing us to classify the object or event under discussion in given ways, in order that we may feel or act in the ways suggested by the terms of the classification.*

There is a simple technique for preventing such directives from having

their harmful effect on our thinking. It is the suggestion made by Korzyb-
ski that we add "index numbers" to our terms, thus: Englishman$_1$,
Englishman$_2$, . . . ; cow$_1$, cow$_2$, cow$_3$, . . . ; Frenchman$_1$, French-
man$_2$, Frenchman$_3$, . . . ; communist$_1$, communist$_2$, communist$_3$, . . .
The terms of the classification tell us what the individuals in that class
have in common; THE INDEX NUMBERS REMIND US OF THE CHARAC-
TERISTICS LEFT OUT. *A rule can then be formulated as a general guide*
in all our thinking and reading: Cow$_1$ IS NOT *cow$_2$; Jew$_1$* IS NOT *Jew$_2$;*
politician$_1$ IS NOT *politician$_2$, and so on. This rule, if remembered, pre-*
vents us from confusing levels of abstraction and forces us to consider
the facts on those occasions when we might otherwise find ourselves
leaping to conclusions which we may later have cause to regret.

"TRUTH"

Most intellectual problems are, ultimately, problems of classification
and nomenclature. Some years ago there was a dispute between the
American Medical Association and the Antitrust Division of the Department of Justice as to whether the practice of medicine was a "profession"
or "trade." The American Medical Association *wanted* immunity from
laws prohibiting "restraint of trade"; therefore, it insisted that medicine
is a "profession." The Antitrust Division *wanted* to stop certain economic practices connected with medicine, and therefore it insisted that
medicine *is* a "trade." Partisans of either side accused the other of perverting the meanings of words and of not being able to understand plain
English.

Can farmers operate oil wells and still be "farmers"? In 1947 the
attorney general of the state of Kansas sued to dissolve a large agricultural co-operative, Consumers Co-operative Association, charging that
the corporation, in owning oil wells, refineries, and pipe-lines, was
exceeding the statutory privileges of purchasing co-operatives under the
Co-operative Marketing Act, which permits such organizations to "engage in any activity in connection with manufacturing, selling, or supplying to its members machinery, equipment or supplies." The attorney
general held that the co-operative, under the Act, could not handle, let
alone process and manufacture, general farm supplies, but only those
supplies used in the marketing operation. The Kansas Supreme Court

decided unanimously in favor of the defendant (CCA). In so deciding, the court held that gasoline and oil *are* "farm supplies," and producing crude oil *is* "part of the business of farming."

"This court," said the decision, "will take judicial notice of the fact that in the present state of the art of farming, gasoline . . . is one of the costliest items in the production of agricultural commodities. . . . Anyway, gasoline and tractors are here, and this court is not going to say that motor fuel is not a supply necessary to carrying on of farm operations. . . . Indeed it is about as well put as can be on Page 18 of the state's Exhibit C where the defendant (CCA) says: *'Producing crude oil, operating pipe-lines and refineries, are also part of the business of farming. It is merely producing synthetic hay for iron horses. It is "off-the-farm farming" which the farmer, in concert with his neighbors, is carrying on. . . .* Production of power farming equipment, then, is logically an extension of the farmers' own farming operations.'" (Italics supplied.)

Is a harmonica player a "musician"? Until 1948, the American Federation of Musicians had ruled that the harmonica was a "toy." Professional harmonica players usually belonged, therefore, to the American Guild of Variety Artists. Even as distinguished a musician as Larry Adler, who has often played the harmonica as a solo instrument with symphony orchestras, was by the union's definition "not a musician." In 1948, however, the AFM, finding that harmonica players were getting popular and competing with members of the union, decided that they were "musicians" after all—a decision that did not sit well with the president of AGVA, who promptly declared jurisdictional war on the AFM.

Is aspirin a "drug" or not? In some states, it is legally classified as a "drug," and therefore can be sold only by licensed pharmacists. If people want to be able to buy aspirin in groceries, lunchrooms, and pool halls (as they can in other states), they must have it reclassified as "not a drug."

Is medicine a "profession" or a "trade"? Is the production of crude oil "a part of farming"? Is a harmonica player a "musician"? Is aspirin a "drug"? The way in which such questions are commonly settled is by appeals to dictionaries to discover the "real meanings" of the words involved. It is also common practice to consult past legal decisions and all kinds of learned treatises bearing on the subject. The decision finally rests, however, not upon appeals to past authority, but upon *what people want*. If they want the AMA to be immune from antitrust action, they will go to the Supreme Court if necessary to get medicine "defined" as a "profession." If they want the AMA prosecuted, they will get a decision that it is a "trade." (They got, in this case, a decision from the Court that it did not matter whether the practice of medicine was a "trade" or not; what mattered was that the AMA had, as charged, *restrained* the trade of Group Health Association, Inc., a co-operative to *procure* medical services for its members. The antitrust action was upheld.)

If people want agricultural co-operatives to operate oil wells, they will get the courts to define the activity in such a way as to make it possible. If the public at large doesn't care, the decision whether a harmonica player is or is not a "musician" will be made by the stronger trade union. The question whether aspirin is or is not a "drug" will be decided neither by finding the dictionary definition of "drug" nor by staring long and hard at an aspirin tablet. It will be decided on the basis of where and under what conditions people want to buy their aspirin.

In any case, society as a whole ultimately gets, on all issues of wide public importance, the classifications it wants, even if it has to wait until all the members of the Supreme Court are dead and an entirely new court is appointed. When the desired decision is handed down, people say, "Truth has triumphed." *In short, society regards as "true" those systems of classification that produce the desired results.*

The scientific test of "truth," like the social test, is strictly practical, except for the fact that the "desired results" are more severely limited. The results desired by society may be irrational, superstitious, selfish, or humane, but the results desired by scientists are only that our systems of classification produce predictable results. Classifications, as amply indicated already, determine our attitudes and behavior toward the object or event classified. When lightning was classified as "evidence of divine wrath," no courses of action other than prayer were suggested to prevent one's being struck by lightning. As soon, however, as it was classified as "electricity," Benjamin Franklin achieved a measure of control over it by his invention of the lightning rod. Certain physical disorders were formerly classified as "demonic possession," and this suggested that we "drive the demons out" by whatever spells or incantations we could think of. The results were uncertain. But when those disorders were classified as "bacillus infections," courses of action were suggested that led to more predictable results. Science seeks only the *most generally useful* systems of classification; these it regards for the time being, until more useful classifications are invented, as "true."

ANATOL RAPOPORT

From Science and the Goals of Man, *by Anatol Rapoport. Copyright, 1950, by Harper & Brothers. By permission of Harper & Brothers.*

What Do You Mean?

Let us return to our two patriots arguing about the respective merits of their countries. We are dealing with Jones and Ivanov, discussing U.S.A. and U.S.S.R., as many Joneses and many Ivanovs actually did in Teheran, Berlin, Fairbanks, Poltava, wherever they met and whenever an interpreter turned up.

As long as they are saying, "My country is a better place to live in than yours," they are making value judgments, talking about themselves. They can, of course, agree to disagree by recognizing the fact that they are not talking about their countries at all. But although it is easy to agree to disagree about caviar and remain friends, it is not so easy to disagree about a "way of life" and remain friends. "Ways of life" have a way of spreading and their spreading invites resistance. Thus, each of our friends wishes to make the other "see the light."

"My country is a democracy," says Jones, "and yours is a dictatorship."

"On the contrary," counters Ivanov.

As they are saying it, the discussion seems to be on the hopeless 'tis-'tain't level. Yet, as we have seen in the preceding chapter, there *is* an area of agreement. Both Ivanov and Jones believe that "democracy" makes a country good to live in and its ideals worth while to defend.

If it were possible for each of them to "prove" to the other that his country has some aspects of "democracy," they would have to agree that there are at least some good things in the ways of life of both. But the potentialities for agreement are not realized, because "proofs" are rejected *in toto* by each opponent.

"Ours is the *real* democracy; yours is a sham one," each of them says.

They are not communicating, because the experiences that have led to the word "democracy" for Jones are not similar to the experiences that have led to that word for Ivanov. The words are the same, but their meanings are different. The agreement on the principle "Democracy makes a country good to live in" is only a *verbal* agreement. For Jones "democracy" means the two-party system, Fourth of July speeches, stories of newsboys becoming millionaires, Town Hall meetings, informality, hot dogs, trailer camps, soapboxes, the Inquiring Reporter. For Ivanov "democracy" means the one-party system, full employment, social security, stories of peasant boys becoming engineers, aviators, and concert violinists, shop meetings, May Day parades, quick action by the state against individuals who become rich by illegitimate means (by means illegitimate for Ivanov but legitimate for Jones), and the line of people in Red Square waiting to see the embalmed body of Lenin.

Even without studying semantics, Jones and Ivanov may still take another step toward agreement. Each may ask the other to *define* democracy. But here other pitfalls await them. They may think they agree on a definition "Democracy is a form of government where the people rule." But again this agreement is only verbal. The experiences that Jones summarizes in the expression "the people rule," are different from those which Ivanov summarizes by the same words.

For thousands of years philosophers have inquired into the "real" meanings of words, with no agreement to show for their efforts. From the semantic point of view, to inquire into the *real* meaning of any word, whether democracy or tyranny, friendship or virtue, taxation or education, is senseless.

Take the word "rot." To a German it means "red," to a Russian "mouth," and to us you know what. How good a philosopher do you have to be to discover the "real" meaning of "rot"?

One may object to this example, since there is nothing remarkable in the fact that a similar sound may have different meanings in different languages.

Take, then, the word "rod," and consider what it means to a land surveyor and what it means to a gangster, both presumably speaking

English. Words do have a variety of sometimes unrelated meanings, and these are not inherent in the words themselves but in their *usage*. Usage depends on the experiences associated with the *use* of words. The various meanings of a word may overlap in spots. But it is no less important to know that other areas of their meanings may be far apart.

There is a mistaken belief that the etymology (ancestry) of a word is somehow a key to its "real" meaning.

Some time ago the Ukrainian delegate to the United Nations charged the government of Greece with "antidemocratic" motives in wanting to demilitarize the Bulgarian border. The Greek undersecretary of foreign affairs replied:

"Democracy is a Greek word, and Greece knows better than anyone else how to interpret it."

Sigmund Freud once pointed out in a lecture on hysteria that men as well as women were often subject to its symptoms. A distinguished Viennese professor upon hearing this walked angrily out of the hall.

"Never have I heard such nonsense," he fussed. "Men subject to hysteria! Why the very word 'hysteria' is derived from the Greek word for *womb!*"

Both the Greek diplomat and the Viennese professor were making the same common mistake: they were confusing words with the things to which words are supposed to refer.

Words are invented by human beings, and their meanings are attributed to them by persons. These meanings arise out of experience. Different sets of experiences may map on the same word.

DEFINITIONS OF DEFINITIONS

How, then, can the meaning of a word be made clear? Obviously by indicating the experiences associated with it. But how do we communicate experiences? By words. Are we in a vicious circle? It looks serious, but there may be a way out.

The question "What do you mean?" asks for the meaning of some words or expressions you are using. Meaning is associated with experience. So actually the question "What do you mean?" is a request to share the experiences associated with the words you are using. In answer to such a request, a definition is usually made.

We shall examine several types of definitions and gauge their usefulness from the standpoint of sharing experience.

1. *Defining a word by giving a synonym.*

Pocket dictionaries are full of such definitions. Asked to define "man" a pocket dictionary will often tell you that a "man" is a "human being."

2. *Making a definition by classification.*

Such definitions haunt the classroom. Pupils who can rattle off "Autocracy is a form of government in which power is concentrated in the hands of one man" and "Capitalism is an economic system based on competition and free enterprise" are most likely to get an A in civics. In the days of Aristotle (about 350 B.C.), "man" was often defined as a "rational animal," also a definition by classification. Such definitions tell first what sort of thing the word you are defining refers to (capitalism is a sort of economic system; man is a sort of animal) ; then it tells how to distinguish the *special* thing the word refers to (not *any* kind of economic system, but one based on competition and free enterprise; not *any* kind of animal, but a rational animal).

3. *Defining a word by enumerating words to which it refers collectively* (definition by enumeration).

Spices are cinnamon, cloves, paprika, ginger, and such.

The kings of the house of Stuart were James I, Charles I, Charles II, and James II.

4. *Defining by exhibiting an example.*

That is the way Robinson Crusoe taught English to Friday. He would point to a hairy animal and say "goat," to the strange object he carried and say "umbrella," etc. Friday learned fast. Children also learn to speak this way.

5. *The Operational Definition.*

Such definitions are commonly used in modern science. A physicist asked to define, say, the "Joule-Thompson effect" will *usually describe the experiments,* in which this effect can be *observed.* A more homely example of an operational definition can be found in the *recipe.*

An operational definition tells *what to do* in order to experience or to recognize the thing to which the word defined refers.

Now let us see how the different kinds of definition serve their purpose. We recall that a definition is used to answer the question "What do you mean ?"--a request to *share experience.*

Definition by synonym is useful only if the synonym is closer to our experiences than the word defined. Sometimes this is the case. People for whom "abdomen" is just a noise, may know very well what "belly" stands for. But the opposite situation is rare.

If you have used pocket dictionaries a great deal, where words are defined by synonyms, you must have experienced the disappointment of finding a synonym that means no more to you than the word you have looked up. The disappointment may grow into a minor frustration if you look up the synonym only to find it defined by the original "sticker."

Definitions by classification are more often useful than definitions by synonym. Their usefulness depends on the familiarity of the person who asks for the definition with the *class* of things into which the word defined is placed. For instance, Jones can explain the grapefruit to Ivanov, who may never have seen one, by such a definition.

> A grapefruit is a citrus fruit, more sour than an orange and less sour than a lemon, larger than both, and canary yellow.

Ivanov has eaten both lemons and oranges. He can form at least some idea of what a grapefruit is like. The shortcomings of a definition by classification is that it does not *necessarily* bring the word defined closer to experience.

A Jabberwock can be defined by "classifying" it.

> A Jabberwock is an animal with "jaws that bite and claws that snatch."

But the definition does not bring us any closer to an actual experience with a Jabberwock.

Similarly, one can define anything one pleases by stringing words together in such a way as to make it appear that one is clarifying meaning. Here are a few examples. It is easy to invent them.

> An irresistible force is a causative agency, able to overcome all obstacles.
> The First Cause is that event which was preceded by no other.
> The Good is what all things aim at.
> The devil is a being who is responsible for the existence of evil.
> Love is that affection which, being compounded of animal desire, esteem, and benevolence, becomes the bond of attachment and union

between individuals of the different sexes, and makes them enjoy in
the society of each other a species of happiness which they experience
nowhere else.

Definitions which by their sentence structure seem to be clarifying
something, but actually are not, resemble useless patent medicines. The
harm of patent medicines is often not in themselves but in that the
addicts keep hoping they will be helped and delay seeking competent
advice and effective measures. Similarly, the addicts of definitions by
classification (Aristotelian definitions) are often pedantic in "defining
their terms" without realizing the futility of such definitions.

Definitions by enumeration are useful in defining classes of things if
the names of the members of the class defined are closer to experience
than the class itself. A person may not know to what the Pentateuch
refers, but he may be familiar with Genesis, Exodus, Leviticus, Numbers,
and Deuteronomy. He may have seen frogs, newts, and salamanders, but
he may not know that biologists refer to all of them collectively as
amphibia.

As a rule, definitions by enumeration do carry words closer to experience, because terms referring to collections of events are less directly connected with experience than the events themselves. We have used this
sort of definition above when we defined Jones's democracy by Town
Hall meetings, etc., and Ivanov's democracy by May Day parades, etc.

The weak spot in this sort of definition is that some words seem to
refer not to classes, as, for example, the sun, and some classes are too
large to enumerate. If I wanted to define "man" by enumeration, I would
have to put down some two billion names, a fourth of them Chinese, a
difficult and rather useless task. Fortunately, in some cases only a few
examples are needed to make the meaning of the class clear. An "etc."
placed at the end of such a partial list is a reminder that the class has not
been exhausted.

A great advantage in making definitions by *exhibiting an example*
is that one cannot define fictions that way. Just try to define Jabberwock
or the First Cause by pointing to something and see how sticking to
definition by exhibiting an example protects you from believing in ghosts.
However, this advantage becomes a disadvantage when one wishes to
define something which is not immediately at hand or something more
abstract than objects to which one can point. Jonathan Swift made great
fun of definition by example. He describes in his satire, *Gulliver's*

Travels, how the academicians of Lagado decided to do away with spoken language altogether, arguing that

> . . . since the words are only names for things, it would be convenient for all men to carry about them such things as were necessary to express the particular business they are to discourse on . . .

Accordingly, says Swift, the learned men of Lagado

> adhere to the new scheme of expressing themselves by things, which hath only this inconvenience attending it, that if a man's business be very great, and of various kinds, he must be obliged in proportion to carry a greater bundle of things upon his back, unless he can afford one or two strong servants to attend him.

The great value of making a definition by exhibiting an example is that it does bridge the gap between words and experience. This, in fact, is the only purpose of definition. Definition by synonym and definition by classification may indirectly bridge this gap if the words used in the definition are closer to experience than the words defined. But this is not necessarily so. In the case of definition by example it is *necessarily* so, because what you exhibit is *not* a word. Still a difficulty remains, quite aside from Swift's objections, to this kind of definition. Many words refer to real things, and these may not be at hand to point to, or one may not point to them at all. Here are a few examples:

electric current	hydrogen
standard deviation	habeas corpus
the French language	mumps
acrophobia	sonata
chiaroscuro	taxes

The *operational definition* succeeds most effectively in connecting such *abstract* words with experience.

In discussing operational definitions of abstract physical concepts, Philipp Frank says:

> These sentences [operational definitions] contain the abstract words of the physical principles like "current" . . . also the words of the everyday English language. Obviously, they contain words like "wire"

and other words which describe the apparatus by which the intensity of a current is actually measured.[1]

Note how the operational definition works. One cannot point to an ampere of electric current (the most one could point at would be the wire that carries it). But one does not dodge the issue by defining a word with other words without bothering to determine whether they are any closer to experience. One gives a set of *directions,* in words, to be sure, but words almost certainly closer to experience than the word defined (wire, magnet, etc.). If one follows these directions, one has the experience summarized by the words "one ampere of electric current."

Sometimes a definition that sounds like an Aristotelian one performs the job of an operational definition. If I say "Acrophobia is a mental disturbance characterized by a fear of high places" I seem to be making an Aristotelian definition. But it can easily be translated into an operational one: "Question a great many people on how they feel about high places, and you will find that a certain percentage of them will declare that they are 'afraid' of high places. Furthermore, if such a person happens to be on a roof or a mountaintop, he usually exhibits a quickening of heart beat and expresses a desire to get down. Such people are said to suffer from acrophobia."

Let us see what happens when we apply an operational definition to a fiction. A vampire, for example, can be defined by a good Aristotelian definition: "A vampire is a person who habitually sucks other people's blood." If we attempted to translate this definition into an operational one, we would have to say something like this: "Have a great many persons watched at night, and you will find that some go abroad and suck blood out of sleeping people, usually from a small lesion in the neck. Such people are called vampires." This operational definition is formally as good as the one of acrophobia except for one thing: you will probably not find any people with blood-sucking habits.

So it appears from the operations prescribed by the operational definition that if any "meaning" is to be attached to the word "vampire," it cannot refer to a person (since no such persons are observed). The operations have revealed that the Aristotelian definition of a "vampire," although formally flawless, is meaningless.

Practically all operational definitions say in fact "Do so-and-so, and

[1] Philipp Frank, "Science Teaching and the Humanities."

you will find . . ." They *predict* an experience. They may also be called definitions by prediction.

In modern semantic literature, definitions by synonym and by classification are often called "intensional definitions," while those by enumeration, example, and operation are called "extensional definitions." From the standpoint of bridging the gap between words and experiences, extensional definitions are to be preferred. As a matter of fact, if that gap is bridged at all, somewhere a definition by example or an operational definition is involved.

The definition by example need not involve language at all. The syntactic structure of an operational definition involves an imperative form of a verb (do so-and-so) and a predictive assertion (you will find . . .). This structure is sometimes clumsy and may be discarded for the elegant structure of the Aristotelian definition (a so-an-so is a such-and-such which is characterized by a this-and-that) ; but if a definition is to serve its purpose (sharing experience), an indication of experience must be involved.

"The stockyards are an area where animals are processed into meat" is a short, elegant definition of the stockyards. But the *reality* of the stockyards is implied in another, clumsier definition, which I would give to a vistor in Chicago if I wanted to bring the stockyards within the range of his experience.

"Take the Halsted Street car to 39th St., etc. . . ."

"Hell is the place where the wicked go when they die" also looks like a definition. But when you try to translate it into operational terms you will immediately get into difficulties. You will be at a loss to indicate a proper procedure in order to experience hell.

Just as assertions about things must be traced to the experiences that gave rise to them, the meanings of words must also be traced in this way.

Words which fail to show an ancestry of experience may nevertheless be well "defined" by intensional definitions, that is, by other words. But they usually cannot be defined by extensional definitions, especially by exhibiting an example and by the operational definition, because these, by their very nature, imply connection with experience.

Extensional definitions, therefore, especially the operational ones, are more generally valuable for the purpose for which definitions are intended—to bridge the gap between words and experience.

An operational definition can do everything all the others can do and often more. In some cases only an operational definition can bridge the gap between words and experience. Its drawback is that grammatically it is not very elegant. Therefore, if one is concerned with literary style, one might avoid the operational definition; but if one is concerned with communicating meaning, one should use it at the slightest indication that the meaning is otherwise not clear.

Granted that a way can be found to map experience on language, how can the infinite variety of experience to which we are subject be mapped on a language of only a few thousand words, to which the vocabulary of most people is limited?

QUESTIONS FOR REVIEW OF PART SIX

1. What are some of the reasons why the meanings of words are not fixed? If they are not fixed, how is it that we are able to communicate with each other?
2. How does Laird distinguish among referent, symbol, and meaning?
3. Look up "signal" in a dictionary. What is the difference between a signal and a symbol? Can you cite an example of a person having a "signal reaction" to a symbol?
4. What does Hayakawa mean when he says that a word is an abstraction? How do we abstract? How do our interests and previous experiences affect the way in which we abstract?
5. In what ways would it be beneficial and in what ways harmful to man if he lost his power to abstract?
6. How is the abstraction ladder similar to the main idea, topic sentences, and details of a written composition?
7. How is the process of classification dependent upon the process of abstraction? Why do our classifications tend to be dependent upon our interests and previous experiences?
8. What does Hayakawa mean when he writes "Cow$_1$ is not cow$_2$"? Supply an example from your own experience.
9. Hayakawa writes that "society regards as 'true' those systems of classification that produce the desired results" and that "classifications . . . determine our attitudes and behavior toward the object or event classified." What is the significance of these two statements, taken together, for a democratic society?
10. In what respects is the process of definition the same as the process of classification?

11. Some people have charged that dictionaries and that intelligence tests which depend on vocabulary items tend to favor a certain socio-economic group. For example, they cite the third grade intelligence test which asks what an elevator is and offers among the multiple-choice answers "a machine for raising people inside a tall building" but not "a round building for hoisting and storing grain." What kinds of people do you think tend to construct dictionaries and intelligence tests, and how do you suppose their experiences may affect their products? What kinds of people may well resent their products?

12. What basis does Rapoport provide for making definitions appropriate to the readers or listeners for whom the words are being defined?

13. Do you agree with Rapoport that the "extensional definition" is superior to the "intensional definition"? Why, or why not?

SUGGESTIONS FOR INDIVIDUAL PROJECTS AND CLASS DISCUSSION

1. If the brain makes decisions as Laird describes, do you suppose that man ever has freedom of choice?

2. Construct an abstraction ladder, beginning with a word other than the ones Hayakawa uses.

3. According to Aristotle, a definition consists of the *genus* (class) and the *differentia* of the concept. That is, the concept is referred to the genus at the next higher level of abstraction, as in "A library is a building . . . ," and then it is differentiated from the other species of concepts in that genus, as in ". . . where books are kept." A classical definition, then, would be "A library is a building where books are kept." Rapoport calls this an "intensional definition." Write classical or "intensional" definitions of three different concepts; then, beneath them, write "extensional" definitions for the same concepts, exhibiting an example for one, enumerating members of the class for another, and using an operational definition for the last.

   Here are some further suggestions for making your classical definitions accurate:

   (a) Make the definition applicable to all individuals included in the concept but to no others.

   (b) State essential and primary attributes of the concept, not accidental or minor attributes.

   (c) Do not use another form of the name of the concept in defining that concept.

   (d) Avoid vague and figurative language.

   (e) Phrase the definition in the affirmative if that is possible.

SUGGESTED WRITING ASSIGNMENT

Write 300-500 word paper defining an abstract concept like "wealth" or "justice." In the introduction, raise the question of what the term means. In preparation for writing the body of the paper, list 25 or 30 concrete things or actions that the term suggests to you. Then imagine that you are a person with markedly different experiences and make a second list of the 25 or 30 concrete things or actions he might list. You may wish to construct a third list for a still different person. Using the ideas you have listed, develop paragraphs presenting the meanings of the term for each of you. In your conclusion, draw together the points of similarity in the different definitions, ending with an abstract definition which is meaningful to both or all three of you.

PART VII

Logic

Consideration of general semantics has provided a background for the following readings on logic. General semantics deals with
the meaning of words and utterances—in a
sense, with their "truth" for different people
under different circumstances. Logic, on the
other hand, deals primarily with "validity,"
with the reasoning which relates terms and
statements. Thus the logician is not concerned
with language features relevant only to the
English language; his insights are pertinent
to almost any language. The universality of
logic in no way diminishes its importance for
English, of course, and these *Introductory
Readings* would present an incomplete picture of our language without attention to
some of the elements of logic. In Part VII,
then, John C. Sherwood provides an "Introduction to Logic" and a brief discussion of
"Induction," following which Manuel Bilsky considers "Deduction: Is Your Argument
Valid?"

275

JOHN C. SHERWOOD

From Discourse of Reason: A Brief Hand-
book of Semantics and Logic, *by John C.
Sherwood. Copyright ©, 1960, by John C.
Sherwood. By permission of Harper &
Brothers.*

Introduction to Logic

Even for the most skeptical, belief is an absolute necessity for practical
experience. At the very least, we have to have faith that the material
world will continue in its accustomed ways, that tomorrow as today iron
will be hard and clay soft, that objects will continue to fall toward the
earth instead of flying off into the sky. Even in the less certain and less
easily analyzed realm of human character, we constantly act on beliefs—
that a soft answer turneth away wrath, that a veteran soldier will fight
bravely, that a mother will love and protect her children, that the mail-
man will deliver the mail instead of stealing it. Without belief, action
would be paralyzed; we should never know what to do in a given situation. What really distinguishes the rational from the irrational thinker
is not the presence or absence of belief, but the grounds on which belief
is accepted.

There are some sources of belief which are either absolutely unsound
or to be resorted to only when all other methods fail. A "hunch" is not
an absolutely useless guide, because it may be based on knowledge which
has temporarily slipped our minds, but we would be foolish to trust a
hunch when objective evidence was available. Our casual impression of
a prospective employee may be useful, but full knowledge of his previous
record is more valuable. Tradition may be a proper guide in some areas
of life, but we cannot accept witchcraft or even the Newtonian physics
because our forefathers did. All too often we believe simply because we
want to believe. It is comforting to think that "there is always room at

the top" or that "there are no atheists in foxholes" or that "football makes good citizens." But such beliefs are the most treacherous of all beliefs, because we tend to protect them by ignoring contrary evidence until at some crisis the brute facts force themselves on our attention. An unfounded belief is not merely wrong morally; it is an unsafe guide to conduct.

What then are the legitimate sources of belief? In a scientific age we instinctively answer, evidence or investigation. We believe that a worker is reliable because we have seen him at work frequently over a considerable period of time; we believe that a certain remedy will cure a certain disease because trained observers have watched its operation in a large number of cases (here, as often, we have to trust the reports of others' investigations); we believe that haste makes waste because we have seen it happen so many times. In effect, we infer from a certain number of instances of a thing that a characteristic of the thing we have observed in these instances will also appear in other instances. This is the process of *induction*. Somewhat less often (unless we are very much given to theoretical reasoning) we use *deduction*. Where induction puts facts together to get ideas or *generalizations*, deduction puts ideas together to discover what other ideas can be inferred from them. If John is the son of David who is the son of William, then John must be the grandson of William—we know this without asking. If a student must pass composition to graduate, and Mr. X has not yet passed it, then Mr. X cannot yet graduate. In each case, given the first two ideas or *premises*, we know that the third—the *conclusion*—must be true; no further investigation is needed. (If the conclusion proved not to be true, then we would assume that one of the premises was wrong; perhaps a student must take composition unless excused.)

In every mind there will be a few beliefs which cannot be proved either by induction or deduction: basic standards of value, ultimate articles of faith, matters of inner conviction which we would be hard put to prove but without which we could scarcely think or act. Religious principles might be thought of as the most obvious example, but philosophy and even science illustrate the same necessity. In plane geometry we must begin with axioms and postulates from which the rest of the system is deduced. It is an article of faith that "things equal to the same thing are equal to each other"; we must believe it or give up plane geometry. Virtually all induction, and hence all scientific conclusions

and practically all action depend on a faith in the uniformity of nature
—that the laws of matter will be the same tomorrow as today. It seems
only common sense to assume that water will continue to freeze at 32°
Fahrenheit hereafter, but there is no way of proving the assumption theoretically.

Induction and deduction are not merely the tools of the philosopher
and the scientist, but in rough-and-ready half-conscious forms are part of
the everyday thought processes of all sane human beings, however limited
their education. It is not infrequently argued that logic in the more
formal sense is neither necessary nor useful for human life, since "common" or "horse" sense can serve us far better in practical affairs. All this
involves a half truth. In the first place, we might question whether logic
and common sense are really so opposed. If common sense has any value,
it is because it is based on "experience"; in other words, having generalized from a series of seemingly like instances observed in the past, we
apply the generalization to a further instance that has just come to our
attention. What really distinguishes common sense from logic is that it
tends to take short-cuts; it seldom bothers to work out all the steps in the
argument. Certain processes work in our brains, and we acquire a sudden
conviction that something is true. It is fortunate that we have common
sense and "intuition" to depend on, for time does not always allow us to
work things out logically or go hunting for evidence. It is certainly better to investigate a prospective employee thoroughly, but if we have to
fill the job on the spot, we shall have to trust our impressions of his
character. Very rarely (if we are wise) we may even trust our common
sense in preference to what seems to be scientific evidence. Many a parent
or teacher has finally nerved himself to go against the "scientific findings"
of a child psychologist or educator. (But perhaps here what is wrong is
not really science but its interpretation by self-appointed prophets.)
Whole areas of human decision lie outside of the range of logic and
sometimes even of common sense. One may be able to prove by critical
principle that a book has every virtue that belongs to a masterpiece, and
the book may in fact be quite readable. Science has not conquered all
areas of human life. It is useless to tell a young man that a certain girl
has all the qualifications of an ideal wife if he happens to hate her.
Nevertheless, to scorn logic and hold to "horse sense" is a dangerous
business. An appeal to common sense—or worse yet, intuition—all too
often represents an attempt to evade the responsibility of looking at

evidence or working out the problem rationally. Common sense sometimes tells people peculiar things about such matters as family life and
racial and economic problems. If by common sense we mean a kind of informal, everyday logic, then it is an absolute necessity of rational existence; but if by it we mean a defiance of logic, it ought not to exist at
all, and it is unhappily true that most of us use logic too little rather than
too much.[1] To come down to the practical problem of communication—
which after all is our basic concern here—our personal intuitions are
probably of very little interest to our readers or listeners, who may even
not be much impressed by our common sense, however much they may
value their own. What they expect from us is logic and evidence.

By its very nature, logic deals in statements or *propositions;* they are
the materials of deductive reasoning and the products of inductive reasoning. By a proposition we mean a group of words which can be affirmed
or denied—of which it can be said it is either true or false. (Even if it is
false, it is still a proposition.) Not all sentences are propositions. A question or command is not a proposition; we cannot say that "Who is
there?" is true or that "Do your homework!" is false. A proposition is
roughly equivalent to the grammarian's *declarative sentence,* though not
exactly equivalent, since a declarative sentence might contain several
different propositions ("The sky is blue, and the grass is green") or
express what is really a question or command ("The audience will
leave quietly").

Another important distinction is that between a proposition which is
merely factual and one which implies a *judgment.* "He served at Valley
Forge" and "He was a loyal soldier" are both statements, but not of the
same kind. The first is a matter of fact: either he served or he did not,
and there is the possibility at least of proving the matter one way or
another to the satisfaction of all. The second is a little different; it passes
a judgment since the word "loyal" implies praise for something the
speaker approves of or judges good. Another speaker, fully apprized of
the same facts, might differ because of a differing conception of what constitutes loyalty, and absolute proof one way or another is impossible, since

[1] Perhaps we should distinguish between common sense, which does involve
some conscious reasoning on evidence, from intuition, which involves no reasoning at all, but only a "feeling" that something is so. Intuition certainly ought
to be a last resort, but sometimes there is nothing else to follow. Often, if the
intuition is sound, one can find evidence or construct an argument to confirm
it. One ought to be able to defend it rationally, however irrational its origins.

an element of personal feeling will always enter in. We should not confuse this distinction between *fact* and *judgment* with the distinction between *established truth* and *mere opinion*. Fact here means "piece of
verifiable information"; what makes it a fact is the concrete quality which
makes conclusive proof at least theoretically possible. "Columbus died in
1491" and "Martians have six legs" are in this sense factual, though the
one statement is known to be false and the other is at present impossible
of verification. "George Washington was loyal" still involves a judgment, however much the statement is confirmed by evidence and
however universally it is believed. A British writer in 1776 might
plausibly have called Washington disloyal, and while we could find
plenty of arguments to challenge the writer with, it is very possible that
we should never come to an agreement with him. Unhappily for logic,
the distinction between fact and judgment is far from clear-cut. The
statement "He is intelligent" certainly contains an element of judgment;
yet it is susceptible of confirmation by means of standard tests and might
approach the status of a fact. It may be especially hard to distinguish
between judgments and generalizations derived from a number of facts.
Generalizations, like statements of single facts, differ from judgments
in not necessarily implying any approval or disapproval. "A 1.5 concentration of alcohol in the blood usually impairs reactions" is a generalization; "It is wrong to drive in such a state" is a judgment.

Needless to say, judgments are not to be condemned; they are merely
to be recognized for what they are. It may not always be easy to do this.
When the educator says "The learner cannot be considered aside from his
environment," he seems to be stating a generalization. But a little reflection reminds us that, rightly or wrongly, pupils are often judged without reference to their environment, and that to make sense the sentence
must read "The learner *ought not* to be considered aside from his environment"—a form which clearly identifies it as a judgment. "Good
children brush their teeth" has the form of a generalization and might
actually represent the result of investigation on the dental habits of
children known to be "good." Probably, however, it is a judgment, telling how the speaker thinks children ought to behave, and in a certain context the sentence might amount to a command. What is important is to
make our meaning clear in the first place, and to show our readers that
our evaluations have been rational. Judgments may be supported by evidence and argument; they need not be mere emotional reactions. The

statement "He was loyal" can be supported by a definition of loyalty and instances of loyal conduct.

It goes without saying that one cannot work logically with a statement which does not have a clear-cut, ascertainable meaning. Puritanical logicians sometimes deny cognitive meaning to any statement which cannot be proved true or false (or at least shown to be probable or improbable) by reference to material facts. Since such an assumption would throw out much philosophy and theology, we should hardly wish to go so far, but we should at least try to avoid those statements, all too common in controversy, which do nothing more than express feeling or prejudice. The following is technically a valid argument: X is a no-good rat; No-good rats should be hung; X should be hung. But we should hope that no jury would follow such reasoning. . . . One cannot deduce anything from a feeling.

JOHN C. SHERWOOD

From Discourse of Reason: A Brief Handbook of Semantics and Logic, *by John C. Sherwood. Copyright ©, 1960, by John C. Sherwood. By permission of Harper & Brothers.*

Induction

Induction has already been defined as the process by which we generalize from examples; generally, we have said, it involves the assumption that examples we encounter in the future will be like those we have encountered in the past. There are, as it happens, some few examples of "perfect induction," that is, generalizations which do not involve any element of prediction, because all the possible examples of the type have been examined. "All members of the present class passed the examination" might be such an example of perfect induction, provided we have actually checked the grade of every student. "Honor high school graduates do well in college" is a different sort of generalization; we could hardly have examined all possible past cases, and yet we expect that unexamined past as well as future cases will tend to confirm the generalization. At the same time we allow for the possibility of exceptions at all times, and even for the possibility that in the future changing circumstances may invalidate the whole generalization. The statement is sufficiently probable so that an admissions officer can act on it, but it is far from certain.

That inductive generalizations are probable rather than certain is a truth that we no doubt recognize clearly enough as far as it is applied to the common-sense generalizations of everyday life. We have enough faith in the notion that "Dogs are friendly" or "Tigers are dangerous" to avoid the latter and pet the former, but we know that there is nothing eternal or immutable about the propositions: dogs were once wolves, and tigers are occasionally tamed. The propositions of science, at least of the physical sciences, would seem on the other hand to be not merely probable but in some cases absolutely certain. Who would question the freezing point of water or the atomic weight of gold? But in theory even scientific generalizations possess not certainty but only an unusually high degree of probability. Although it may be a metaphysical quibble to say that we cannot after all know for certain that the constitution of the universe will not change tomorrow, the fact remains that scientific theories are in a constant state of revision. Newton's theory of gravity once seemed eternal truth, but it has been superseded by Einstein's. For practical purposes, the layman may well accept scientific theories as certain, but the knowledge that an inductive generalization never really gets beyond a high degree of probability may give him a healthy skepticism toward the generalizations he deals with in everyday life. In practice it is usually not dangerous to speak of true and false generalizations, but it would be more accurate to speak of degrees of probability or improbability.

Induction is generalization from evidence; manifestly we cannot (or ought not to) generalize without evidence which is both authentic in character and sufficient in quantity. The question of the authenticity of the evidence can be very simple or very complex. The sources of evidence can be virtually comprehended under the categories of *observation* and *authority*. Sometimes, in other words, the evidence comes from our own observations, either casual or systematic. Having been repeatedly pleased with the purchases made at a certain store, we reasonably infer that goods bought there will be satisfactory. This is a more or less casual, common-sense inference. At the other extreme we have the operations of science, in which the evidence is collected through elaborate, repeated, and carefully controlled experiments. It might seem as if we could always depend on our own observations, but unhappily in ordinary life our senses and our memories often deceive us, as the confusion of witnesses in court trials depressingly illustrates. Even in science errors of observation, though carefully guarded against, are not entirely unknown. The "canals" of Mars have actually be "seen" by only a few observers, who by some trick of vision identified some rather vague bands as straight lines. Another reputable scientist *thought* he had overthrown Einstein on the basis of some measurements of the speed of light which no other experimenter was ever able to duplicate. There is always the danger that we will see only what we want to see, even though the error may not be deliberate. A bigot with a deep prejudice against a racial or religious group will manage to notice and remember incidents where members of the group behave badly and pass over those where they behave well. The questionnaire is an important tool in some kinds of investigation, but unless a questionnaire is skillfully worded it may be quite deceptive as to the actual situation. A group of good students asked "Do you cheat frequently?" might hesitate to answer at all, since even a *no* might leave the impression that they did *some* cheating. (The old gag "Have you stopped beating your wife?" illustrates the same point.) Observation is in fact an art, and wherever something important is at stake, as in research, we must observe according to the rules of the field.

Of course most of the information we work with in academic matters, especially student papers, does not derive from observation but from indirect means, especially books. The use of second-hand information constantly raises the question of authority: how far are we justified in believing the learned lecture or the printed page? In general we expect to depend on authorities who are competent in the field and, as far as possible, unbiased. Advertisements, political propaganda, casual gossip are "authorities" which we should use only when every other source fails us. The question of competence can be a rather complicated one. We naturally trust the man who is discussing his own field of study and distrust the man who claims to speak in an area where he has no special

qualifications. There are doubtless incautious people who really accept
movie stars as authorities on tobacco and baseball players as authorities
on diet, but wiser thinkers remember that men as great as Henry Ford
and Thomas Edison possessed some surprising beliefs: Ford was aggres-
sively ignorant of history and Edison had some odd ideas about gravity
which are now being advocated by a man whose proper area of competence is the stock market. Recently it has been necessary to remind ourselves that scientists who venture into the fields of politics and ethics
have just as much competence there as other educated men, but no more.
That businessmen make good public officials is almost an article of
faith with one of our political parties, but a belief not always borne out
by the facts. In the end we usually have to accept the weight of the
received opinions of the body of experts in the field. If the whole member-
ship of the Modern Language Association is convinced that Shakespeare
wrote his own plays, their opinion will have to outweigh that of an
eccentric who holds that the plays were written by Queen Elizabeth.
A quack may loudly proclaim that his cancer cure is being suppressed by
a conspiracy of the American Medical Association, but a sane patient will
take the word of the doctors. Even the authority of George Bernard
Shaw, who was opposed to vaccination, cannot outweigh the pronounce-
ments of the whole medical profession. If a novelist claims to have found
a way to detect water underground or a minister a way to find oil (and
such things have happened), we should do well to question them about
their training in geology.

The problem of the *adequacy* of evidence is equally complicated since
it varies so much according to the particular problem or field. We could
imagine situations in which a single piece of evidence would be sufficient
to establish a generalization, if not with absolute certainty (which is
impossible anyway), yet with a high degree of probability. We would have
to be dealing with phenomena whose operations are regular, to be sure
that the example is absolutely typical and to be careful not to draw a
broader generalization than is warranted. If we once succeeded in dis-
solving gold in *aqua regia,* we should assume that we could do it again,
since chemical reactions are reliable; although, because of the possibility
that chance factors such as impurities or variations in temperature might
operate, a careful scientist would be anxious to accumulate instances before making a pronouncement. If a student produces a good theme, we
can safely say that he is capable of writing well, but this does not assure

us that he will always write well—the one good theme might have been the result of an isolated inspiration. Generally speaking, the more evidence available, the more convincing the conclusions, since the likelihood of a chance factor is decreased. Statisticians have elaborate formulas for determining the number of instances needed in a given case; if, for instance, comparison were to be made of the performance of groups of students taught by varying methods, we should probably not want to work with groups of less than one hundred.

Mere quantity, however, is insufficient. Instances prove nothing or next to nothing if the investigator has accumulated only the instances that confirm his theory and has ignored the contradictory examples. We do not prove that high school training in English is inadequate by pointing to the (admittedly considerable) number of incompetent writers in college classes; this number must be balanced against those who seem to be competent. It is important, too, that by a process of *sampling* we make sure that the instances are typical and represent the proper range and cross-section. If we are comparing two groups of one hundred students each, we must make sure that the two groups represent equal ability and that all the abler students do not turn up in one group. If the one class were scheduled at eight o'clock, for instance, there is at least the possibility that indolent students would avoid it. If one wanted to get the average views of the whole student body on athletics, one would not merely poll the football team or the members of Phi Beta Kappa. It has been suggested, perhaps wrongly, that the Kinsey Report might give a faulty impression of American sexual habits because only a rather uninhibited person would consent to be interviewed at all. Whether it is safe to judge of the quality of the fruit in a basket by sampling the top layer depends on the honesty of the farmer.

Many useful generalizations can be reached by the simple method of accumulating positive instances and considering the number and importance of negative instances. "Dark clouds are a sign of rain" and "Contour plowing reduces erosion" are propositions of this kind. Often, however, induction is more complex, involving a process of elimination; we must show what a thing is not before we can say what it is. If two sections of a college course vary greatly in their performance, it is easy to jump to the conclusion that the one instructor is more effective than the other; but actually we should never come to such a conclusion until we have eliminated all other factors, such as the native ability and prior training of the students. The students in High School *A* showed a markedly higher average performance on a standard English test than those in High School *B*. One might suppose that instruction was better in *A*. Investigation showed, however, that the students of High School *B* were of lower general ability than those of High School *A*, and this general weakness, not any deficiency in the English training, was the real cause of the lower English scores.

The problem of the performance of the students at High School *B* is complex in another way. The statement "Students from High School *B* are usually weak in English" is a simple descriptive generalization, stating that the members of a certain group tend to have a certain characteristic. When we say that this situation is due to low general ability, we are no longer merely trying to describe but wish to establish a causal relationship. It is notable that most of the more troublesome inductive problems are causal; they are problems in which we try to prove that one phenomenon is the cause of another. Hasty errors in analyzing cause and effect are much too common—so common that one type is described by a standard logical term, *post hoc ergo propter hoc* ("after this therefore because of this"—said of a faulty argument which assumes that *A* caused *B* simply because it preceded it in time). Statistics seem to show that business executives have large vocabularies, and unwary English teachers have sometimes suggested to their students that a large vocabulary might be a help to business success. The relationship may, however, be quite different; perhaps success causes the executive to acquire a large vocabulary through the variety of his business and social contacts, or success and vocabulary both may be the results of some other factor, such as intelligence or education. From the fact that juvenile delinquency is supposed to be less common in Italy than in the United States and that the Italian father is said to have more authority than the American father, some may conclude that lack of paternal authority is the sole cause of juvenile delinquency. A careful social scientist, even if he were willing to assume the greater docility of the Italian child and the greater forcefulness of the Italian father, would want to consider what other factors might be operating. Even if two phenomena occur so frequently together that it seems safe to say that there is some causal connection, we should still have several possibilities to consider: that *A* caused *B*, that *B* caused *A*, or that both *A* and *B* were caused by some third factor. To feel sure that *A* caused *B*, we should not only observe that

B regularly follows *A*, but we should make sure that there is no third factor *C* that consequently accompanies both.

In practice, it is usually not possible to proceed far with an inductive study without some sort of preliminary theory. Instead of looking at phenomena simply with the idea of seeing what is there, we look to see whether an opinion we have tentatively adopted is confirmed. If not, we modify it or discard it in favor of a more promising theory. Tests would never have been conducted to establish the connection between tobacco and lung cancer if the suspicion had not already existed that there was such a connection.

Part of the art of induction lies in the accurate statement of conclusions, mainly in distinguishing between generalizations supposed to be universally true and those not intended to be more than generally true. In the physical sciences most generalizations have something like universal validity, but in the social and even the biological sciences and certainly in common life they seldom have it. The two types can be clearly distinguished in terms of the effect of discovering an exception. A universal generalization would be overthrown by the discovery of a single clear exception, while a looser generalization would presumably stand as long as it proved true more often than not. Much trouble arises from forgetting that a particular generalization was never meant to be one hundred per cent accurate. During the recent Communist scare, many politicians seemed to operate on the assumption that all Communists are invariably spies and traitors, though the evidence could hardly have been stretched to prove much more than that a substantial number of Communists might reasonably be suspected of such activity. To avoid clumsiness we may state generalizations such as "Cows give milk" and "Babies cry" without naming all the qualifications and exceptions and special circumstances, but we need to keep in mind that such qualifications and exceptions exist. To say that all *A* are *B* is emphatically not the same as saying that most *A* are *B* or that *A* tends to be *B*.

One word more: proof in the strict sense is usually not possible within the confines of the ordinary student essay or speech. Perhaps on a very limited topic the writer might be able to accumulate enough instances to establish a generalization, and on some topics he might be able to report the results of research done by others; but generally his evidence will be at best of the kind and quality offered by Hazlitt in the following quotation:

Criminals are not to be influenced by reason; for it is of the very essence of crime to disregard consequences both to ourselves and to others. You may as well preach philosophy to a drunken man, or to the dead, as to those who are under the instigation of any mischievous passion. A man is a drunkard, and you tell him he ought to be sober; he is debauched, and you ask him to reform; he is idle, and you recommend industry to him as his wisest course; he gambles, and you remind him that he may be ruined by his foible; he has lost his character, and you advise him to get some reputable service or lucrative situation; vice becomes a habit with him, and you request him to rouse himself and shake it off; he is starving, and you warn him if he breaks the law, he will be hanged. None of this reasoning reaches the mark it aims at. . . . To argue with strong passion, with inveterate habit, with desperate circumstances, is to talk to the winds.

The instances cited, which are hypothetical anyway, could hardly suffice to prove the generalization "Criminals cannot be influenced by reason"; rather they illustrate it by showing clearly what is meant and by making the point seem plausible and reasonable. In much of our writing, we have to be content with illustration; but though we must sacrifice the quantity of proof, we can still be sure that the instances are relevant, typical, and numerous enough to make some sort of case. If we do not take at least these precautions, we are simply adding to the world's stock of useless "hasty generalizations."

HYPOTHESIS

It is customary to group under the forms of induction one kind of inference which differs from ordinary generalization, namely, *hypothesis*. By hypothesis we do not mean primarily a tentative theory (the popular meaning, though the two tend to overlap), but rather a conjectured state of affairs which, if it proved to be true, would explain a phenomenon which we already know to exist. The process is that of working back from a known effect to an unknown cause. The sudden disappearance of the moon from the sky would lead us to assume that a cloud bank was passing even if we could not actually see the clouds as such; unless we assume the clouds, we would have no plausible explanation for the disappearance of the moon. Graphic—though, from a strictly logical point of view, often very unsound—examples of this kind of reasoning overflow in the average detective story. Here, for instance, is the celebrated Sherlock Holmes at work:

> With a resigned air and a somewhat weary smile, Holmes begged the beautiful intruder to take a seat, and to inform us what it was that was troubling her.
>
> "At least it cannot be your health," said he, as his keen eyes darted over her; "so ardent a bicyclist must be full of energy."
>
> She glanced down in surprise at her own feet, and I observed the slight roughening of the side of the sole caused by the friction of the edge of the pedal.
>
> "Yes, I bicycle a good deal, Mr. Holmes, and that has something to do with my visit to you to-day."
>
> My friend took the lady's ungloved hand, and examined it with as close an attention and as little sentiment as a scientist would show to a specimen.
>
> "You will excuse me, I am sure. It is my business," said he, as he dropped it. "I nearly fell into the error of supposing that you were typewriting. Of course, it is obvious that it is music. You observe the spatulate finger-ends, Watson, which is common to both professions? There is a spirituality about the face, however"—she gently turned it towards the light—"which the typewriter does not generate. This lady is a musician."
>
> "Yes, Mr. Holmes, I teach music."
>
> "In the country, I presume, from your complexion."
>
> "Yes, sir, near Farnham, on the borders of Surrey."

In other words, since cycling could cause a roughened shoe, and playing the piano flatten the fingers, we conjecture that a person showing these effects is likely to be a cyclist and a musician. When Robinson Crusoe found the footprint on the shore, he had to assume the presence of another human being on the island in order to account for it.

There are certain inherent difficulties in handling hypotheses. By their nature, they tend to have only a fair degree of probability, since for every effect there are usually a number of different possible causes. Holmes himself acknowledged that typing might be the cause of his client's spatulated fingers and had to resort to the "spiritual look" (whatever that is) to prove her a musician. A policeman who found a man lying unconscious in the gutter outside a saloon might reasonably suppose alcohol to be the cause of the catastrophe, but he would be grossly negligent if he did not consider illness or injury as possible explanations. It is part of the normal machinery of the detective story to tempt the reader into forming a false hypothesis and then to reveal the right one, quite unexpectedly, at the end.

Such considerations might lead us to despair of any kind of certainty in dealing with hypotheses, but the situation is by no means so desperate. In the first place, a hypothesis usually does have somewhat the status of a provisional theory which can be confirmed or overthrown by further investigation. Holmes confirms his hypotheses by getting his client to acknowledge that she is indeed a cycling pianist from the country, and a doctor could establish whether the man in the gutter was ill or drunk. If we see a man shabbily dressed, we probably could not immediately tell whether the disarray was due to poverty, miserliness, absent-mindedness, a sick wife, or some dirty job to be done, but a little inquiry would easily establish the true situation or at least eliminate some of the possibilities. In science, systematic testing in the laboratory is the natural way out; if the conjectured cause can be made to produce the known effect regularly, the problem is solved.

There are times, of course, when the nature of the situation does not permit final confirmation, but even then we can at least look for degrees of probability. The man who feels drops of moisture falling from the sky assumes rain without stopping to consider the improbable possibility that a practical joker is showering him from a helicopter. The conduct of Hauptmann, who was executed for the Lindbergh kidnapping, could hardly be explained except on the assumption of his guilt: he spent some of the ransom money, the ladder used in the kidnapping was made from wood from his house, the ransom letters were in his handwriting, and the child's sleeping jacket was in his possession. Edmund Pearson, in discussing the case, mentions some other celebrated criminals who were also found in circumstances that only one reasonable hypothesis could explain: George Joseph Smith, three of whose wives (insured) drowned in the bathtub, and Dr. Crippen, who suddenly fled abroad with his typist, leaving fragments of his wife behind. Simplicity and inherent plausibility are the proper criteria to employ in judging between hypotheses incapable of confirmation or still to be confirmed. We *can* explain the existence of Shakespeare's plays on the hypothesis that the playwright Christopher Marlowe, whom history records as having been murdered before many of the plays were produced, actually was spirited abroad, wrote the plays, and sent them back to England to be produced under Shakespeare's name. But the hypothesis that Shakespeare wrote his own plays is a good deal simpler and, considering the vanity of authors, inherently far more plausible.

As a logical device hypothesis is susceptible to all kinds of abuses; careless or unscrupulous thinkers constantly offer us hypotheses which, without genuine confirmation, they regard as proved simply because the hypotheses explain known phenomena after a fashion. Some of the examples are merely comic, as is the case with the controversies over the authorship of Shakespeare's plays. A little more serious is the recent furor over the "flying saucers." It may be true that the presence of Martian observers in saucer-shaped vehicles in our upper atmosphere would explain the undoubted fact that honest observers have seen objects of a certain seeming shape and speed in the sky. But there is no real evidence for the existence of rational life on Mars, and the simpler and therefore more acceptable hypothesis would be that the observers were deceived by known phenomena such as weather balloons. (Here we notice that, short of an actual landing by Martians, final confirmation is virtually impossible.) The saucer scare may be considered harmless, though it acquires a sinister aspect when the Air Force is accused of plotting to suppress evidence on the matter. It is characteristic of a certain kind of paranoid mind to explain in terms of "plots" all sorts of things for which rational people find simpler explanations. Notorious is the case of the unhappy victim of a Congressional investigation who was told that his repeated public denunciations of Communism did not save him from the suspicion of being a Communist agent, since the public utterance might simply have been intended to distract attention from secret subversive activities. The old belief in witchcraft was in a sense a kind of hypothesis to explain such undoubted facts as sickness and crop failure, for which our ancestors simply did not possess the scientific explanations we accept today. Nor does the existence of an accepted scientific explanation necessarily deter some men from continuing to manufacture alternative hypotheses. To most of us, fossils in ancient rocks point to the former existence of the corresponding animals, but the fossils have also been accounted for on the hypothesis that they were placed in the rocks by the devil to tempt unwary scientists into infidelity. Much racism is based on some shaky hypothesis—for instance, the belief that the relative vigor of various European nations is determined by the amount of Nordic blood in the people. Since tribes speaking Germanic languages (if that is what is meant by "Nordic") wandered over all of Europe at the time of the fall of Rome, the theory is hard to refute, but neither is it susceptible of any kind of proof. (Here the problem—national greatness—is so complex as almost to defy an absolutely satisfying explanation and so vast as to exclude the use of controlled experiment. The fall of Rome has been explained as caused by everything from slavery and malaria to unchastity and poor cavalry.) Often we have to work with unprovable hypotheses, but we should not put any more stock in them than we can help.

There is scarcely any civilized activity that does not depend upon induction. It is the basis of science and of human learning generally. Even at its best, however, it never attains absolute certainty, and the practical generalizations we employ in everyday life must always be handled with caution and humility. Induction has, moreover, certain inherent limitations. It cannot solve basic questions of value, nor perform the basic operations of deductive logic. . . .

MANUEL BILSKY

From Logic and Effective Argument, *by Manuel Bilsky. Copyright ©, 1956. By permission of Holt, Rinehart and Winston, Inc., publishers.*

Deduction: Is Your Argument Valid?

THE NATURE OF DEDUCTION

Up to this point, in a sense, we have been clearing the ground. To write a good argument, as you have seen, one must first contend with a stubborn barrier, language itself. Before we can argue effectively, we must be able to communicate clearly. We may think of an effective argument, but when it comes to putting it down on paper, frequently the language we must use to put our thoughts into communicable form is extremely troublesome. Consequently unless we are constantly on the alert, clarity, so very important to successful communication, is often no more than an ideal.

We turn now from the study of language to the study of argument proper. What do we do when we try to present an effective argument? Briefly, we use reasons; we think by means of reasons. We believe that a certain statement is true, that it corresponds to the facts, but we want to prove it, so we give reasons to support the belief. These reasons are evidence for the belief; we may call the reasons proof and the belief a conclusion. I believe, say, that the next chancellor of the University of Chicago will be a woman. "A ridiculous idea," you reply. So I try to convince you that my belief is a true one. I do this by giving you reasons, or evidence. The degree to which I can get you to believe what I believe depends, of course, on the kind of evidence I can give you. Remember that in this book we are interested exclusively in what I called in Chapter I legitimate arguments. I could beat you over the head with a club—some arguments don't amount to much more than that—or perhaps resort to a spurious type of argument and get you to agree with me, but such means of persuasion are entirely foreign to the spirit of this book. We are interested in being logical, in being reasonable; and here this means depending on the truth, on what actually is the case.

Argument, then, is a way of using language, and it involves reasons. Indeed most of our discourse is argument. But there are kinds of discourse, ways of using language, which do not involve reasons, at least not in the same sense as they do when we are presenting an argument. Suppose, for example, you have to write an exposition—what Main Street looks like back home, say—in this case you don't worry about reasons. All you do is think of what the stores looked like, and then try to write down as accurately as possible what you see in your mind. You are describing something; you don't have to worry about giving reasons, proving anything, or solving problems.

Or suppose you have to write about the most exciting thing that happened all summer, another old chestnut that usually hits you in the face the minute you walk into an English class after a summer vacation. What you produce will probably be some form of narration, another kind of exposition. Or take reverie—the random thoughts that go through your head when you are listening to a symphony concert or to an economics lecture. We can also call this exposition, although it rarely gets put down on paper, except by such writers as James Joyce. Most poetry and history are also exposition. I do not mean to say that these forms of writing are entirely free of argument. Actually in some cases, Upton Sinclair's *The Jungle,* for example, the author is mainly motivated by the desire to produce a convincing argument. This can be said of almost all forms of writing: they are mixtures of poetry, description, argument, narration. But the ones I have just mentioned are mainly discourse without inference, that is, without reasons to prove a point. And that is the distinction between argument and exposition: one tries to prove a point or a belief, the other reports a series of events; one gives reasons, the other reports facts or ideas.

A deductive argument is one kind of argument. There are other kinds, inductive and analogical, as we shall see in the following chapters. A deductive argument has a certain form of structure. In this kind of argument we lay down first certain statements which we know or strongly believe are true. We then use these statements to get to others. This process of "getting to," under certain conditions, is enough to prove that the other statements are true. We know they are true because the first ones are. Suppose, for example, you know that all the people in your English class are under thirty years of age. This would be the first statement, the one that you know; this would be the statement that you lay down. Now what statement can you "get to" from this one? That is, what other statement will you know is true simply because you know that this first one is true? An obvious example is that Mamie, the blond that sits next to you, is under thirty. To know this, you don't have to ask her. All you have to know is that the first statement is true.

This procedure is called deduction, or a deductive argument. If we are justified in going from the first statement to the second, then we can say that the second statement *follows from* the first, or that we *infer* the second from the first, or that the first *implies* the second. When are we justified in making such an inference? When is it logical to go from one such statement to another? There are certain rules which govern such inferences. The purpose of this chapter is to explain what these rules are. I shall try to describe the conditions under which you can legitimately go from one statement to another. A mastery of this will enable you to do two things: find out whether your own arguments are valid, that is, whether they satisfy the rules governing deduction, and find out, or test, the deductive arguments you read in other writers.

A deductive argument, then, has parts. First, although they do not necessarily come in this order, there is the evidence. This consists of the statements that you know are true, or that you strongly believe are true. These are the premises of your argument. Second, there is the conclusion. This is the statement that you deduce, or infer, from your premises. This is the statement that you don't have to investigate: you know it is true if it follows from true premises. And if it really does follow from the premises, we say that your argument is valid, that you have proved your conclusion. But if you have made a mistake in your reasoning, if you haven't followed all the rules of deduction, we say that your argument is invalid. Finally, if your premises are true and your reasoning is valid, your conclusion cannot possibly be false. At this point you don't need to worry about the precise nature of truth. That question will be discussed in detail in the next chapter. Here the important thing is whether the conclusion of a deductive argument follows validly from the premises.

THE IMPORTANCE OF FORM

In a deductive argument, if the premises are true and if the reasoning is valid, then the conclusion is necessarily true. It follows from the premises. This is so because in deduction the important thing is the form of the argument; indeed the whole secret of deduction is form. What exactly is this form? We can look at any statement from two aspects: its form and its content. The first is the relation that exists between the different parts of the statement. Take the statement, "Swallows are birds." Two important parts are "swallows" and "birds." What is the relation between these two? Simply that all the swallows there are form a group or class, and this class is part of a larger class, namely, birds. The form of the statement, that is, the order in which the words appear, tells us that this relationship exists. Suppose we change the statement to "Sharks are fish." Is the form different? No. The content has changed: the first statement deals with swallows while the second deals with sharks. But the form, the relation between the two parts of each statement, stays the same. If we let "A" stand for the first part of each statement and "B" for the second, in both cases we can symbolize the relation by saying "A is a part of B," or, more precisely, "A is included in B."

There are four kinds of logical form. But before we take them up, some preliminary matters require attention. I have been using words like "term," "class," and "statement" on the assumption that you have a rough idea of what they stand for. But now I must try to make them more precise. They are important to a discussion of deduction; we will be using them constantly throughout the remainder of this chapter.

First: a term. This refers to the subject or the predicate of a statement. In the above statements the terms are "birds," "swallows," "sharks," and "fish." A term does not have to be one word: it is, rather, the whole of the subject and the whole of the predicate, not counting the verb. Thus in "The boy next door is a member of a medical fraternity," one term is "the boy next door," and the other is "a member of a medical fraternity."

Second: a class. This refers to a group, a collection of things or people. The collection has one characteristic which is the same for all the members of the class. This is what makes them members of that class. What, for example, do all birds have in common? The fact that they all possess feathers. Sometimes there are classes which do not have any members— they are empty. "Dragons" is an example. In Chapter I these were instances of classes with connotation but no denotation.

Finally: a statement. This is a group of words which shows clearly what the logical form of that particular statement is. Although there are certain puzzling philosophical difficulties involved, we will not go far wrong if we refer to a statement sometimes as a sentence, sometimes as a proposition. Besides the two terms in a statement, there are two other important parts. The first is the verb, and the second is the word which tells how many are involved in the subject term. In the statement, "Swallows are birds," the word "are" is of course the verb. The word which tells how many does not appear in the sentence as it stands, so we supply it. In this case it would be "All." The complete statement would then read, "All swallows are birds."

We are now in a better position to talk about the four kinds of form. They are usually referred to by the capital letters A, E, I, and O. An example of the A-form is "All Baptists are Protestants." If we let A stand for the subject term and B for the predicate term, the statement becomes "All A's are B's." This means, as we have seen before, that the class of A's is included in the class of B's. We can show this on a diagram:

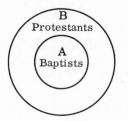

You can see by the diagram that the circle labeled A, class A, the class of Baptists, is wholly included in, or contained in, class B, the class of Protestants.

"No Catholics are Baptists" is an example of the E-form. Using our capital letters, we see that this becomes "No A's are B's." The corresponding diagram is:

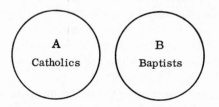

This diagram shows that no member of class A is a member of class B. The I-form is "Some Baptists are Americans," which becomes "Some A's are B's," and the diagram:

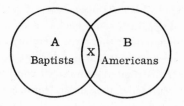

The cross shows the A's which are also B's. Finally, the O-form: "Some Catholics are not Americans," or "Some A's are not B's." The diagram for this is similar to the last one.

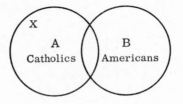

The cross of course indicates the A's which are not B's.

All these statements are called categorical; they have no conditions attached to them. Each categorical statement, or proposition, has what is called *quality* and *quantity*. If you ask what the quality of a statement is, you are asking whether it is affirmative or negative. Thus the A and the I statements are affirmative; the E and the O negative. If you ask what the quantity of a statement is, you are asking whether it refers to all members of the class or to some of them. The A and E refer to all the members; they are called universal statements. The I and O refer to some members; they are called particular statements. Statements which refer to an individual, by the way, are regarded as universal statements. "President Eisenhower is a Republican" is an example. Read this as "All the President Eisenhowers there are are Republicans," and you can see why.

Before we turn our attention to the syllogism, we need to know about one more concept: distribution. This is a rather difficult notion, but it is extremely important, as you will see when we get to the syllogism. In the first place, forget about the way you ordinarily use this word "distribution." In logic it has a special meaning. To say a term is distributed means that it refers to all the members of the class it designates. For example, the term "all books" is distributed since it refers to all the members of the class "books." But "some books" does not refer to all the members of the class designated; this term therefore is undistributed.

The subject terms in statements do not present a problem: it is easy to tell whether they are distributed or not. All you have to do is look at the quantity word that precedes the subject term, and you can tell immediately. If "all" precedes it, the term is distributed; if "some" precedes it, the term is undistributed. Hence in the A-form statement, "All Baptists are Protestants," the subject term is distributed. In the E-form, "No Catholics are Baptists," the subject term is also distributed since it refers to all the members of the class Catholics, although in a negative way. It denies something about all of them. The other two, the I and the O, both say "Some A's"; both subject terms are therefore undistributed.

The predicate terms are a little more troublesome, since they don't have labels the way the subject terms do. In the A-form statement, "All Baptists are Protestants," however, you can see rather easily that not all Protestants are referred to, since there are many more Protestants besides Baptists. The predicate term, therefore, of the A-form is undistributed. In the E-form, "No Catholics are Baptists," however, since the whole of the one class is entirely excluded from the whole of the other, the predicate term is distributed. The I-form, "Some Baptists are Americans," does not distribute its predicate term: obviously there are many more Americans than those who are Baptists. Finally, the O-form: "Some Catholics are not Americans"; here the predicate term is distributed, because the "Some Catholics" referred to may be Portuguese Catholics, and the entire class of Americans is outside the class of Portuguese Catholics. The following table summarizes this discussion of distribution:

	Subject Term	*Predicate Term*
A-form	D	U
E-form	D	D
I-form	U	U
O-form	U	D

THE SYLLOGISM

Everything in this chapter has really been a preparation for the study of the syllogism. And since the syllogism is the basic form of deductive reasoning, we have been preparing for the study of deduction. A syllogism is a kind of deduction, a deductive argument with a certain structure, or form. There are other kinds of deduction—mathematics, for example—but we will not be concerned with them.

A syllogism contains three statements. The first two are the premises and the third is the conclusion. Here is an example:

> All dogs are animals.
> All spaniels are dogs.
> Therefore, all spaniels are animals.

This is called a categorical syllogism since all the statements in it are categorical, that is, they are statements without conditions, or qualifications. "If I finish my work, I'll go to the movies" is an example of a statement which is not categorical. To talk about the syllogism we need some special words. The *major term* is the predicate of the conclusion, which in this case is "animals." The *minor term* is the subject of the conclusion: "spaniels." The *major premise* is the one which contains the major term, in this case the first one. The *minor premise* is the one which contains the minor term. The *middle term* is the term which appears in both premises: "dogs." Every valid syllogism has three terms, no more, no less. In the course of the argument each of them turns up twice.

Using the same letters that we used with statements, we can symbolize the syllogism. The above syllogism symbolized looks like this:

> All A's are B's.
> All C's are A's.
> ∴ All C's are B's.

The same circle diagrams that show the structure of statements show the structure of syllogisms:

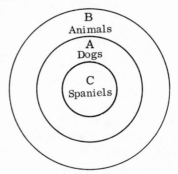

This diagram shows that class A, the class of dogs, is included in class B, the class of animals. That is the first, or major premise. Class C, the class

of spaniels, according to the diagram, is included in class A, the class of
dogs. That is the minor premise. The conclusion also appears on the
diagram: class C, the class of spaniels, is included in class B, the class of
animals.

A deductive argument is valid if the conclusion follows from the
premises. Whether it is valid depends solely on its form. The validity
has nothing to do with the content, that is, with what the argument is
about. Consequently we can have a valid syllogism even when one or
more of the statements in it are false. Here is an example of a valid
syllogism in which the premises are both false and the conclusion is true.

> All angels are animals.
> Juan Peron is an angel.
> ∴ Juan Peron is an animal.

And here is an example in which all three parts are false and yet the
reasoning is valid:

> All angels are butterflies.
> Al Capone is an angel.
> ∴ Al Capone is a butterfly.

Hence if a syllogism is to be entirely satisfactory, we must ask whether
the premises are true. Such a syllogism must, as a matter of fact, satisfy
two conditions: (1) the premises must be true, and (2) the reasoning
must be valid. When both these conditions are satisfied, we can be sure
that the conclusion is true. Whether a premise is true depends on its content. In a deductive argument we can remove the content, that is, symbolize the argument, and still decide whether it is valid. In this chapter
we are concerned mainly with validity. We want to know how to tell
whether a deductive argument is valid, whether the conclusion has been
correctly deduced from the premises. In the next chapter we shall examine the ways to prove that a statement is true or false.

Studying deduction helps you to construct effective arguments of this
sort. If you learn the form, the structure of a valid deductive argument,
a good part of the job is done. This gives you a sort of outline: major
premise, minor premise, conclusion. What you have to do then is supply
the flesh, fill in the substance. Your premises will be either definitions—
e.g., "All dogs are animals," "All Frenchmen are Europeans"—or gen-

eral observations which you build up from experience—"Salk's vaccine prevents polio"—or particular observations like "Fido is a dog." And if your reasoning is valid, you will have proved your conclusion.

One of the most important things, then, about the study of deduction is that it helps in constructing valid arguments. The other important thing is that it provides a means of testing deductive arguments, your own and those of others, to see whether they are valid. Sometimes you may think of an argument in defense of a position, but when you get it down on paper in symbolized form, you might discover that it is not valid. This applies equally to the arguments of others, thereby supplying a valuable means of refutation. How, then, do we test deductive arguments of the syllogistic sort?

One way of doing this is by using circle diagrams. You have already seen these in operation, so that by now you should have a certain amount of familiarity with them. Here are a few more samples of the circle method of diagramming syllogisms. Of course, to become perfectly familiar with this method, you must construct such diagrams yourself. First I will put down the syllogism, next the symbolization, and finally the circle diagram. Remember that we treat an individual statement as a universal one.

> All dogs are animals.
> Fido is a dog.
> ∴ Fido is an animal.

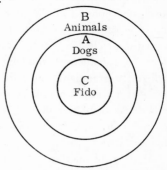

All A's are B's.
All C's are A's.
∴ All C's are B's.

The diagram shows that the argument is valid, that the conclusion follows from the premises. The circle labeled C is wholly contained in the larger circle, the one labeled B, and that is what the conclusion says.

Thus we have a test of the validity of this particular argument. We can literally see that it is valid.

Now try a syllogism which uses as its major premise a form other than the A:

> No Catholics are Baptists.
> All Jesuits are Catholics.
> ∴ No Jesuits are Baptists.

No A's are B's.
All C's are A's.
∴ No C's are B's.

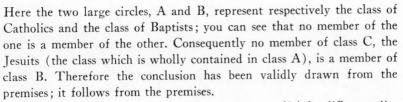

Here the two large circles, A and B, represent respectively the class of Catholics and the class of Baptists; you can see that no member of the one is a member of the other. Consequently no member of class C, the Jesuits (the class which is wholly contained in class A), is a member of class B. Therefore the conclusion has been validly drawn from the premises; it follows from the premises.

Syllogisms with particular premises present a slightly different diagramming problem. Take the following one:

> Some Japanese are Shintoists.
> No Texans are Shintoists.
> ∴ Some Japanese are not Texans.

The symbolized and diagrammed versions are:

Some A's are B's.
No C's are B's.
Some A's are not C's.

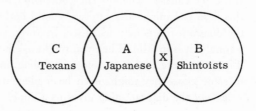

Instead of concentric circles, here we use overlapping ones. Since the A's, the Japanese, are sometimes Shintoists, the B's, the two overlapping circles on the right show that some people are both Japanese and Shintoists, and the cross shows this. The circle on the left, C, the Texans, shows that no member of this class is a member of B, and this is what the minor premise says. Consequently the conclusion, namely, that some Japanese are not Texans is valid, as we can see from the diagram. The cross, again, indicates those Japanese who are not Texans.

Here is an example which shows how the diagrams reveal an error in reasoning:

> All Chicago freshmen are brilliant people.
> All geniuses are brilliant people.
> ∴ All Chicago freshmen are geniuses.

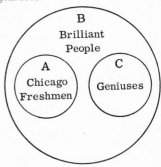

All A's are B's.
All C's are B's.
∴ All A's are C's.

The large circle, B, the brilliant ones, contains both class A, the Chicago freshmen, and class C; the geniuses. But, as the diagram shows, the conclusion is invalid since circle A is not *necessarily* included in circle C, although the conclusion of the syllogism asserts that it is.

There are some general rules, fairly easy to apply, to which syllogisms must conform in order to be valid. Given any syllogism, if we apply these rules, we can see whether the conclusion follows from the premises. If this is so you might ask why we should bother with the diagrams. What the diagrams do is help us to see, literally, where the syllogism has gone wrong if it is invalid. Then you might ask why bother applying the rules. The point here is that in some cases diagrams might be misleading, and in some cases they might even be inadequate. So the application of the rules *and* the diagramming gives us a double check on the validity of the syllogism. There are a number of these rules, but here I discuss only the three most important ones, the three that are most frequently responsible for mistakes in reasoning.

The first rule is that a syllogism must contain three and only three terms, and each of them must be used in the same sense throughout. A violation of this rule is called the Fallacy of Four Terms. It may occur in either of two ways. In the first the use of four terms is obvious and quite easy to detect. An example is the following syllogism:

> Some statesmen are good novelists.
> All psychologists have insight into human nature.
> ∴ What?

Count the terms; you can see that there are four. It is therefore not even a syllogism, and it is impossible to conclude anything. But sometimes an argument seems to have only three terms when it really has four. The trouble arises when the same word is used in two different senses. Here is an example:

> Moderate people avoid intoxicating things.
> The fragrance of orange blossoms is intoxicating.
> ∴ Moderate people avoid the fragrance of orange blossoms.

Since "intoxicating" means two different things, there are really four terms. Again, this is not really a syllogism.

According to the second rule, the middle term should be distributed at least once. A violation of this rule is called the Fallacy of the Undistributed Middle. This violation is the source of many of the spurious arguments we read in the newspapers. Most of the "guilt by association" arguments rest on this fallacy. A typical example is the following:

> Stalinist agents supported the League against War and Fascism.
> Professor Potshot supported the League against War and Fascism.
> ∴ Professor Potshot was a Stalinist agent.

Here the middle term, "the League against War and Fascism" is undistributed in both premises. A circle diagram quickly reveals the fallaciousness of this argument.

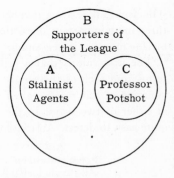

All A's are B's.
All C's are B's.
∴ All C's are A's.

You can see by the diagram that even though the A's and C's are parts of B, this is no reason to conclude that A is the same as C.

The third rule states that if a term is undistributed in the premises, it can't be distributed in the conclusion, that is, if it doesn't refer to all the members of the class when the term appears in a premise, it can't refer to all the members when it appears in the conclusion. If it did, it would be going beyond what the term covers in the premises. The previous rule applied to the middle term; this one applies to either of the other two. A violation of this rule is called an Illicit Process. Here is an example of syllogism which commits this fallacy:

> All Chicago undergraduates are lovers of Aristotle.
> No Harvard men are Chicago undergraduates.
> ∴ No Harvard men are lovers of Aristotle.

The major term, "lovers of Aristotle," is undistributed in the first premise, but in the conclusion it is distributed, so an illicit process has taken place. Again a diagram will show this clearly.

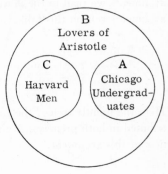

All A's are B's.
No C's are A's.
∴ No C's are B's.

The fact that the C circle is outside the A circle is no reason to argue that it is outside the B circle. It may be outside it, but it doesn't necessarily follow from the premises that it is.

ORDINARY LANGUAGE AND THE SYLLOGISM

We now have a means of testing the validity of deductive arguments. Given almost any deductive argument that can be put into the form of a syllogism, after a certain amount of practice you should be able to use what you have learned in this chapter as a tool, an instrument with which to check whether the conclusion really follows from the premises. But there is one difficulty—a question that has probably come up in your own mind. The deductive arguments you encounter seldom appear in the pat form that this discussion seems to have implied they do. Nobody talks or writes in syllogisms. If someone did, for any length of time anyway, people would start looking at him queerly and wondering whether he had been seeing the right kind of doctor. Similarly in your own writing. Suppose your assignment were to write an argument defending social fraternities. If you were to hand your English teacher a sheet of paper with a beautifully valid syllogism on it, you would probably get "A" for validity, but "F," for the theme, and you would be spending the next few days writing an argument in ordinary language. But don't throw that syllogism away. It will serve as a model, a form, a skeleton. For the finished theme your job will simply be to fill out the form with some substance.

In reverse this works the same way. When you read someone else's deductive argument, before you test, before you feed it into the machinery we have set up, you have to change it into the kind of form that is appropriate for such testing. You have to reduce the argument that you find to a syllogism, and then it is ready to be tested. This reducing process, this cutting down to size, must take place in two areas: the statements themselves and the syllogistic argument as a whole.

The statements that make up the different parts of the syllogism should look as much as possible like the ones we have been working with. Your job, then, will be to change what you find into something closely resembling the A, E, I, and O-form statements. Sometimes this is very difficult, and the ability to do so efficiently rarely comes without a great deal of practice. Here are a few of the ways that you can change ordinary language into the language of the syllogism, into statements that can easily be recognized as having the A, E, I, or O-form.

The verb should always be a part of the verb "to be." This means that whenever you come across verbs which are anything besides "to be," you must change them to this verb. For example, the sentence, "Stalinist agents supported the League against War and Fascism," does not contain "to be." Here it is a simple matter to make the change. In its new form the sentence becomes "Stalinist agents were supporters of the League against War and Fascism." Now it is easy to identify the subject and predicate terms. One more example should be enough to take care of this problem. Suppose you have the sentence, "Chicago undergraduates love Aristotle." Again the solution is simple. All you have to do is change the verb "love" to some part of the verb "to be"; in this case it is the present tense: "Chicago undergraduates are lovers of Aristotle." And again, in its new form the sentence allows you to identify more readily the classes involved.

Sometimes you have to change the grammatical structure of the sentence. Take the sentence, "To play tennis well requires much practice." Here you must change the infinitive phrase which starts the sentence to a pronoun with a modifying clause. The subject term then becomes "Those who play tennis well." Again, we change the verb to "to be," and the complete sentence becomes "Those who play tennis well are those who spend much time practicing." When your original sentence uses a passive verb followed by a prepositional phrase, you must change the voice to active and make the object of the preposition into the subject of the sentence. "Much pleasure is produced by symphony orchestras" because "Symphony orchestras are producers of much pleasure."

In all cases you must supply the quantity word if it does not appear in the original sentence. The two sentences in the preceding paragraph would then begin with "all," and would read "All those who play tennis well are those who spend much time practicing," and "All symphony orchestras are producers of much pleasure." Notice how easy it is now to change such statements into the symbolized form: both become "All A's are B's."

Finally, to indicate clearly the class designated by the predicate term, we must frequently supply a predicate noun where the original sentence contained a predicate adjective. In the sentence "A miracle is incredible," the predicate adjective "incredible" would become "an incredible thing." Then, when we supply the quantity word, the sentence becomes "All miracles are incredible things." Sometimes the predicate word is missing entirely as in "Birds fly." In such cases we must supply a predicate word. The sentence then becomes "All birds are flying things."

These are not all the difficulties that ordinary language presents, but enough so that now you have a fairly good basis for changing the sentences you come across every day into sentences you can use in checking the validity of a deductive argument. The syllogism as a whole also presents problems of this sort. Actually it is very rarely that a complete syllogism appears in the arguments of everyday language or even in the arguments of the natural sciences. They appear rather in an elliptical fashion, that is, parts of them are frequently missing. An argument of this sort, in which one or more of the parts are missing, is called an enthymeme. To test such an argument you must of course first supply the missing part. Let us look at a few examples of enthymematic, or incompletely stated, deductive arguments.

In our first example the argument might appear something like this: "Father Jacob's Nectar cured George's cough; it ought to do the same for mine." If we put this in the form of a syllogism, we see that we have the minor premise and the conclusion:

> Father Jacob's Nectar cured George's cough.
> ∴ Father Jacob's Nectar will cure my cough.

The major premise is therefore missing, but it's not much of a problem to supply it. The brackets show the missing, or suppressed, part.

> [All medicines curing George's cough will cure my cough.]
> Father Jacob's Nectar cured George's cough.
> ∴ Father Jacob's Nectar will cure my cough.

It is now almost ready for the testing job. If you put it into the form suggested above, you will then be ready to apply the syllogism tests.

Here is an example of an enthymeme with a missing minor premise: "All drunkards are short-lived; Herman won't live long." The complete syllogism looks like this:

> All drunkards are short-lived.
> [Herman is a drunkard.]
> ∴ Herman will be short-lived.

And finally, the conclusion may also be left out. In most cases of this sort it is implied so strongly that it is hardly mistakable. For example: "I say cheating on exams is immoral, and what Henry did yesterday was certainly cheating." The syllogism would look like this:

> Cheating on exams is immoral.
> What Henry did yesterday was cheating.
> [∴ What Henry did yesterday was immoral.]

QUESTIONS FOR REVIEW OF PART SEVEN

1. How does Sherwood differentiate induction, deduction, faith, and common sense? How, if at all, does he differentiate "hunches" and intuition? What distinction does your dictionary make between "hunches" and intuition?

2. What does Sherwood mean when he writes ". . . in theory even scientific generalizations possess not certainty but only an unusually high degree of probability"? Give an example of such a generalization other than one Sherwood offers.

3. What are some of the criteria of sound evidence or "proof"? Where in the article does Sherwood summarize the criteria he has in mind? Are there any criteria which he suggests previous to the summary but does not include in the summary?

4. Using your dictionary or a science text, distinguish among "law," "theory," and "hypothesis." What criteria does Sherwood suggest "to employ in judging between hypotheses incapable of confirmation or still to be confirmed"? Can you think of any former hypotheses, since accepted as theories or laws, which did not seem to meet his criteria when they were still hypotheses?

5. What distinction does Bilsky draw between exposition and argument? Which of the requirements under the first of the "Suggestions for Individual Projects and Class Discussion" is the one clearly pertaining to argument rather than to exposition? Which of the sample propositions in that same assignment can be proven deductively, and which can be proven inductively?

6. What are the four types of categorical statements, and what is an example (original with you) of each type? In which are the subject terms distributed, and in which are they undistributed? In which are the predicate terms distributed, in which undistributed?

7. What are the three rules which the Bilsky article states that a valid syllogism must follow?

SUGGESTIONS FOR INDIVIDUAL PROJECTS
CLASS DISCUSSION

1. List five statements of fact and fifteen propositions. Make the first five of the propositions, propositions of fact ("Smoking causes cancer"); the second five, propositions of policy ("Utopia College should offer classes in the evening"); the third five, propositions of value ("Ernest Hemingway was an excellent novelist"). Label each set of statements clearly. Here are some requirements of an effective proposition:

   a. The proposition should present a statement which is *arguable*.
      Poor examples: Army won the Army-Navy football game in 1936.
      Football is better than track.
   b. The terms of the proposition should be *clear and restricted*.
      Poor examples: The automobile is not what it used to be.
      Socialized medicine would be bad for the country.
   c. The proposition should present a *single* judgment.
      Poor examples: Fraternities have become so undemocratic that they should be abolished.
      As long as Red China continues to demonstrate that it wants war, it should not be admitted to the United Nations.
   d. The terms of the proposition should be *unprejudiced*.
      Poor examples: Traitors should not be allowed to teach at Utopia College.
      Only students with a high sense of morality should be admitted to Utopia College.

2. List five statements presenting universal truth, five presenting probable truth. Label each set of statements clearly.

3. Following the suggestions which Bilsky makes under "Ordinary Language and the Syllogism," carefully construct a syllogism from each of the following enthymemes. Beneath each syllogism, state whether or not the premises are true and the reasoning valid.

   a. Of course it's the right number; I just looked it up in the telephone book.
   b. Being a Negro, he has musical talent.
   c. It is no wonder that he is a juvenile delinquent; his mother and father were divorced three years ago.

    d. Because war has existed since man's earliest years, it is ridiculous to expect that we will ever abolish it.

    e. Since there is no scientific basis for it, no one should harbor any racial discrimination.

    f. Communists favor socialized medicine, and so does that Joe Jones character.

    g. Who says our national health standards are low? Don't our boys in the army get the best medical services of any army in the world?

SUGGESTED WRITING ASSIGNMENT

Write a 500-word paper convincing a particular group of readers of some idea with which they have disagreed or on which they have not formulated a strong opinion. Begin planning your paper by formulating carefully a proposition of policy. Then ask yourself what the "stock issues" are: (1) Are your readers involved in a problem which needs solution? (2) Will the proposed solution be workable? (3) Will the proposed solution bring your readers the satisfaction they desire? And, if necessary, (4) will the proposed solution introduce new problems worse than the problem it is designed to solve? List several reasons supporting your viewpoint on each of these questions, anticipating the kind of evidence you will need to support each of your reasons: instances, statistics, analogies, or the testimony of authorities. After you have worked out a careful outline of this type, write a rough draft of the paper. In the first paragraph, move directly into your position on the first stock issue and state your proposition clearly by the end of that paragraph. In subsequent paragraphs, state your position on each of the other stock issues, supporting your stand with valid reasoning and relevant, typical, and sufficient evidence. In the conclusion, summarize your reasoning and restate the proposition in clear and emphatic terms. Before copying your paper into its final form, study it carefully to make sure that it contains no missing (implied) premises which you and your readers do not accept.

Style
and Rhetoric

Style is concerned with a person's characteristic manner of choosing words and figures
of speech, forming them into sentences, and,
in written work, punctuating and spelling—
all features of language in which it usually
makes a great difference whether one is using
English or another language. It is curious,
then, that so many books on the English language contain little or nothing directly about
style. George Orwell's "Politics and the English Language" begins Part VIII as an illustration of one writer's reaction to the stale,
inflated style of many people writing modern
English.

Rhetoric, the art or science of prose composition, tends to be a broader conception,
including style within its province, but also
concerned with organizational features of
language, means of proof, and the like. Because for decades many school and university
English departments have tended to devote

most of their attention to grammar and literature, while speech departments have continued their strong interest in rhetoric, many people associate "rhetoric" with speech only, or, pejoratively, with artificial and elaborate speech. But this pejorative meaning is nothing new, for the master of all rhetoricians—Aristotle—inveighed against that kind of language in his *Rhetoric,* selections from which form the concluding reading in this book.

GEORGE ORWELL

Politics and the English Language

Most people who bother with the matter at all would admit that the English language is in a bad way, but it is generally assumed that we cannot by conscious action do anything about it. Our civilization is decadent and our language—so the argument runs—must inevitably share in the general collapse. It follows that any struggle against the abuse of language is a sentimental archism, like preferring candles to electric light or hansom cabs to aeroplanes. Underneath this lies the half-conscious belief that language is a natural growth and not an instrument which we shape for our own purposes.

Now, it is clear that the decline of a language must ultimately have political and economic causes: it is not due simply to the bad influence of this or that individual writer. But an effect can become a cause,

reinforcing the original cause and producing the same effect in an intensified form, and so on indefinitely. A man may take to drink because he
feels himself to be a failure, and then fail all the more completely because
he drinks. It is rather the same thing that is happening to the English
language. It becomes ugly and inaccurate because our thoughts are
foolish, but the slovenliness of our language makes it easier for us to
have foolish thoughts. The point is that the process is reversible. Modern
English, especially written English, is full of bad habits which spread by
imitation and which can be avoided if one is willing to take the necessary
trouble. If one gets rid of these habits one can think more clearly, and to
think clearly is a necessary first step towards political regeneration: so
that the fight against bad English is not frivolous and is not the exclusive
concern of professional writers. I will come back to this presently, and
I hope that by that time the meaning of what I have said here will have
become clearer. Meanwhile, here are five specimens of the English
language as it is now habitually written.

These five passages have not been picked out because they are especially bad—I could have quoted far worse if I had chosen—but because
they illustrate various of the mental vices from which we now suffer.
They are a little below the average, but are fairly representative samples.
I number them so that I can refer back to them when necessary:

(1) I am not, indeed, sure whether it is not true to say that the Milton
who once seemed not unlike a seventeenth-century Shelley had not become,
out of an experience ever more bitter in each year, more alien [*sic*] to the
founder of that Jesuit sect which nothing could induce him to tolerate.

> Professor Harold Laski (Essay in *Freedom of Expression*).

(2) Above all, we cannot play ducks and drakes with a native battery
of idioms which prescribes such egregious collocations of vocables as the
Basic *put up with* for *tolerate* or *put at a loss* for *bewilder*.

> Professor Lancelot Hogben (*Interglossa*).

(3) On the one side we have the free personality: by definition it is not
neurotic, for it has neither conflict nor dream. Its desires, such as they are,
are transparent, for they are just what institutional approval keeps in the
forefront of consciousness; another institutional pattern would alter their
number and intensity; there is little in them that is natural, irreducible, or
culturally dangerous. But *on the other side*, the social bond itself is nothing
but the mutual reflection of these self-secure integrities. Recall the definition
of love. Is not this the very picture of a small academic? Where is there a
place in this hall of mirrors for either personality or fraternity?

> Essay on psychology in *Politics* (New York).

(4) All the "best people" from the gentlemen's clubs, and all the frantic fascist captains, united in common hatred of Socialism and bestial horror of the rising tide of the mass revolutionary movement, have turned to acts of provocation, to foul incendiarism, to medieval legends of poisoned wells, to legalize their own destruction of proletarian organizations, and rouse the agitated petty-bourgeoisie to chauvinistic fervor on behalf of the fight against the revolutionary way out of the crisis.

Communist pamphlet.

(5) If a new spirit *is* to be infused into this old country, there is one thorny and contentious reform which must be tackled, and that is the humanization and galvanization of the B.B.C. Timidity here will bespeak canker and atrophy of the soul. The heart of Britain may be sound and of strong beat, for instance, but the British lion's roar at present is like that of Bottom in Shakespeare's *Midsummer Night's Dream*—as gentle as any sucking dove. A virile new Britain cannot continue indefinitely to be traduced in the eyes or rather ears, of the world by the effete languors of Langham Place, brazenly masquerading as "standard English." When the Voice of Britain is heard at nine o'clock, better far and infinitely less ludicrous to hear aitches honestly dropped than the present priggish, inflated, inhibited, school-ma'amish arch braying of blameless bashful mewing maidens!

Letter in *Tribune*.

Each of these passages has faults of its own, but, quite apart from avoidable ugliness, two qualities are common to all of them. The first is staleness of imagery; the other is lack of precision. The writer either has a meaning and cannot express it, or he inadvertently says something else, or he is almost indifferent as to whether his words mean anything or not. This mixture of vagueness and sheer incompetence is the most marked characteristic of modern English prose, and especially of any kind of political writing. As soon as certain topics are raised, the concrete melts into the abstract and no one seems able to think of turns of speech that are not hackneyed: prose consists less and less of *words* chosen for the sake of their meaning, and more and more of *phrases* tacked together like the sections of a prefabricated hen-house. I list below, with notes and examples, various of the tricks by means of which the work of prose-construction is habitually dodged:

DYING METAPHORS. A newly invented metaphor assists thought by evoking a visual image, while on the other hand a metaphor which is technically "dead" (e.g., *iron resolution*) has in effect reverted to being an ordinary word and can generally be used without loss of vividness. But in between these two classes there is a huge dump of worn-out metaphors which have lost all evocative power and are merely used because they save people the trouble of inventing phrases for themselves. Examples are: *Ring the changes on, take up the cudgels for, toe the line, ride roughshod over, stand shoulder to shoulder with, play into the hands of, no axe to grind, grist to the mill, fishing in troubled waters, on the order of the day, Achilles' heel, swan song, hotbed.* Many of these are used without knowledge of their meaning (what is a "rift," for instance?), and incompatible metaphors are frequently mixed, a sure sign that the writer is not interested in what he is saying. Some metaphors now current have been twisted out of their original meaning without those who use them even being aware of the fact. For example, *toe the line* is sometimes written *tow the line.* Another example is *the hammer and the anvil,* now always used with the implication that the anvil gets the worst of it. In real life it is always the anvil that breaks the hammer, never the other way about: a writer who stopped to think what he was saying would be aware of this, and would avoid perverting the original phrase.

OPERATORS OR VERBAL FALSE LIMBS. These save the trouble of picking out appropriate verbs and nouns, and at the same time pad each sentence with extra syllables which give it an appearance of symmetry. Characteristic phrases are *render inoperative, militate against, make contact with, be subjected to, give rise to, give grounds for, have the effect of, play a leading part (role) in, make itself felt, take effect, exhibit a tendency to, serve the purpose of, etc., etc.* The keynote is the elimination of simple verbs. Instead of being a single word, such as *break, stop, spoil, mend, kill,* a verb becomes a *phrase,* made up of a noun or adjective tacked on to some general-purposes verb such as *prove, serve, form, play, render.* In addition, the passive voice is wherever possible used in preference to the active, and noun constructions are used instead of gerunds (*by examination of* instead of *by examining*). The range of verbs is further cut down by means of the *-ize* and *de-* formations, and the banal statements are given an appearance of profundity by means of the *not un-* formation. Simple conjunctions and prepositions are replaced by such phrases as *with respect to, having regard to, the fact that, by dint of, in view of, in the interests of, on the hypothesis that;* and the ends of sentences are saved by anticlimax by such resounding commonplaces as *greatly to be desired, cannot be left out of account, a develop-*

ment to be expected in the near future, deserving of serious consideration, brought to a satisfactory conclusion, and so on and so forth.

PRETENTIOUS DICTION. Words like *phenomenon, element, individual* (as noun), *objective, categorical, effective, virtual, basis, primary, promote, constitute, exhibit, exploit, utilize, eliminate, liquidate,* are used to dress up simple statements and give an air of scientific impartiality to biased judgments. Adjectives like *epoch-making, epic, historic, unforgettable, triumphant, age-old, inevitable, inexorable, veritable,* are used to dignify the sordid processes of international politics, while writing that aims at glorifying war usually takes on an archaic color, its characteristic words being: *realm, throne, chariot, mailed fist, trident, sword, shield, buckler, banner, jackboot, clarion.* Foreign words and expressions such as *cul de sac, ancien régime, deus ex machina, mutatis mutandis, status quo, gleichschaltung, weltanschauung,* are used to give an air of culture and elegance. Except for the useful abbreviations *i.e., e.g.,* and *etc.,* there is no real need for any of the hundreds of foreign phrases now current in English. Bad writers, and especially scientific, political and sociological writers, are nearly always haunted by the notion that Latin or Greek words are grander than Saxon ones, and unnecessary words like *expedite, ameliorate, predict, extraneous, deracinated, clandestine, subaqueous* and hundreds of others constantly gain ground from their Anglo-Saxon opposite numbers.[1] The jargon peculiar to Marxist writing (*hyena, hangman, cannibal, petty bourgeois, these gentry, lacquey, flunkey, mad dog, White Guard,* etc.) consists largely of words and phrases translated from Russian, German or French; but the normal way of coining a new word is to use a Latin or Greek root with the appropriate affix and, where necessary, the size formation. It is often easier to make up words of this kind (*deregionalize, impermissible, extramarital, non-fragmentary* and so forth) than to think up the English words that will cover one's meaning. The result, in general, is an increase in slovenliness and vagueness.

MEANINGLESS WORDS. In certain kinds of writing, particularly in art

[1] An interesting illustration of this is the way in which the English flower names which were in use till very recently are being ousted by Greek ones, *snapdragon* becoming *antirrhinum, forget-me-not* becoming *myosotis,* etc. It is hard to see any practical reason for this change of fashion: it is probably due to an instinctive turning-away from the more homely word and a vague feeling that the Greek word is scientific.

criticism and literary criticism, it is normal to come across long passages which are almost completely lacking in meaning.[2] Words like *romantic, plastic, values, human, dead, sentimental, natural, vitality,* as used in art criticism, are strictly meaningless, in the sense that they not only do not point to any discoverable object, but are hardly ever expected to do so by the reader. When one critic writes, "The outstanding feature of Mr. X's work is its living quality," while another writes, "The immediately striking thing about Mr. X's work is its peculiar deadness," the reader accepts this as a simple difference of opinion. If words like *black* and *white* were involved, instead of the jargon words *dead* and *living,* he would see at once that language was being used in an improper way. Many political words are similarly abused. The word *Fascism* has now no meaning except in so far as it signifies "something not desirable." The words *democracy, socialism, freedom, patriotic, realistic, justice,* have each of them several different meanings which cannot be reconciled with one another. In the case of a word like *democracy,* not only is there no agreed definition, but the attempt to make one is resisted from all sides. It is almost universally felt that when we call a country democratic we are praising it: consequently the defenders of every kind of régime claim that it is a democracy, and fear that they might have to stop using the word if it were tied down to any one meaning. Words of this kind are often used in a consciously dishonest way. That is, the person who uses them has his own private definition, but allows his hearer to think he means something quite different. Statements like *Marshal Pétain was a true patriot, The Soviet Press is the freest in the world, The Catholic Church is opposed to persecution,* are almost always made with intent to deceive. Other words used in variable meanings, in most cases more or less dishonestly, are: *class, totalitarian, science, progressive, reactionary, bourgeois, equality.*

Now that I have made this catalogue of swindles and perversions, let me give another example of the kind of writing that they lead to.

[2] Example: "Comfort's catholicity of perception and image, strangely Whitmanesque in range, almost the exact opposite in aesthetic compulsion, continues to evoke that trembling atmospheric accumulative hinting at a cruel, and inexorably serene timelessness. . . . Wrey Gardiner scores by aiming at simple bull's-eyes with precisions. Only they are not so simple, and through this contented sadness runs more than the surface bitter-sweet of resignation." (*Poetry Quarterly.*)

This time it must of its nature be an imaginary one. I am going to translate a passage of good English into modern English of the worst sort. Here is a well-known verse from *Ecclesiastes:*

I returned and saw under the sun, that the race is not to the swift, nor the battle to the strong, neither yet bread to the wise, nor yet riches to men of understanding, nor yet favour to men of skill; but time and chance happeneth to them all.

Here it is in modern English:

Objective considerations of contemporary phenomena compels the conclusion that success or failure in competitive activities exhibits no tendency to be commensurate with innate capacity, but that a considerable element of the unpredictable must invariably be taken into account.

This is a parody, but not a very gross one. Exhibit (3), above, for instance, contains several patches of the same kind of English. It will be seen that I have not made a full translation. The beginning and ending of the sentence follow the original meaning fairly closely, but in the middle the concrete illustrations—race, battle, bread—dissolve into the vague phrase "success or failure in competitive activities." This had to be so, because no modern writer of the kind I am discussing— no one capable of using phrases like "objective consideration of contemporary phenomena"—would ever tabulate his thoughts in that precise and detailed way. The whole tendency of modern prose is away from concreteness. Now analyse these two sentences a little more closely. The first contains forty-nine words but only sixty syllables, and all its words are those of everyday life. The second contains thirty-eight words of ninety syllables: eighteen of its words are from Latin roots, and one from Greek. The first sentence contains six vivid images, and only one phrase ("time and chance") that could be called vague. The second contains not a single fresh, arresting phrase, and in spite of its ninety syllables it gives only a shortened version of the meaning contained in the first. Yet without a doubt it is the second kind of sentence that is gaining ground in modern English. I do not want to exaggerate. This kind of writing is not yet universal, and outcrops of simplicity will occur here and there in the worst-written page. Still, if you or I were told to write a few lines on the uncertainty of human fortunes, we should probably come much nearer to my imaginary sentence than to the one from *Ecclesiastes*.

As I have tried to show, modern writing at its worst does not consist in picking out words for the sake of their meaning and inventing images in order to make the meaning clearer. It consists in gumming together long strips of words which have already been set in order by someone else, and making the results presentable by sheer humbug. The attraction of this way of writing is that it is easy. It is easier—even quicker, once you have the habit—to say *In my opinion it is not an unjustifiable assumption that* than to say *I think*. If you use ready-made phrases, you not only don't have to hunt about for words; you also don't have to bother with the rhythms of your sentences, since these phrases are generally so arranged as to be more or less euphonious. When you are composing in a hurry—when you are dictating to a stenographer, for instance, or making a public speech—it is natural to fall into a pretentious, Latinized style. Tags like *a consideration which we should do well to bear in mind* or *a conclusion to which all of us would readily assent* will save many a sentence from coming down with a bump. By using stale metaphors, similes and idioms, you save much mental effort, at the cost of leaving your meaning vague, not only for your reader but for yourself. This is the significance of mixed metaphors. The sole aim of a metaphor is to call up a visual image. When these images clash—as in *The Fascist octopus has sung its swan song, the jackboot is thrown into the melting pot*—it can be taken as certain that the writer is not seeing a mental image of the objects he is naming; in other words he is not really thinking. Look again at the examples I gave at the beginning of this essay. Professor Laski (1) uses five negatives in fifty-three words. One of these is superfluous, making nonsense of the whole passage, and in addition there is the slip *alien* for akin, making further nonsense, and several avoidable pieces of clumsiness which increase the general vagueness. Professor Hogben (2) plays ducks and drakes with a battery which is able to write prescriptions, and, while disapproving of the everyday phrase *put up with,* is unwilling to look *egregious* up in the dictionary and see what it means; (3), if one takes an uncharitable attitude towards it, is simply meaningless: probably one could work out its intended meaning by reading the whole of the article in which it occurs. In (4), the writer knows more or less what he wants to say, but an accumulation of stale phrases chokes him like tea leaves blocking a sink. In (5), words and meaning have almost parted company. People who write in this manner usually have a general emotional meaning—they dislike one thing and want to express solidarity with another—but they are not interested in the detail of what they are saying. A scrupulous writer, in every sentence that he writes, will ask himself at least four questions, thus: What am I trying to say? What words will express it? What image or idiom will make it clearer? Is this image fresh enough to have an effect? And he will probably ask himself two more: Could I put it more shortly? Have I said anything that is avoidably ugly? But you are not obliged to go to all this trouble. You can shirk it by simply throwing your mind open and letting the ready-made phrases come crowding in. They will construct your sentences for you—even think your thoughts for you, to a certain extent—and at need they will perform the important service of partially concealing your meaning even from yourself. It is at this point that the special connection between politics and the debasement of language becomes clear.

In our time it is broadly true that political writing is bad writing. Where it is not true, it will generally be found that the writer is some kind of rebel, expressing his private opinions and not a "party line." Orthodoxy, of whatever color, seems to demand a lifeless, imitative style. The political dialects to be found in pamphlets, leading articles, manifestos, White Papers and the speeches of under-secretaries do, of course, vary from party to party, but they are all alike in that one almost never finds in them a fresh, vivid, home-made turn of speech. When one watches some tired hack on the platform mechanically repeating the familiar phrases—*bestial atrocities, iron heel, bloodstained tyranny, free peoples of the world, stand shoulder to shoulder*—one often has a curious feeling that one is not watching a live human being but some kind of dummy: a feeling which suddenly becomes stronger at moments when the light catches the speaker's spectacles and turns them into blank discs which seem to have no eyes behind them. And this is not altogether fanciful. A speaker who uses that kind of phraseology has gone some distance towards turning himself into a machine. The appropriate noises are coming out of his larynx, but his brain is not involved as it would be if he were choosing his words for himself. If the speech he is making is one that he is accustomed to make over and over again, he may be almost unconscious of what he is saying, as one is when one utters the responses in church. And this reduced state of consciousness, if not indispensable, is at any rate favorable to political conformity.

In our time, political speech and writing are largely the defence of the indefensible. Things like the continuance of British rule in India, the Russian purges and deportations, the dropping of the atom bombs on Japan, can indeed be defended, but only by arguments which are too brutal for most people to face, and which do not square with the professed aims of political parties. Thus political language has to consist largely of euphemism, question-begging and sheer cloudy vagueness. Defenceless villages are bombarded from the air, the inhabitants driven out into the countryside, the cattle machine-gunned, the huts set on fire with incendiary bullets: this is called *pacification*. Millions of peasants are robbed of their farms and sent trudging along the roads with no more than they can carry: this is called *transfer of population* or *rectification of frontiers*. People are imprisoned for years without trial, or shot in the back of the neck or sent to die of scurvy in Arctic lumber camps: this is called *elimination of unreliable elements*. Such phraseology is needed if one wants to name things without calling up mental pictures of them. Consider for instance some comfortable English professor defending Russian totalitarianism. He cannot say outright, "I believe in killing off your opponents when you can get good results by doing so." Probably, therefore, he will say something like this:

"While freely conceding that the Soviet régime exhibits certain features which the humanitarian may be inclined to deplore, we must, I think, agree that a certain curtailment of the right to political opposition is an unavoidable concomitant of transitional periods, and that the rigors which the Russian people have been called upon to undergo have been amply justified in the sphere of concrete achievement."

The inflated style is itself a kind of euphemism. A mass of Latin words falls upon the facts like soft snow, blurring the outlines and covering up all the details. The great enemy of clear language is insincerity. When there is a gap between one's real and one's declared aims, one turns as it were instinctively to long words and exhausted idioms, like a cuttlefish squirting out ink. In our age there is no such thing as "keeping out of politics." All issues are political issues, and politics itself is a mass of lies, evasions, folly, hatred and schizophrenia. When the general atmosphere is bad, language must suffer. I should expect to

find—this is a guess which I have not sufficient knowledge to verify—
that the German, Russian and Italian languages have all deteriorated in
the last ten or fifteen years, as a result of dictatorship.

But if thought corrupts language, language can also corrupt thought.
A bad usage can spread by tradition and imitation, even among people
who should and do know better. The debased language that I have been
discussing is in some ways very convenient. Phrases like *a not unjustifiable
assumption, leaves much to be desired, would serve no good purpose, a
consideration which we should do well to bear in mind,* are a continuous
temptation, a packet of aspirins always at one's elbow. Look back through
this essay, and for certain you will find that I have again and again
committed the very faults I am protesting against. By this morning's post
I have received a pamphlet dealing with conditions in Germany. The
author tells me that he "felt impelled" to write it. I open it at random,
and here is almost the first sentence that I see: "[The Allies] have an
opportunity not only of achieving a radical transformation of Germany's
social and political structure in such a way as to avoid a nationalistic
reaction in Germany itself, but at the same time of laying the foundations of a co-operative and unified Europe." You see, he "feels impelled"
to write—feels, presumably, that he has something new to say—and yet
his words, like cavalry horses answering the bugle, group themselves
automatically into the familiar dreary pattern. This invasion of one's
mind by ready-made phrases (*lay the foundations, achieve a radical
transformation*) can only be prevented if one is constantly on guard
against them, and every such phrase anaesthetizes a portion of one's
brain.

I said earlier that the decadence of our language is probably curable.
Those who deny this would argue, if they produced an argument at all,
that language merely reflects existing social conditions, and that we cannot influence its development by any direct tinkering with words and
constructions. So far as the general tone or spirit of a language goes,
this may be true, but it is not true in detail. Silly words and expressions
have often disappeared, not through any evolutionary process but owing
to the conscious action of a minority. Two recent examples were *explore
every avenue* and *leave no stone unturned,* which were killed by the
jeers of a few journalists. There is a long list of flyblown metaphors
which could similarly be got rid of if enough people would interest themselves in the job; and it should also be possible to laugh the *not un-*

[handwritten annotation:] ↓ Won't someone, please, do the same
with a window of opportunity and ro
model in the late 1990s?

formation out of existence,[3] to reduce the amount of Latin and Greek in the average sentence, to drive out foreign phrases and strayed scientific words, and, in general, to make pretentiousness unfashionable. But all these are minor points. The defence of the English language implies more than this, and perhaps it is best to start by saying what it does *not* imply.

To begin with it has nothing to do with archaism, with the salvaging of obsolete words and turns of speech, or with the setting up of a "standard English" which must never be departed from. On the contrary, it is especially concerned with the scrapping of every word or idiom which has outworn its usefulness. It has nothing to do with correct grammar and syntax, which are of no importance so long as one makes one's meaning clear, or with the avoidance of Americanisms, or with having what is called a "good prose style." On the other hand it is not concerned with fake simplicity and the attempt to make written English colloquial. Nor does it even imply in every case preferring the Saxon word to the Latin one, though it does imply using the fewest and shortest words that will cover one's meaning. What is above all needed is to let the meaning choose the word, and not the other way about. In prose, the worst thing one can do with words is to surrender to them. When you think of a concrete object, you think wordlessly, and then, if you want to describe the thing you have been visualizing you probably hunt about till you find the exact words that seem to fit it. When you think of something abstract you are more inclined to use words from the start, and unless you make a conscious effort to prevent it, the existing dialect will come rushing in and do the job for you, at the expense of blurring or even changing your meaning. Probably it is better to put off using words as long as possible and get one's meaning as clear as one can through pictures or sensations. Afterwards one can choose— not simply *accept*—the phrases that will best cover the meaning, and then switch round and decide what impression one's words are likely to make on another person. This last effort of the mind cuts out all stale or mixed images, all prefabricated phrases, needless repetitions, and humbug and vagueness generally. But one can often be in doubt about the effect of a word or a phrase, and one needs rules that one can rely on when instinct fails. I think the following rules will cover most cases:

[3] One can cure oneself of the *not un-* formation by memorizing this sentence: *A not unblack dog was chasing a not unsmall rabbit across a not ungreen field.*

(i) Never use a metaphor, simile or other figure of speech which you are used to seeing in print.

(ii) Never use a long word where a short one will do.

(iii) If it is possible to cut a word out, always cut it out.

(iv) Never use the passive where you can use the active.

(v) Never use a foreign phrase, a scientific word or a jargon word if you can think of an everyday English equivalent.

(vi) Break any of these rules sooner than say anything outright barbarous.

These rules sound elementary, and so they are, but they demand a deep change of attitude in anyone who has grown used to writing in the style now fashionable. One could keep all of them and still write bad English, but one could not write the kind of stuff that I quoted in those five specimens at the beginning of this article.

I have not here been considering the literary use of language, but merely language as an instrument for expressing and not for concealing or preventing thought. Stuart Chase and others have come near to claiming that all abstract words are meaningless, and have used this as a pretext for advocating a kind of political quietism. Since you don't know what Fascism is, how can you struggle against Fascism? One need not swallow such absurdities as this, but one ought to recognize that the present political chaos is connected with the decay of language, and that one can probably bring about some improvement by starting at the verbal end. If you simplify your English, you are freed from the worst follies of orthodoxy. You cannot speak any of the necessary dialects, and when you make a stupid remark its stupidity will be obvious, even to yourself. Political language—and with variations this is true of all political parties, from Conservatives to Anarchists—is designed to make lies sound truthful and murder respectable, and to give an appearance of solidity to pure wind. One cannot change this all in a moment, but one can at least change one's own habits, and from time to time one can even, if one jeers loudly enough, send some worn-out and useless phrase —some *jackboot, Achilles' heel, hotbed, melting pot, acid test, veritable inferno* or other lump of verbal refuse—into the dustbin where it belongs.

Extreme form of mysticism proposed by Miguel de Molinos and more moderately by Fénelon and Madame Guyon. Its essence [is] passivity of soul before God for sake of achieving unity with Him. This involves abandonment of effort, reason, motion, sacraments, even of prayer. Fundamental principle is common in Oriental religions.

Selections from The Rhetoric of Aristotle

BOOK 1

1. [Scope and Purpose of the Art.] Rhetoric is the counterpart of Dialectic [—that is, the art of public speaking and the art of logical discussion are co-ordinate, but contrasted, processes]; for both have to do with such things as fall, in a way, within the realm of common knowledge, things that do not belong to any one science. Accordingly, everybody to some extent makes use of both Dialectic and Rhetoric; for all make some attempt to sift or to support theses, and to defend or attack persons. Most people do so, of course, either quite at random, or else merely with a knack acquired from practice. Success in either way being possible, the random impulse and the acquired facility alike evince the feasibility of reducing the processes to a method; for when the practised and the spontaneous speakers gain their end, it is possible to investigate the cause of their success; and such an inquiry, we shall all admit, performs the function of an art.

. . .

But the art of Rhetoric has its value. It is valuable, first, because truth and justice are by nature more powerful than their opposites; so that, when decisions are not made as they should be, the speakers with the right on their side have only themselves to thank for the outcome. Their neglect of the art needs correction. [A proper knowledge and

327

exercise of Rhetoric would prevent the triumph of fraud and injustice.]
Secondly, [Rhetoric is valuable as a means of instruction]. Even if our
speaker had the most accurate scientific information, still there are
persons whom he could not readily persuade with scientific arguments.
True instruction, by the method of logic, is here impossible; the speaker
must frame his proofs and arguments with the help of common knowledge and accepted opinions. This method has been noted in the *Topics,*
in our remarks on popular discussion. [See Aristotle's *Topica* 1.2.]
Thirdly, in Rhetoric, as in Dialectic, we should be able to argue on
either side of a question; not with a view to putting both sides into
practice—we must not advocate evil—but in order that no aspect of the
case may escape us, and that if our opponent makes unfair use of the
arguments, we may be able in turn to refute them. In no other art do
we draw opposite conclusions; it is characteristic of Rhetoric and
Dialectic alone that, abstractly considered, they may indifferently prove
opposite statements. Still, their basis, in the facts, is not a matter of
indifference, for, speaking broadly, what is true and preferable is by
nature always easier to prove, and more convincing. Lastly, if it is a
disgrace to a man when he cannot defend himself in a bodily way, it
would be odd not to think him disgraced when he cannot defend himself
with reason [in a speech]. Reason is more distinctive of man than is
bodily effort. If it is urged that an abuse of the rhetorical faculty can
work great mischief, the same charge can be brought against all good
things (save virtue itself), and especially against the most useful things
such as strength, health, wealth, and military skill. Rightly employed,
they work the greatest blessings; and wrongly employed, they work the
utmost harm.

.   .   .

2. [Definition of Rhetoric. Modes and Means of Persuasion.] So let
Rhetoric be defined as the faculty [power] of discovering in the particular
case what are the available means of persuasion. This is the function of
no other art [save Dialectic]. The others are each instructive or persuasive with regard to some special subject-matter. Thus medicine informs us about the conditions of health and disease; geometry about the
properties of magnitudes; arithmetic about numbers; and so with the
rest of the arts and sciences. But Rhetoric, it would seem, has the function of discovering the means of persuasion for every case, so to speak,

that is offered; and hence we say that the art as such has no special application to any distinct class of subjects.

Proofs [persuasions] are of two kinds, artistic and non-artistic. [Or we might call them "scientific" and "unscientific." Aristotle distinguishes means of persuasion that inherently belong *in* the art, and those that, while associated with it, are really external and adventitious.] By "non-artistic" proofs are meant all such as are not supplied by our own efforts, but existed beforehand, such as witnesses, admissions under torture, written contracts, and the like. By "artistic" proofs [means of persuasion] are meant those that may be furnished by the method of Rhetoric through our own efforts. The first sort have only to be used; the second have to be found.

Of the means of persuasion supplied by the speech itself there are three kinds. The first kind reside in the character [*ethos*] of the speaker; the second consist in producing a certain [the right] attitude in the hearer; the third appertain to the argument proper, in so far as it actually or seemingly demonstrates. [Under all three heads, and explicitly under the third, Aristotle makes room, with the scientific branch of Rhetoric, for devices related to those of the sophistical branch. As in the *Poetics,* we see that the artist may use elements that are somewhat external to the art itself, in a more artistic way rather than a less.]

The character [*ethos*] of the speaker is a cause of persuasion when the speech is so uttered as to make him worthy of belief; for as a rule we trust men of probity more, and more quickly, about things in general, while on points outside the realm of exact knowledge, where opinion is divided, we trust them absolutely. This trust, however, should be created by the speech itself, and not left to depend upon an antecedent impression that the speaker is this or that kind of man. It is not true, as some writers on the art maintain, that the probity of the speaker contributes nothing to his persuasiveness; on the contrary, we might almost affirm that his character [*ethos*] is the most potent of all the means to persuasion.

Secondly, persuasion is effected through the audience, when they are brought by the speech into a state of emotion; for we give very different decisions under the sway of pain or joy, and liking or hatred. This, we contend, is the sole aspect of the art with which technical writers of the day have tried to deal. We shall elucidate it in detail when we come to discuss the emotions.

Thirdly, persuasion is effected by the arguments, when we demonstrate the truth, real or apparent, by such means as inhere in particular cases.

Such being the instruments of persuasion, to master all three obviously calls for a man who can reason logically, can analyze the types of human character [*ethe*], along with the virtues, and, thirdly, can analyze the emotions—the nature and quality of each several emotion, with the means by which, and the manner in which, it is excited.

.   .   .

4. . . . Of the subjects upon which all men deliberate, and upon which deliberative orators speak, the chief ones, we may say, are five in number, to wit: (1) ways and means; and (2) war and peace; next, (3) national defence; and (4) imports and exports; finally, (5) legislation.

Accordingly, one who is to make recommendations on ways and means must know the sources of the public revenue, what they severally are, and their respective value; so that if any of them is being neglected, it may be added, and if any is too small, it may be increased; and he must know all the public expenses, so that any useless outlay may be cut off, and any excessive outlay reduced. Men become richer not merely by adding to their capital, but also by cutting down their expenditures. One cannot get a comprehensive view of these matters, however, from domestic experience alone; for the ends of deliberation, one needs insight also into devices of finance that have been tried abroad.

With regard to war and peace, one must know the forces of the State, their actual strength, and the strength they can develop; also the kind of forces now existing, as well as any additional kind that can be brought into existence; further, what wars the State has waged, and how they have been conducted. Not only with respect to one's own State must one know these things, but with respect to bordering states also, or, more particularly, those states with which there is likelihood of war, so that one may cultivate peace with the stronger, and have the option of making war on the weaker. And one must know whether the alien forces are like or unlike ours; for in this point also we may have, or lack, the advantage. As regards these points, too, one must have studied the issue, not only of our own wars, but of the wars waged between alien states as well; for like conditions naturally lead to like results.

Further, with regard to national defence, one must not be ignorant of details, but must know the extent and character of the protection, and the situation of the forts (a matter which calls for a practical knowledge of the country), so that an inadequate preparation may be increased, and any superfluous defence reduced, and special care given to strategic positions.

Again, for the means of subsistence, one must know what total outlay will suffice for the State, the nature of the supplies produced at home or obtainable from without, which articles the citizens need to export, and which must be imported; these last, in order that treaties and agreements may be made with the proper states; for there are two sorts of alien powers with which we must see to it that our citizens maintain good relations—the stronger, and those that are useful for commerce.

For the stability of the commonwealth, the deliberative speaker must be an able student of these matters; but, above all, he must be competent in legislation, for the salvation of the State is in its laws. Accordingly, one must know how many types of government there are; what conditions are favorable to each type; and what things, inherent in the type itself, or antagonistic to it from without, naturally tend to destroy it. When I speak of destruction by causes inherent in the type itself, I mean that, save for the best type, they are all ruined by getting unstrung and by over-tension. [The figure is that of a stringed instrument.] Thus democracy grows weaker, not only by relaxation, until it ends in oligarchy, but also by excessive tension [intensification, exaggeration, ending in anarchy]; just as the aquiline or the snub nose, as its curve is relaxed, comes toward the intermediate type, but when the hook or the snub is violently intensified, it assumes such a shape as to lose all resemblance to a nose.

For the ends of legislation, it is helpful to understand what type of government is desirable, and to learn this not only from the history of our own State, but also by studying the forms of government abroad, observing how the different forms are suited to different peoples. And hence, obviously, books of travel will be of use with respect to legislation, since from them one may learn the laws and customs of foreign nations; while histories [since they deal with human actions] should be read for their bearing upon counsels of state. All these inquiries, however, belong to Political Science, not to Rhetoric.

These, then, are the chief subjects upon which the intending deliberative speaker should be well-informed.

•   •   •

BOOK 2

18. [General Recapitulation.] The function of all persuasive utterance is realized in some decision—for when we know a thing, and have reached a decision about it, there is no need of further argument. Such is the function of speaking, even to a single listener, when you urge him on, or try to turn him—as you do if you tax an individual about his conduct or seek to alter his views. The individual man is as truly a judge or decider as an entire audience; so, in the wider sense, whoever it is you have to persuade is "judge." Nor does it make any real difference whether you are addressing an actual opponent or merely arguing against an impersonal thesis. However impersonal the case, what you say must function like a speech; you have to upset the opposite hypothesis, and you frame your discourse against that as if it were your opponent. [That is, any kind of persuasive discourse must observe the method of rhetoric; of written discourse—of ordinary prose—the reader is the "judge." You aim to make the reader "decide" in your favor.]

•   •   •

20. [Means of Persuasion Common to All Branches of Speaking.] We have now discussed the [four] special means of persuasion [belonging to the three kinds of speaking (epideictic, forensic, and deliberative)]; it remains to discuss the means that are common to all [three]. These common [universal] means are generically two [—that is, under one genus there are two species, namely,] Example and Enthymeme. As for the Maxim [which some take to be a third species], it is to be included under the Enthymeme. Accordingly, let us first speak of (1) the Example; for [in Rhetoric] the Example corresponds to the process of induction [in Dialectic], and induction is the basis [of all reasoning].

There are two kinds of argument by example. One consists in the use of a parallel from the facts of history; the other in the use of an invented parallel. This last may take the form of a comparison [parable, invented by the speaker], or one may employ fables such as Aesop's or the African beast-tale. The use of the parallel from history would go as follows. The speaker, say, is urging us to arm against the King of Persia, and not let him conquer Egypt; then the argument from parallels would be: "Darius in his day did not cross [the Aegean] until he had seized Egypt; but once he had seized it, he crossed [the sea against us]. And Xerxes, again, did not invade us until he had seized Egypt; but once he had seized it, he likewise crossed [against us]. And so this man, if he seizes Egypt, will cross, too. We must therefore prevent him."

Instances of the invented comparison are those employed by Socrates. Let us suppose the speaker to be urging that public officials should not be chosen by lot. He may argue this: "It is like choosing athletes for a contest by lot, instead of picking those who can play the game; or it is as if the choice of a helmsman from a crew had to go by the toss of a coin, and not to the man who knows how to steer."

· · ·

22. . . . We have already stated that the Enthymeme is a syllogism, and in what sense it is so. And we have noted how enthymemes differ from the syllogisms of Dialectic: [when you wish to persuade,] you must not begin the chain of reasoning too far back, or its length will render the argument obscure; and you must not put in every single link, or the statement of what is obvious will render it prolix. These are the reasons why uneducated men are more effective than the educated in speaking to the masses—as the poets say [cf. Euripides, *Hippolytus* 989] that the unlearned "have a finer charm . . . for the ear of the mob." Educated men lay down abstract principles and draw general conclusions; the uneducated argue from their everyday knowledge, and base their conclusions upon immediate facts. Our speaker, accordingly, must start out, not from any and every premise that may be regarded as true, but from opinions of a definite sort—the [actual] opinions of the judges [audience], or else the opinions of persons whose authority they accept. And the speaker must make sure that his premises do appear in this light to most, if not all, of his audience. And he must argue not only from necessary truths, but from probable truths as well.

Now, first of all, let this be understood: Whatever the subject on which we have to speak or reason—whether the argument concerns public affairs or anything else—we must have some knowledge, if not a complete one, of the facts. Without it, you would have no materials from which to construct an argument. How, let me ask, could we advise the

Athenians whether they should go to war or not, if we did not know
their forces, whether these were military or naval or both, the size of
these forces, what were the public revenues, and who were the friends
and foes of the State, what wars it had waged, and with what success
—and so on?

.   .   .

. . . Consequently, as may be seen in our treatise *On Topics,* the
speaker must, first of all, be provided with a selection of premises [facts]
from which to argue on the possible and most timely subjects he may have
to discuss; and in emergencies he must seek his premises in the same way,
by referring, not to vague generalities, but to the facts of the subject
on which he is speaking, including just as many of the most pertinent
ones as he can. The more facts he has at his command, the more easily
will he make his point; and the more closely they touch the case, the
more germane will they be to his purpose, and the less like sheer commonplace.

.   .   .

BOOK 3

1. . . . We have next to treat of Diction [i.e., Style, and the like];
since it is not enough to know *what* to say—one must also know *how* to
say it. The right way of doing this contributes much to the right impression of a speech. It was natural that we should first investigate the subject which comes first in the natural order—the facts themselves as a
source of persuasion. But next comes the question, how to state [set
out] these facts in language. A third question would touch the art of
correct delivery; for success in delivery is of the utmost importance to
the effect of a speech. . . . Strict justice, of course, would lead us, in
speaking, to seek no more [of an emotional effect] than that we should
avoid paining the hearer without alluring him; the case should, in
justice, be fought on the strength of the facts alone, so that all else
besides demonstration of fact is superfluous. Nevertheless, as we have
said, external matters do count for much, because of the sorry nature of
an audience. Meanwhile attention to style necessarily has some real, if
minor, importance in every kind of exposition; it does make a difference
in the clearness of an exposition whether you put a thing in this way or

that—and yet not so much difference as people think, since all these devices of style and the like are of the imagination, and meant for the ear. No one uses them in teaching mathematics!

. . .

2. [The Qualities of Style.] We may therefore assume the general observations of the *Poetics,* and regard it as settled that a good style is, first of all, clear. The proof is that language which does not convey a clear meaning fails to perform the very function of language. The style, again, should be neither mean nor above the dignity of the subject, but appropriate; the poetical style, say, is not mean, but it is unsuited to prose. Clearness is secured through the use of name-words [= nouns and adjectives] and, verbs, that are current terms; freedom from meanness, and actual embellishment, through the use of the other terms mentioned in the *Poetics.* These deviations from ordinary usage make the style more impressive. Words are like men; as we feel a difference between people from afar and our fellow townsmen, so is it with our feeling for language. And hence it is well to give the ordinary idiom an air of remoteness; the hearers are struck by what is out of the way, and like what strikes them. In verse there are many things to produce this effect, and to verse they are fitting; for there the subject-matter—both things and persons—is more remote from daily life. But in prose such devices are far less often to be used, since the subjects are humbler. Even in poetry, it is hardly appropriate if fine language is used by a slave or a very young man, or for very trivial matters; even in poetry, the language, if it is to be appropriate, must rise and fall with the subject. Thus we see the necessity of disguising the means we employ, so that we may seem to be speaking, not with artifice, but naturally. Naturalness is persuasive, artifice just the reverse. People grow suspicious of an artificial speaker, and think he has designs upon them—as if someone were mixing drinks for them.

. . .

7. [Propriety.] We turn to propriety. Your language will be appropriate, if it expresses (1) emotion and (2) character, and if it is (3) in proportion with the subject. By proportion is meant that weighty matters shall not be treated in a slipshod way, nor trivial matters in a solemn way; nor should ornamental epithets be attached to commonplace nouns,

or the effect will be comic, as in the poetry of Cleophon. He used phrases as absurd as it would be to say "O Lady Fig-tree!"

For emotion, if the subject be wanton outrage, your language will be that of anger; if you speak of impiety or filth, use the language of aversion and reluctance even to discuss them; if of praiseworthy deeds, the language of admiration; if of piteous things, that of dejection; and similarly for the other emotional states. The appropriateness of your language to the emotion will make people believe in your facts. In their souls they infer, illegitimately, that you are telling the truth, because they, in a like situation, would be moved in the same way as you are; accordingly, even when the facts are not as the speaker says, the audience think he is right. Indeed, they are always in sympathy with an emotional speaker even when there is nothing in what he says; and that is why many an orator tries to stun the audience with sound and fury.

· · ·

9. . . . The periodic style in which the sentence is divided into members is of two kinds. The members are either (1) simply divided, or (2) antithetical. Thus, (1) divided: "I have often wondered at the conveners of national assemblies, and the founders of athletic contests" [—from Isocrates, *Panegyricus* 1]. When the style is (2) antithetical, in each of the two members (*a*) an opposite is balanced by an opposite, or (*b*) two opposites are linked by the same word. For example [cf. *ibid.* 35, 36]: "They served both parties—both those who stayed behind and those who came with them; for the latter they acquired additional territory larger than that at home, and to the former they left land enough at home." Here the contrasted terms are "staying behind" and "coming with them," and "enough" and "larger." So [cf. *ibid.* 41]: "Both to those who want to have money, and to those who wish to enjoy it"; where the contrast is between enjoyment and acquisition. Again [cf. *ibid.* 48]: "It often happens in such enterprises that the prudent fail, and the fools succeed." Or [*ibid.* 72]: "They immediately received the crown of valor, and soon won command of the sea." Or [*ibid.* 89]: "To sail through the mainland and march through the sea, by bridging the Hellespont and digging through Athos." Or [cf. *ibid.* 105]: "By nature citizens, by law bereft of their city." Or [*ibid.* 149]: "Some of them perished in misery, others were saved in disgrace." Or [cf. *ibid.* 181]: "In our private households keeping foreign servants, as a public measure

letting thousands of our allies live in foreign slavery." Or [cf. *ibid.* 186]: "To enjoy in life, or bequeath at death." Take, again, what some-one said in court of Peitholaus and Lycophron: "These fellows while at home used to sell you; now they are here, they've had to buy you." All these passages have the structure described above. This kind of style is pleasing, because things are best known by opposition, and are all the better known when the opposites are put side by side; and is pleasing also because of its resemblance to logic—for the method of refutation [of the refutative syllogism] is the juxtaposition of contrary conclusions.

. . .

10. [Lively Sayings.] We may now regard the questions above as settled, and must take up the question how to devise lively and popular sayings. Of course, the actual invention of these is a matter of natural talent or long practice; the affair of this treatise is to explain them. Let us proceed by enumerating them in full. And we may start from the principle that we all take a natural pleasure in learning easily; so, since words stand for things, those words are most pleasing that give us fresh knowledge. Now strange words leave us in the dark; and current words [with the things they stand for] we know already. Accordingly, it is metaphor that is in the highest degree instructive and pleasing. When Homer calls old age "stubble" [—"but natheless I ween one might see from the stubble what the grain has been" (*Odyssey* 14.213-4)], he makes us learn, gives us a new concept, by means of the common genus; since both things [old age and stubble] fall under the genus "withered."

. . .

13. [Arrangement, or *Taxis.*] A speech has two parts. Necessarily, you state your case, and you prove it. Thus we cannot state a case and omit to prove it, or prove a case without first stating it; . . . . Well, then, the indispensable constituents are simply the Statement and the ensuing Argument. These are the essential elements of a speech; at most, the parts cannot exceed four—Proem, Statement, Argument, and Epilogue.

. . .

14. [The Proem or Introduction.] The Proem is the beginning of a speech; it answers to the prologue in poetry, or to the prelude in music

for the flute. All three are beginnings, and, as it were, pave the way for what follows. Thus the musical prelude is like the proem in ceremonial [epideictic] speeches. A flutist will take some brilliant passage that he can play, and using this for a prelude, will link it on to the opening notes of his theme; just so should the author proceed in an epideictic speech. He should begin with whatever he likes to say, and then strike up his theme with a connecting link. It is precisely what they all do; for illustration take the proem to the *Helen* of Isocrates—there is no inner bond between the disputatious dialecticians [with whom he begins] and Helen. Meanwhile, even if you stray far from your point, it is better so—not to have the whole speech in a single vein.

.   .   .

This, then, is the superlative function of the proem, this its distinctive task: to make clear the end and object of your work. And hence, if your matter is plain and short, a proem really should not be employed.

Other kinds of proem are used, but they are all in the nature of anti-dotes; they lack the distinctive function. [They are remedies against the defects of the speaker, or of his audience or his subject, or against the strength of his opponent.] These proems have their source in (1) the speaker, (2) the audience, (3) the subject, and (4) the opposition. Those that concern (1) the speaker or (4) his opponent have to do with removing or exciting prejudice. But here we note a difference be-tween one who is defending a position and one who is attacking it. The defendant will deal with prejudice at the beginning; the accuser will reserve such effort for the close of the speech. Nor is the reason for this obscure. When a defendant is about to present his case, he must dislodge whatever stands in his way, and so any prejudice against him must be removed at the outset. But if prejudice is to be excited, this should be done at the close, for then what you say will be better remembered.

Appeals (2) to the hearer aim at securing his good will, or at arousing his anger; sometimes at engaging his attention, or, on occasion, at divert-ing it—since engaging it is not always an advantage, and for that reason a speaker will often try to set his audience laughing.

You may use each and all of these means, if you like, in your proem, with a view to making your audience receptive, and withal give an impression of yourself as a good and just man, for good character always commands more attention. Men pay attention to things of importance, to their own interests, to anything wonderful, to anything pleasant; and hence you must give the impression that your speech has to do with the like. If you wish to divert their attention, make them think that the matter is trifling—in no way concerns them—is displeasing.

But we must not forget that such things are, every one of them, extraneous to a speech. They are for the audience, an audience that is weak enough to accept utterances beside the point; and if audiences were not what they are, there would be no need of any proem beyond a summary statement of the matter in question; thus the body of your speech would have a head as well. And further, if the hearer's attention must be caught, this may have to be done in all parts of the speech; the interest throughout is more relaxed than just when you begin to listen. So it is absurd to prescribe that the thing should be done at the outset, when every one listens with most attention. At any point in the speech, therefore, when occasion demands, it is proper to say: "Now I draw your attention to this, which concerns you as much as it does me"; or: "I'll tell you that, the like of which you ne'er before heard"—for terror, or for wonder. This is doing as Prodicus said: "When the audience gets drowsy," to "slip in for them a bit of the fifty-drachma course." . . .

Proems in political [deliberative] speaking are drawn from the materials used in the forensic proem; but, by the very nature of political speaking, proems are here least in order. The subject to be discussed is already known; the facts of it, then, need no introduction. Still, the speaker may, at the beginning, have something to say on personal grounds, or because of his opponents; or because the matter is taken less seriously, or more, than he wishes. Thus one may have to excite or remove prejudice, or to magnify or diminish the importance of the facts; either of these aims may call for a proem. Or the aim may be that of adornment; you may use a proem for fear that without one the speech may appear slipshod. Gorgias' *Eulogy of Elis* may so appear, for without even working his elbows—with no preliminary sparring at all—he starts right out with "Elis, fortunate city!"

         .   .   .

17. [The Arguments and Their Order.] Your arguments should have the effect of demonstrations; and, as there are four possible issues in a dispute, your attempt at demonstration must directly bear upon the issue that really is in dispute. Thus, if the point is (1) that an act was not

committed, then your primary concern at the trial is to show just that. If the point is (2) that the act did no harm, there is the thing you are to prove; and similarly with the issues (3) that the harm was less than is alleged, or (4) that the act was justified; whichever (2, 3, or 4) is the point, that is your primary concern, and as much your concern as if the issue were (1) whether or not the act was committed. But bear in mind that this first issue [—Was the act committed?] is, of the four, the only one in which it can be true that either the defendant or the accuser is necessarily a rogue. Here ignorance cannot be pleaded, as it might be if the parties were disputing whether the act was justified or not. In the first case, then, proofs that your adversary must be a rogue may be used, but not in the others. . . .

In Deliberative speaking, you may contend (1) that a certain thing cannot be done; or, granted that the thing urged by the opposition can be done, you may contend (2) that it is unjust, or (3) that it will do no good, or (4) that it has not the importance the opposition gives it. Note any false statements your opponent makes in matters apart from the issue; they can be made to seem proofs that his major statements are false. Argument from examples is best-suited to Deliberative speaking; argument by enthymeme is more characteristic of Forensic speaking. Deliberative speaking is concerned with the future, to which the speaker must find parallels [as "examples"] in events that are past. Forensic speaking has to do with matters of fact—now true or untrue, and necessarily so; here strict proof is more feasible, since the past cannot change. But the enthymemes should not be given in an unbroken string; interweave them with different matter, or your arguments will damage each other's effect. . . . Nor should you try to argue [find enthymemes] on every point; otherwise you will be doing just as some in philosophy do, who by syllogistic process reach conclusions more familiar and obvious than the premises from which they are drawn. And avoid using the enthymeme when you are trying to stir an emotion, for it will either dispel the emotion or itself be futile; simultaneous motions of the soul tend to efface each other, and, if not mutually destroyed, are mutually weakened. Nor, again, should you resort to an enthymeme in a passage where your aim is to depict character; demonstration is devoid of both character [*ethos*] and moral purpose. Maxims, however, should be employed in the proofs; here their use has an ethical value, as it has in narration: "All the same I let him have it, though well I knew the maxim, 'Trust no man.' " If your aim is emotional, put it thus: "And I have no regrets, wronged though I have been.—'His the gain, mine the justice.' " . . .

If you have proofs of your case, then use them, and speak from moral character [use moral suasion] as well; if you have nothing for enthymemes, then rely upon moral suasion alone. After all, it is more in keeping with true worth to reveal yourself as a man of probity than as sharp in argument. Refutative enthymemes are better-liked than demonstrative; the refutative process always makes the conclusion more striking, for setting opposites side by side renders their opposition more distinct.

A "Refutation of your Opponent" is no separate division of the speech; it belongs to the Argument. You are to break down his arguments, partly by objection, partly by counter-syllogism. In Deliberative speaking, as well as in court, if you are the first speaker you should first present your own arguments, and then meet the opposing arguments by direct refutation or by pulling them to pieces in advance. If, however, the opposition has many proofs of its case, then begin with these, as Callistratus did in the Messenian assembly. First of all he demolished the arguments they were going to use against him, and then he presented his own. If your turn comes later, and especially if the opposing arguments have been well received, you will have to deal first with them, by the method of refutation and counter-syllogism; for, as the mind of the hearer rejects a man against whom it has taken a prejudice, just so it refuses an argument if the opposing speaker has made a good impression. You should therefore make room in the minds of the audience for the argument you are going to offer; and this will be done if you demolish the one that has pleased them. So combat it—every point in it, or the chief, or the successful, or the vulnerable points, and thus establish credit for your own arguments. . . .

So much for the Arguments [persuasion by proofs]. Let us turn to *ethos.* [The distinction (still under the head of Argument) is between convincing the audience by process of reason and convincing them by your character. Here the treatment of *ethos* concerns the character of the person speaking, and may be called subjective; for the treatment of character on the more objective side, in relation to the audience, see 2.12-17, and in relation to persons represented, see 3.7.]

There are things which, if you say them of yourself, will bring you dislike, or will be tedious, or will arouse contradiction; and things which, if you say them of another, will make you appear abusive or ill-bred. Such things, if said, should be put into the mouth of a third person.

.   .   .

19. [The Epilogue.] The Epilogue is made up of four elements. (1) You must render the audience well-disposed to yourself, and ill-disposed to your opponent; (2) you must magnify and depreciate [make whatever favors your case seem more important and whatever favors his case seem less]; (3) you must put the audience into the right state of emotion; and (4) you must refresh their memories.

When at length you have shown the truth of your case, and the falsity of your opponent's, it is in the natural order of things that (1) you should commend yourself, censure him, and drive the difference home. In doing this, you must aim at one of two things. You must reveal yourself as a good man, and him as a bad one, in this particular case, or yourself as a good man, and him as a bad man, absolutely. How you are to present men in either light—the *topoi,* that is, which you are to employ in representing them as good, and as bad—this has already been discussed.

And again, now that the facts have been established, the next step (2) naturally is to magnify or depreciate [to increase or diminish their alleged importance]. The facts must be admitted before one can discuss their importance; if bodies are to increase, they must be in existence. The means of magnifying and depreciation, the *topoi,* have already been set forth.

This done, and now that the nature of the facts, and their importance, are alike clear, the next thing (3) is to make the audience feel the right emotions—pity, indignation, anger, hatred, envy, emulation, antagonism, [or whatever the case requires]. The *topoi* for these, too, have been previously discussed.

All that remains, then, is (4) to recapitulate what has been said. Here you may properly do what some wrongly advise doing in the earlier parts of the speech; they bid you reiterate your points so that the audience may learn them well. Now what you should do in your introduction is to state the subject, so that the issue to be judged may be perfectly clear; whereas in the Epilogue you should give a summary review of your proofs. In this review, you begin by noting that you have done what you undertook to do. So then you must state what you have said, and why you have said it. One way of doing this is by a comparison of your opponent's argument with your own; and here you may contrast what he said and you said on the same point, or not do it point by point. Thus: "My opponent said this, and I that, on this point, and my reasons were these." Or ironically: "Of course he said this, and I said that"; or, "How content he would have been to prove all this instead of merely proving that!" Or put it as a question: "What has not been proved?" or, "What *has* my opponent proved?" Your recapitulation, then, may take this form of direct contrast; or you may follow the natural order, that of the arguments as they were given, first taking your own, and then separately, if you like, those of your opponent.

You may in fitting style close your speech with an asyndeton; it will mark off the Epilogue as a true peroration. "I have done; you all have heard; you have the facts; give your judgment."

QUESTIONS FOR REVIEW OF PART EIGHT

1. What are the types of "swindles and perversions" Orwell finds lazy writers using to construct stale, imprecise prose? Give an example of each type.
2. What is it about the purpose of much political writing which, according to Orwell, inevitably makes it tend to be trite and inflated?
3. Doubtless Orwell labels as stale or hackneyed some expressions which seem all right to you. Perhaps your English instructor has marked "trite" opposite some phrases which you were not previously aware were overused. How do you account for the fact that such people recognize triteness when you do not?
4. Aristotle seems to state in Book 2, Section 22, that an enthymeme helps to link speaker and listener together when the speaker uses an enthymeme the unstated premise of which is obvious to the listener as well as to the speaker. In what other ways does Aristotle suggest that the speaker take the listener into account?
5. What does Aristotle mean by *ethos?* Which of the writers represented in this book of readings do you think has the most *ethos?* Why? How do you suppose you can increase your *ethos* as a writer and speaker?
6. Which of the readings in this book do Aristotle's ideas seem to anticipate?
7. Do you find that Aristotle tends in places to take a demeaning attitude toward the common man, an attitude which Orwell criti-

cizes in the politicians of our own time? Defend your answer by referring to specific passages in each selection.

SUGGESTIONS FOR INDIVIDUAL PROJECTS
AND CLASS DISCUSSION

1. Working from one of your textbooks or from the printed speech of some major political figure, quote several brief passages of the type Orwell criticizes, and rewrite them in fresh, precise language. You may wish to follow Orwell's suggestion and use his own writing as a source of bad examples.

2. Aristotle lists five chief subjects upon which the men of his time deliberated. Revise his list to make it appropriate for our times, including in your list no more than ten subjects. Then, as he does with all five subjects, list under one of the subjects you have selected, the things a person must know in order to understand that subject.

SUGGESTED WRITING ASSIGNMENT

Write a 400-500 word paper explaining your own philosophy of language (your own rhetoric), interpreting the meaning of that term as you see fit.